ONCE A
CHAMPION

ONCE A CHAMPION

Legendary Tennis
Stars Revisited

by Stan Hart

DODD, MEAD & COMPANY
New York

For
Stan Murphy
and
Dick Craven

Picture credits: 1. Dick Darcy; 2. Author; 3. Author; 4. Pictorial Parade; 6. Author; 9. Author; 10. N.Y. Times News Service; 11. Art Seitz; 12. Author; 13. Author; 17. Author; 18. FPG International Photoworld; 20. Author; 22. Art Seitz; 23. Bettmann Archives; 25. David Walburg; 29. AP Wide World Photos; 30. Author; 31. Bettmann Archives; 32. Rich Collins; 33. Rich Collins; 34. Author; 35. FPG International–Keystone View Co.; 37. Author; 38. Author; 39. Bettmann Archives; 40. Author; 41. Bettmann Archives; 42. Author; 43. Author; 44. Author; 45. Author; 46. Max Peter Haas; 47. Fox Studios; 48. Thelner Hoover, Los Angeles; 49. Author; 50. Author; 52. Author; 53. Bettmann Archives; 54. Author; 57. Author; 58. Bettmann Archives; 59. Author; 60. Bettmann Archives; 61. Bettmann Archives.

Published by Dodd, Mead & Company, Inc.
79 Madison Avenue, New York, N.Y. 10016

Distributed in Canada by
McClelland and Stewart Limited, Toronto

Manufactured in the United States of America

Designed by Terry Antonicelli
First Edition

LIBRARY OF CONGRESS CATALOGING IN PUBLICATION DATA

Hart, Stan.
  Once a champion.

    1. Tennis players—Biography. I. Title.
GV994.A1H37 1985   796.342'092'2[B]   84-21173
ISBN 0-396-08544-X

Contents

Acknowledgments

I should like to acknowledge a debt of gratitude to my editor, Allen Klots, who read my manuscript with fresh eyes and made it better. Also I owe a large "thank you" to Al Hart, my agent, who took on my project with enthusiasm. I wish to thank both Peter Schwed and Ned Chase for their advice. Also I wish to state that without George Plimpton's "participatory journalism" and Roger Kahn's *Boys of Summer,* the idea for my book would never have crossed my mind. Hence, to both writers I am in debt.

I am forever grateful to Dick Craven for his constant encouragement and buoying nature as well as for his comments concerning the text.

Finally I must acknowledge my gratitude and love for my three youngest children who live at home and who had to endure my distractions, absent-mindedness, and changes in temperament as the book-in-progress continued to grow. I refer to Sloan, Max, and Sam Hart.

Introduction

I saw my first tennis game when I was five or six years old. That would have been in the late spring of 1935 or 1936, and it was played on a clay court that had been built behind a neighbor's home. It was in New Britain, Connecticut, and the reason I remember the game is because my father was playing with his cousin, Tod Hart. They were both wearing long, white flannel pants and long-sleeved, white shirts—the kind you would wear in an office under a suit coat, only the two men had rolled their sleeves up to their elbows. I kept the memory of that game with me for many years, and it comes back to me now as I think of this book I am starting to write. I was standing there near the court along with our maid, my constant companion, Mary, and there was something in that match that was important to me because I was forever asking my father, "When are you going to play tennis again?"

As far as I know, that was the one and only time I watched my father play tennis. He was always complaining about his back, his neuralgia, his bursitis, or his stomach. By the late 1930s, I think he had given up the game. In any case, I never saw him play after that one glorious time. The men looked so neat and dashing in their whites, the game itself was fast and crisp (both my father and Tod Hart were good athletes), and the privacy of the court made it unique: a lovely clay court separating a spacious lawn from the edge of a golf course—the grown-ups had it all to themselves and could play as long as they liked. It is very probable that I remember the game because it was exciting to see my father doing something—something so fast and with such power. For he was a businessman in those days, and the customary picture of him that I carried in my mind was of a man getting into his automobile to drive to work. Even on Saturdays, he drove to work, to the Hart and Cooley Company in New Britain, and I know I felt a sense of loss whenever he drove off down the driveway. That it happened all the time surely deadened my disappointment, but I nevertheless missed him, and I continued to do so until I was finishing grade school and had caught up with my own sports and my own friends.

So I started off idealizing tennis. Tennis took my disappearing father and gave him white clothes and set him loose at a game in which he ran and propelled a ball so that his opponents could not return it. To a little kid, he looked splendid out there, and when he hit a winner, his partner—and maybe his adversaries as well—would yell out, "Nice shot!" Such enthusiasm would only affirm what I always felt: my father was a great man.

Allow it to stand that my first tennis game was played almost fifty years ago in a small manufacturing town in Connecticut and that it stayed in my head because of my father. That match set me up for what has become in my own middle age a fine passion. I love to play tennis, and I admire the people I play with. Sometimes I used to think it was a singular enthusiasm, special only to me, but as I continue to play, I find that my feelings are shared by many, in fact by almost every partner or opponent. In the summer months, the phone rings and rings, and if it is ringing for me, it usually means a tennis player is looking for a game. And that means he is looking for the same thing I look for—a workout, competition, and friendship. Over the years, other tennis players and I reaffirm our friendship. No one stops and says, "Okay, we are friends; we don't have to play anymore." We just keep on playing and liking it, and it just goes on, getting better all the time.

But I don't want to oversentimentalize this. I just want to establish why tennis has such a hold on me, why I am smitten by the feelings I get when I play the game, and where those feelings come from. And, too, let me add that I know of no other game I can play. I am, at middle age, stuck with tennis, for I cannot play any other sport at all well. I do not think it is a coincidence that the only game I can participate in with some ability is the only game I ever saw my father play with style and charm. I loved my father, I loved the way he looked on that sunny afternoon back in the Depression, and I have taken up his sport. On that golden afternoon, my father and a game were joined. For me it only happened once, but that was enough. My father died some thirty years later, but the game would go on. That he never played in my presence again only makes everything more deeply etched in my memory.

* * *

x

Age should be an equalizer. If I am fifty-four, someone pushing seventy should be an easy mark. I am thinking of Bob Feller. He is probably in his late sixties now, and I would lay odds that I can drive his best pitches deep into the outfield, if not put them out of the park. Surely his arm would be dead. And you can take Joe DiMaggio. I would bet that I can shag flies better than he and bat better than he. Near Feller's age, he wouldn't have the strength, the timing, or the endurance. What I am trying to say is that there comes a time in most sports when a significantly younger, mediocre athlete such as myself would be able to catch up to an older athlete who in old age is losing his abilities. Between Joe DiMaggio and Bob Feller and me, there is a gap somewhere between twelve and twenty years. If I use that age gap as a yardstick and look around at other sports, I could probably beat out Clint Frank or Sammy Baugh at football. What would it be like to box Jersey Joe Wolcott? How about George Mikan on a basketball court? Could I get by him for a lay-up? Probably.

But when I look at the so-called country club sports, this age gap does me little if any good. A seventy-three-year-old golfer will shoot his age. Just imagine my trying to play golf with Sam Snead. I can't break 90. A good squash player twenty years my senior would destroy me. And a tennis player? Well, that is the test. I *can* play tennis—though, lamentably, I have seldom risen above the B-level: good but not *really* good. I was number seven on a six-man team at college. It was a college unknown for its tennis teams, Wesleyan University in Middletown, Connecticut, where it rained all spring and where all there were were outdoor courts. In the Air Force, where I served for four years, I managed to take the number one position on a team that had no good players, only one World War II hero down on his luck, two black lieutenants, and two sergeants who were ex-fist fighters. But they liked the game for reasons that eluded me at the time. One weather officer, a major who had taken up the game somewhere in his career and plugged away at it to keep in shape for his sweetheart from Kentucky, became my friend, and we encouraged each other. It was a ragtag group that traveled together around northern California and was regularly beaten. Once, however, during 1954, I did play a superb player. Our Mather Air Force tennis team contested Modesto Junior College. At Modesto Junior College, they had three Mexican Davis Cup players and one ranked junior named Gerald Moss. I played their number two man, Esteban Reyes. He was at least four years younger than I and was so good that I hardly ever reached the ball, nor was I able to stroke it to keep it in play. At that time, I was made painfully aware of the great difference that existed between a fairly good hacker and a great player. No matter what I did or how hard I might practice, I would never, never get close enough to Reyes to give him a contest.

So tennis came and went in my life. I picked it up in the Air Force as a way to get off duty and to pal around with officers. We played on the officers' tennis courts, which were right beside the pool of the officers' club. I found I could pass myself off as a lieutenant and use both the pool and the club as I wished so long as I was coming or going to or from the tennis courts dressed in civilian clothes. And I guess in the back of my mind was some hope that I might learn the game and have it to play through the years ahead, but that thought was buried beneath a larger consideration. The main thing was that I could play tennis, as well as semipro softball, for the base team, and with two sports going on at the same time, my regular duties would fade away. The Korean War had ended long before. Air Force life was very much like a civilian job but, without the pay and with no war tension, had become a bore. People tried to escape the tedium by any means available. So I played tennis.

I went back to college after the service, and I did try out for the team but failed to get my letter. In the summers on Martha's Vineyard, I played at the East Chop Tennis Club and once around 1957 won a trophy for runner-up in men's doubles. That was my shining hour until 1977. During those twenty years, I played tennis sporadically, usually to sweat out excesses of the night before or because I was locked into a game twice a week after work and was happy to play for the exercise it gave me. I worked in Boston, and playing tennis in the evening was a way to fight against the big lunches I enjoyed. I did not think much about friendship, teamwork, or camaraderie in those days. I could have been going to an exercise class.

But in the early fall of 1977, things changed, and I became caught up in a game that was surely, for me, a lifesaver. A gentleman named Walter Charak, then about as old as the year, approached me in a bakery on Martha's Vineyard and said he heard that I had once played tennis. He wondered if I could make a fourth at a court owned by Roger Baldwin, founder of the American Civil Liberties Union. It was late September, and he couldn't get anyone else. Walter Charak had once been a publisher and had brought Ezra Pound back to the United States, and there he was pleading with me. I remember thinking that I'd never known anyone who knew Ezra Pound, and so I went out there onto that wonderful clay court in the woods. (It was clay-based but covered with a green substance called Har-tru, and you could find it at the end of a winding path that meandered through the woods to a small hollow right near the edge of the great Wequobosque Cliffs that front on the Atlantic Ocean.) As I soon discovered, this was a treasure of a court—so beautifully situated and wind-free. And I liked Walter immensely. Other players whom I met through him and with whom I played were the late Dan Lang, a *New Yorker* writer and author of many books; Michael Straight, writer and editor and man of the world, whom I still play with; Paul Moore, the Episcopal bishop of New York City; Robert Morgenthau, attorney general for Manhattan; and many others. Jonathan Schell comes to mind. The brilliant author of

The Fate of the Earth was brought to the court by his mother, Moxie, who played in that first game with Walter Charak and me. Hollis Chenery, once with the World Bank and co-owner of the great race horses Riva Ridge and Secretariat, played there; as did Victor Gurevich, an internist; and Bob Siffert, a world-famous orthopedic surgeon. Lou Harris, the pollster, played up there, and so did Rose Styron, whom I got to know and who led me on to another group of players with whom I play three times a week during the summer.

I want to pause here to say that I intend to identify people whose names show up in the pages of this book. I have always found it uncomfortable and incomplete to read the name of someone and not know what is behind the name. Who is he or she? Am I supposed to know? Also, I think it is important for the reader to get the idea that the game of tennis and the people who play it go hand in hand all the way back to my first match, the one I saw played by my father.

It was a great bunch of accomplished people at Martha's Vineyard. Sometimes as many as twelve of us would meet on a summer's afternoon and play in turn in groups of four. It was there at Windy Gates that I began to recognize the camaraderie, the feeling of loyalty. I began to care deeply for the other players regardless of how good they were. Soon my game improved, and I began to rank myself number one of the Windy Gates tennis group. Michael Straight fell to me, and so on occasion did Victor Gurevich. Hollis Chenery and a London banker named Charlie Goodheart played doubles with Julius "Dooley" Rosenwald and me. Dan Greenbaum, whose father had brought Svetlana Stalin to New York and to Harper and Row, came for the month of July, and his good nature cut the hot air like an ocean breeze—and what is important is that while I won, I really understood that winning was very much secondary to the good feeling I was getting from playing with such enjoyable people. Sometimes on a July afternoon, it was a hundred degrees on the court, and we would be out there banging away. Engaged in the same enterprise of playing tennis in the heat, we were, regardless of court position, all on the same team. It brought me close to the others, and I felt that I had discovered something about myself. By playing tennis with people I liked, I began to feel happy and worthwhile from the inside out. My chance meeting with Walter Charak in a bakery on Martha's Vineyard saved my life. Where once I had been self-deprecating and rudderless, I now felt energized and fit. Other people and good health had entered my summer days. Tennis was my vehicle to a recognition of self-worth and to love. And in a way, my father, the memory of whom I had buried or shied away from, was back, and with him were the high spirits I'd witnessed once as a little boy on a tennis court in New Britain, Connecticut.

* * *

I did not know how naive I was when I undertook the writing of this book. All I wanted (and I thought it so easy and accessible) was to play tennis with some older ladies and gentlemen and then to interview them.

I'd always venerated champions. I had a friend from my youth who became an intercollegiate boxing champion back in the late 1940s. I like him unequivocally because of this. I particularly admire champions who, as time passed, slipped out of memory so that if you mentioned Louise Brough (one of the most consistent of tennis champions), even sports fans would have trouble remembering who she was. Barbara Ann Scott, the great Canadian figure skater, comes to mind, as does Debs Garms, who won the National League batting title in 1940. How about Frankie Flichock or Arky Vaughan? They are all people who excelled at a sport and then disappeared into the bigger world and dropped from sight. As a fan, I asked myself how are they doing *now?*

So I valued the sense of rediscovery, and tennis was ideal for me. It was a game I could play, and if I could lure Alice Marble onto a court, the world would thank me for describing her as she stroked a ball, moved along the baseline, and executed her serve. I am a fan who would track down some of the best of the best old-timers and then tell my readers how they are doing now. What would these giants of the game be like now? I asked myself, and then I resolved to find out.

S. H.
September 21, 1983

PART ONE

The Eastern Swing

1

Pauline Betz Addie:

"You Fight Your Way Up."

When I made my first list of ex-champions with whom I would play tennis and then interview, I thought of people who were on the Eastern seaboard, men and women I could meet conveniently in a way that would save me money and time. Thus I set up a schedule that would take me to Sidney B. Wood, Jr.,* who lived, I thought, on Long Island; to Althea Gibson, in New Jersey; then to Don Budge on the New Jersey-Pennsylvania border. After seeing Don Budge, I would fly to Washington to play Pauline Betz Addie and Margaret Osborne duPont. From there I'd fly to Florida to see Gardnar Mulloy and Doris Hart, and finally to Jamaica where I had been told Fred Perry was director of a tennis club. After seeing Fred Perry, I would return home to write the first section of my book. Once that was completed, I would head out to the West Coast to find the Californians, with a stop in Las Vegas, where some almost forgotten news story had alerted me to the whereabouts of Pancho Gonzales.

I was unsure of anyone's precise address and was guessing—guessing on shaky evidence such as the fact that people had told me that Don Budge and Sidney Wood owned a laundry in the New York area and that you could see laundry vehicles out on Long Island and even in the city with the names

---

* A Wimbledon singles winner in 1931 by default. His opponent, Frank Shields (Brooke's grandfather), had sprained his ankle the previous day, getting to the finals.

"Budge and Wood" on the side of the panel trucks. I thought Margaret Osborne duPont lived in Maryland because a cousin of her husband William had said she "had a feeling" that is where she lived but didn't know exactly. People said Althea Gibson lived in New Jersey because years ago Governor James Byrne had appointed her to some job related to urban problems. And so it went. I based my itinerary on hearsay and then went for the addresses. I had already typed out a basic letter that, with a few appropriate changes, would go to each player on my list. It was late September and time to move. With not much to go on, I called my friend Dick Craven, who lives in Manhattan and plays tennis there. Craven is a sports trivia expert who might be able to help me.

As it turned out, he did. He, in turn, knew a man named Steve Flink, who is editor of *World Tennis* magazine, a man obsessed with statistics about tennis players. It was Flink who came up with the first few addresses. The first one was the office of Sidney B. Wood, Jr., in Woodside, Long Island, New York.

I wanted Wood because he was a man my father often said was a player who "wasn't the best, mind you, but who tried hard and was likable and quite probably a gentleman whom you'd like to know." Wood held an image for me that was informal—the kind of guy who at seventy-two or so, were he to visit Martha's Vineyard, would call me up to set up a game of doubles. During the summer, I had played quite a bit with Mike Wallace, and for a while back in June, I had been playing with Walter Cronkite. The idea of a nice elderly gentleman, all but forgotten by the world, actually wanting to play with me did not seem out of line. My head had been turned, as it were, by being a fairly popular doubles player there on the Vineyard. I saw no reason that Wood, who had won the singles championship at Wimbledon back in 1931 at nineteen years old, would not welcome me to his court, to his home, and to his heart. Once he read my letter, I thought, he would want to be in my book.

So I waited two weeks and then a few more days and did not get an answer to any of my letters. Frantically I called the Tennis Hall of Fame in Newport, Rhode Island, where I hoped for an updating on addresses and maybe some home phone numbers. Luckily I did get Wood's home number from Newport and called him at once. His wife could not have been nicer. I talked to her at least four times without getting her husband. Alas, her seventy-two-year-old spouse had become a whirlwind of business activity and was never home. He rose at 5:00 A.M. and returned home at 9:30 P.M. "too exhausted to think, much less talk with anyone on the phone," said his wife. "The best idea," she finally told me, "is to call Sidney on Saturday mornings. He's always home on Saturday mornings."

Assuming Wood would see me sometime during the following week, I called Pauline Betz Addie who, I had learned, worked at the Cabin John Indoor Tennis Courts in Bethesda, Maryland, just outside of Washington, D.C. I called her on a Friday, and she said that she could see me early in the next week but not later. She was tied up on business matters, but she sounded very friendly on the phone. She had read my letter and she felt bad about not answering it. Pauline had won singles at Wimbledon once, in 1946. And during the war years when Wimbledon was canceled she won the United States Lawn Tennis Association's singles championships at Forest Hills four times—1941, 1943, 1944, and again in 1946. She had a very pleasant voice and I made a date to play her Tuesday night, October 11, and would take her to lunch for my interview the following day.

On Saturday morning I called Sidney Wood. While I was seeing Pauline, he was going to be in Georgia on business. However, if I could be at the Pan American Motor Hotel in Queens (a favorite of his, "Where I put up my friends") on Thursday morning, he would call me, and we could set up a time to meet. I was overjoyed. Though no one else had answered me I could see two Wimbledon winners in a row, and surely one or both would open doors to others on my list. I had a beginning to work with. And remember, it was now early in October and all of my tennis friends who had come to the Vineyard in the summer were gone. I had thought of the idea for this book back in July, and though I had done nothing concrete other than talk to my agent about it, by Columbus Day weekend, I had grown very impatient. Between talking to my agent and finding a suitable publisher and agreeing to terms, months had slipped by. I wasn't going out without a contract only to be taken as some insane fan. I wanted to be sure that the subjects of my book understood that I was a legitimate writer. All of this had taken time. It was now autumn, and I was eager, and so with two firm commitments, I left Martha's Vineyard at noon on a Tuesday to fly to LaGuardia to catch the shuttle to Washington, where Mike Straight would meet me, and then I would be whisked away to Cabin John for a game with Pauline Betz indoors under the lights.

I was not sure where things would go once I saw Wood, so I had packed enough clothes for a three-week trip. I had just gotten through to Gardnar Mulloy by that time, and he was amenable. "Call me when you are in town," he said. "I'll fix up something. Don't worry about it." And Fred Perry, the great British champion from the mid-1930s, had also come through. He was *not* in Jamaica nor in England, but in Pompano Beach, Florida. He would see me, he said, but he was a bit guarded. I sensed that he felt he couldn't turn down a man who would travel so far for an interview but that he did not welcome the intrusion. And playing tennis with him was out. "I am under doctor's orders," he said. It was a thread, only a thread of encouragement but enough for me to feel elation. I had Betz, Wood, Mulloy, and Perry lined up. And somewhere in East Orange, New Jersey (I'd been able to narrow it down), was Althea Gibson. I had hopes for her, but they were growing dimmer. I left a few days open to work on Gibson, and with a briefcase full of notes, a camera, and a tape recorder, I flew to Washington.

The day I left, the weather on Martha's Vineyard was perfect. It was in the seventies, and as I stood at the airport, I thought of swimming on the island's south shore. I could feel myself riding in the surf, something I had done almost every day since the end of summer. I had also taken up jogging, and with only a few people on the beach, usually nude, I had run day after day with my dog, an Ohio nondescript named Lexi, beside me. I had lost maybe a few pounds and had assumed an allover tan that made my skin feel tighter and gave me a strange inner feeling of being much younger than my age. I was one month shy of my fifty-fourth birthday but felt about thirty-five, and as far as tennis went, I was at the top of my game. I had beaten Dick Craven three sets running, and then Don Davis, a summer tennis friend who had come down for a weekend, twice in succession. I was hitting hard and with accuracy. Pauline, who would be in her sixties, would be no match.

I thought about that on the way down to Washington and realized that I had missed the point. I wasn't going to compete with players older than I. I was going to *play* them or play *with* them. My book was to deal with friendship and insight into the souls of champions, not with a sports fan's contest with someone far his senior in age. What I was aiming at was something deeper. I wanted to become friends. I repeated that—I wanted to become friends with a few people whom I had idolized and maybe romanticized since youth; in some cases (Budge, Perry, Wood), with people I had idolized almost from infancy.

A true baseball fan, for instance, doesn't want to go out and challenge Joe DiMaggio to a batting contest against some pitching machine set up in Yankee Stadium. A fan of my age should want to go out and have dinner with Joe DiMaggio. Maybe the next day, he could throw a ball around and talk about batting stances, but not to see who could hit a ball out of the park. A baseball fan like me would want to say he *knew* Joe DiMaggio. That would be more than enough. And as I wrote in my introduction, tennis gave me the opportunity for knowing my idols, and it gave me the chance to exchange a few ground strokes, maybe play a set, maybe not. That should be a plus factor, a fringe benefit, and surely a kind of Plimptonesque gimmick for my book but not the overriding purpose. The actual playing would be what Hollywood calls "the hook," something to hang my story on.

It was my pleasure, therefore, that Mike Straight agreed to play doubles with Pauline and me, and after a phone call or two, a young local pro named Rob Arner agreed to be our fourth. We met at 7:00 at Cabin John. My two plane rides had landed on time. The traffic in the District of Columbia was

6

fierce, but Mike got us to his home in Bethesda with a half hour to spare. We dressed and drove to the indoor courts.

The Cabin John Indoor Tennis Courts were at the Cabin John Shopping Mall on Democracy Boulevard in Bethesda. The courts were in a building that looked like a warehouse. It was a structure that could have housed several bowling alleys and in no way projects even a hint of glamour or a suggestion that the manager and one-third owner of the building is a former world-class champion, a woman who had been on the cover of *Time* magazine, someone who as a young woman had fallen for the actor Spencer Tracy and had been Jack Dempsey's girl friend.

Inside, in a small lounge, I saw her. She was standing near a young man, laughing at some private remark. Mike went to her, his hand out, and said, "Hello, Bobbie," which I gathered was Pauline's nickname. Later I asked her about this, and she said some of her friends from the old days called her "Bobbie" and so did a few local people such as Mike. Others called her "Pauline." I called her "Pauline" because that was the name I had read in the papers and in magazines forty years ago. When we were introduced, I found myself shaking a firm hand and looking into a grandmotherly face, a face that reminded me of the supporting actress Marjorie Main. It was a Depression face, the kind Walker Evans might have considered for a photograph but rejected as being too healthy. Saying the usual trite things one says after an introduction, I thought, "I bet she was born in Oklahoma or Kansas," and reminded myself to get her family background at lunch the next day when I interviewed her. She was wearing long-legged running pants and a pink polo shirt. Her hair was short and blond, and her arms were reddish-tan and freckled. At her elbows were the telltale wrinkles of her age, which was sixty-three. The wrinkles would have given her age away had her face been lifted or beautied up in some manner. She was down-home-looking all the way and very pleasant. When not talking to Mike and me, she mingled with other guests, laughing and conversing with an easy familiarity. She was quite simply who she was: Pauline Betz Addie, the widow of the late sportswriter Bob Addie, and she ran six indoor tennis courts in Bethesda. She was totally unassuming and genial and plain and warm, and had there not been the obligatory photographs on the back wall of the lounge, this would have been the image you would take with you. But in one picture, a print of herself playing doubles with Pancho Gonzales, you see the old star. They were both professionals then, and Pancho was in the forecourt with Pauline behind him, ready to stroke her return shot. Her hair in the photo is long and blond, she is in whites, and her legs are slim and graceful. The picture was taken some twenty years ago at a benefit tournament that she and Gonzales had entered. When I turned back from the framed photograph hanging as a testament to her style and ascendancy in tennis, we were ready to play.

1. Pauline Betz and Pancho Gonzales on the attack

She chose me as her partner, and Mike and Arner took the other court. At once I could see the imbalance that would pervade our game. Rob Arner, who is probably twenty-two or -three, is short (about five-five) but extremely agile and had developed a skill that was far above anything Mike and I had to offer. As for Pauline, she showed the most effortless strokes I had ever seen on a tennis court and glided along the baseline as though wired to a pulley. Her backhand lob was perfection, lofting the ball over her opponents' heads to land an inch or two in their backhand corner. Even Rob Arner couldn't catch it. Her forehand was hard and flat, and you could hear the smack of the ball when she would slip in from her backhand court into the middle to take a shot, and the ball went back over the net hard and with power. But she was no longer a runner or a scrambler. She had that smooth glide, and she covered her side of the court, but she could not make up for my almost stationary performance and tightness, which made me pile errors on top of errors. And, of course, Rob was too strong. When he had the chance, which was often, he could slam the ball away or drop it over the net. Neither Pauline nor I could fend off his youthful exuberance, which made him look like a man springing off a rubber band. As for Mike, whom I had played almost every day out-of-doors throughout the whole summer, he suddenly flowered and was nearly errorless. At sixty-seven, he looked thirty-seven in his shorts and polo shirt in the odd light, and he just returned anything we hit his way, complementing his active partner very well. They beat us 6–4, but I think that even had I played better, they would still have won. A young man as good and as strong as Rob Arner made it very difficult for Pauline and me ever to get going. Only her lobs, her effortless, classic backhand, and an occasional hard forehand kept us in the game. The game was much more lopsided than the score indicated.

For the second set, Mike's glamorous wife, Nina, took his place. I had played with Nina every once in a while in the summer and figured that her game was surely worse than mine, and with her facing us, Pauline and I could just "play her" so that even the bounding Arner could not save the day. However, as with her husband, Nina Straight in suburban Washington was not the woman I knew from Martha's Vineyard. For one thing, she looked stunning: she was in a purple running outfit with some kind of lace hanging down over her wrists. Her dark hair was kind of blow-dried so that it dazzled you in a controlled, messy fashion. And her face, often photographed, is undeniably pretty. Her tennis was superb. She was hitting strong shots, low and controlled, and had a slice backhand that took away my serve as I kept serving to her backhand corner, assuming an error would follow. Instead she would slice it back to my backhand, and Arner would move to center court and put my weak return away. I yelled and cursed at myself, but Nina had confounded me, and there was no use in trying to pressure her. She was too good (all of a sudden) and like Mike seemed born for indoor tennis. And age was beginning to count. Nina and Rob together added up in years to maybe a touch more than Pauline alone, and then I had to add almost fifty-four years on top of that. The two of them had us completely on the defensive, and I felt a great deal of mortification that I had not risen to the challenge at all, that I had let Pauline down, that I was not moving, not covering my side of the court, not going to the net, not serving with any sting, and unable to return Rob's twisting serve at all. I had written to Pauline (as I had to others) that I was "an upper B-level player." I was playing at a lower B-level, and I feared some kind of remark from Pauline to the effect that I might have overrated myself. I also expected a few tips—some friendly advice from a pro that would have been ill-taken because I was so furious at my ineptitude. Neither was forthcoming. She just glided along, her backhand a thing of beauty, her occasional forehand hard as a teenager's but her reflexes slowed by time and unable to take on Rob Arner's placements and speed and sometimes Nina's slices, while I just stood around and felt out of place. They won 6–3 in a game that should have been 6–0. Pauline was able to win her serves, and maybe we took Nina once.

Pauline's serve, by the way, was relatively soft but well placed. It hit the forehand corner and then went down the center line just enough to keep Rob Arner on his toes and Nina a bit apprehensive. Rob often would lob it over my head at net, and it would drop a winner because I was too immobile to step back and crunch it with a leap, and Pauline was no longer fast enough to go from corner to corner behind me. When the game ended and we all shook hands, Nina was redolent and Pauline was grinning. She had had a good workout, she said, and she liked it very much. It was a good time. "Thank you all," she said, and then we left the court. Arner, an ebullient, cheerful type, was full of comments and quips, and he too seemed to have enjoyed himself. All of this good cheer lifted my spirits. I knew that playing indoors for the first time in a few years of constant outdoor play had disoriented me. "So what!" I thought. It really doesn't matter, and it didn't. We had played together, Pauline and I, and that was what I had come for. But I still did battle within my mind.

I didn't want her to think I had overrated myself. If she thought that on the solid evidence at hand I had misled her, there was nothing I could do about it now. I hated to be thought of as being a braggart. I wanted her to like me and to trust me. The next day at lunch, I felt that she did, and later when I rehashed my experience at Cabin John, I reasoned that I had just had a bad day—it happens to everyone. But damn, why did it have to happen on my first match with a world-class champion whose picture hung on the wall, with a remarkable blond woman at the ready, her glowing good looks and power backing up the incomparable Pancho Gonzales? "Damn," I thought, "why couldn't I have played like Gonzales for her sake, for my own sake?" But in the back of my mind, I was beginning to realize that there was no way in the world I was going to play like Pauline Betz, much less like the great Pancho. Both Mike and Nina had risen to the occasion and had acquitted themselves beautifully while I had regressed. Those were the facts. I kept telling myself to forget the aspect of competition, of winning. "That's not why you're here, Stan," I said to myself. But at heart, I knew I was lying. Once on the court, I wanted to shine—especially in front of an idol, a legend from my childhood.

The next morning, I called a cab around 11:30 and arrived at Cabin John in ten minutes or so. While Pauline made some arrangements and tidied up, I chatted with her assistant, a young woman of about twenty-two. Finally she asked me, "Just who really *is* Pauline Betz?"

She had never known that her employer had once been famous. I told her. I said, "For a time, she was the best woman tennis player in the world. She won Wimbledon and several U.S. titles and countless minor tournaments and then turned professional. Also," I added, "if memory serves me, she was very good-looking. You might say she had a large following in pretelevision America. It was a time when you could separate a hero or heroine from a celebrity. Today," I said gravely, "we have celebrities. There is a difference."

"Wow! She won Wimbledon?"

"And Forest Hills," I said. "Several times."

"No wonder people ask about her," said the young woman. "I just never knew."

Of course, all this was great for me. It was precisely what I was looking for. I was finding someone contemporary America had forgotten. At least, Pauline's own assistant had not even known in order to forget. Presumably when she took the job, no one had said, "Well, young lady, you'll certainly have a famous boss." The point had been confirmed that Pauline wasn't famous anymore, and that was all to the good. I could pretend that I was Frank Buck and would bring them back alive through my prose. I thought of this as we entered a cul de sac delicatessen for lunch in a shopping center close to the tennis courts. Also, I had thought, "Wouldn't it be nice if Pauline should emerge from the women's locker room wearing a dress ready to go into Washington for a real lunch in a great restaurant?" But no. This trim five-seven or so woman with a western twang to her voice came out in her long running pants and her tennis shoes. If there were still shades of the old days in her life, she was not showing them to me. She worked, took a short lunch, and went back to work. I would have to fit myself into her schedule. And so I did.

Pauline was raised in Los Angeles and went to Los Angeles High School, where her mother was a physical education instructor. All her young life, she had played sports, and her mother had been her guiding force. Her father came from Dayton, Ohio, and her mother was from Kansas (which pleased me because I had first thought that Pauline was from somewhere near Oklahoma—at least her mother was). Though she was born in Ohio in 1920, the family moved soon after to Los Angeles. By the time she was fourteen, she was entering junior tennis tournaments, and in her third tournament she became a winner. Apparently after that victory, there was little doubt in her mind that she would reach the top and become the best tennis player in the world. "It came as a shock to me that it took so long," she said with a slight smile. And right then I saw a similarity to another Kansan born in Denison, Texas: Dwight D. Eisenhower.

As she talked on about her junior career and racking up wins in southern California, I thought of Eisenhower and recognized in Pauline that same sense of inner confidence and self-possession I had seen in the late general back in the mid-1960s. His son John and I and Sam Vaughan, an editor from Doubleday (Eisenhower's publisher), had gone to Gettysburg to talk to the general. We tried to get him to agree to switch a vast amount of personal material from Doubleday to Little, Brown and, moreover, to turn everything over to his son so that his son could write the big book on the Western Alliance that Eisenhower, himself, was willing to commence but was then (or so it was thought) too old and often too infirm to pull off. It was a rather extraordinary adventure in publishing because we were trying tactfully to suggest to Eisenhower that it would be better for everyone if John wrote "the big book" based on his father's material than to have the father write it himself. Even the general's own publisher had concurred since Eisenhower's health was suspect and the project would be a long one. (John and I had hit it off, and I worked for Little, Brown.) That was the nub of it all, and I had high hopes and was thrilled to be meeting Eisenhower. The only trouble was that when we all sat down at a large conference table along with several aides and the general entered the room, wearing a sharply creased blue suit and flashing that famous grin of his, I froze. He had such an inner sense of authority and command that I dared not speak lest I say something that would turn the smile on his face into a frown. With such a man, I did not know how far I could go or how far I could press, and I was scared to death that whatever I might say would lead him to think that I thought he was too old to do the work that his son could do with time and ease. So I sat mute. He made me too nervous to be tactful.

Pauline had that same inner authority. I would rather rob a bank than tease her, and teasing attractive women had become a habit of mine. So I was halting and cautious in our conversation. Her hazel eyes had seen so much more than I would ever see. Her athletic supremacy had been stupendous. And, finally, she had those Kansan roots, and here we were so close to the White House, and memories of my stage fright with Eisenhower flooded through my mind.

But she went on, oblivious to my remembrances. She said that she doubted that good character had much to do with the making of a champion. She said that competitiveness and motivation were the keys, and that if anything, probably it was a *defect* in character that propelled people to the top. By *character*, she meant moral and ethical ideals that people "with character" adhered to. A champion, then, was someone who wanted to win. You could leave it at that.

By the time she was eighteen, she was on the road traveling with a young woman named Jane Stanton. She went to Florida to enter some tournaments and then up to New York for the National Indoor Championships. It was 1939, and she won. "We had good players in California," she said. "Alice Marble was probably the best woman around, but there was another girl named Barbara Winslow, who died at eighteen of amoebic dysentery. I am convinced she would have been the greatest tennis player in the world, maybe as good or better than even Helen Wills and Helen Jacobs."

Going east with $35 in her pocket and a guaranteed $25 in expenses at each tournament was exciting stuff for the young woman, a fresh-faced California blonde who could run down almost any shot and just loved to play and play and play tennis. By 1941 she again won the indoor singles but also won the ladies' doubles, playing with a college teammate, Dorothy "Dodo" Bundy. Rollins College in Florida had come through with a tennis scholarship, and she was playing for Rollins' men's tennis team, amassing a string of wartime victories, winning at Forest Hills in 1942, 1943, 1944, and 1946 and the indoors again in 1943 and 1947, and also taking the doubles in 1943 with a partner in her fifties, Hazel Hotchkiss Wightman. At Wimbledon's first tournament after the war, Pauline won the ladies' singles in 1946. By the end of 1947, she turned professional.

If she had a major competitor during that time, the record indicates it was either Sarah Palfrey Cooke or Margaret Osborne duPont. Apparently Sarah Palfrey (who now prefers to be known for tennis purposes by her maiden name) did not intimidate Pauline, but Margaret Osborne did. Although Pauline was able to beat her, she always had the fear that she might not since Margaret Osborne duPont was too steady and strong.

Pauline signed on as a professional because, she said, "I had won what I wanted to win. There wasn't anywhere else to go." She was teamed up with Sarah Palfrey, Don Budge, and Bobby Riggs. Of Riggs, she says, "I liked Bobby better than anybody. If anyone was in trouble, he was always there to give people money." He was also her all-time favorite men's doubles partner, and her childhood friend Budge Patty was a close second. "Budge Patty and I grew up near each other in California. He was about four or five years younger than I, and when he was twelve and I was around sixteen, we were even. He was a tremendous player to practice against." As for grand-slam winner Don

13

Budge, she says, "I liked Don. I loved his backhand. That's where I got my backhand from, Don Budge." And as everyone knows who has played with her, her backhand is the strongest part of her game. As for the last member of the professional foursome, Sarah Palfrey, Pauline says that Sarah was her favorite woman partner. In all, it must have been a happy group that toured together after the war.

It was during this period that she joined the Hollywood crowd. She liked Spencer Tracy and dated him. "Not before or after Katharine Hepburn . . . during a hiatus." She also went out with Jack Dempsey. "He was really a soft man. I liked him a lot. One time when we were entering the Stork Club, I met an old beau of mine coming out. He said to Jack, 'If you don't leave my girl alone, I'll punch you in the jaw.' Jack laughed, and we walked in. I liked that."

She particularly liked Palm Springs and played at the Racquet Club. "I practically lived there," she said, and one can imagine those free-spirited years that seem almost unbelievable now, when World War II was just over, the world was at peace (presumably for at least a lifetime), and every day was full of exuberance as young people reassembled their lives with grins on their faces and carefree hearts. No doubt Pauline was enveloped in those heyday years, and, of course, she was famous. After winning Wimbledon, she made the cover of *Time* magazine. To the editors at *Time*, she surely personified the outdoor California look as well as American dominance in the world. She was a superior twenty-six-year-old woman just as America was then the superior nation, and Henry Luce at *Time* must have loved that cover as much as Pauline loved the exciting life that was opening up for her.

After all, she had been born poor. She had two devoted parents, a brother, and a sister, and she used the public tennis courts of Los Angeles, especially Griffith Park, which was near her home, where she could play until her young legs finally grew tired. "I figured I had the best of all worlds. I had a great childhood, and if I had it to do all over again, I'd only ask for a better volley and overhead. No," she said, "I would not have wanted money. I was lucky to be born poor. If you are from a poor family, you fight your way up. That was the best thing that could have happened to me."

And then came a tennis scholarship to Rollins College. She played for Rollins and later at Columbia, where she had an academic scholarship through which she pursued a master's degree in economics. All this had come, she said, from "fighting your way up." It all added up to a nice package, and later on before she began to tour with Gussie Moran ("a very good player whose game was overlooked because of her 'panty publicity' "), this rather well-rounded woman—equipped with an advanced education, exposure to the world, athletic ability, good looks, and brains—was noticed by sportswriter Bob Addie. They met at Al Schact's restaurant in New York. Not too long

14

after that, in 1950, they were married. "My husband was recalled into service during the Korean War, and I went on tour with Gussie. Later when he was discharged, we settled in Washington because he was writing for *The Washington Post*."

She became a club pro, working at different places around the nation's capital, and began having her family, five children. It was a pleasant life and especially so because of her husband. I asked her a question from a list I had drawn up: "Now as you reflect upon your life, who are the men and women you admire the most?" Without hesitation, she said, "My husband. He was the most admirable of men, the most compassionate . . ." and then her voice trailed off. After a pause, she said, "I don't spend too much time thinking about public figures. I guess you'd have to put Eleanor Roosevelt on the top of a public list. And all writers. Not just sportswriters but all writers." Another pause. "Grantland Rice (a famous sportswriter, nevertheless) comes to mind." Then she said, thinking about it some more, "I loved comedians. Men like Milton Berle. I knew him and liked him. And Spencer Tracy." And then the subject was dropped.

As I led her back in time, she pulled at her memory. "My most memorable victory was in 1942 in the finals at Forest Hills when I beat Louise Brough. I was not supposed to win." She was twenty-two then and upset Miss Brough 4–6, 6–1, 6–4.

I went down my list of questions: "If you had a chance to relive your life, what would you change?"

"I'd get a better serve and volley," she said. "And if there were anything else I would have liked to have become, I would like to have been a stand-up comedian." But she never tried show business or the movies. She just kept at tennis until her marriage and family life took over.

"What about world events? Would you want to see poverty erased and see an end to the threat of nuclear war?"

"I used to be involved in that sort of thing when I was young. I was a socialist in college and all for the labor unions. Now I guess I am more cynical. I suppose I should think more about politics, but I don't. I'd like to learn how to write braille—you know, books for the blind. Someday I'll get back to that. I am too busy now . . . but someday I *will* get back to that."

And busy she is. In a day, she will be off to Stuart, Florida, where she owns her own tennis club. She has her private lessons to give, Cabin John to run, and her seven-bedroom home in Bethesda to keep in order. She also has her ninety-year-old mother (the one real hero in her life) to look after. "I just got her Mustang fixed up," she says proudly, implying a mother full of grit, from the old Kansas background of cornsilk and moonglow, from the California Depression years of clean air and physical education—all that background now an obvious asset. She speaks of her mother with a moving sense of respect.

And she believes in God. She is a Catholic from German-Scotch stock, and she attends Mass. Norman Rockwell and Horatio Alger come to mind. And you can add to that a touch of 1940s Hollywood when good people won out in the end. She drives a Thunderbird, a throwback to the open roads of the West.

I asked her if she resented the fact that current tennis players were making so much money while she had received so little. "No. I would rather be number one and not making any money than number four and making millions. The only thing I *would* resent would be if the men were making the money and the women weren't. But that isn't the case."

As for any wisdom to impart, she said, "My philosophy of life is this: You never know what is good for you or what's bad. When anything terrible happens to me, I look at it that way. It may turn out for the best."

"Who was the greatest player you ever saw play?" I asked.

"Don Budge. Maybe Jack Kramer was next, behind Don."

Asking an obvious question, I said, "How would you compare yourself in your prime to the women tennis stars of today?"

"Who knows?" she answered. "But I will tell you one thing. I would like to play Billie Jean and Martina, people who come to the net, rather than Tracy or Chrissie, who stay back. But then," she paused, "after seeing Martina this year, I am not so sure about her." Years back she had beaten a younger champion, Althea Gibson, who was a serve-and-volley player. And at that time, Pauline had just had her fifth child. So I nodded, recognizing that the so-called "big game" was up her alley but that all the way back to Margaret Osborne, who was a baseline player, it was the conservative opponent who gave her the most trouble.*

Her sports interests now? "I'd rather play golf now than tennis. Any good athlete or good tennis player should be able to switch over to golf. Unfortunately there is not enough similarity in the swing; otherwise I would be a better golfer."

I mentioned Ellsworth Vines, who beat Bill Tilden, the best tennis player in the world, and then went on to beat Ben Hogan, the best golfer in the world in a playoff in Chicago at the Tam O'Shanter. "Oh, yes," she said, "but think of a woman, Mary K. Browne. She was a winner in tennis and a semifinalist or finalist in golf at the same time. In *amateur tourna-*

---

* Margaret Osborne duPont does not consider herself a baseline player. She was also a serve-and-volley player when she chose.

ments, but at the same time. She didn't leave one sport and then go on to practice at another. That was the greatest feat I know of if you're talking golf and tennis ability, switching sports—to be at the top at the same time, simultaneously."

(Mary K. Browne's name will come up often in this book. Ranked first in the United States in 1913 and 1914, she was induced to turn professional in 1926 and play the incredible French champion, Suzanne Lenglen, on tour in the United States. And so began the age of the touring tennis professional in this country. Earlier in her career Miss Browne had amazed the world of sport by taking a set from Helen Wills in the finals of a major grass tournament— the only set that Miss Wills had lost in a year. Then within two weeks, Mary K. Browne went on to beat the best woman golfer of the time, Glenna Collett, in the semifinals of a golf tournament. As Pauline Betz Addie said, Mary K. Browne was superb in two sports "simultaneously." Clearly this back-to-back feat places her with Ellsworth Vines in the legends of great athletic achievements.)

By now it was time to stop. She had a lesson to give, and I had a flight to catch for New York. The hamburgers we had eaten and the pot of coffee were gone. I was smoking a cigarette and asked if it bothered her. "If it doesn't bother you, it doesn't bother me," she answered with a smile.

2. Pauline Betz

I took a picture or two of her outside the Cabin John Indoor Tennis Courts. I saw again her long feminine arms freckled in the misty overcast afternoon. There was no noticeable trace of muscle in them, and her figure still held its curves. These may have been crass thoughts—looking at the outer beauty of a woman. But she had her charms, there was no doubt about that; her lined actress face was prettier now than it had been when I saw her in the evening. I was not thinking of Marjorie Main when we parted. I was thinking of splendor on cement courts out there in southern California: a blond perpetual-motion machine who could run anything down, return any shot. I imagined her at Rollins, where she waited on tables to get money to live on and played tennis and was still able to earn her degree that got her to Columbia University graduate school. And I saw her as a businesswoman who studied tax law at night so that she could be more effective with her tennis enterprises. But mostly I just saw her as another human being who is very likable and who has learned to use her skills.

If you didn't like Pauline Betz Addie, there had to be something wrong with you. But I wouldn't want to say that to her face. I didn't, and waved good-bye.

CHAPTER

2

Althea Gibson:

Looking Straight Ahead

By the time I reached National Airport the rain was descending through a deep cloud cover. I soon found that the LaGuardia shuttles had been backed up by hours. I had intended to catch a 4:00 flight but caught one scheduled for 2:00. A friend, David McCullough, who has won several prizes for his writing (*The Great Bridge, The Path Between The Seas, Mornings On Horseback*), was to fly up with me. From my cab, I saw him go into the terminal and then lost him. When I found I had a chance for a plane about to leave, I grabbed it, thinking David had done the same. He was not on board. I crammed myself into the rear of the aircraft and waited for takeoff—another ninety minutes of sitting out on the flight line.

At LaGuardia I learned that my overload of luggage had not arrived with the plane. I had written Alice Marble, Ellsworth Vines, and Louise Brough, all living out in the Palm Springs area, that I would be coming out. If things ran thin in Florida, that was where I would go. Although I had Mulloy and Perry lined up, I was still uncertain. Suppose they changed their minds? I wanted Vines and Marble in particular because I felt they had the highest name recognition. After being stalled by Don Budge (he said he'd see me in November), I was prepared for whatever might come. But for now, I waited for my suitcases to arrive.

Finally another shuttle from Washington made it through the murk of

Long Island skies, and I saw both David McCullough and a tennis agent named Ray Benton emerge from the arrival ramp. Benton had been Don Dell's partner and was well known in the sports world as representing hot property tennis players. I made a note that I might have to call him someday if I needed help. McCullough just waved and said he had to rush. He was to give a presentation of his one-man show on Teddy Roosevelt for the New York Historical Society, and he was already very late. And then as I paced about, I saw Mike Straight. He was going back to Washington, having been in New York for a full day of business. I waved good-bye to him as he dashed down the departure ramp still looking trim and neat in a suit, as unruffled as he was on the tennis court, and I was reminded of my bad play once more.

I stayed at the Pan American Motor Hotel because that was where Sidney B. Wood, Jr., would call me in the morning. I went to bed early, reading myself to sleep with Joe McGinnis' *Fatal Vision* and wondered if I would ever be able to write a book as good as his. I wished I'd started earlier in life, not waited until middle age. Then I turned off the light and fell asleep.

There was no call from Sidney Wood. Finally I called his office in Woodside and was told by his secretary that he could not see me. He was having directors' meetings all day. I persisted a bit, and she said nicely that Wood had instructed her to tell me that he couldn't see me—period.

I had been anticipating this rejection. I don't know how, but people can sense a delaying action. Of course, it had cost me extra money to go down to Washington from Massachusetts and then back again. I could have scheduled Pauline *after* New Jersey, on my way to Florida. And in my anticipation of being rejected by Wood, I decided to call Althea at her home.

Over the preceding two weeks, I had been able finally to reach her. I'd gotten her home number from Don Budge, who said to say hello. At the time, I thought he'd given the number to me to get me off the phone. She told me in turn that she didn't discuss matters such as interviews without getting the approval of her business manager, Sydney Llewellyn. In Washington, calling from the Straight's home, I had gotten the green light from Sydney Llewellyn with one proviso: I had to pay Althea Gibson money. This is how the resolution to this situation came about.

After carefully explaining the purpose of my book, which is that I was attempting to look up the tennis legends of my youth and play with them, he began to talk about Althea. He said that she was apt to be negative at first, but if I could break through this barrier, I would find a very warm and generous human being. So I said, "Why don't I ask her if she will give me a tennis lesson? She is, after all, a pro, and she can help me with my game as I talk with her." Sydney Llewellyn chuckled at my ploy and confided that my idea would probably work. I'd have to pay, he said, but if I called her with this approach, she could hardly refuse. After all she *does* give lessons. He agreed to my proposal and said I could see her with his permission.

So by Thursday morning, I had Althea in my pocket at a cost of $100 ($50 for the lesson, $50 for an hour of talk). We were to meet on Sunday morning at 10:00 A.M. at the Rallye Racquet Club in East Orange, New Jersey. Wood's avoidance of me was therefore not catastrophic. All I had to do was idle about Queens or New York City from Thursday morning until Sunday morning.

Of course, I went directly into the city. I called Dick Craven and went to stay with Dick and his wife, Carol. And as things turned out, this was a wonderful visit. I don't think I'd seen New York with a completely sober eye in years. Usually when I visited the city, it was to party about and then return home tired and feeling somewhat ill. But this trip was to be a teetotaling one, as I wanted all my senses to be as sharp as they could possibly be.

On Saturday Dick and I drove out with David Smith and Hank Rowley to the Rockaway Hunting Club for a full day of tennis on simulated *en tout cas* courts. We played right across the road from the great grass courts of Cedarhurst, site of the over-sixty-five finals, where Riggs had recently beaten Gardnar Mulloy. Eventually a fifth player showed up, and we began to switch off, although I did not get a break. I played almost five hours of doubles, and my game sharpened. I felt very healthy out there near the Atlantic Ocean under very bright skies. It was like being on a sailboat. The wind blew constantly, and the sun boiled through salt air. We had a short lunch in the clubhouse and heard long tales from a man who had known Bill Tilden. By the end of the day, I was on fire to play Althea and felt in trim. Although I had not been planning on going out on the town, that full day of tennis may have saved me from doing so. I hate idling about for too long, but now, full of good feelings, I set off for East Orange to stay in a motel for the night. I wanted to be nearby for my match or my lesson or whatever was forthcoming with Althea.

East Orange is a predominantly black city. On weekends (it was Saturday night), almost every white person is gone. What East Orange looks like is an urban ghost town. I'd hired a driver who had gotten lost finding a motel, and we drove for perhaps a half hour down side streets and along back roads, where a few blacks ambled in the night, enjoying the weekend. When we found Central Avenue, the main street, we found a thoroughfare devoid of life. Shops and banks and stores lined this street, but not a soul could be seen. We finally arrived at the Royal Inn, and as I signed the registration, the young black clerk told me not to go outside for a walk. But she knew who Althea Gibson was, and her eyebrows rose when I said I would be seeing Gibson the next day. As she spoke, I had the feeling that Althea Gibson was a local hero. This would be a little different from Pauline Betz Addie, who goes unnoticed in Bethesda. I went to bed in a deserted motel, a onetime Holiday Inn, eager for tomorrow.

The next morning, Althea Gibson drove her elongated Mercury sedan into the parking lot. I was just about to ascend the steps when I turned and saw her: a woman alone, a rather large, handsome, brown face behind the windshield. She was wearing glasses. "East Orange is a long way from Lawrence Welk," I thought. This project of mine had begun because of names heard in my youth, names of tennis players that were bandied about our living room. But Althea belonged to my generation. My father (who in his later years watched Lawrence Welk on TV), were he still alive, would not have been interested in her. She was not Alice Marble, and her skin was brown. He would have liked Evonne Goolagong, who is also brown-skinned, but Evonne is Australian. American blacks were invisible to my father's crowd; there was no plus or minus attached to them, they just were not there. I liked Althea Gibson *because* she was American and was a black and had done what Pauline Betz Addie extolled: she had fought her way up. You mention Althea Gibson, and you also think of Martin Luther King, Jr., and Jackie Robinson.

She was taking her time in the front seat of her car, and I stood and waited, thinking of my thoughts at breakfast. I had eaten in the coffeeshop at the Royal Inn, eating alone amid a scattered group of what looked to be affluent black businessmen already scanning their Sunday papers.

I was in the Air Force when I first heard of Althea Gibson. She caught my attention because she was a black person who might do for tennis and the entire country club sports world what Jackie Robinson had done for the mass sport of baseball. Marion Motley and Bob Willis had integrated pro football for the Cleveland Browns, both becoming NFL all-stars just as I was entering the service, and before that Yale had elected Levi Jackson as its football captain. Everything was beginning to open up—even the armed services themselves where, at least in the Air Force, black airmen enjoyed complete equality, and the segregated companies of World War II were over with. But tennis and golf—the kind of games I might play at a later date—were still untouched with what I, a middle-class white youth, romantically called "brown grace." It was hard to conceive of an American black playing lawn tennis or joining the pro golf tour to play alongside Texans Ben Hogan and Byron Nelson. As a matter of fact, it was hard to think of an American Jew who was doing that. Yet by 1952, Althea was gaining a reputation. She was cleaning up in the American Tennis Association—the black tennis league. In 1950 she made the papers because she had broken through the color screen, was being sponsored by the American Tennis Association, and was the recipient of a favorable letter backing her from the great Alice Marble. She was allowed to enter a tournament, the Eastern Indoor at the 369th Regiment

Armory at 143rd Street and Fifth Avenue (Harlem) in New York.* She won that tournament and later entered Forest Hills. In 1951 she entered Wimbledon. All that had impressed me as a kid in the service, and this impression was augmented by my relationship with members of the tennis team at Mather Air Force Base near Sacramento.

In the spring of 1954, I joined the team because I had discovered that if a person kept playing sports, authority figures, such as first sergeants and squadron commanders, lost track of you. I had played semipro softball, football, and basketball by then, and as stated the Korean War was over. Fervent patriotism was a thing of the past. My work load became fuzzy at best as I was forever going off to practice or to a game. Eventually I was ignored, and the entire Air Force base became like some giant exercise yard. Whatever training I had received was eroded by a jump shot or an overhead or a line drive. I served my last year of a four-year hitch on the playing fields; peace had come again, and it was not hard for me to rationalize myself away from duty.

The tennis team had two black officers, both lieutenants. I was playing number three or four on the team at that time, and among the group we had a major and a couple of sergeants—one a huge man named Frankie Kovac, who had sunken knuckles from years of fighting and boxing. Our schedule sent us off to towns such as Modesto and Yuba City, where we played junior college teams. We also played in Reno, Nevada, against Stead Air Force Base and around Sacramento. One time, returning from a tennis match, we stopped to eat dinner at some roadside restaurant. It was, after all, 1954, and we were in California. But our black second lieutenants would not be served. Kovac rose to his full height and went to the bartender who had instructed the waitress "to get them out of here" and with one arm Kovac lifted the bartender from behind the safety of his bar and drew him across so that his face was staring at Kovac's other fist, clenched. Kovac didn't say anything. He just held the man and then pushed him back and turned to us and said, "Let's get the hell out of this dump."

I could not forget that and my remembering it lent a certain piquancy to my meeting with Althea Gibson.

Althea came from her car looking at me, her eyes alert with curiosity. I had the feeling that she didn't think I would show up—that I was some crank who had pestered her into commitments and pestered her business manager, Sydney Llewellyn, as well. She was pulling a metal carriage like a shopping cart, only it was constructed for tennis pros and was filled with old tennis balls. "She actually is going to give me a lesson," I thought, and looking at

* Months later I played there along with Dick Craven. One could not help but think of Althea and the man who came in her wake, Arthur Ashe, who also played in that same armory.

3. Althea Gibson

her array of balls, I imagined her standing patiently at the net, hitting me easy shots, and I would flail about awkwardly trying to hit them back. I had told her in my introductory letter that I could play fairly well, but then she had not read my letter—that was obvious from the phone conversations and now from the ball carriage.

We went onto the court, she in maroon warm-up clothes and I in my tennis shorts. We were the only ones at the Rallye Racquet Club other than an assistant manager, who sat around and listened to rock music from a transistor radio. "Dick Craven and his friends in New York should know about this place," I thought. They could come out on a Sunday morning and play all day. Just bring some food and drink and make a day of it. No one else in East Orange was interested, or so it seemed. (As a matter of fact, when we broke off the interview more than two hours later, the six courts were still empty.)

"Don't leave anything in the locker room," Althea warned me. I was going to leave a pair of pants and a sweater down there, but I took them to the court instead. This was black America in 1983. Someone would swipe the trousers, thinking there was petty cash in the pockets. It *was* a long way from Lawrence Welk or the Vineyard, for that matter, and for a second I thought I was involved in some kind of reverse integration. Althea offered no comment as I piled my pants up along the end of the net. She stopped at midcourt and began hitting soft shots at me.

But that morning, I was a little more familiar with the lights than I had been with Pauline Betz Addie. I began to line a few back at her and then passed her a couple of times, and she backed up to her own baseline. She told me I didn't bend my knees, which was true. She also said I "pushed" my backhand because I would not change my grip. She showed me how to change the forehand grip to a backhand grip and then went back to hit again. I stayed with my old ways, and she admitted that if I was comfortable that way and only played for fun, what did it matter? After I made her stretch for a few hard shots, she suggested a pro set. In a pro set you must get eight games to win, and you must win by two. I happily agreed.

Althea's game is strong, and she goes right for the corners. Her net game is her calling card, and at five ten and one-half she has surprisingly long arms, longer than the men I had been used to playing who were taller than she. Once at net, it was hard to pass her, and I dared not lob because she had me always on the run and on the defensive, and I couldn't trust myself. It was also more fun to try to get it by her. I hit one great backhand with the grip she said had no power, and she just watched it whiz by and said, "Nice shot," and she looked, briefly, amazed. But she was winning; she was ahead 4–1.

I broke Althea's serve then, and I even aced her and was able to win points by hitting it deep and making her run—and began to come back. Eventually at 5–4, I had her serve broken again—almost. She sent a deep shot to my forehand corner, which bounced high and away. I had seen it coming, however, and caught it on the dead run. I hit it as hard as I could down to her backhand corner. She was almost at net, and my shot came into her court from a wide angle. It was impossible for her to reach it. It caught the inside of the line, and we were at 5–5, with my serve coming up and my spirits soaring. "Out!" she yelled, and I looked at her, stunned. She walked slowly back to where my ball had struck, where I had seen it land, having had a perfect view of the shot while she had to twist her head around to see it, and she said, "It was a pretty shot, but it just landed outside." I made a mental note to ask her about her glasses. How was her eyesight? I didn't think she would consciously cheat, but damn it, the ball was in.

We ended with her winning 8–6. Both of us were sweating, and Althea was grinning as she walked to the net. "You play a lot better than I thought you would," she said. I told her I played better outside, that I was disoriented by the indoor lights, which was the same excuse I had used with Pauline. She nodded, and we went inside to talk.

Althea was born in a little town called Silver, South Carolina, where her family picked cotton. When she was about one year old, she was brought to Harlem by her aunt. On the streets of New York, she played the sports that were available: "I was blessed with natural ability and body coordination and natural timing. Prior to my becoming a tennis champion, I was a bowler, a softball player, and a basketball player. I played Ping-Pong, shot pool—I did anything that took timing and coordination. I even became a semiprofessional basketball player. But it was Harlem paddle tennis that got me into real tennis."

Althea lived on 143rd Street, where the Police Athletic League (PAL) had its paddle tennis courts. "One day I picked up the paddle, one summer morning . . . and I started to play. Tennis just evolved out of what I was doing on 143rd Street. The PAL did a lot for me."

Althea also went to school, to a trade school where she learned to fix sewing machines because of "the dexterity in my hands. Sewing came natural to me." It took eye-hand coordination, but she dropped out. Sports took over as she began winning the American Tennis Association championships—ten in a row as it turned out.

"The ATA decided that I was their national champion, and in 1950 the ATA people called a meeting and got together with the United States Tennis Association officials and discussed my entering a USLTA-sponsored tournament. Open letters were sent in my behalf, and Alice Marble in particular sent one admonishing the USLTA for not permitting me to play. Well, they relented, and I played my first indoor tournament, the Eastern Indoor, at the 369th Regiment Armory, also on 143rd Street."

Althea won that tournament, and that was the beginning. In 1950 she entered the tournament at Forest Hills, and soon she was ready for her first trip to Wimbledon. It was 1951, and a black community leader named Dean Hoxie invited Althea to his youth camp in Detroit. In Detroit a group of people got together and raised enough money for her trip to England. "They had a fund-raising affair at the Plane Showbar, and at that time Joe Louis used to have a suite at the Gotham Hotel in Detroit. Upon learning of this endeavor (to get me to England), he gave me a round-trip ticket he had but wasn't going to use. So that was his contribution."

The Detroit group put Althea up at a hotel, the name of which she has long forgotten, but she will never forget the friendship of her Detroit supporters. "Although the war had been over since 1945, they still didn't have any meat in England. So they flew steaks over for me so I wouldn't have to sustain myself on fish and poultry.''

Althea ate well and kept up her strength, and when she was ready for her first match, she vowed to keep her mind only on tennis—never mind the fact that she was the first black person to play on Wimbledon grass.

"My first opponent was Pat Ward, one of their top players, and the match was scheduled for center court. The grass was beautiful; it was so velvety and plush. It was easy on the feet, and I decided that all I was going to watch was the ball and not notice the 19,000 people who were sitting there to watch me, and I wasn't even going to watch Pat Ward. 'Just watch the ball,' I said over and over, and I concentrated so hard I won the first set 6–0. Now, after winning the first set, I looked around as if to say, 'Now, how do you like that?' I was a novice to them, a novelty I should say. The second set, I lost 6–0 'cause I stopped watching the ball. I was in my glory on the hallowed grounds of Wimbledon, and I had won my first set. Now however it was a battle. I eked it out 7–5.''

She lost in the second round however to a young Californian, Beverly Baker Fleitz. "She was ambidextrous and had no backhand. She'd switch hands, and that gave me fits. And, as a matter of fact, it always did. She beat me more consistently than anyone else, as time went on.''

Althea would not win at Wimbledon for six years—not until 1957—but she had generated support within the black community. She was still winning her ATA tournaments and had found a pair of benefactors from the South: two doctors, one named Ekins from Wilmington, North Carolina, and another named Johnson from Lynchburg, Virginia. These two men had come into her life back when she was with the American Tennis Association, winning, of course, but young and with an unsure future. They saw her play in a tournament in Xenia, Ohio. "They were watching the match, and I went over afterward and sat between them, and they said, 'How would you like to play Forest Hills?' by which they meant with the United States Tennis Association. I said, 'Huh?' and that started it. I went back to high school to Wilmington, North Carolina, in 1946 and graduated three years later. I kept playing tennis, and it was because of the love and concern of these two tennis buffs, tennis players, that I got my entry into Forest Hills.''

Indeed Althea's life was a mosaic, with the pieces slowly—sometimes almost simultaneously—beginning to fall into place. First the great natural ability displayed in Harlem and the career at paddle tennis that led to regular tennis; then the tournaments with the black tennis league; and finally the black doctors who took her life into their hands and also the intervention of people such as Alice Marble and the officials of the ATA, who pressed for her entry into USLTA tournaments. All of this came to a head in Forest Hills and a year later at Wimbledon. All of this rather random but somehow orchestrated movement in time brought her to center court, where she beat Pat Ward in 1951.

She practiced at the 369th Regiment Armory. She played on wood at the armory, "which is the fastest surface of all." Her game was (and still is) serve and volley. "I also had a great overhead, and I was fast. No one could hardly pass me, especially if I got the ball deep. I won on all surfaces: grass, hard court, and clay, as well as wood. People thought I was ruthless, which I was. I didn't give a darn who was on the other side of the net. I'd knock you down if you got in the way."

It was not surprising that by the mid-1950s, the State Department had caught on to this peppery athlete from what used to be called the wrong side of the tracks. She epitomized the promise of America, and she began a worldwide journey as a public figure representing the United States. As an "ambassador-at-large," she played in tournaments in Sweden, Germany, France, Monaco, Burma . . . the list seemed endless, and always she was improving. In 1956 she won the French Women's Singles Championship, her first victory in one of the four major tournaments. Later that year, she won at Wimbledon, for the first time playing doubles with Angela Buxton. In 1957 she won the singles at both Wimbledon and Forest Hills. In 1958 she repeated this, as well as winning the women's doubles for the third straight year at Wimbledon, each time with a different partner. In 1957 she won the U.S. mixed doubles, playing with the now all-but-forgotten Swede, Kurt Nielsen.

By the summer of 1958, Althea Gibson was thirty years old. Like so many black athletes, her career had been slowed by segregation. She had ten years running in the ATA and had beaten the best in the world in tournaments across the world. She had also represented America in the Wightman Cup against Great Britain and had gone everywhere for the State Department. By late summer, after her last victory at Forest Hills, the world was at peace, the Eisenhower years were winding down, a young Jack Kennedy was waiting in the wings, and black athletes were achieving stardom across the country, and Althea Gibson, thirty years old, gave up tennis. She wrote a book called I Always Wanted To Be Somebody with sportswriter Ed Fitzgerald, and she took up golf.

"You couldn't make a living playing tennis—remember, it was amateur tennis—you had to make a living outside of tennis, and you had to devote your time and energy to being a champion. So after I repeated . . . defended my title successfully at both Wimbledon and Forest Hills, by that time I had a book coming out, and I had a movie offer [the movie was called The Horse Soldiers and starred John Wayne—Althea Gibson played a slave girl], and a lot of things were happening to me. I had to devote a lot of time to the book, the movie and couldn't concentrate on tennis, and since I wasn't making any

4. Althea in overdrive

money at it, I decided that I would retire undefeated, and I did. I went into the movies and in 1960, I picked up golf."

But golf was not to be the answer to her money problems. "I *almost* won two tournaments in seven years I was a golf pro. But when I first went on the tour, my aspirations were high. Because I was strong, I could hit the ball long. The only trouble was, I didn't know where it was going. I can hit a ton, but I always hook or slice. At first they all compared me to Babe Didrikson Zaharias."

After seven years of fun but little success, she retired. And it wasn't all fun. In Midland, Texas, for instance, she was not allowed to use the clubhouse because of her color. Her roommate, Marlene Bauer Hagge, and others finally said that if Althea were to be segregated in any way, they would not play. The barriers slipped slightly downward, and the tour continued. In Midland, Texas, they said that Althea could use the clubhouse to change her shoes.

Oddly enough, Althea Gibson was able to have her professional status as a golfer rescinded. She is now, once again, an amateur because "I love the game and want to play in amateur tournaments around New Jersey. I felt no necessity in remaining a professional golfer when I wasn't going on the tour." Her status as a tennis player, however, is strictly professional. She gives lessons, having been a professional for many years. "Actually," she said, "in 1973 I was a pro at an indoor court in Bergen County (New Jersey) called the Valley View Racquet Club. I was also part owner, and I hired me an assistant, a young fellow. We would get out between lessons and my duties, and we'd practice every day for about three hours. This young fellow really drove me— you know, stinging forehands, smashing overheads, and moving me side to side. I mean, I began to feel fleet of foot again, and my serve was just as big as it always had been.

"So I made the suggestion to Billie Jean King and the Women's Tennis Association that I might make a comeback at forty-five years old. And I think I would have done well. But the thing that turned me off was when I applied to play, you know, at Forest Hills, I had to qualify. Now, how can you tell a world champion she has to qualify? I felt that the public would be delighted to see me after fifteen years of being away. And how would it look for a world champion qualifying against someone up-and-coming and lose? But I wouldn't have, but *just suppose?* So that turned me off, and I didn't pursue it any further."

We had been talking for over an hour. Althea was loose and chuckling a good deal as we slipped and slid over issues and memories of her career and her life. Finally I brought out my list of questions, which was similar to the list I had gone over with Pauline Betz Addie. I asked her the following:

"What are you doing now?"

"Well," she said, "I have a job with the city of East Orange as manager of the Department of Recreation. And, as a matter of fact, one of the things I am trying to do is to interest young people in tennis. But black boys think it is not manly enough, and their girl friends don't take it up because they are told that they will get muscles. So it is hard to get them going, although we have the facilities."

I had seen public courts, empty as was the racquet club, on my way to meet her. And now I looked at her own physique. She did not appear muscular, although she had put on some weight since her days of competition. I asked her if that was the reason that, except for her and Arthur Ashe, you just didn't hear of black tennis players, although she had broken the color barrier back in the early 1950s. "I suppose so," she said. "At least from my talkin' with the young people, it's a . . . sissy sport. And for the girls, it gives them muscles." I had thought that poor black kids eschewed tennis because they wanted to concentrate on sports that would get them scholarships to college and maybe a professional career in basketball, football, or baseball. Tennis scholarships are rare. I took issue with her for a minute, but she stuck to her guns. From her experience, the main thing was the nature of the game itself and the supposition that it gave a masculine look to the women. I let it lie and went on to the next question.

"What was your greatest tennis match?"

"Oh, that is easy. It was in 1958 when I defended my title at Forest Hills. Darlene Hard, whom I had always beaten, was ready for me that day. She came out attacking me, serving, volleying, I mean outwitting me, outplaying me, and everything else. That is, until I threw up five perfect lobs, and they landed on the chalk of the baseline. Every time she came to the net, I'd throw up a lob and make her run back to retrieve them and then, of course, after five times in a row, five straight times to no avail, it was all over."

"As a youth, did you have any heroes?"

"Alice Marble. As a matter of fact, she was my inspiration. I first saw her as a teenager, when she and Bobby Riggs gave an exhibition at the Cosmopolitan Tennis Club, the elite tennis club in Sugar Hill in Harlem. The way she played simply inspired me. She served and volleyed and had a great overhead. And, outside of tennis, of course, there were Joe Louis, Sugar Ray Robinson, Roy Campanella, Larry Doby—athletes, all athletes, and Ralph Bunche. I admired him."

"Now as a mature person, a woman who has traveled the world and seen so much, now as you look back over your life, who are the people you admire the most?"

"Franklin Delano Roosevelt, John F. Kennedy, and Martin Luther King. I remember exactly where I was when I heard that Dr. King had been shot. I was coming from a golf course in Raleigh, North Carolina, with Dr. Ekins. I couldn't believe it, I was so shocked. There were two times when I cried openly with whomever I was with—once when Kennedy was shot and then later when I heard about Dr. King."

"If you could do it all over again, is there anything you would change or see change?"

"No, I wouldn't change a thing, except that I would be more of a winner."

"But you won almost everything. Even down under, in the Australian Championships in Melbourne, you won the doubles playing with Shirley Fry in 1957."

"But Shirley Fry beat me in the singles final. Of course, I beat her later in Perth on the tour," she added.

I looked at her. Her hair was black save for a wisp of gray over her left forehead. "I haven't decided whether to let it all hang out. I feel this way: as long as I am in the public eye, I don't want to look my age. When I let it all hang out, I'll look all gray and distinguished, but now is not the time."

And those glasses: "Simple prescription glasses with removable lenses. I'm nearsighted." (I thought of the missed call that cost me the game—she couldn't see where it landed!) I also thought of her phrase "as long as I am in the public eye." What public eye? Here she is in East Orange, running the Department of Recreation. She is no longer competing as a tournament tennis player. She is going to try golf again but as an amateur. She lives alone and in an apartment. She said that she is a private person. "I lead a private life." Sometimes she appears at tennis tournaments as a spectator, and the camera zooms in on her in the audience. Just last night, American Express had her as a guest for an anniversary party at the Statue of Liberty. In a way, she *is* in the public eye but not really. Her fame now rests with the public in East Orange, New Jersey. She is a local hero. I had noticed that earlier. A famous citizen. For Althea that was enough to keep her self-image intact, or so it appeared.

"Are you religious?"

"I believe in our Creator. You have to think that there is someone or something that made us the way we are. I believe we were put here on this earth for a purpose. My purpose was to be a great athlete because of all the attributes that go with being an athlete: tall, lanky, and well-coordinated."

"What about racial prejudice? Why does it linger on so long?"

"Well, the only thing I can say is that when I was growing up I never thought about race problems . . . I played with any kid on the block. It didn't matter whether he was white, brown, black, or yellow. And the only time I really thought about race problems was when I was back in high school in North Carolina, when I got on the bus, and they had a big sign up there. They didn't say blacks then: they said niggers, coloreds sit in the back. Thank God, it's all gone now, but I think it stems from the colonial days from the South when there were plantation owners."

"Why doesn't it go away?"

"Because it's in the teaching over the generations. It's passed on down the line until it gets to the generation that says: 'Hey, what is the difference, really?' So it's up to that last generation to say that they have had enough."

"In this residue of prejudice, there must still be a fear in the hearts of many people against people of another color. Why is there a lingering fear?"

"I haven't a clue," she said.

"Do you ever have any thoughts about the meaning of life? Any words of wisdom to impart?"

"You know, Stan, I used to travel quite a bit on the road by myself. Especially if I was on the golf tour, and during those times many things would run through my mind. Many, many things as I traveled down the road, and I don't remember any of them. I've got the tape deck on, I got music on in my car, air conditioner on, and I'm driving on, concentrating on the road. I'm like a person with blinders on. I'm looking straight ahead. I've thought of many philosophical things, but I tell you that they only occurred at the time when I'm driving. I don't remember them now."

One last question: "At the top of your form, how do you think you would do against the great women of today?"

"I would win."

"You think you could beat Martina Navratilova?"

"I would win."

We walked out to her Mercury, talking as we went. Althea was going to drive me back to the Royal Inn. She said she was going to watch the Giants and the Jets that afternoon on TV and she asked me what I was going to do. For a second, I thought she might be suggesting that I come back and watch the games with her. I could have followed her along and hinted that I would like to do so, but I let it drop. I was not writing a full profile of her. I was trying to stick to describing my relationship, as a fan, with the subject of my veneration. I wanted to be a friend, but at the same time, I still wanted to keep my distance—to stay a bit on the outside. I could not risk letting familiarity dilute my sense of awe. I took some pictures of her and made a two-dollar bet on the football games. She wanted New York in each case. I would be happy to take her money.

In the car, we passed a housing project for senior citizens. Her work in a previous job for the Department of Human Services had brought her into contact with the elderly. "You know, I could live in any one of those apartments," she said. "They are all clean, roomy, and fit to live in. I've been up there in them." She was proud of what East Orange had done for the aged.

"Someday," she added, "I would like to own my own house. That is my dream. To afford my own house."

I nodded sympathetically and thought, "She has an apartment and is already contemplating the possibility that when she gets old, she will be living in the project we have just passed. She wants her own house but can't afford it. She went from Harlem to Wimbledon to Hollywood to the great golf courses of America and now works as a functionary for the city of East Orange. It doesn't seem fair; something went wrong somewhere down the line. She was enjoying herself, obviously proud of East Orange, pointing to landmarks, and I didn't probe. She'd like a house, but it almost didn't seem to matter, her spirits were so high. It was a throwaway comment that I could do with as I pleased.

Althea was laughing about something as we made the turn to my hotel. She had a good, deep laugh. She was loose and very warm, and I felt that we had known each other for a long time. I was drawn to her, and when we parted, I said to myself, "I don't want to go."

I dropped by Althea's office the next morning to say good-bye and see where she worked. She was all smiles and shook her head as I entered her office. "You know, I could hardly get out of bed this morning. My body just hurts from our match."

And that made my day. Althea Gibson had placed me on the one level I would be able to comprehend completely. We had competed and were friends because of it.

CHAPTER

≈ *3*

Sarah Palfrey:

"Who *did* write
LORNA DOONE?"

To me playing tennis is a celebration of the spirit, and no one better epitomizes that sentiment than Sarah Palfrey. Sarah Palfrey, born in 1912, is still game to play, even though she suffers from osteoarthritis of the hip. Working for *World Tennis* magazine, she is a whirlwind of tennis news and tennis remembrances, and she is enthusiastic about life in general. Her spirits seem to soar from a face that is always responsive. In her early seventies, she is inspirited by a sport, and the sport of tennis is just part of a basic zest she has for life.

Had it not been for Steve Flink, an editor at *World Tennis*, I might have overlooked her. I remembered Sarah Palfrey but had trouble placing her because she had played under two married names, Fabyan and Cooke. And doubtless, because of the overlay of two married names and now a third—she is very happily married to Jerry Danzig—I had omitted her from my pantheon of great champions. The women players who were still alive and whom I was anxious to meet all had name recognition to me. I was thinking of Marble, Betz (at first I was unaware that Pauline Betz had married Bob Addie and, in any case, when she was winning amateur tennis she was just plain Betz—a name that had a good hearty ring to it like a casino), Wills, Gibson, Brough, Moran (as in Gussie), Hart, Fry, and Margaret Osborne duPont (the duPont coming after Osborne did not obscure matters since she played and won under that name for years).

The case of Sarah Palfrey was different. Her reputation was unfortunately diluted in appeal because of this lack of consistency in what people called her. I was soon to learn that she was aware of this herself and instructed me always to refer to her as Palfrey, which I will do. As she said, "I want to be remembered as Sarah *Palfrey*. Though I owe much to my earlier husbands and in particular to Elwood C. Cooke, who helped me with my game, I want the tennis world to know me for myself." Animated by the thought that she could be rediscovered after many years of name confusion and the lack of a concrete image, she was happy to participate in the writing of this book. After all, she won 39 national championships and 24 foreign titles for a total of 63 victories in major tournaments around the world. And had not Steve Flink mentioned her at the Harvard Club in New York where Dick Craven brought us together, I would have missed her. It would have been a severe loss to my project.

I had come back from New Jersey in a rented car, owned and driven by a man who worked for the Tel Aviv Private Car and Limousine Service, Ltd. I mention this only because carrying a good deal of luggage about and being somewhat irritated at the thought of boarding buses and then disembarking to hail a cab and paying for one mode of transportation after another, I used the Tel Aviv service, and it was exceptional. It also gave me a sense of tone that was in keeping with having played Althea Gibson the day before and, though losing, giving her a tough match and, hell, I felt uplifted. I would indulge myself.

I had a date in Manhattan with Sarah at 3:00 that afternoon. Her apartment was on Park Avenue in the eighties. She lived with her husband of thirty-two years, Jerry Danzig, a prosperous man in the communications field. Their rooms were book-lined and trophy-filled from Sarah's victories. It was a cultured residence complete with a piano and set of drums belonging to their son. Whoever lived here, I thought, is no jock athlete but rather a worldly person, someone who has been around and reads and has heightened sensibilities. I looked over the bookshelves: *A Stillness at Appomattox, Silent Spring, Guide to the Metropolitan Opera, The Selected Works of Sigmund Freud.*

Sarah had been very cordial on the phone and said that if everything worked out (meaning that if we got along), I might be able to hit with her at the Grand Central Tennis Club on the third floor of the old railroad terminal, *and* if someone canceled out, I could play in a doubles game with employees of *World Tennis*, who reserved the court once a week for a company game. I knew from Steve Flink that she had bad arthritis problems, and I could only *hope* that we might play. The doubles game would be a bonus because I always wanted to play at the old Vanderbilt courts, as they had been called. They were supposed to be very expensive to rent, and I had read that good players such as Dick Savitt and Hank Greenberg played there often. If things worked out, I could have a few moments that would rival my experience out at the Rockaway Hunting Club. It seemed to go along with the rented car—a touch of high life that I enjoyed thoroughly.

It was a fine style, or what used to be called the "upper crust," that attended Sarah Palfrey. I was no longer at an empty racquet club in East Orange, New Jersey, nor was I with Pauline Betz, recalling the public courts in Los Angeles and the $35 she took with her when she set out across the country to enter tournaments before World War II. Sarah Palfrey's life had been different. "I don't want to sound snobbish, but it happens to be the truth. In my day, I was the only socialite, the only Easterner to make a national name." Born near Boston, in Sharon, Massachusetts, she had gone to the exclusive all-girls Winsor School in Brookline, and her father, a noted lawyer, had Oliver Wendell Holmes as a client. From a background that was decidedly proper Bostonian, she and her four sisters and one brother were handed the Longwood Cricket Club on a silver platter. They were members—it was their home base.

Longwood was the home of the national doubles for years, a tennis heaven with many courts, constant competition, and a girls' tennis program arranged by the estimable Hazel Hotchkiss Wightman.

It was Wightman who took Sarah and her sisters under her wing. She found them partners in mixed doubles, oversaw their development, and tutored them in the game—she was a constant support. Hazel Hotchkiss Wightman originated the Wightman Cup, a trophy earned by the winner of English and American women team matches. It is an annual event and alternates between America and Great Britain, depending on who is host, the winner from the preceding year. Wightman was also a great champion herself, winning major tournaments over an extended period of time. As an example, she first won the United States Tennis Association's Singles Championship in 1909. In 1943, thirty-four years later, she won the indoor doubles, playing with Pauline Betz. She was a fine power of example to young Sarah Palfrey, who took her advice to heart and played herself on to stardom, even though she was from New England where the weather precluded play for much of the year.

"We *did* practice indoors sometimes, on a surface that was covered with something like linoleum. But I was playing other sports such as field hockey. Practically speaking, tennis only came with the warm weather. We were at a great disadvantage from, say, the Californians."

Particularly, if not solely, because of Wightman's encouragement, Sarah was able to win the National doubles nine times in a twelve-year span. She played with Helen Hull Jacobs, Alice Marble, and Margaret Osborne. In mixed doubles, she won with Fred Perry, Don Budge, and Jack Kramer, three of the greatest players to ever hold a racquet. She also won the U.S. singles in

1941 and 1945 and the indoor singles in 1940. She prevailed at Wimbledon with Alice Marble two years in a row, 1938 and 1939. Across the board, there had never been a player from New England who could come close to Sarah Palfrey. With support from four tennis-playing sisters and a brother and from the venerable Hazel Wightman, she practiced and played in the short spring and summer seasons. When Sarah was twelve, Wightman got her Bill Tilden as a partner in a tournament near Boston. They reached the semifinals in her first *senior* tournament, when Tilden was at the top of his form and she was still a child. It was an exciting, heady life around the courts at Longwood. Hazel Hotchkiss Wightman had a protégé, and the protégé was willing.

There is a portrait of Sarah on the wall of her living room. It shows a young woman with a strong jaw, dark hair, and a pair of determined eyes. It is still a good likeness though painted over forty years ago. The hair remains dark, the eyes are more sparkling now than in the portrait, and her jaw will be forever strong. Her face and the luminosity in her eyes tell you that lethargy is a dirty word, and this is so both in the portrait and in person. It is a face from the British Isles and old Yankee Boston. A person thinks of Concord and Lexington and "The White Cliffs of Dover," the song from World War II when Bundles for Britain were being collected in America and when the old

5. Sarah Palfrey

Anglo-Saxon families in the East lived securely atop the hill, their values the unquestioned values of the American establishment. She played against England on ten Wightman Cup teams, and one can visualize her Anglo-Saxon features blending in with the crowd at Wimbledon. Now at seventy-one, she is part of the old regime but also in the old guard of tennis champions. Her office testifies to this. It is crammed from wall to wall with folders and files and paperwork—a vast enterprise that reflects her heritage.

Sarah shut the door on her office, giving me "just a peek." I was not to ask what she does. I was amazed at the immense profusion of writing and notes and letters and who knows what else. I could only guess that what was in there reflected a Boston past and an ongoing commitment to tennis, a blending of dual interests that dominated our conversation.

Currently Sarah is the advertising consultant for *World Tennis*, and her entry in *Who's Who* is filled with positions held, including her election in 1953 as Massachusetts' greatest woman athlete. There is another listing that befits a society matron: chairman, annual benefit for the Visiting Nurse Association of New York City. And then a further listing states that she was chairman for special events for the Child Study Association of America, 1963–1967. She is a member of the English Speaking Union, belongs to a country club in Pawling, New York, and holds honorary memberships in many organizations including the Longwood Cricket Club in Brookline, Massachusetts, where memories pile on memories: Helen Jacobs, Helen Wills, Bill Tilden, Alice Marble, Don Budge, Fred Perry, and others.

"I started playing senior tennis at twelve, but I didn't become a good singles player until my late twenties. You see, early on I got married to Marshall Fabyan, and when that marriage didn't work out, then I took up tennis more and more, working on my ground strokes. When I was twenty-six, I had Alice Marble at match point in the semifinals at Forest Hills, and that showed that I had potential.

"After meeting my second husband, Elwood Cooke, I started to work on my ground strokes and took lessons for my backhand out in California with Don Budge's coach, Tom Stow. It all paid off in 1941 when I beat Pauline Betz in the finals at Forest Hills for the National Championship.

"Of course, in doubles I had done fine, going undefeated for four straight years with Alice Marble as a partner. I played the deuce court, and Alice Marble had what I didn't have. She had the flashy put-away, and I had the consistency, and we kept on winning."

Wimbledon was suspended during the war from 1940 through 1945, and in the United States the war caught up with Sarah Palfrey, even though the nationals at Forest Hills continued right through the hostilities. She had her first national tournament victory at Longwood in 1930 when she was eighteen, playing doubles with Betty Nuthall. By 1941 her record in doubles

6. Sarah Palfrey, the Pride of Boston

showed nine championships in America and two successive triumphs at Wimbledon. Now with a singles win over Pauline Betz behind her, she went off to the Navy with her husband, Elwood Cooke, with whom she had won the French mixed doubles title in 1939. They lived in Navy towns such as Pensacola, Florida; San Diego and La Jolla, California; and, for a while, Athens, Georgia. For the whole war, "my Navy years," she lived in a warm climate. The Cookes had a daughter in 1942, but being a mother did not keep Sarah off the court. For once she had a climate that was conducive to tennis year round, and she used it to her advantage.

"I worked on my game for five to six hours a day. In California Bill Tilden came through for me, and we practiced together. Elwood, who was on duty, managed an hour or two a day. By the end of the war, I was sharper than I had ever been. My ground strokes at last were working well, and I felt confident as a singles player."

Meanwhile, Pauline Betz had played competitively throughout the war. Ranked number one in the world, Pauline was favored to win the nationals once again in 1945 for her fourth successive title. Sarah Palfrey Cooke, however, pulled a stunning upset and at thirty-three years old with a singles game that was unbeatable, she took back the crown that she had won in 1941. "Everybody thought I was all through," she says. "But you see, all that practice had paid off. I was playing better than ever."

In 1946 she stopped playing amateur tennis and instead wrote a book, which Doubleday and Company published under the title *Winning Tennis and How To Play It*. She also became enamored with Hollywood and had several auditions, but nothing came of them. She turned her attention to television and did some shows, but soon Pauline Betz came back into her life. "Pauline is so unaffected, so natural, a nifty girl," she says of her friend. They decided to tour together as professionals and played exhibitions at colleges and country clubs and schools. "Sometimes we were paid $300 an event, and we thought that was wonderful."

By the summer of 1947, Sarah and Pauline were teamed with Bobby Riggs and Don Budge, and they toured Germany. She had the time of her life, now commemorated by a single scrapbook marked *Germany*, and in it are exceptional photographs of a young Sarah Palfrey; the California blonde, slightly glamorous Pauline Betz; and the two great stars of the day, Bobby Riggs and Don Budge. Don Budge was famous for winning the first grand slam in tennis history—all four major tournaments in one year—but Sarah had her own version of the grand slam. In 1941 she won all three national titles—"won the singles beating Pauline, the doubles playing with Margaret Osborne, and the mixed doubles with Jack Kramer." Although her accomplishment was minor in comparison to later women stars Maureen Connolly and Margaret Smith Court, both of whom equaled the great around-the-world feat of Don Budge, it placed her on a very special pedestal shared by the greatest of women players of all time: Helen Wills, Helen Jacobs, and Alice Marble prior to Sarah; and later on, Doris Hart in 1954 and Billie Jean King in 1967.

By the late 1940s, competitive tennis was behind Sarah. She had become involved with benefits and sold advertising for charities. Her marriage to Elwood C. Cooke was fading away, and in 1951 she married again, this time to her husband with whom she has lived now for thirty-two years, Jerry Danzig. She enjoys a comfortable Park Avenue, New York, life, working for *World Tennis*, first under Gladys Hellman and later for CBS, which bought the publication and retained her past retirement age as a consultant. Her life is full. She plays the piano, and her husband plays the saxophone. Her son, young Jerry, who is an advertising copywriter, plays the drums. There are many friends, and everyone stays busy. It is the kind of life one thinks of when one dreams the New York dream: enough money, status, popularity, and a life of distinction.

I looked around Sarah's dining room where we had seated ourselves. Her dining room table was filled with scrapbooks, and trophies from her career stood in a blaze of shining silver against the wall. I wondered where the Wimbledon trophies were and asked to see them. She looked for a while and then shrugged, "They're somewhere around here, somewhere buried," she said, smiling.

It was getting late. She had phone calls to make, and I was eager to get to some direct questioning. Again, as I had done with Pauline and Althea, I looked over my list.

"As a girl growing up in Boston, who were your heroes?"

"The opera star, Kirsten Flagstaff, Helen Wills, Bill Tilden, Francis Quiment, the golfer—and Katharine Hepburn. We were very good friends, and I stayed with the Hepburn family in Hartford. She wanted to be a tennis champion, and I wanted to be an actress."

"Anyone else?" I asked.

"Oh, there must have been some writers. Who wrote *Lorna Doone*, for crying out loud? I loved *Lorna Doone*. And Robert Louis Stevenson, but who *did* write *Lorna Doone*?"

I, too, had forgotten and made a note to find out. (It was R. D. Blackmore, a good name for a trivia contest, I thought, and so told Sarah by phone some time later.)

As for looking back from the vantage point of age and experience and selecting people she admired, she singled out Ernest Schelling, who had run the children's concerts in Boston when she was a child. "Under Ernest Schelling, I played the piano with the Boston Symphony Orchestra at the Conservatory of Music. He was very important to me and a wonderful man. But I am mixing my personal life with public figures. Of course, Winston Churchill comes to mind, and so does Theodore Roosevelt." (As an aside, she mentioned that her brother had married Teddy Roosevelt's granddaughter.) She then said that she admired Jack Kennedy very much, a man she had known. "He made my brother an atomic energy commissioner. We all went to the White House for the swearing-in. It was very impressive."

On the greatest match of her career: "In 1945 when I beat Pauline Betz in the finals at Forest Hills in three sets. When I beat her in 1941, it had been windy and neither of us played very well. In 1945 they thought I was all through."

"Who was your favorite woman partner?"

"That would have to be Alice Marble, because we went for four years without losing a match. I liked Helen Jacobs very much, but we didn't play as well as a team."

"And your favorite male partner?"

"Fred Perry was sheer delight. We won at Longwood, beating Ellsworth Vines and Helen Jacobs. That was in 1932 on the same day as my sister's wedding. I missed the wedding because of the match. On the other hand, Don Budge was great fun to play with, too, and Enrique Maier from Spain was charming. We won in 1936. I was still married to Marshall Fabyan then." (She was Sarah Palfrey with Fred Perry and Sarah Cooke with Jack Kramer in 1941.)

"Was there anyone in woman's tennis who scared you, someone you hoped would be in the other half of the draw so you wouldn't meet her until the finals?"

"No. I was nervous going into a match, but it was the event that made me nervous, not any particular player. I played Helen Wills when I was thirteen at Essex. And I thought I would beat her. I was surprised when she beat me 6–1, 6–3."

On contemporary players: "Could you have held your own against the best women of today?"

"I think that Alice Marble and Pauline and I could hold our own against Chrissie and Tracy and Martina. But Martina at her best, I couldn't have handled. I would try to break her up, but I don't know. At her best, she would have won. Other than Martina, in 1945 when I came back (remember that I had been playing singles against men for a long time during the war), I could have handled both Tracy Austin and Chrissie Evert. But on *clay*, no one would have beaten Chris Evert Lloyd. I was talking about grass."

"Is there anything you would have changed in your life?"

"I would not have married all those times, but," correcting herself, "had I not married Elwood, my game would not have improved, and Marshall Fabyan was a very nice man. It was, well . . . we couldn't have children. So if I changed all that, I would not have had my tennis career or my daughter with

Elwood. Let's just say that I'd have everything as it was except for my arthritis, osteoarthritis. I could do without that."

"Do you believe in God?"

"Yes, but I am a Unitarian, and that gives me some leeway. I don't have to believe in all those precepts."

"Do you have any wisdom to impart?"

"Help your fellow man. Every day. And love people and stay in good health. That would be my advice or words of wisdom."

Sarah had said to take the elevator to the third floor. I was to enter Grand Central from the Vanderbilt Avenue entrance. I did this and quickly found the elevator. But I went up the wrong side of the building, getting off at the third floor where the custodians had their locker room. I was directed across a catwalk affair that went along the inside face of the building, and from it I could see out onto Vanderbilt Avenue and down into the station itself through opaque plastic tiles. Walking thusly and feeling a touch of vertigo, I fancied the ghosts of Grand Central on the old radio show "Grand Central Station," the millions of people who have gone through it, each one with worries and dreams. I had flashes of recall of my own experiences, my anticipation, the glory that Grand Central carried at Christmastime when you heard carols from the loudspeakers and people rushed by carrying brightly wrapped presents. And the heartbreak. The ghosts of broken hearts: people, defeated, leaving the city, an affair terminated, a job lost, a career in ruins. And for me, the remembrance of the long trips on the *Montrealer* up from Washington, over to Grand Central, then down to catch the Old Colony line for Woods Hole, and then to Martha's Vineyard.

At the other end of the catwalk, I went through a door, and suddenly the gray colossus of Grand Central, its girdered immensity vanished in a fecund display of green—green plants, green upholstery, green walls. The tennis club was like a garden inside a battleship. A young woman smiled up at me from her desk, and when I said that I was there as a guest of Sarah Palfrey and *World Tennis* magazine, she smiled again. I would have the run of the facilities, and finding the men's locker room, I changed into my tennis clothes.

Sarah arrived about twenty minutes before the hour, and we went directly to a court that was open. There were two courts there, both padded and separated from each other. When you start to play, it is like playing in a giant padded cell. Even the whack of the ball becomes a modulated thud. I found that the green floor was not as fast as the two indoor courts I'd previously played on, and I was able to get loose and set up for my shots to really stroke the ball.

Sarah took a volley position about six or seven feet back from the net. She stood in the middle on the center line and told me once again that she couldn't run (due to her osteoarthritis). I was back near my baseline, and we

44

began to hit at each other. She would take a step forward, one back, one to the left, two to the right, her eyes sparkling even more now from the pure joy of hitting the ball, of holding her racquet again, of getting some fairly hard shots at her stomach, and then dropping her returns about two feet on my side of the net. She practiced her drop shots for a while, and once when she hit one a little deep, she called, "Could you have gotten that?"—hoping I would say no, that indeed it was a put-away, but it really wasn't. I was still far back when she dropped it, but I knew because of its depth and because it bounced high that I could have returned it for a point. I said, "Yes, I could have reached it." She smiled and said, "Oh," and then dropped another that angled just over the net and died, and I saw her lovely reflexes at work. She just stood there moving a step here and a step there and returned everything with a champion's touch.

We played like that for about twenty minutes, and I was stroking the ball well and was receiving compliments from her. "No wonder you gave Althea a game of it," she said. In that soft light and on that lovely, hard green surface, I felt that I could do almost anything with the ball. I wanted to show off, to atone for bad play with Pauline Betz and so-so play with Althea Gibson, but we just kept on hitting until three other players showed themselves, and then Sarah Palfrey walked off the court to sit on the sidelines to watch us play doubles. And I couldn't believe my luck. One player had canceled out. I would be in the game.

She was almost as intense in watching us as she was in slicing her drop shots. "She loves tennis," I thought, "even if her arthritic hips keep her off the courts. She's not in the least bitter, or so it seems." She shouted directions to the others, and finally in the second set when I made an error, she said, "That was your first error." She had noticed. I almost called to her, "You see I'm okay. Do you think I can play Gardnar Mulloy in singles?" But I held my tongue. I was getting so enthusiastic that I did not want to catch my ride with Tel Aviv to my Miami flight. I hung on to the last minute, playing like a child in a room full of Christmas presents. It felt so good. I knew again the celebration of the spirit—that high ride of exaltation that tennis can bring when everything is working. And you feel light as the tennis ball itself, almost springing along the back of the court, not breathless, all good health and happy.

At the end, I waved good-bye to my partner, a young woman named Cindy who worked for the magazine, and our two opponents, Pete and Nancy. I had played better than I thought I would play and was very pleased. Sarah not only had hit with me, she had also displayed a set of reflexes far above anything I had hitherto experienced save for Pauline Betz and Althea Gibson. I learned what perhaps most middling club players do not know: a world-class player has reflexes so well honed and shots so instinctive that a mediocre competitor will never have a chance regardless of other advantages, such as youth and strength. Partially immobilized by arthritis, Sarah was able to do with my hardest strokes as she wished, provided I hit them within her reach. A man such as Gardnar Mulloy would simply crush me. Never mind that Mulloy would be almost seventy years old. "Sarah is seventy-one," I thought. "She plays with a Prince racquet that she won in a raffle and dearly loves. She always hits the ball on the sweet spot. She is so beautifully coordinated." So was I at one time, but I never had the will to practice, the will to get anywhere with what I was born with. I did not capitalize on my assets. Indeed, it seemed that in this matter of will, there lay the difference between a hacker and a champion. It all had to do with some inner resolve, some sense of self-possession that had eluded me from the days of my youth. I contemplated the gulf that divides ordinary people like me and the marvel that was Sarah Palfrey Fabyan Cooke Danzig.

Sarah Palfrey had won titles under both Fabyan and Cooke and under her own name as well, and even though she had been in the Tennis Hall of Fame for years and had come from the famous Palfrey family that produced five sisters, each of whom had won at least one national tennis title, I had forgotten her. I would never forget her again.

Gardnar Mulloy:

"I keep telling you,
you've been playing with girls."

The Tel Aviv limousine driver was to meet me at 6:30 in front of the Hotel Lexington, which was only a few blocks from Grand Central. I had spent the night there for almost $100, an unpardonable sum given the tawdry dimensions of the hotel. Both nights in New Jersey had added up to only $80, and in neither place did I have to contend with a mob scene of foreign tourists and long lines at the desk. Analyzing the tourists milling about in the small lobby of the Lexington, I wondered how these rather plain-looking people could possibly afford the place, especially with the dollar showing strength and the exchange rate advantageous to Americans.

I just wanted to get out. If I could live as Sarah Palfrey lives, perhaps New York City would be a possibility, but shuffling around as I had been doing, the city struck me as an insane asylum full of victimized human beings, screaming sirens, and filthy air. I was impatient to be on my way to Florida, where Gardnar Mulloy, Fred Perry, and Don McNeill awaited me.

New York is untenable, I thought. I'd lived there before, in the late 1950s, and it was bad then. It still is rotten and dirty beyond description—and costly beyond admissable limits. I had just left a green paradise on the third floor of Grand Central, and the contrast between the life that the old Vanderbilt courts reflect and the teeming jungle of the Hotel Lexington was unsettling. The Tel Aviv man showed up exactly on time, and I left the city.

On the plane, I took hold of myself to glue together my emotions that were threatening to unravel. The problem was that now I had material! Three separate experiences to write down. And instead of writing, I was on the move again. I was worried that I would lose everything, that my memory would not hold the impressions and the details. I feared that I would lose the nuances, that I was in a small whirlwind of movement, and that when I at last got home, it would all be a jumble of facts and feelings and the identities would merge. It was clear that I could not possibly go to California on this trip. Ellsworth Vines and Alice Marble would have to be held in abeyance. So too would Louise Brough and Margaret Osborne duPont. I had not yet written to Jack Kramer and Bob Falkenburg and Gussie Moran.

I thought of the three women I had met. All three had two things in common. First, they had always believed in themselves. Second, they were very nice people. In each case, I had been treated warmly and with enthusiasm. Once we played, Althea became very friendly and open and almost vulnerable. I did not move into her private world, nor did I press her to talk about her childhood and the uprooting of a young girl who was brought to New York from South Carolina. Did she ever go back to find her parents? I did not know. What was her personal life like? I had not a clue.

I equated Pauline Betz Addie with Eisenhower because of her mother's Kansan heritage and because of a feeling I got that told me not to go too far. She is the kind of attractive woman a man would want to flirt with in a teasing way. "Uh, uh," I thought. I would not want her eyes to flash in anger at me. She had a personality that carried with it a sense of command. Old fears of authority rose within my heart, and I was happy to keep things on the surface where she was friendly and helpful and full of humor.

Sarah Palfrey reminded me of many women I had known. She had told me that one of her ancestors was George Washington's postmaster general and that the first Palfrey arrived from England soon after the *Mayflower*. She was a daughter of the American Revolution, just as I was a son, and I sensed that though this stroke of fate was meaningless, it was still, deep down, something we were proud of, and it created a bond between us.

When we met for tennis, Sarah had brought a list of people whom she admired, people she had not thought of during our talk in her apartment. On the bottom, she had written, "my mother, a most remarkable woman." Pauline Betz had said the same thing. Both had been greatly helped and influenced by mothers they loved.

All three shared a Hollywood connection. Althea had made a movie, and Sarah had auditioned for one. Pauline did neither but for a while was part of the Hollywood crowd and thought of the Racquet Club in Palm Springs as her second home.

Sociologically they constituted a cross section of America. Althea Gibson was born black down south in cotton country. Pauline Betz was born white and poor and Catholic in Dayton, Ohio, and then taken off to California to grow up using public tennis courts. Sarah Palfrey was born into a large, established Boston family that personified America's ruling class. She attended the right schools—even Radcliffe for a while before tennis took over—and (I had forgotten) had access to the family tennis court built next to their summer house in the country, in Sharon, Massachusetts. This is in addition to Longwood and Hazel Wightman and the Boston Symphony Orchestra with Schelling's children's concerts. All three women had had to fight long and hard to get to the top of the tennis world, but ironically Sarah, who had all the advantages, probably had to persevere the most. Sports to her were consuming, but there were in her life so many other interests and interferences, not the least of which was the New England climate.

Now I had three men ahead of me. Would they have anything in common? For one thing, I would not be able to just breeze into their lives as I had with the women. I held the opinion that great male athletes view writers with distaste, tempered with a layer of indulgence. Deep down I felt very insecure. I was a guy who had never even gotten his letter in college. As far as athletics went, I was a nobody. And as a book writer, I had no reputation. As a fan, I was one of thousands. What I had to be was a salesman, and I had never been a salesman in my life. Somehow I had to sell myself, to get three older men who had known glory to like me.

I spent the night at the hotel that sits in the middle of Miami International Airport. I had called Gardnar Mulloy's home the day before to confirm with his wife that I would be down that night. I was told to call him for an appointment in the morning—early. "He's up and out soon after 8:00."

I called at 7:45, and the conversation went like this:

Mulloy: Ohugh. [supposed to be "hello"]
Hart: It's me, Stan Hart. Did I wake you up?
Mulloy: Yes.
Hart: Your wife said to call before eight. Am I in trouble?
Mulloy: Not much. [Pause] Where are you?
Hart: I am at the hotel at the airport.
Mulloy: What are you doing there?
Hart: Waiting to find out when we can meet and when I can see you.
Mulloy: Look, I have to go to the bank in North Miami. It's near the airport. I'll pick you up at 9:30.
Hart: How will I know you? [Oops] I mean, I would know you anywhere from your pictures and all, but . . . ah . . .
Mulloy: I'll be in a white Buick station wagon. A compact.

Hart: Fine. I'll be out front.

Mulloy: Yes, stay right out front. Not on the lower level. On the level even with the hotel entrance.

Hart: I got it. The upper level.

Mulloy: Just not the lower level.

Hart: Good-bye.

Mulloy: Good-bye.

Already I am taking orders. I wasn't in much trouble, just *some* trouble. All I'd done was to follow his wife's directions. I had the feeling that communication was not a strong suit among the great male tennis stars. Neither Sidney Wood nor Don Budge had replied to the letters I'd sent to them. Mulloy had a way of making me feel like a nuisance. So did Don Budge. And I'd really given up on Wood. Maybe, I thought, I should just stick to the women.

Mulloy arrived in his Buick, easing into a wide opening directly before me, where I was standing holding my briefcase. He left his driver's seat and came around. I tendered my hand, and he shook it but without much enthusiasm. He was tall and had short, gray hair and was wearing tennis clothes. "Christ," I thought, "what a life. He gets out of bed and puts on tennis clothes, drives off to work, spends the day playing tennis, giving advice, directing others at his new club, which would open soon." Mulloy's new club was called Boca Grove Golf and Tennis Club, and his wife said that Gardnar was over there working on it all of the time, getting ready for the season.

I loaded all my luggage into his Buick, and he almost scowled. "You don't travel light," he said. I told him that I had once planned on going on to the West Coast, but this did not satisfy him. He had spent an adulthood going to the four corners of the world and probably traveled with some tennis clothes, a few racquets, and maybe a sport shirt to go with what he had on his back. I felt uncomfortably like a dud amateur thrown in with the consummate professional. We drove along, and I explained to him the purpose of my book.

Mulloy had a friend who ran the Atlantic Car Rental, which was near the airport, and we pulled in. I leased a Ford Escort, and within a few minutes, we were back on the highway, I following him to his old club where he still had an office—the California Country Club.

All this was to the good. He'd met me, gotten me a car, and seemed amenable to a long interview and, indeed, promised we would play tennis. My George Plimpton streak would soon be activated, and this laconic man was right on course even though he gave the impression that I was a bother and maybe a klutz who had to be looked after.

We rode into the large parking lot in tandem, and when I got out of my car, Mulloy looked at me with a pained expression. "Where did you learn to drive? I sure wouldn't want you following me across the state!"

I explained. "Hell, I haven't been in city traffic for two years or more, and besides, this Escort has no power. I had you in sight all the time, though. You don't think I was going to let you get away with all my luggage."

This made Mulloy stop for a minute, and he smiled slightly as though he hadn't thought of that—that he was carrying my worldly goods in the back of his station wagon.

Mulloy wanted to talk out by the courts, and we found a round wooden table between two red clay *en tout cas*-looking playing surfaces, courts that were laid out in a row—six of them with more on the other side of the road—all designed by Gardnar. There was shrubbery to break the wind, swaths of green grass were under our feet between each court, and the clear, white tropical sky with a fierce sun burning from above.

Inside, I had been introduced by Mulloy as a man "who is writing a book about me." I met his assistant pro, a woman named Bonnie Smith, who is a national tournament competitor. Men walked over and shook Gardnar's hand, and each time he would turn to me and say, "Meet Stan Hart. He is writing a book about me."

One man came in, saw Gardnar, and said, "Hi, God." Others laughed, but I knew what the man meant. "God" Mulloy stood there considerably taller than everyone else, looking more than six feet one, and he was trim as a two iron and brown as a chestnut, and he had a pair of gray swamp-rat eyes that reflected bemusement toward us mortals. Then someone called him "Mr. Wonderful" amid guffaws, but I noted that there was deep affection for him in that small waiting room by his office. The world was full of ungainly part-time sportsmen or tennis players, but there was only one Gardnar Mulloy. I think the banter made him uncomfortable, but he was used to it. A month shy of his seventieth birthday, he moved slowly about the room, somewhat regal but not self-conscious. It was just the luck of the draw. He did what others could not do. He could do a Gardnar Mulloy because, alas-alack, that is what he was.

Back in the Depression, Gardnar, who had played number one for Miami High School's tennis team, received a football scholarship to the University of Miami. An all-around athlete, Gardnar had played football, boxed, was a second-string basketball player, played baseball, and captained the tennis team. Like Sarah Palfrey, he grew up with a tennis court in his backyard. His family lived in Miami, and his father built a clay court and had young Gardnar playing with him and his male cronies until Gardnar was twelve, at which time the son took over the game, beating the grown-ups and playing himself out of his father's doubles. He had become too good.

But at Miami, where he was a backup quarterback ("I think I would have made a good T-formation quarterback, but they didn't have the T formation then"), he was able to switch his scholarship from football to tennis, where he was appointed coach and was encouraged by the college president, Bowman

51

Ash, to develop a first-rate squad. To this end, he found both Jack Kramer and Bobby Riggs and enticed them to enter the University of Miami. Mulloy had lost to Riggs in five sets in the National Clay Court finals in 1937, and he knew both young men from his having toured the circuit. "Kramer stayed about a week,* and Bobby maybe a month. They were too good. But Bob had a plan. He went to Dr. Ash and proposed a deal. He said, 'I will tour the world for four years, playing tennis for the University of Miami. Then after four years of publicizing the university, you will give me a diploma.' He was thrown out of college after that, and I suppose that was Bob's first hustle."

Miami was a small private university then, back in the Depression. There were about 600 undergraduates, and surely the place was too small for both Kramer and Riggs. "Bobby was too good to be playing college tennis. Hell, Kramer came and went so fast." But you have to remember that Miami even then looked kind of odd. The university had bought two bankrupt hotels and covered them with cardboard paneling. "We called it Cardboard College after that. We'd walk around and punch holes in the cardboard with our fists . . . you know, athletes kidding around."

But the tennis team didn't kid around. In the spring, Gardnar took his teammates and headed north. The football team, meanwhile, was languishing in the minor leagues, as it were. Their fall schedule included Stetson, Rollins, Southwestern Louisiana, and Furman. Gardnar Mulloy sat on the bench in the first Orange Bowl classic when Miami beat Manhattan 7–0. He knew, as did Dr. Ash, that if there were a chance for Miami to rise into big-time competition, it rested with the tennis players, even without Riggs and Kramer. So when spring came, Gardnar, acting as coach, took his team north to the great Ivy League and other prestigious schools of the East. Gardnar had scheduled

---

* Gardnar gave the impression that he was still in college when he had Riggs and Kramer entered at the University of Miami. When Jack Kramer was in Miami he says he played *at* the University but has no recollection of *enrolling* in it.

As far as Gardnar is concerned, he was the coach, but by Kramer's time he was out of college. He is, after all, seven years older than Kramer. His teams that went north and were so victorious were teams that he coached, but they did not include him as a player. Thus, I drew a misconception from talking with him; I thought he meant that he was a playing coach. He said that his team played Rollins when Pauline Betz was on that college's tennis team. Indeed, that is true, but Gardnar was not a player.

Going back to Kramer: he did go to Rollins (not Miami) and knew both Pauline Betz and Dorothy Bundy, two Rollings stalwarts, but Jack did not play for the Rollins team because as a freshman he was ineligible (as was the custom in those years). He lasted one semester and left.

Kramer also tried U.S.C. but told me that "college was not for me." Just prior to the war, Jack Kramer went on tour to South America—a tour sponsored by Nelson Rockefeller. The group included Dorothy Bundy, Don McNeill, and Elwood and Sarah (Palfrey) Cooke. When they returned, the war was on, and "everything changed."

Miami against Princeton, Yale, Harvard, Cornell, Williams, Colgate, and Pennsylvania. "The football players and other athletes just laughed at us. Of course, they couldn't compete against those kinds of colleges, but I just loaded everyone into a station wagon, and off we went. We won 9–0, 8–1 everywhere we went. When we came back to Miami, they gave us a big parade down Flagler Street. You know, I had to keep calling so as to tell them where we were as we got nearer and nearer to the city. We ended up at the courthouse, with the mayor giving us a speech in honor of Miami's first undefeated team. Well, we did the same thing for two more years, returning from our trip north undefeated. Finally, Dr. Ash—he was a great man—came into my office. I was making out the schedule again, and Dr. Ash said, 'The only thing worse than winning all of the time is losing all the time.' A light bulb lit in my head. I realized that what he was saying was that I was taking a team that practiced all year to play a bunch of northern players who maybe had two weeks' practice before we arrived. It was then that we began to schedule competition, and we went through the South to Rollins, Tulane, and Texas, and then on to UCLA, California, Stanford, and USC. We split matches with Texas, lost to UCLA and USC, and won against the others. I guess that tour was more in keeping with what Dr. Ash meant."

Gardnar Mulloy's college days from undergraduate work through law school took place right in the depth of the Depression, but when you hear him talk, there is no suggestion that he endured any hardship. He had his health and his youth and his sports and, looking back from 1984, a student athlete's life at Miami appears so uncomplicated, so uncluttered, so innocent. Although Mulloy had no money (Gardnar's father, who was in the lumber business, was having a very hard time of it), in hindsight the entire world seemed to him like some open range where opportunity was like a nugget hiding under tumbleweed, in spite of mass unemployment.

Gardnar, now an ex-college athlete, graduated fourteenth in a class of fourteen at Miami Law School. "I was at the bottom of the totem pole," he says, "but I went right into a law firm, Palette, Silver, and Mulloy, as a senior partner. I was on the tour, and my biggest asset was to bring business into the firm." As the war years edged ever closer, as the Depression began to lose its teeth, and as Miami grew, Gardnar Mulloy, the tennis-playing lawyer who was to practice law for thirty years, was making contacts wherever he served an ace or lofted a lob.

At fifty-four years old, in 1968, Gardnar was still playing at Wimbledon in both singles and doubles.* Still an amateur, he was irritated by the hypocrisy

* In 1984, Gardnar is still competing. He is closing in on seventy national titles, by far a record for men.

that attended the tournaments he entered. "We all got money under the table," he said. "I'd been getting money under the table for years, and so had the others. It was illegal, but it was the club officials, themselves, who paid us. For instance, the officials of the United States Lawn Tennis Association all come from member clubs around the country. Now, if I was asked to go to southern California to play in a tournament there and was offered the standard, legal expense money of $15 per day, I would say, 'Well, I have to be in a tournament in Dallas over that weekend, where I am getting $150.' Then, of course, the offer would come in for maybe $500 under the table for me to forget about Dallas. Well, it was all crazy, and I was talking at the big International Club banquet during the National Championships at Forest Hills. I was talking with the head of the All-England Tennis Club, and I told him that I thought we ought to go open, let the pros and the amateurs play together for money, prize money. To my surprise, this gentleman (whose name now escapes me) said, 'Listen to my speech. I am going to tell everyone that Wimbledon is going open,' and that is when open tennis came in. Around 1968 or so."

With open tennis, there was no longer a need for Mulloy to protect his "amateur" standing, to continue the masquerade, as it were, and he too became a professional, accepting a job as tennis pro for the Fountainbleau Hotel in Miami Beach.

Playing tournaments was his "life blood." Years earlier Bobby Riggs had asked him to turn pro and to go on the tour, along with Jack Kramer. The offer was for $25,000 a year, and Gardnar would play number one doubles with his long-standing partner, Billy Talbert, and number two singles. He talked it over with his father, "who was truly a great man, and I decided to turn it down. Professional tennis in those days meant one-night stands. There would be no more tournaments; they were left to the amateurs."

But now he could have it both ways. He had his tournaments, and he could make money legally. After the original hue and cry over Wimbledon's move to professionalism, things quieted down, and Gardnar could tour with the senior circuit, making some money by playing as much as he would like but, of course, coming along far too late for the big money available to world-class players forty years his junior.

When World War II broke out, Gardnar enlisted in the Navy and rose to the ranks of lieutenant commander. He was captain of an LST and made six landings, including Anzio, Salerno, and Normandy. He received the Navy Citation and a number of battle ribbons cluttered with campaign stars. And while all of this was good for his country and most probably gave him an immense satisfaction as a patriot, it was not exactly good for his tennis game. He did get a leave to play with Billy Talbert at Longwood in 1942. The record books list him as Lieutenant Junior Grade Gardnar Mulloy, and with Talbert (who was 4-F because of diabetes), he won his first tournament at Longwood. He would repeat his wins in 1945, 1946, and 1948, and win Wimbledon with Budge Patty in 1957 at forty-three years old. As a doubles player, he knew few if any peers, but in singles he had a hard time at war's end when, as he says, he was no longer "tournament tough."

Gardnar started playing immediately after his discharge but was losing everywhere. Finally in one semifinal, he ran up against Talbert, who won the first set 6–0. Talbert was leading the second 5–0 when Mulloy said to himself, "Nobody, but nobody, can beat me love and love," and he strained as hard as he could to get one game, but he lost love and one. He told Talbert later that he was going to quit. But Billy Talbert urged him on, and together they reestablished their doubles supremacy.

But all along, it was Gardnar Mulloy's dream to play for the Davis Cup team. He had tried out for it in 1939 but missed making the squad, and then it was canceled because of the war. In 1946, however, Mulloy was picked with his partner Billy Talbert (they were the National champions), and with Jack Kramer, Ted Schroeder, Tom Brown, Jr., and Frank Parker to journey to Australia to win back the cup. No one was allowed to bring his wife. (Gardnar, an agnostic, had married the former Madeline Cheney of New London, Connecticut, a Catholic, and had told the priest who shook his head over the impossibility of a church wedding, "What are you, a gutless wonder? Get the Pope to grant a dispensation," which the Pope, to the amazement of one and all, did.) Frank Parker brought his wife anyway and had worked out a special deal that stated that he was guaranteed a slot as one of the two singles players. This confusion, or exception, regarding Frankie Parker foreshadowed the problems that would follow. It was not long before everyone knew that the doubles team of Mulloy and Talbert was not going to get the attention that Schroeder and Kramer were receiving, even though Mulloy and Talbert had been national champions the last two years, 1945 and 1946. Parker was also losing favor as a singles representative.

Perry Jones, the venerable president of the Southern California Tennis Association, clearly favored the Californians, Kramer and Schroeder, and he had considerable control over Walter Pate, the team captain. It was not long before Billy Talbert broke the news to Gardnar that they would not be the doubles team. Talbert eventually left the squad for "other commitments."

They had played many tune-up matches around Australia, and Gardnar recollects he won most consistently, followed by Kramer, Parker, Talbert, Brown, and at the end, Ted Schroeder. And they shifted doubles partners. Mulloy was given Frankie Parker, and the two of them beat the team of Kramer and Schroeder "every time." Yet when the final selections were made, the doubles team of Kramer and Schroeder was elected as a furious Frankie

Parker "took a walk," furious at losing the singles shot to Schroeder, whom both Jack Kramer and Perry Jones had been pushing even though Frank Parker thought he had been guaranteed a position. Although Mulloy was out of the doubles, he did play one match against Dinny Pails in a bid for an American sweep, once the victory had been assured.

"I made a bet with Kramer, then, that I would beat Dinny Pails, their national champion, worse than he would—and I did." Although on the surface this was just a good-natured bet made by overconfident Americans, it underlined a certain testiness that swirled through the American camp, an undercurrent of contempt for Walter Pate, the California-influenced squad captain, an influence that had caused both Billy Talbert and Frankie Parker to quit and irked both Mulloy and Talbert.

And one factor that surely exacerbated the situation was what Gardnar calls "abominable table manners" displayed by Ted Schroeder, the "fair-haired boy," who Gardnar considered to be the weakest player on the team. "One time we were all eating together, and Schroeder reached over and stuck his fork in my salad and started to eat it. I told him, 'Don't do that, Ted.' Then he stuck his fork in again. I told him, "Don't *do* that, Ted,' and when he did it a third time, I dumped the salad on his head."

"One other time, Tom Brown, who liked to get all his courses at once—you know, steak, milk, salad, dessert, all at the same time—was called to the phone and Schroeder took Tom's steak and began eating it. I didn't say a word, no one did. Well, Tom comes back and asks, 'Where is my steak?' I thought Tom was going to kill him. He said, 'I am not going to eat with you again.' Then after that, Schroeder dipped into my tomato soup, and I dumped it on his lap."

But they won every match that year, and Gardnar played on the next three victorious American teams. In 1950 the Australians retrieved the cup by beating the Americans 4–1 at Forest Hills. Again there was confusion, if not dissension, on the team. At Longwood in the national doubles, a tournament that preceded the Davis Cup play by only a week or so, Mulloy and Talbert, in search of their fifth championship, were upset by the Australians, Bromwich and Sedgman, in five sets. Apparently this was enough to turn the Davis Cup captain, Alrick Man, away from them as the American doubles team. Instead Mulloy was paired with Schroeder, and Billy Talbert was dropped. Schroeder was to play number one for the Americans, and Mulloy and Tom Brown had to fight it out for number two position. They competed up to the day before the tournament was to begin and Man, the captain, said that he was still unsure of his choice. With literally just hours to go before the Americans had to defend the cup, he made Tom Brown and Gardnar Mulloy go out for another five-set elimination match. "At something like 8–8 or 9–9, I told Tom, I said, 'Look, I am already in the doubles. If I win, I can't walk

7. Lt. Commander, Ret., Gardnar Mulloy looking very young in 1946

much less play tomorrow. If you win, you will lose your edge for tomorrow the same as I will.' I then walked off the court and conceded it to Tom Brown."

The tired Brown did win one match (against Ken McGregor), but everything else went to the Australians; Mulloy and Schroeder were beaten by Bromwich and Sedgman in five sets. The Davis Cup was returned to Australia.

We had been sitting outside with small tropical birds chirping by our table, and an occasional shout from a nearby court cut off the conversation. It was getting hotter, and Gardnar Mulloy was obviously enjoying himself. He *went* with clubs like this one, the California Country Club. The Boca Grove Golf and Tennis Club in Boca Raton was lucky to get him. At an age when most men are retired, he was just starting out on a new enterprise. He'll launch a new resort. The man went with south Florida the way palmetto palms went with the vast rangelands and alligators went with the Everglades.

Gardnar wanted to talk at some length about his war experiences because they were extensive, and in a Mister Roberts fashion, they were leavened with humor. As I listened, he reminded me of the actor James Garner, only his hair is snow white. But he had an actor's voice and a slow, penetrating style of talk. If I interjected a comment or two or got off on one of my own exploits, he would wait patiently for a moment and then gaze off into the distance. It was his club, his life, and his show.

I asked him about the money being made in tennis today. He is not too excited by it. "Look, we did all right in the old days, considering the money we received under the table. And the dollar went so much further then. I guess some of the boys are envious; they think they are not getting their fair share, having been pioneers and so forth. But it doesn't bother me. There were no taxes . . . we did all right."

"Would you rather be a tennis star known to tennis fans and sports fans, or a celebrity, seen on TV, appearing in *People* magazine?"

"I'd rather be a star, not a celebrity. I think it all started with Bjorn Borg. He had his groupies; you know, bobby soxers, and became an idol."

"What was your greatest tennis match?"

"The most satisfaction I ever got out of a tennis match was when Billy Talbert and I won the National USLTA Championships for the third time and retired the bowl. Kramer and Schroeder had won it twice, as we had, and we were supposed to meet them in the finals at Longwood. If the same team wins it three times, they retire the bowl. It had all those names on it, a real prize. This would have been 1946. They'd won the year before, but Frank Guernsey and Don McNeill upset them in the semis. So we had to play

8. Gardnar, the mature athlete

Guernsey and McNeill. We beat them 20–18 in the fifth set. We were down
six break points, with Talbert serving, and he pulled it out.

"Another doubles match that sticks in my mind was when Budge Patty
and I won Wimbledon. We were unseeded at Wimbledon, and in the finals
we beat Lew Hoad and Neale Fraser, 8–10, 6–4, 6–4, 6–4. They were ranked
number one in the world.

"The best I ever played was in Australia with Talbert, and we beat
Ashley Cooper and Mal Anderson in straight sets—4, 3, and 2, something
like that. Then afterward someone came up and said, 'You know, Gardnar, in
the whole match you only missed four returns of service.'"

On the question of heroes, he said, "Well, since I was born in Washington [he had moved to Miami as an infant], I always liked the Washington
Redskins and the Washington Senators. But I liked Jack Dempsey a lot. I was
always sports-minded."

"As you look back on your life, who are the men and women you most
admire?"

"I can't remember." (I pressed him a bit . . . he paused, and then spoke
slowly again; his voice had a touch of gravel in it.) "The person I most admired was my father. I think he was a great man. He was the person who in-

59

sisted that I go to college, no matter what—he never went to college—and he had great advice for me. I remember once when I was fifteen or sixteen, I was playing for the Dade County Championship, and I was playing a guy named Carroll Turner, who was the preeminent champion. Nobody could beat him. But there we were, deep in the fifth set at maybe 4–all, and there was a disputed call, and the umpire lost control, and Turner and I were arguing over it. All of a sudden, I saw my father come out of the stands, and he took my racquet from me. His name was Robin Mulloy [with whom Gardnar had won three National USLTA Father-Son Tournaments, 1939, 1941, 1942] and I said, 'Dad, I can win this match.' He said, 'You don't want to play tennis. You want to fight.' He sent me home. That night he sat on the edge of my bed and gave me a two-hour lecture. I never again got enraged and used profanity on a court.

"Another time I was in a tournament, and I saw the chart, and I started complaining because I wasn't seeded. My father tapped me on the shoulder and said, 'Son, if you are going to win this tournament, you should be able to beat everyone in it. So what does it matter, first or last, what does it matter where you are in the draw?' I never forgot that and never complained again about the draw."

"If you had your life to live over again, would you change anything?"

"No, I wouldn't change anything. I'd like to have not made any mistakes, but then I'd have been perfect. No, I would want to go to a small college as I did, and play all the sports as I did, and get to know everybody as I did. I never worried about money, even though there wasn't always very much of it."

"Do you believe in God?"

"I'm an agnostic. I believe people should say what they feel. Those who go to church, Christians, and politicians always talk about God. You never hear anyone talk about not believing in God. I say I believe in evolution and science."

"Do you have any wisdom to impart?"

"I think the world is too dishonest. I believe you should be honest with yourself and with your beliefs. When things go wrong, it's due to dishonesty. When you think about nuclear war, it's incredible that in light of that, leaders of nations have chips on their shoulders. I fought against the Germans in the war, and when I go to Germany, the people are fine. If people get along . . . why can't nations? Everything is politics. Why don't we feed the world? And look at McEnroe. He is going to get maybe $100,000 to play, and he is berating a linesman who isn't even getting paid anything! What kind of behavior is that?"

Gardnar's father was his role model, but Robin Mulloy passed away about twenty years ago. "I have a mother who is ninety-four and who lives up

60

in North Carolina in a cabin, living alone. She's got a couple of dogs and is an artist, and she enjoys living up there—it's kinda woodsy." He told me how he worried about her, and it was obvious that he came from a solid, loving family.

"Could the stars of today beat the great players of yesterday?"

"I don't know. There have been some changes. For instance, the serve. The players today cross over the baseline on their follow-throughs. That would have been a foot fault in our day. And we amateurs had to play all three matches at each tournament: mixed doubles as well as men's doubles, and there weren't any jets then!" I imagined Don Budge going all the way around the world by boat for his grand slam. I thought of the three weeks that players spent on deck waiting to get to Australia and of the strain of travel, long in duration, and little time to practice. Could the younger players today take all that effort? Were they patient enough?

On John McEnroe: "His father should have spoken to him when he was a kid the way mine did when I ranted and raved at the Dade County finals against Carroll Turner."

"Was there anyone on the tour you did not like?"

"I already told you—Ted Schroeder."

We'd eaten lunch at the club restaurant. I had a huge hamburger that must have had a half-pound of beef in it, along with french fries and coleslaw. Gardnar had a tunafish sandwich with melted cheese on top. He sat there in his white tennis clothes, and people came to our table to say hello, to pay tribute. They knew he was moving up to Boca Grove. They wanted him to know how much he was liked. If the people here thought of him as "Mr. Wonderful," he didn't act that way. He was always courteous and spoke of personal matters as though he knew each person very well. I sat there and rued the title of the movie *The Right Stuff*, because I would have referred to him as having had that ingredient if I had been able to simply allude to the book by Tom Wolfe. Now with the hype from the movie version, the term had lost its authenticity. Gardnar was from the book, but the movie had turned the term into a cliché. One thing Gardnar Mulloy was not, was trite. He was not anything other than what he was. He had no pretensions that I could detect. I played around with the pun "The Real Mulloy" but let it drop. We ate and discussed current events, and then we went out into the heat to play.

We were the only ones out in that tropical sunshine. It was 1:30 when we began to rally. At once I saw his long strides and how he approached the ball with his backswing already back. There was nothing at all jerky in his motion. He strode the court like a great albino cat—lean and hard and white-topped. If I hit a deep one into the corner, he was already there, his backswing deep behind him. Whoosh, the ball would return down the line, low and hard.

61

He could see that I was not up to his ability in any way, and so when we commenced a pro set, he sent gentle high bouncers to me, balls I could return. His serve was slow and within reach. For a second, before I knew he was just keeping the ball in the court waiting for my shots, I had hopes. We were at 2–all, and I had his serve at break point. He won it, however, and then he began to pull away. He hit drop shots from anyplace on the court without giving them away. He could be at the baseline and look as if he was going deep and, then, oh jeez, the ball would dip over the net and die.

At first I ran for the drop shots but the sun was taking its toll. I felt dizzy and had chest pains. I said to myself, "Okay, you are going to die on a tennis court, playing a four-time* national doubles champion and Davis Cup star

9. Mulloy at seventy; the greatest tennis player for his age
the world would ever see

* His fourth title with Talbert was in the finals at Longwood where they beat Parker and Schroeder in 1948.

62

who won Wimbledon in 1957 when he was forty-three years old. He still looks forty-three years old." I thought they would all say at home, "Good old Stan died playing tennis. If he had to go, that is the way he would want it."

I actually was thinking that way as the french fries gave me terrible heartburn, which I translated into heart attack. And Gardnar just kept going—a drop shot here and a deep high one to my backhand or forehand corners. Once he hit a weak overhead, and I lost it in the glare of the almost platinum sun. He sent up a second one a game or two later, and I did manage to put that one away, but I was awkward in doing so. Another time I gave him my "slither shot," which is a shot I think I've invented, in which I take volley at midcourt and slice it off the cocked face of my racquet with a loose grip; the ball just slithers over the net and spins away. I also got him with a backhand volley with some steam behind it. But that was all. When I served to his backhand, he arced it down the line just inside the tape. It was no contest.

When it ended, I was out of breath, more so than I had ever been. We'd played no more than forty minutes. I couldn't understand it. I'd never felt better playing doubles up at Grand Central or at the Rockaway Hunting Club, and I could have easily played two more sets with Althea Gibson. But now I was a ruined man. I could hardly stand up.

"It's the heat," I said. "I'm not used to the tropics. I just came down from the North, for God's sake."

Gardnar just smiled and replied, "You've been playing with girls," meaning Pauline and Althea and Sarah. When we were in his office and I was dripping wet, I noticed that he had not perspired. I said, "How did you like that forehand volley [my slither shot] you couldn't handle?" He smiled again. So I had gotten a good shot off. Hell. He'd been hitting the ball at half pace. He didn't say that, but I knew it was true. His assistant, Bonnie Smith, looked at me and shook her head. I complained again about being worn out, and he grinned broadly and raised his voice, "I keep telling you, you've been playing with girls."

Gardnar, a couple of weeks before, had lost the men's sixty-fives in Cedarhurst to his old friend, Bobby Riggs, in the finals. Gardnar is still a superb singles player. Bonnie Smith's shake-of-the-head told me that I would have to be crazy to think I could get more than two games from him.

Gardnar called Fred Perry in Pompano Beach for me and set up my appointment. I then called Don McNeill from Gardnar's office, and being with Gardnar enabled me to get McNeill to agree to an interview. The man was an inspiration and a help. I asked Bonnie Smith how far it was to drive to Vero Beach where Don McNeill lived. "About three and a half hours," she said. Mulloy overheard this remark and added, "The way Stan Hart drives, it will take him five hours." He hadn't forgotten how I had hung back in traffic as I trailed him to his club.

63

We said good-bye, and I gave him a last look. He had been an all-around athlete, a lawyer, a world tennis champion, and a club pro. He had a marriage for over forty years, children, and he went to work in tennis clothes. I couldn't get the last thought out of my mind. Miami, now a large city, had at least one man who drives about in a jockstrap, blue shorts, and white sweat socks. He has a long, tanned torso and is slender and eye-catching. Surely he draws envy wherever he goes. People are bound to say, "That guy's got it made." Indeed.

I asked him how he keeps in such good shape. He said, "I don't smoke, I don't drink, and I don't go out with girls who do"—a switch on the old line from the prissy gingham-dressed stereotype of the late 1930s. At least two people in the waiting room guffawed, but Gardnar only smiled slyly and looked away. I believed him.

I called Gardnar the next day to ask if other than the Navy Citation, he had received any medals for heroism while in the Navy. "Just a lot of those things that go on your ribbons, you know, little stars." I told him I was really pretty bad when I played him. I said, "I could do better." He sounded sincere when he said, "I shouldn't have drop shot you so much; that's when you started to sweat and pant."

"Hell," I said, "I should have had them."

"Well," he repeated, "I shouldn't have dropped so many on you."

Gardnar Mulloy asked for Don McNeill's number and told me to tell McNeill that he would call. I almost said, "Good-bye, God," but decided not to.

CHAPTER

5

Fred Perry:

"Showing the flag"

Gardnar was painstaking with his directions so that I would not get lost driving to Pompano Beach. He could see that I was hopeless, a kind of third-string quarterback who might get into a game for a moment or two and then forgets his plays and trips over his own feet, and, of course, fumbles the ball. Mulloy was like a coach. He went over the route I had to take, but it was all gibberish to me: too many turns and I-95s and overpasses and so forth. I really had no idea how to get from the California Country Club to Florida's Turnpike, which would zoom me up to Pompano.

About two hours later, after several wrong turns, I was looking for a place to spend the night. I had a date with Fred Perry at 2:00 the next afternoon. Then I was to drive up to see Don McNeill in Vero Beach. McNeill could see me either that evening, which was a Thursday, or I would have to wait for several days because of his bridge routine. He had taken up duplicate bridge, and his games were inviolate. For some reason, meeting him in daylight wouldn't work. I had to see him on the night of my meeting with Fred Perry.

Meeting Fred Perry would have pleased my father very much. Perry and Budge and Vines and, to a degree, Sidney Wood and surely the late Bill Tilden and Frank Shields were people he had talked about. I think he admired Fred Perry's English charm and style. Shields, as everyone knew, was a flamboyant, very handsome man right out of the Roaring Twenties. There was a part of my father that admired the rake, the good-natured ladies' man that Shields epitomized so well. He was an American athlete who fit tennis into a schedule of late-night carousing with amenable ladies or with rogues like himself. This all fed the fires in men who had settled down but sometimes wished they had not. Perry, on the other hand, was simply one of the best of all time, and whenever he beat Ellsworth Vines or Don Budge, even patriotic Americans were pleased. It was hard not to root for Fred Perry.

For me, though, Fred Perry was a different kind of prospect. When I'd called him from my home, I had taken him by surprise, calling him before I had written him, my unmailed letter a short essay on the purpose of my book. I was sure I had caught him off guard. He had just arrived from England, and only the helpful Mrs. Sidney Wood was able to give me a lead as to where he might be residing. She told me to call a friend of the Perrys, who in turn could give me Fred Perry's phone number. And so I did this, and having Fred Perry's number in hand I had called him, back then in those confusing early days at home.

Perry said he was under doctor's orders not to play, and maybe he would not be able to see me, but, well, certainly if I was in the area he could find a way. He was polite and terse. Eventually Gardnar opened things up with some good-natured banter, calling from his office. But Perry did tell me that he was writing his own book and strongly intimated that he wasn't going to give much away.

After seeing Gardnar I became fired with the excitement of my adventure, becoming increasingly intrigued with the inner depths of the great stars. Yet, I still worried about putting into words what all of this fan-meeting-his-idols business meant. I had to combine my own sentiments and my long travels with the personalities of men and women I was meeting and thus present to the reader a smorgasbord of this and that which would be, as they say, bigger than the sum of its parts. So as I drove on to Pompano Beach for just a short visit with Fred Perry, I was on one level a fan finding a hero—actually his father's hero, and by extension, his—and an optimist who would try to establish a friendship with a man who, under normal circumstances, would be unavailable. I thought of what Washington factotum Clark Clifford had said: it would have been nice to call President John F. Kennedy "Jack." There was something like this in my odd quest. As a baseball fan and working in Boston, I always thought it would be wonderful to call Ted Williams on the phone and say, "Hi, Ted, what are you doing tonight? Why don't we eat over at that new steak house they just opened on Commonwealth Avenue and then take in a movie?"

Perry was calling my room as I came around the corner from the elevator—on time to the minute. He was dressed in a light green Fred Perry polo shirt with his symbol, a gold wreath, on his left sleeve. He wore darker green, pleated beltless trousers and had a strong English face with a body that was still athletic-looking. He was a compact man, just over six feet tall. His hair, of course, was thinning, but at seventy-four he looked fit as a soldier. In fact, that is what he reminded me of—a British general in civilian clothes. He appeared friendly but somewhat official. He wanted to get right down to business, and so we walked very quickly into the restaurant of the Beachcomber Hotel and took a table. It was just after 2:00, and I ordered a pot of coffee, and we began to converse.

In Fred Perry's honor, I had purchased a nice-looking pink Fred Perry polo shirt and was sitting across from him, assuming he would notice it. I knew he must have, but modesty kept him from any comment, so I asked him about the business that bore his name. I even said (with some brashness) that though I had worn Fred Perry tennis shoes for years, they had a way of wearing out very quickly. This did not faze him, and he went into a long, very complicated synopsis of his relationship with sporting clothes, tennis shoes, racquets, and gut stringing. It was a litany of corporate involvement that included the Mac-Intosh Corporation of England, his own corporation that licenses his name, and the fact that for a while he used to go on promotional tours for which he was "in charge of the bullshit department." It was impossible for me to follow it all, and had I felt obliged to ask questions, I had the feeling that we would have spent the better part of an hour talking about the mechanics of endorsement, which was not what I was looking for.

I switched the line of talk to tennis and asked him about the players of today and how they would stand up to the players of his day and those that followed after the war. I showed him a "draw" in which a tennis writer, Gianni Clerici, had taken the best players of all time and placed them in a mythical tournament.* In this tournament Tilden met Laver in the finals. Perry beat both Jack Crawford and Don Budge but lost to Henri Cochet in the semifinals.

Perry studied the draw as it progressed to its conclusion, and I could sense an incipient scoff underneath his comments. He said, "In any game it is one to one. You never know who is going to win in a tournament like the one you have here. The real question is, where is this game going to be played? Do we play on grass, for instance, or on clay? And remember, when we served, we had to have both feet behind the baseline and one foot on the ground at all times until after impact.

"Now, to me the game is a question of control: control of yourself, con-

---

* "The All-Time Tournament" from *The Ultimate Tennis Book* by Gianni Clerici. Clerici does not give the name of the winner.

trol of your emotions, control of your opponent. You can only serve the ball into the court with control at a certain speed. We clocked Ellsworth Vines, who had one of the fastest serves in the game at 118 miles per hour. Now that means he can't hit it in at 120. Not with any control. So what would happen is that you would move up on a man who hit like Vines to shorten the angle—or else you'd never get it—and "fiddle it back" to the side to make the guy reach down for a low volley off his foot and then you pass him on the next one when he comes up for air. Now, under present regulations, you can jump into the court, swing over with your back foot, have both feet off the ground, switch feet as Hoad would do, be like Newcombe used to be (he served as if he were in a rocking chair, and got up to about twenty-five miles an hour, and then let fly), be like Arthur Ashe and start two feet behind the line and throw the ball up in the air and jump at it. Because of the rule change, the contemporary server can get about a foot and a half closer to the net. He can cross over the line in the process of serving. This we could not do.

"This means that the return of service that once went to the toe now hits you on the knee. You have therefore eliminated the low volley. What went to the waist now goes to the chest. The 'fiddle' has disappeared. So the server hits the hell out of the ball and grunts, and the receiver hits the hell out of it and grunts, because that is the only chance the receiver has got, and that's the end of the point.

"Now, when we played, there was no sitting down for three to five sets. No chairs, no anything. So when you talk about comparing players, you have to establish the ground rules. Would the players of today want to play with our rules? Would they go five sets without sitting down? How long could they last with the low volley? With no rest, they would not be able to keep getting to the net. Remember, they've lost that one-and-a-half-foot advantage. The 'fiddle' would come into play."

Perry paused for a moment to let his words sink in. There was no doubt that the change in the rules allowing for crossing over the service line made it hard to accurately compare the great players. I remembered that Gardnar Mulloy had said the same thing. Were Don Budge in his prime to play John McEnroe, one or the other player would have to be retrained. If McEnroe served from a foot-and-a-half back so as not to foot fault in accord with the old rules, how would he handle a return of service, a low volley to his toe? If he served softly in order to get to his accustomed close position to the net, then, of course, Don Budge or Fred Perry would adjust his return of service and take advantage of that. And the rest periods: that had brought a touch of irritation to Fred Perry, but he went on to something else for a moment.

He was talking about playing for a team.

"You played on a team for your country. Your national tennis association sent you overseas and paid your way. Now, if you were wealthy on your own, you could go solo as Tilden did, but generally speaking, we went as a team. You were proud to wear the blazer ascribed to your country. Now, I am talking about New Zealand, Australia, South Africa, Belgium, France, the United States, countries from South America—we all were part of teams. If Vines or Budge went to Wimbledon, they went as members of the American team.

"The problem today is that open tennis is show business. Players today are in vaudeville, just as George Burns and Gracie Allen were. As years went by, more and more people went into tennis hoping to achieve greatness at the game with the ultimate idea of turning professional. The idea was to get a job in a club in the United States, which was the mecca for teaching professionals. Of course, one of the greatest players in the history of the game was *always* a pro: Karel Kozeluh.*

"What you have now is this: look at the U.S. Open this year. Connors versus Lendl. Connors leaves the court for six minutes. Three minutes is the maximum allowed. Lendl sits there like a bump on a log not knowing what the hell is going on. No one explains anything to him. It is 91 degrees in the shade. But no one in his right mind is going to disqualify Connors. You wouldn't have a match. On prime time TV with two hours of dead air? No way. And the trouble is, the players know that. That's why it's show business.

"But going back to our day. The only way to go overseas was on a team. You had to have permission. If you didn't have permission, you didn't go. It was like the Olympics. There was a captain, and you did what he told you to do. You represented your country. You behaved the way you were told to behave. There were four men and a captain. Every time Budge or Vines or Allison or Van Ryn or Tilden went overseas they wore the coat and the badge. They represented the United States of America. They weren't representing McDonald's or Orange Crush or some business."

And then Perry went back to Connors, leaving the court for six minutes: "Bill Tilden was a stickler for the rules. He knew them inside out and sideways, what could be done, what could not be done. If you tried to bend the rules a little bit, he jumped you quick. Now it would have been interesting to see what Tilden would have done had he been in Lendl's place. He would have declared himself the winner, or he would have quit. It is unlikely that he would have been intimidated by television. Tilden wasn't intimidated by anything. In my view Bill Tilden was the greatest player of

---

* In 1928, Karel Kozeluh, "always a pro," arrived in the United States to tour with Vincent Richards. Richards won on grass, a surface with which the Czech was unfamiliar. On other surfaces Kozeluh established his superiority. A year later he beat Richards on grass for the professional title. Some consider Kozeluh as good as, or even greater than, Bill Tilden.

10. Fred Perry showing the flag and unbeatable

all time. But the greatest player since the war was Rod Laver. That's my personal opinion."

In Fred Perry's time—the mid-1930s—there was hardly anyone as good as he. He won the singles championships at Wimbledon in 1934, 1935, 1936; the mixed doubles playing with Dorothy Round in 1935 and 1936; and the U.S. singles at Forest Hills in 1933, 1935, and 1936.* He won the French singles in 1935 and the Australian singles in 1934; the French doubles in 1933, the Australian in 1934 both with his Davis Cup partner, Pat Hughes. Usually he is bracketed by Ellsworth Vines, who came just before him, and Don Budge, who succeeded him in supremacy. And also the venerable Australian, Jack Crawford, whose name slips into the winner's column, along with the other three great players, though less often.

It was a time for competing openly in a free world. Fred Perry, whose father was a Labour Party member of Parliament, took up table tennis at thirteen. At nineteen he won the championship of the world, playing in Budapest. One can imagine the excitement generated by a hometown favorite leaving for overseas competition. As Fred Perry spoke, I could almost hear the enthusiasm that sent him off from England on his way to Hungary, a representative of the Crown, a youngster who had a chance to win it all for Great Britain. If there was a latent hostility in the world, it did not intrude upon the lives of athletes. A nation's pride rode on their backs, but a universal appreciation of skill attended their eager meetings in far-off lands.

Perry won his championship in table tennis in January 1929 and qualified that spring for Wimbledon in tennis, a game that had been secondary to him up until then. It took him four years to win a major tournament in singles, which he did in the United States. The great Bill Tilden had turned professional, and Ellsworth Vines was about to do so. Perry prevailed over a group including Gottfried von Cramm, Wilmer Allison, and Jack Crawford and the young Don Budge—names now enshrined in tennis history.

Perry turned professional in 1936 and toured with Ellsworth Vines. He says that, give or take two or three matches, they were even. In 1937 at Madison Square Garden, they played before a crowd of over 18,000 spectators, a record until Bobby Riggs played Billie Jean King in what Perry calls "their soiree" in the 1970s.

"I won the first match at Madison Square Garden, the second one in Cleveland, and the third one in Chicago. After that we were about even." As for a carousing night life, he said, "I never drank in my life, and I only smoked a pipe. Concerning cigarettes, I won a few silver cigarette cases in my time but

---

* Fred Perry is the only man in history to win the All-England championship and the U.S. championship three times.

never used them." In short, this was a serious business to Fred Perry. He was making a good living as a touring professional.

Two years later, Perry and Vines put up the money for Don Budge to turn professional, and then along came Frankie Kovacs and Bobby Riggs to join the group. It all ended for Perry in Madison Square Garden when he was playing Riggs, and going for a shot, he fell and broke his right arm. "That was the end of it . . . There was no serious tennis after that fall."

It was a good time for the waitress to interrupt us. She wanted me to sign the check so that she could have a couple of free hours prior to dinner. We sat there alone in the quiet green dining room, festooned with potted plants and dripping water that lent a lush aura to the restaurant. Rather than continue chronologically into World War II, Mr. Perry, as I called him, began to reminisce about the old days when he was a young tennis player and started to travel for England.

"You went down to Southampton for America, and there was a certain glamour about it. You had your steamer trunks. You'd get on the boat with your own cabin. We traveled A-number-one, first class. Best hotels, best everything. You'd be a week in each place, but you didn't have to worry about details, because it was all done for you. From the West Coast of America, you would get on another boat and go for a day in Hawaii, and then you'd board again and go to Pango Pango or someplace on your way to New Zealand, where you'd stay two or three weeks because we played matches against New Zealand. Then you would go to Australia, and when you left Australia, it was five weeks by boat before you got back to England. We'd stop off in Colombo, Ceylon (now Sri Lanka); Bombay, India; the Suez . . . but you're on the boat all of the time—that full moon, you know, and the first time you go, you run around like a chicken with its head cut off, checking the merchandise. But the more you do it, the more you would hold off and sort of sort yourself out. You see, there would be six weeks of tennis play in America and four days just going across by train to Los Angeles. There would be movie people on the train, and you'd get to a place like Gallup, New Mexico, and kids would line up outside the train to get autographs from the movie stars.

"But the boat trips gave us a chance to unwind. You would restore your batteries at sea and begin pointing toward the next championship, usually the Australian. It was a different ball game then . . . you see."

I looked at Perry and I saw. I saw the British team and the American team and all the other teams crossing the oceans to play a great game. I could visualize the smug half-smiles of patriotism and the good-natured rivalries. I asked him if players ever traded their blazers or their patches that signified nationality.

"Oh, no! That's what soccer-football teams do when they play for the

Gold Cup. They exchange their jerseys. The Italians had the most beautiful patches. No, we would never trade."

I went on. "What do you think you would have become had you not taken up tennis?"

"I have no idea," he said, as though the thought had never occurred to him. He had been in tennis in one way or another for over fifty years. To conceive of himself as a barrister, shopkeeper, dentist . . . was impossible.

In World War II, Perry served with the U.S. Army Air Corps in rehabilitation work, stationed in California. "I was with Joe DiMaggio for a couple of years," he said as an aside. "I had been over here since 1936 and never went back to England to stay." In 1937 he started the Beverly Hills Tennis Club with Ellsworth Vines. It was then that his fame as a tennis player crossed with others of international luster, namely members of the movie colony. He did not talk about this period, and I surmised that this was one section, perhaps the juicy section, of his life that he was saving for his own book. He did mention that his friends were Clark Gable, Loretta Young, and Gary Cooper. "Errol Flynn was a great friend of mine," he added.

So I asked Perry what his greatest tennis match was.

"For any individual, your greatest moment has to be when you win your national title. For me that was Wimbledon, but it was both the national title and the world title at the same time. I beat Crawford the first year and von Cramm the next two years. I won all three in straight sets."

I asked Perry about his famous win over Don Budge at Forest Hills in 1936. By beating Budge, he became the only foreigner to win the U.S. title three times. It took two hours and forty-five minutes to complete and the scores were 2–6, 6–2, 8–6, 1–6, 10–8. He brushed my question off because it was irrelevant. By winning against Budge, he was not winning the All-England Championship. Although it had been one of the greatest matches ever played, it did not qualify within the framework of his memory. When you win at home—that is the important thing. You keep the title at home where it belongs. Beating Budge was beating Budge. Winning on the center court at Wimbledon was winning the World for Great Britain.

Perry did go on to say that it was impossible for him to think that a losing effort could ever be considered your best match. "I don't think anybody who loses to somebody is going to say that was the greatest match I ever played in my life. It would upset your ego. In any one-on-one sport—take boxing—you go into it expecting to beat the hell out of the other fellow."

And that, I thought, was a champion's remark: you don't want to recognize defeat. I thought of myself and realized how wide the gulf was between us. If I were ever lucky enough to play a player much better than I and by sheer exuberance and through an immense effort were able to extend the match to the last possible moment prior to defeat, I should look on that as my finest

11. Fred Perry with Don Budge: what a pair!

moment on a court. Because Fred Perry was, on any given day, the best that ever played the game, to lose was to fail. Never mind the excitement of the game, the sheer drama that might have transpired. The truth that he would have to deal with was the fact that he had lost, and that was the kind of truth he would rather suppress.

As with Gardnar Mulloy and Pauline Betz, Perry could relate to boxing. I remembered that Gardnar had actually been on a boxing team and that Pauline had dated Jack Dempsey and still recalled him with a good deal of affection. Several times Perry had used the term "one-on-one." Tennis, like boxing, was one-on-one, and it was clear when I looked into his narrow eyes that this genial man could be tough. I thought of golf, a game in which your main battle is with yourself. In a racquet game, you are like a boxer. You attack and exploit another man's weakness. And a five-set singles match would be like going fifteen rounds.

"I got fed up with team sports, which I played as a kid—football-soccer and cricket—I was an individual." As a kid, by the time he turned twenty, Perry had fought four general elections with his father for his father's seat in Parliament. After the fourth election, Perry swore he would never be involved with politics again. His heroes as a youngster were jockeys and race-car drivers. If he had any heroes outside the sports world, they were the royal family. "You must remember, we were steeped in tradition." George V, having ascended the throne the year Fred Perry was born, ruled Britain. Except for the great athletes of his time, Fred Perry would admit to no admiration other than for his ruling monarch. Steve Donahue, the jockey; Juan Fangio, the race-car driver; and the royal family; other people were mere mortals who did not excite him to extremes.

Rocking back in his seat at the restaurant of the Beachcomber, Perry said he had never thought about—had never put into words—his admiration for men and women who influenced the history of his time. I suggested Churchill, and he said, "Oh, yes, of course Churchill. But I'll tell you. There is one American who did a hell of a job. I mean Truman. But I go back to the era of the maharajahs of India who would pay £25,000 per year, when the pound was equal to $5, for polo uniforms alone. This was to me something . . . I mean, where do I go from here, Charlie? It's not respect; it's awe, really . . . that these things existed or could exist."

If Perry could have changed anything in his life, go back to age ten and start over, he showed little interest. "You have a pride in knowing that you did what you did with what you had," he said. "At least, whatever I managed to do, I did. In hindsight I probably would have done the same things I did. We were pioneers. These boys today aren't. Budge and Vines and Richards and Tilden . . . we were the pioneers. We were completely persona non grata. We were finished, ended. We couldn't play tournaments, anything. So we had to build. After the war, the old format of one-night stands was over. We had to start tournaments. Apart from Lacoste, we were the first people in the shirt business. We were the first to start outfitting players. So you might say [since tennis attire was so much a part of his history], if I could have done it all over, I would do it with more managerial expertise. We had no managers in those days after the war."

Perry is not a religious man. "I take it as it comes. I assume that there is something beyond my ken, you might say, but I don't worry about it. I have to stick to tennis because it is all that I am mixed up in, yet it goes further than that. For instance, when I give clinics to younger players, I do give some advice. I say, 'You have to respect the job that you do. You have to respect the school that you're in and the authority that is placed over you in that school.

75

Later on, you should go into some business that you like. If you work at what you like, you will do a much better job.'

"Now, the modern tennis player has a God-given gift to work at a job that he likes, that has become, suddenly, a gold mine. And, above all, you have to respect yourself and the game or the job that you do—and to repeat—the authority that runs that game or that job."

On the influence of his parents, Perry said, "They brought me up well, nicely, correctly. They did the best they could for me. We had a very close family, and we didn't particularly have to work at it. My two sisters, who are still alive . . . we don't see one another for a long period of time, but when we do get together, we start right where we were before. I had a solid home, and I looked up to my father. He worked very hard at the job he did and did a lot of pioneering in the labor movement. As far as my father was concerned, if you were told to be home at night for dinner at 7:30, you had better be there. I'd been around the world five times or so, but when I returned to England, I always stayed at the house. And it was just like being twelve years old again: 'What time are you coming in?' "

Perry has been married to the same woman for over thirty-five years. But he adds, "I was first married to a movie actress for my sins, a woman named Helen Vinson." The Perrys have a married son, who lives in Beverly Hills with four children, and a married daughter, who lives in England. He has been an American citizen since 1938, and his legal residence is in Pompano Beach, although he and his wife keep a cottage in Sussex.

In the not-so-old days, Perry was with Tommy Armour at Boca Raton and took golf lessons from the great professional. Perry was able to get down to a three handicap, and this led him to say that it was not that difficult for a man who played a racquet sport to switch to golf. However, he had never heard of a golfer who had taken up tennis and done well. I agreed and mentioned Ellsworth Vines, who went from tennis to golf, having beaten Tilden at tennis and then Ben Hogan in a playoff. "Ellsworth Vines is the one guy who beat the world's best golfer *once* and the world's best tennis player *more* than once. I beat Tilden many times, but you must remember that I was a hell of a lot younger."

I asked Perry if there was any time in his youth when he thought he might go all the way to the top. He said, "To me there is no prize for coming in second. I always thought I would be the champion, or otherwise I would not have gone on."

"Was there anyone who scared you, someone you hoped would not be on your side of the draw?"

"No. But I did worry about two things. One was playing on grass. You could always get caught in the first two or three days at Wimbledon, playing on an outside court that had been left uncovered and could be wet. Bad condi-

76

tions are great levelers, and the unknown player will go all out on a slippery court because he has a chance to make a name for himself—he has nothing to lose—and you, if you're seeded, can get hurt playing under wet conditions against someone who goes all out and doesn't care about himself. I saw Mal Anderson get hurt going for a wide one and go sliding off the court under a chair. He was injured, and he would have won it that year. But he didn't.

"The other thing was that I was always leery, not scared, but leery of the big serve-and-volley guys who would hit their ground shots as hard as they could—just swing and hope—because if they broke your serve, you had a hell of a time breaking back. If you lost your serve to Frank Shields, you could be in trouble. Another one was Berkeley Bell."

I asked Perry about the legendary Shields, who had the image of a swashbuckler. "Frank Shields was flamboyant, but if he had changed, he wouldn't have been Frank Shields, now would he? He was a great server, marvelous control," he said, "but so was Tilden. Tilden was not the fastest server in the world; not as fast as Vines, say, but from the same throw he could hit it three different ways, so you couldn't tell what was coming from the throw. Don Budge once asked me why I thought Tilden was so great. I said, with him you always have to think. Now when you watch the players of today, the pattern is 90 percent the same. Every time Connors plays Lendl, it's the same pattern as the last time. Every time Connors plays McEnroe, it's the same pattern as the last time. With Tilden it never was the same. You were always thinking."

Perry's mind was back at the end of the Tilden era. He recalled a Wimbledon finals in 1931 that went to Sidney Wood by default. "Wood beat me in the semifinals, and Frank Shields beat Jack Crawford in their semifinals, only Shields in winning, sprained his ankle. Wood won by default, and there was no final match." For some time, I had heard that Shields had showed up with a painful hangover, and after hitting one ball, he walked off the court. Perry said, "No." They did not even appear on the court, Shields having capitulated the previous day, unable to run.

Perry did not play men's doubles with much success. He did play mixed doubles, usually with Dorothy Round, and in 1932 he played with Sarah Palfrey, and they beat Ellsworth Vines and Helen Jacobs in the finals at Longwood. "Sarah would return Vines' serves as fast as he served them to her."

And going back to the big serve again, he said, "If you hit a good serve to one of these big serve-and-volley guys, he would take a Godawful belt at it. If you served it faster than he expected, the racquet was late, and the ball would go down the line. If you hit it softer than he expected, he'd hit early and crosscourt you. None of those shots was planned, so if they didn't know where they were aiming, how in hell were you supposed to find out? The thing I was very leery of was the roof falling in, to be very frank about it!"

I asked Perry what it was like to travel so much. As a young man, he had spent eight to nine months a year touring for his country over a four-year period.

"I was a bit of a loner. I didn't go in for sightseeing too much. We left home for South America, South Africa, to teams all over Europe—going, coming, going, coming—to America, then on to New Zealand and Australia. There was no one whom I couldn't get along with. We were always a team, and we stuck together, but I kept to myself a good deal.

"Later, though, as a professional when I toured with Bill Tilden, Vincent Richards, Karel Kozeluh, George Lott, and Bruce Barnes, we were much more together. I was no longer a loner; we were in business together, and we went to shows together. And with Bill, the atmosphere was always interesting. He had a circle of friends that was really extraordinary. And he, with Vincent Richards, between them they knew everyone who was in sports."

Perry gave an example of how he operated within this fellowship of athletes. "When I was still mixed up with sportswear and going on promotion tours, showing the flag and glad-handing, that sort of thing, my wife and I went to Stuttgart, and Max Schmeling had the soft drink concession in Hanover, and often we would have dinner with Schmeling and then late at night drive on to Munich." Serious differences in national policies did not intrude upon this fellowship. Because of tennis and particularly because of Bill Tilden, Perry knew everyone who was anybody in the only world that mattered. Dempsey, Gehrig, DiMaggio . . . the list was endless, the socializing taken for granted.

Thinking of Schmeling and the 1930s, Perry went back again to his many crossings of the Atlantic. "We would board the *Mauritania* or the *Leviathan* or the *Olympic* at Southampton. The smallest liner, which was the *Mauritania*, was 35,000 tons, the others considerably larger, with the bridge ninety feet above the water. Of course, we dressed for dinner. We were like the navy in peacetime, showing the flag, representing Great Britain."

In America Perry enjoyed going to Newport and to Long Island when they had their coming-out parties, and he and his teammates in dinner jackets would cause a considerable flutter.

"You must have had some interesting times," I said. "I can imagine a few hearts were broken along the trail."

"No," he answered. "We were never in one place long enough." He smiled like a fox when he said that and seemed content to let the days of debutante parties rest. He had told me enough.

I took a couple of snapshots of Perry outside the restaurant. He was impatient to be gone. No doubt it was one thing to reminisce with Don Budge but another to try to get across the excitement of his youth to a man like me. He looked taxed, and I waved good-bye as he walked out to his car. Then I raced after him. I wondered how he supported himself now that he was in his seventies. "Oh, I still get an income from the sportswear," he said. No doubt there was other income; surely he had made a healthy profit on the sale of the Beverly Hills Tennis Club. He lived in a quiet section of Pompano Beach, which I was able to locate on a local map. His cottage in Sussex no doubt was also comfortable.

The weather in south Florida seemed to be to his liking. He smiled a good deal as we talked, and he looked fine although he had collapsed just last summer in the hospital where he had gone because of feeling ill while doing television commentary at Wimbledon. There was no trace of illness when I saw him. I saw a full chest and strong English face, the kind you associate with tough taskmasters at English public schools or maybe drill instructors at Sandhurst.

For a short period in the 1930s, Fred Perry was the greatest tennis player to walk the earth. He knew royalty, movie stars, the leading athletes of his age, and within the guidelines that he had set for himself, he had gone to the top and had done it first class. It had all started with table tennis, which I mis-

12. Fred Perry

takenly referred to as Ping-Pong. "No," he said rather sternly, "there is a difference."

As Fred Perry drove off in his car, I looked back at the small pool in front of the restaurant. I saw some happy American tourists talking among themselves at the pool's edge. There is a difference all right, I thought. About the time Fred Perry won the world table tennis championship in Budapest, my father began to build a Ping-Pong table for our new house in New Britain, Connecticut. Where I came from, nobody would ever call what we played anything other than Ping-Pong. Over the long haul, my life and Fred Perry's life would seem as different as TWA from the Cunard Line. I was the kind of guy who read about the things that Fred Perry had done.

With Fred Perry gone, I went up to my room and changed into a pair of bathing shorts. I had an hour or so of sunlight and went down to the broad beach at Pompano, which was almost barricaded by an unending line of condominiums and hotels, and ran toward the pier at the end of Atlantic Avenue. I swam along the way, diving under the weak breakers into the cloudy ocean, knowing that it was not clean, that I would get freshened all right, but I would not feel that wonderful, purifying sensation I got at home on Martha's Vineyard. Yet it was very nice. I *did* feel at home the more I thought about it. For the first time that I could recall, I felt at home in Florida, the line of condominiums and the ocean clouded with their effluence notwithstanding.

No doubt I felt that way because of being with Fred Perry. I started going to Florida on my own in 1950. Since then I have been in that state too many times to count. But I was always on the outside looking in: either a young man living alone in a rooming house on Sunrise Avenue (Palm Beach, 1958), or living on my Gloucester schooner with my wife and friends (1971–74), staying at a girlfriend's house (also in Palm Beach in 1956 and 1957), or going into the Everglades fishing with a great outdoorsman, Homer Rhode, and the writer Allan Eckert (the mid-1960s).

But with Fred Perry I felt different. I realized that this was so because I was working, I had a mission to perform and therefore had a bona fide reason for being there. I had never been the kind of person who was happy very long just hanging about. I had to belong to a place or to a project to feel right. So, I reasoned, that was why I felt so at ease and could flow along on the flat beach and on a curl of a wave.

I remember that my parents had been to Florida twice. I was very young when they first went down to Key West and stayed at a hotel called the Casa Marina. They liked it, and my father came back with rhumba music to play on our stand-up Victrola in the hallway.

Later, around 1939, they went to the Hillsborough Club in nearby Hillsborough, Florida, which was the next town up the coast from Pompano Beach. They hated it there, and my father grumbled for days about how snooty everyone was. I believe that the Casa Marina had been taken over by the Navy by that time and, of course, Miami was out. He felt that Miami was full of the wrong kind of people, which was a veiled phrase meaning Jews from New York. Connecticut Yankees like my father got along with big-city Jews only at a distance, and even then they managed poorly. My father thought that although there were plenty of good Jews, some right in New Britain, Connecticut, there was little chance of finding a good one from New York, and so Miami was out, and they tried the Hillsborough Club.

But my father, who was mechanically oriented and could do wonders working with wood and loved to fix things, was ill at ease with smooth talkers and those soft, rich people from old families who did not know what made an internal combustion engine work. People who affected the mannerisms of high society and who have their expensive coming-out parties weren't his type; they talked with a Long Island accent, as though they had cheeks full of marbles, and couldn't sail a boat and didn't know how to clean fish, and probably the men had not served in the trenches in World War I as my father had done, though he never talked about it, and they were in their way snooty. Left to their own devices, they never would have passed muster. They wouldn't have made the grade. My father might have thought that way but would not have said it. He was often a silent man, but he could seethe inside. Sanctimonious, pompous, or stuffy people gave him what he called "the willies."

Then, too, my mother was slowing down with a dreaded disease, which would soon be diagnosed as multiple sclerosis. On top of that, probably in her panic at not knowing what was wrong with her, she had taken to drink. You don't need too much imagination to see my father leading an unsteady woman into dinner and getting odd, lofty, all-knowing looks. So for them, Hillsborough was an embarrassment, and they never returned to Florida again.

But I was thinking of Hillsborough for my own purposes. I wanted to go there just to see what it was like and to see if I would get the "high snoot" that my father had talked about. I also wanted to go there to inquire about the club tennis professional, Doris Hart. I wanted to play Doris Hart, Wimbledon champion, and had called her from my home only to get an absolute no-bones-about-it rejection. She said that she never gave interviews—period, and didn't play tennis anymore—period, except once in a while, and was too busy period to see me—period. But I thought that if I caught her off guard at her club and she saw that I was a disarming kind of vulnerable guy, I might win her over.

Alas, as I thought about it and wondered if I should give it a try, the time slipped by, and after one more lazy jog on the beach, it was too late to go. Don McNeill was waiting for me at 8:00 that night. Also, it was still October. Doris Hart might be around the club but surely not yet working. It was out of season in Florida, which was why I was paying only $27 a day at the Beachcomber and had the run of the beach, the pool, the cocktail lounge, and the restaurant. Although I really had no choice when it came to crashing the Hillsborough Club to see Doris Hart—she wouldn't be there, would she?—I still worked the proposition over in my mind and then said the hell with it. What I really wanted was to see the place that had snubbed my parents. I changed clothes quickly and left for Vero Beach and Don McNeill.

I don't like road signs that are mounted in cities to lead you out to a large interstate highway. Almost always they begin in order, one every few blocks, but then maybe halfway out of town, they fizzle out, and from then on you are going blind. I want directions to continue right to the end or not begin at all, in which case you are forced to buy a map and do your own thinking. So I got lost driving out of Pompano Beach looking for the Florida Turnpike. Somewhere at a shopping mall, about 7:00, I called Don McNeill from a phone booth, dropping a fistful of coins into the slot like a compulsive gambler in Reno.

I told him where I was and that I would be an hour and a half overdue . . . something on that order. "You see, I got lost," I said weakly. "Oh," he said, "I wish I'd never heard of you," he said then, and he sounded furious.

Fortunately for me, Dick Craven had known McNeill years back when they both worked on the Four Roses account at Young and Rubicam and had given me the name of a close friend of Don McNeill's, a neighbor back in Darien, Connecticut, named Jerry Palmieri.

I quickly told McNeill that Jerry Palmieri said to say hello and for me to extend his warmest wishes.

"How in hell do you know him?" asked McNeill. "Jerry Palmieri was my neighbor years ago, a good guy. How do you know him?" he repeated.

I told him about Dick Craven, and this seemed to calm him down.

"Well, I've blown the night anyway," he said. "I'll leave the light on for

13. Don McNeill

you. It will be the only light on on the whole street. Don't come after 9:00—I'll be going to sleep."

His caustic attitude seemed to fit what I had heard. I had been told that he was dead, that he had had a stroke, and that he was an alcoholic. Gardnar Mulloy said, "Gee, Don McNeill was around and winning and then all of a sudden he wasn't at any tournaments anymore. I used to ask, 'Where is McNeill?' and no one ever knew. He just dropped from sight."

So I had halfway expected a rather sour man and did not like making that call to tell him I had lost my way. A hopeless bungler was I—another dub he would have to talk with, some dumb hacker who couldn't find his way out of Pompano Beach.

I drove on into the night, finding the turnpike and keeping that Ford Escort at 65 all the way. I thought about Don McNeill. He was not on my original list. His tenure had been so brief. But I had looked at his record. He won the French singles title in 1939, the U.S. singles in 1940, beating Jack Kramer in the semifinals and Bobby Riggs in the finals. He won the national doubles in 1944 as Lieutenant Don McNeill, playing with the charismatic Bob Falkenburg. After the war he won the indoor singles title in 1950 and took the indoor doubles three times in a row with Billy Talbert 1949–1951. To beat Kramer and Riggs in the same tournament was a genuine feat, but what interested me was the old idea of rediscovery. Let's face it, I thought as I drove along, everybody has forgotten Don McNeill. After 1951 he vanished. Getting McNeill to talk excited me, and driving on toward his home my sense of expectation rose with each mile.

When I rang his doorbell, it was just after 9:00. I heard the gait of a man with a limp slowing him down, coming to the door, and then when he opened

84

it, I saw his large head with very bright blue eyes and a formidable nose, and he said, "I've met you somewhere before." He thrust his face at me and his pallid complexion took me unaware.

I entered the house and watched him slowly cross back to his chair where he sat himself, and after a few customary comments, I placed my tape recorder on a table near him and sat down, and we started to talk. It was true that we *had* met before, but where and under what circumstances, I did not remember nor did he. When I saw a picture of his wife, I knew I had met her, too. She was more familiar than he was. I reasoned that it must have been back in the late 1950s when we were both working in New York and had probably gone to the same party. I had the feeling that our meeting had not been pleasant. I seemed to remember a scene of some kind either with Don or with his wife. But then, we could have met in suburban Connecticut. I had friends in the New Canaan-Darien area. Surely there had been a good deal of drinking, and doubtless neither of us would ever remember the details. We had met, it had been unpleasant, and now years later we were meeting again. It was curious, but this old business had a positive effect on me. I liked him almost at once. For better or worse, we had been through something together somewhere, sometime ago. I liked that.

McNeill was born about fifty miles southwest of Oklahoma City in a town named Chickasha. He came from a family that was not too well off but then again not poor, and when they moved to Oklahoma City, he started out like any other southwestern kid—without money, without pretenses. He came from a 1930s middle-class home and had a ready, enthusiastic smile and a rather spectacular skill at hitting a tennis ball.

McNeill hung around the cement courts of Oklahoma City, hitting away at opponents, and then one day Bill Tilden came to town. "I don't know what brought him to Oklahoma City . . . surely not to hit tennis balls with me. I was about twelve or thirteen then, and I was a ball boy at a local club. Bill Tilden got out on one of the cement courts in his street clothes and street shoes, and he hit the ball with me, and it was a great thrill.

"I think he was on a tour, maybe with Vincent Richards. He had passed through a couple of years earlier, playing with Karel Kozeluh, and they played indoors that time. I saw them, but it was nothing like the thrill I got when I played with him, him in his street clothes."

For two years, Don McNeill won the high school singles championships of the state of Oklahoma, and failing to get a scholarship to the University of Texas, which was where he had set his heart, he enrolled in Central State Teachers' College. In his fall semester, fate intervened in the person of Eugene Lambert, the tennis coach for Kenyon College in Ohio. Obscure Kenyon College and Lambert in particular had come up with an idea: Kenyon would field a world-class tennis team and take on the great universities and make a name for itself. Like Rollins before it, Kenyon, a small experimental college, could catch the nation's eye through the relative inexpensive game of tennis. Don McNeill and a fellow Oklahoman, George Pryor, enrolled at Kenyon.

"One of the things that Eugene Lambert did was to drive the tennis team around all summer, and we'd go to tournaments that we'd never have gone to on our own. In this big station wagon of his, we'd drive through the Middle West and to the East one or two times. We did this for a couple of years, and I became ranked number nine in the country. This was in 1938 or 1939, and between my junior year and senior year, I got picked along with three other young players to play on a team that was going around the world. India wanted a team over there, and they gave us a first-class, round-the-world ticket.

"We had Charlie Harris, Owen Anderson, and Bill Robertson and me on that team, and that was before there were transoceanic commercial airlines. We went by ship to Hawaii and Japan and Hong Kong and Singapore, and then we spent three months traveling around India in slow trains, playing in what were called the princely states. We'd stay with the Maharajah Barodah and Maharajah Birphur and play exhibitions. I beat their number-one player, a man named Gos Mohammed, twelve times in a row. Had I beaten him a thirteenth time, I believe they would have given me permanent possession of the man. Anyway, from there we went to Egypt—Cairo and Alexandria—and there I met Baron von Cramm."

By that time, von Cramm had served time in a German prison for the trumped-up charge of sodomy with a male youth—a charge engineered by the Nazis because he would not promote Hitler's demagoguery to the world. Consequently, von Cramm was exiled and languished, as it were, in Cairo, where he ran into the young American, McNeill. Don now says that von Cramm had the best ground strokes in the game, and the two of them hit at each other for hours at a time in the dry Egyptian air. When Don went on to the French Open in June 1939, he was entering that prestigious tournament after practicing with von Cramm, a master, and he was tournament tough, having played in both large Egyptian cities, as well as in Athens and Stockholm. At Roland Garros, the site of the French championships, McNeill ran up against Bobby Riggs in the finals and beat him in straight sets, 6–3, 6–0, 8–6. As a youth, McNeill had played Bobby Riggs "at least ten times, and I never won a set, much less a match from him." But now all of a sudden, Don McNeill was number one in France, and Eugene Lambert's dream of having a ranking tennis star from Kenyon had paid off. "Who is Don McNeill?" and "Where is Kenyon?" were questions asked back to back. Don McNeill would be happy to answer both.

In 1940 everything began to jell for Don McNeill. He graduated from

14. Don NcNeill: Dressed to
kill, ready for stardom

Kenyon and entered the National Clay Courts Tournament in Chicago. In three successive matches, he beat Bitsy Grant, Frankie Parker, and Bobby Riggs. Later he won the National Intercollegiates, beating Joe Hunt. They played at the Merion Cricket Club outside Philadelphia, which has some of the finest grass courts in the world. However, because of NCAA rules, they played on clay. From Merion he went to Forest Hills. In September 1940, he beat Jack Kramer in the semifinals and Bobby Riggs, the defending champion, in the finals. It was McNeill's year: three championships all in 1940.

Added to all this, it should be remembered that as a junior at Kenyon, Don had won the national indoor singles title. This was before he had met Baron von Cramm and before his ascendancy to the top. Even without the polishing from the German master, McNeill, from Chickasha, Oklahoma, had more than fulfilled Eugene Lambert's dream. Like Pauline Betz, he'd grown up playing on hard cement courts and had surprised everyone coming from the hinterlands, but unlike Pauline, he did not grow up in California, where tennis was a way of life. He was from Depression-ridden Oklahoma, an Okie, who in his way would prove once again that America belonged to everyone.

McNeill was drinking wine, and I had helped myself to a couple of drinks, and as the night went on, I was beginning to feel very close to Don McNeill. It was true that he did not radiate the good health so evident in the other players—even Sarah Palfrey with her osteoarthritis. It was true that his pale, angular face gave more than a hint of a man who had made friends with alcohol: his nose was a giveaway. And he was still drinking even though partially paralyzed, "disabled," as he would say. But he was sixty-five and surely had the right to do as he wished. He lived alone, just away from the beach in a modest home in a row of modest homes. He had a car that he could still drive—"not to drive would be a fate worse than death"—and one wall was full of trophies, and pictures of his wife, recently deceased, were on display. There were other mementos about, and he had a pool in the backyard in which he swam every day to keep in shape as best he could. He had taken up bridge with a vengeance, though he admitted being only "a promising junior" at this stage. He did say that Pauline Betz Addie was a life master. "I read that in my *American Contract Bridge Bulletin* that I get monthly." He was impressed by her prowess, and I could see that he hoped someday to get out of the juniors and arrive in the finals in bridge as he had done in tennis.

On the surface, McNeill may have looked as though life had passed him by, but it hadn't. He was still swimming and working at his bridge, and he alluded often to a lady friend. At sixty-five he was doing pretty darn well, I concluded. He was doing as well or better than the older men I had known as a kid in Connecticut. Woefully out of shape, diseased from chronic drinking, the older crowd my father's age were, for the most part, dead issues by the time they had reached sixty-five. I saw them in yacht clubs and country clubs and in California and Florida and in every town and city in which I lived. Such men resided in their memories and pharumphed about, corpuscular and always complaining of minor bodily malfunctions, their slow wits mouthing platitudes. I used to think that the smart alecks in Hollywood invented "I Love Lucy" and "Gunsmoke" and John Cameron Swayze just for my father's crowd. Growing up I got the idea that at sixty-five, it was all over. But then I began to find the exceptions. I found that there were men at seventy who were as spontaneous and quick as I was at thirty, and once when I was covering the Boston Marathon for a newspaper, I saw old men going the distance, their lean bodies tightened by resolve. Don McNeill was not a dead issue. He was a gritty guy. He took a sip of wine, and I rose to get another drink, and then he picked up the story of his life.

With the entry of the United States into World War II, Don McNeill enlisted in the Navy. He had graduated cum laude at Kenyon; his major was economics.* A smart young man with a national reputation, the Navy kept him visible. He was made a naval attaché and posted to Buenos Aires, Argentina. He served there long enough to win four consecutive Argentine championships and eventually was given leave in 1944 to play at Forest Hills, where he and his partner, Bob Falkenburg, won the U.S. doubles title. He wound up his service as an air combat information officer, serving on aircraft carriers in the Pacific.

But as all players over fifty-five are quick to remind me, this was the time of amateur tennis, and McNeill had to find work that would support him and his growing family. He went into advertising and, listening to his clipped speech, his rather abrupt way of talking, I could imagine a razor tongue back in the glory days when Frederic Wakeman was writing *The Hucksters* and Sloan Wilson was writing *The Man in the Gray Flannel Suit*, and all the clever young men with a touch of style thought New York City and advertising was an irresistible combination. And for Don, it was. He thrived at his work, first for McCann-Erickson, then Young and Rubicam (where he met my tennis chum, Dick Craven), and finally at J. Walter Thompson, his last employer, in which company he rose to be vice-president.

In 1950 he won his last major singles title: the national indoor, at the 7th Regiment Armory in New York. He beat Fred Kovaleski, who had been extended until 2:00 that very morning by Billy Talbert. [He is quick to point

---

* In April of 1984, Don McNeill was awarded an Honorary Doctor of Laws from Kenyon. The citation read, in part: "Kenyon should not forget that its most remarkable and successful athlete of all time played tennis." He was lauded as both an athlete and a successful advertising executive.

out that Kovaleski was tired.] By then Don was a weekend player, and in spite of his work and the socializing and the martini lunches, he still had the goods, even though he stresses that Kovaleski must have been exhausted when they met. But McNeill *was* the winner, and it was 1950, not 1938. No other American man in history had come back after twelve years to repeat as a singles champion in the same major national tournament. In 1952, the year that belonged to Frank Sedgman of Australia and both Jack Kramer and Pancho Gonzales had come and gone, McNeill was still able to get to the semifinals at Forest Hills, where he was beaten by Billy Talbert. It is safe to say that by 1952, Don McNeill was burning the candle at both ends, and while one flame was strong, tennis had begun to flicker and grow dim. Tennis became paddle tennis, and work and his family took over his suburban life that began in Orange, New Jersey, and moved into Fairfield County, Connecticut.

But back to tennis. In 1944 the Navy gave him a short leave to play against Bill Tilden in a benefit for the Red Cross. "I think Bill Tilden won the first set, but I won the second. Anyway, we split sets. It was great, no question about that. I don't know how old Tilden was then, probably in his late forties."

I could see a glow in Don McNeill's eyes as he talked about Bill Tilden. He had to be thinking of himself as a kid in Oklahoma City, a ball boy getting a chance to hit a few with the great star. And then, so many years later, with the war raging and he a lieutenant in the Navy, now a champion himself, taking on his idol and splitting sets. Just splitting sets—that gives some idea of Tilden's greatness as a player.

And he remembers 1946, the year Gardnar Mulloy and Billy Talbert won their third national doubles title and retired the trophy. He was playing with Frank Guernsey, Jr., and in the fifth set, which Mulloy and Talbert ultimately won 20–18, McNeill and his partner had Talbert at break point five or six times. "There was one call that Frank thought was out and that would have won it for us, and we went to each other and shook hands and then walked toward Gardnar and Billy to offer our condolences, and the linesman said he hadn't made a call, and the umpire in the chair asked him how it was, and the linesman went like this [and McNeill made a gesture that a baseball umpire makes when he signals "safe"]."

I told him that Gardnar lists that as one of his greatest matches, and McNeill smiled, acknowledging that no doubt it was. I said, "But Gardnar swears he saw the chalk dust fly when Talbert's ball hit the baseline. The shot was *in.*"

"I went down to Houston where Frank Guernsey has pictures of that disputed point," McNeill replied. "But you can't really tell whether it was in or out. It had that little tail on the ball you get in a picture."

"Mulloy says he could see the dust rise," I insisted.

"Well, he's got good eyes then. The ball was on our side of the court and . . ." at which point McNeill snorted in derision.

But as McNeill reminded me, he and his partner had packed to go home and had checked out of their hotel room prior to the semifinals, where they were to meet Jack Kramer and Ted Schroeder, seeded number one. "We blew them off the court in straight sets," he says, "and then we had to go back and check in again and unpack our suitcases, only to lose on a disputed call when we had Billy Talbert broken at match point." He laughed fondly; those were the days.

The night was wearing on, and I was very relaxed. I'd seen Fred Perry that afternoon, run on the beach, was now talking amiably with Don McNeill, but I knew I had a long ride back to Pompano Beach, and I had not eaten dinner. It was great fun. McNeill looked well and was talking with a very slight hesitation in his speech, a vestige of the stroke that had paralyzed his right leg. But he did not appear eager for me to leave, and I thought that he wanted company. So I stayed, and I asked him some questions for the record.

"Was there anyone on the tour who scared you? Someone you hoped would be in the other side of the draw?"

"No. If I'm going to win this thing, I'm going to take them as they come, which I did."

"Who was your favorite doubles partner?"

"Frank Guernsey was my favorite doubles partner."

"Mixed doubles?"

"Probably Dorothy Bundy. I always had to play mixed doubles to stay in the tournament to get my room and board. Dodo Bundy is a marvelous person and was a great partner."

"As you went along playing in tournaments, was there anyone you didn't like?"

"No, I can't say there was such a person. I know that Bobby Riggs irritated a lot of people, but Bobby and I got along fine. He was always a gambler, a hustler. When we were kids and we played each other in junior tournaments, and when I was in college, you couldn't walk along the street without him wanting to lag you for a quarter or a half dollar for a line on the sidewalk. Bobby was quite a character."

I knew McNeill's greatest match had to be his singles victory over Bobby Riggs in 1940 at Forest Hills, to become ranked number one in the country. He lost the first two sets 4–6, 6–8 but won the next three 6–3, 6–3, 7–5. He showed me a copy of the *Kenyon Alumni Bulletin*, in which he is quoted as follows: "Three things stand out in my memory of the last game with Riggs serving at 5–6. Riggs was unable to persuade the umpire that he had not touched the net and ultimately lost the point to make it 0–15. Undecided whether to throw the next point because Riggs swore he hadn't touched the net, I knocked the serve out. Although I had done this unintentionally, the fans cheered wildly, interpreting my bad return as a gesture of good sportsmanship. Score: 15–all.

"On my first match point, Riggs got to the net and made a fine volley, and I fell flat on my face trying to get a fast start for it. Then he had game advantage when I hit an impossible forehand crosscourt passing shot—the best I'd ever hit in my life. It couldn't have come at a better time, as it so unnerved Riggs that he missed two difficult low volleys coming in behind his serve at deuce and match point. I got the feeling he was desperate."

I read the *Kenyon Alumni Bulletin* article, and we talked about it for a while. Don spoke: "Riggs always said that he let me off the hook in that match. I guess he is right." McNeill had beaten Fred Kovaleski indoors because the latter was worn out by Billy Talbert. Now he is saying that he had been let off the hook. He was without bravado, he was no braggart—a quiet man with an honest face, trying to tell the truth.

About his heroes as a youth, McNeill answered as almost everyone else had answered: tennis players. He was in awe of Bill Tilden and venerated Don Budge, who "was the best, and I still look up to him. A true gentleman and a great player. Bill Tilden and Don Budge are two great players to have as your idols."

At sixty-five and looking back over his life, McNeill mentions Winston Churchill as the greatest man in his time. "As far as my personal life goes, I would have to say that my wife has meant the most to me. As far as tennis is concerned, there was one man, Gottfried von Cramm, who meant a lot to me. He played with me for four or five months. We would exchange shots down the line for fifteen minutes; then we'd hit crosscourt forehands, then backhands for another fifteen minutes each. Then after an hour and a quarter of practice, we'd take fifteen minutes at the net, slamming back and forth as hard as we could volley. I maintain that anybody has to be very lucky to get that kind of practice with such a great player. He was very interested in seeing me progress."

"If you had your life to live over again, is there anything you would change?"

"Yes. I'd keep my wife alive. I was very fortunate as a young man and all through my college career and business career, married life and family life. I am just sorry my wife can't be with me now."

McNeill came from a very religious family, but he is an agnostic. In a general sense, he thinks he believes in God but let the subject drop.

As far as any wisdom to impart to the world, he can only advise that young people take up a sport such as tennis. "It is a great sport to play because it can stay with you all your life, through married life and old age. Exercise is the key to anybody's life, or it should be," he added.

Speaking of his parents, he said that his father got him started. "I don't think anybody in Oklahoma had any ideas that I would amount to anything. I think by getting me interested in tennis at eight or nine years of age, he pointed me in the right direction. Both my parents were very influential in that, and we were a relatively poor family."

McNeill's father died twenty years ago, and his mother, who was 100 when we talked, lives in a nursing home in Conroe, Texas, with her sister who is 102. McNeill has a sister who resides twenty miles north of Houston, near the nursing home. He respects the family: Don McNeill was married almost forty years and had three daughters and a son, who died. His sister has been married "about thirty-seven years, with two boys and two girls."

He left J. Walter Thompson in 1966 and went to work selling space to newspapers across the country for a company called Newspaper One. This job lasted for six or seven years, and finally he left the business world altogether. Eventually he and his wife bought a home in Grenada, which he was lucky to sell prior to the hostilities that have enveloped that country. They settled in Vero Beach, and then his wife died on July 5, 1982. His married daughters and four grandchildren are elsewhere, but he has his pool and his duplicate bridge and a sharp mind that does not admit second thoughts about his years in New York and its environs when he drank too much and played too hard and raised a family according to the code of the suburbs. He had come out of nowhere and had done very well in the big city. His wife was good-looking and a continual joy. They shared everything. At the end of our talk, I sensed his loneliness and wondered if he had been an open, sharing kind of person prior to his wife's death. I asked him: "If you were keeping a diary over the years, would you have shown it to your wife?"

"Hell," he answered, "I would have asked her to edit it."

McNeill walked me to the door, and we shook hands. He was leaning on his aluminum cane, and he looked tired. It was after 11:00, and I wanted to say something trite such as, "Hang in there, Champ," and though he was trying to ease me out of his life and go to bed, I really didn't want to leave him alone. But I remembered that he had a lady friend and his bridge pals, and he could still drive. His stroke was now over ten years past, and he had adjusted. "The hell with it," I thought and, driving down the Florida Turnpike, I wondered why I had been drawn into McNeill's life so deeply. Somewhere down the line, I realized that it was very simple. I envied him. I envied the fact that he was old enough to have served in the war, to have ended it off Japan aboard a carrier. I envied his great tennis successes. I envied his marriage, in which he would ask his wife to edit his diary. I liked the fact that he had put himself through the mill and damn near died and was still kicking. He'd lived the kind of life that Sloan Wilson had made famous in *The Man in the Gray Flannel Suit*, and surprisingly I was still envious that I came too late to live it

93

also. He had come along ten years ahead of me and had hit history at the right time. "Damn," I said to myself, "I would have loved to have been a naval attaché in Buenos Aires instead of an Air Force PFC working on the flight line at Mather Air Force Base in Sacramento, California." I recognized that I had romanticized Fred Perry and his transatlantic crossings and his "showing the flag," but with McNeill, it was pure envy. I was not yet fifty-four and wondered where I would be at sixty-five. That was what I thought as I drove back to Pompano Beach.

The next morning I called Don McNeill. I wanted to know when he had had his stroke. It was not in my notes, and I was afraid I had missed asking him. He said, "I want to be honest with you. I didn't have a stroke. I woke one morning, and my right leg was paralyzed. Our doctor came to the house because I couldn't move. Then they took me to the hospital, where I stayed for a couple of weeks. My leg never got better, and when the diagnosis came in, it read: acute deterioration of the cerebellum—from alcohol abuse. I wanted you to know that," he said.

Then he switched the tone of his voice and said cheerily, "I was about to go into the pool for my workout when you called. Keep in touch," he added, and that was it. He had told me that he had brain damage from drinking. The tennis world and even the *Kenyon Alumni Bulletin* had thought it was a stroke. Instead it was something self-inflicted, something to be kept a secret. I wondered about the wine that he was drinking when I saw him, and I imagined moments of pure drunkenness that could have punctuated his heavy drinking days. And then I thought . . . a stroke or brain damage from drinking, what really is the difference?

Don McNeill needn't be ashamed of anything. There had been competitive sports and New York advertising, and sometimes people burned themselves out. I was grabbing at reasons, if not excuses, and I was no longer envious . . . just perplexed by his confession.

Shirley Fry Irvin:

"Little me from Ohio"

It was late in October, and I took one day for myself just to walk the beach and run a bit and loll about the pool. I knew that once home in Massachusetts, it would be a long fall, full of work, and only the evergreens would keep their color. The tall maple trees and the scrub oak would go bare and then the bleak New England winter would roll in, and the wind out of the northwest would chill the island, a wind carrying a cloying wetness from the ocean. It is seldom cold on Martha's Vineyard, but always raw. The greatest thing about Florida was the verdure, the feeling of a swamp that you can get out past town, inland where the edges of central Florida still carried mystery and even alligators and the lush sensuality that I liked. It made me feel like an animal; it lent the illusion that I was sleek and fast and on the loose.

At home I was pale and fat and sloppy, which is how I saw myself, and so I spent one more day in Florida, not out coasting along some inland rivulet among the mangroves, but still there on the beach, idling about in the sun. The sun took away this urge to drive up to West Palm Beach, turn left, and go inland to Lake Okeechobee and then south from there to the Okaloacoochee Slough and lose myself.

Then, too, I had made earlier plans to fly on to California to see Ellsworth Vines and Alice Marble and other tennis stars, and I wondered about that. Could I handle more interviews without a word set down in type? I realized I could not. The more I saw myself in the jungle of interior Florida, the more my mind was working its way free from the hard work, which was to write. I sent some postcards to California informing Louise Brough and Margaret Osborne duPont and Ellsworth Vines that I was canceling my trip. I called Alice Marble on the phone. She was very pleasant and said she would see me when and if I got there. I looked around the pool at a group of dull Americans and did not bother asking them if they had ever heard of Fred Perry, Gardnar Mulloy, or Don McNeill. I had already tried that a few times, and inevitably I had drawn blanks. I had been visiting outstanding people, and nobody knew who they were. The idea was to get to writing, and maybe then someone would care about a fan and his idols, about the men and women who had played on center court and won and then drifted away from the adulation.

I flew home, carrying Miami Dolphin T-shirts and hats and other inexpensive gifts people buy at a souvenir store at the airport. At home I began to type and to listen to the tapes I had made, records of conversations starting with Pauline Betz. There were many questions I had forgotten to ask, many thoughts I could have explored. Each person deserved a full profile, but that was impossible. But I hoped my own feelings were more or less the feelings that any fan would identify with; I surmised they would cut across lines and appeal to anyone who had ever dreamed of playing catch with Bob Feller or of having a drink with Sir Laurence Olivier. Most people have someone out there in stardomland they would like to meet once for just a moment. I was no different, except that I had done it—with tennis. When I thought of Olivier, I saw Fred Perry waving good-bye.

And then the name Shirley Fry came to my attention. I had been playing tennis with Don Davis, a friend of Dick Craven's and mine, who was on the island off-season, enjoying the warm autumn weather that had put the lie to my thoughts that the Vineyard would be cold and dour, and hence I should disappear for a few days into the steamy middle ground of Florida. Davis, who lived near Hartford, Connecticut, knew Shirley Fry and reminded me that she had won quite a few tournaments in her day. She and Doris Hart formed a doubles team that knew few equals in the history of women's tennis. She was a wonderful person, he said, and I should see her. Don Davis can be very authoritative. He is chairman of a company called the Stanley Works, a large tool company founded three generations ago by two of my ancestors. I listened to him and then went to the record books to investigate Shirley Fry.

Briefly, back when I concocted my plan for this book, I thought of her but only as Doris Hart's partner. I did not realize that in 1956 she had won the singles at Forest Hills, as well as at Wimbledon, and was ranked number one in the world. Nor did I know that in 1952 she won both the French and the Italian singles titles and later the Australian singles in 1957. In 1956 she had won the U.S. Clay Court Championships, again in singles. And who was I to scorn doubles victories anyway? I had gone down to Florida to see Gardnar Mulloy, whose reputation rested on his doubles play. And for me, personally, doubles was always the better game to play. I always loved the teamwork, the flow of four players as they kept the ball in play, waiting for the precise moment for the put-away. So why, then, had I let Shirley Fry fizzle away in my mind? I suppose it has to do with celebrity.

Maureen Connolly, who may have been the greatest woman singles player in history, was called by the press "Little Mo," and Little Mo had the clippings and the attention. When Maureen Connolly was winning her singles matches and taking the grand slam (the first woman to win all four major tournaments in the same year), Shirley Fry was winning the doubles with Doris Hart. When Maureen Connolly was felled by her horse, ending her career, Shirley Fry emerged as a singles star. But to many, and surely to me, her status was vitiated by the loss of Maureen Connolly to the tennis world and by the fact that right in her footsteps came Althea Gibson, a serve-and-volley player who played "the big game" and had the coffee-colored skin that made her at once a celebrity, a female Jackie Robinson. Shirley Fry, caught in the middle, became a no-name, whose last win was the Australian singles title, beating Althea Gibson, having teamed with Althea for the doubles title. She was a doubles winner in Australia, but after 1957 there is hardly a mention of Shirley Fry. Only once could I find her and that was in the over-forty category: she won the singles in 1971 playing on grass.

I was only about halfway through my writing when I left home again to drive to Hartford to see Shirley Fry Irvin. Until Don Davis gave me her address, I did not know that she had married. The Tennis Hall of Fame, of which she is a member, has her correctly listed as Irvin, but I had not seen that until just before I left for Hartford, and I only mention this because tennis names and married names were beginning to cause confusion. I was never sure how to refer to a married woman sports star. In the theater, you simply said Miss Davis (as in Bette Davis), regardless of her many husbands.

It was late November, and football was in the air, apple cider stands were along the highway, and the ghost of Norman Rockwell stalked the earth. Shirley Fry Irvin would qualify for the finals in such a master plan of an American fall, so full of old memories, small-town values, ancient woodlands, and general stores along the road from Providence to the Hartford area. But I was unaware of Shirley Fry's wholesome appearance until I saw her smiling face and took a picture of her standing under a basketball hoop before her garage in West Hartford. I had encountered what my father would call "a peach of a girl." No one is perfect, and Shirley Fry may have a dark side that eluded me, but I was soon to discover a fifty-six-year-old woman who still had the grin of a tomboy, the impish good humor that only the actress Katharine Hepburn had ever caught right on the screen. It was an impish allure that had been part of my life wherever girls competed with boys and won and wherever girls could turn the tables and make you glad that they did. I could imagine racing with her as kids across a field full of wildflowers.

I had arrived in Hartford the night before, driving up from the Vineyard. I wanted to see Hartford again, the city where I was born and where I often visited as a young adult and where I was taken as a kid to see the pediatrician. I also got my teeth straightened in Hartford by a man who filled my mouth with rubber bands, charging a small fortune during the Depression and causing my father to say, "The hell with him!"

But what I remember best about the Hartford of my early youth were the Thursday nights when my parents would take me with them to go to the movies. Before the movies, we would dine at the old Bond Hotel, now torn down—so I discovered—and listen to a dance band that played in the style of Vincent Lopez, which is to say the band played very danceable music, the foxtrot that my parents enjoyed. The leader bowed the violin and nodded to our table, often coming over to say something to me, a very small boy who just sat there dressed in clean knickers and a sports jacket. Those were warm evenings back around 1936 or 1937, and my mother was not yet too ill to dance a little and to sit through a movie. We saw *It Happened Last Night, The Awful Truth, The Hunchback of Notre Dame,* and my favorite, *Captains Courageous.* Driving back to New Britain in my father's Buick or Packard, we would rehash the movie we had seen. My mother's favorite actor was Robert Montgomery, and my father and I liked Spencer Tracy. Revisiting Hartford reminded me of those evenings, and I almost went to a bookstore to buy a book that would be full of stills from the old movies so that I could find a few that I had seen to jog my memory. Perhaps I could recall some of the films that starred Robert Montgomery or Madeline Carroll or Irene Dunne or Franchot Tone, who was my very favorite, even better than Spencer Tracy, because he reminded me of my uncle, Foster Upham, for reasons that are now obscure.

In any event, I was back in Hartford on a Saturday night, and coming toward the bridge on Route 44, I saw the city rising out of the flatland along the Connecticut River like the Emerald City of Oz. Once there had been one tall building in Hartford, the Travelers Building, and that was the highest structure north of New York City. Now Hartford stands like a great metropolis in the middle of the prairie. I pondered Omaha as I saw it around the bend, leaving what used to be tobacco country to my right and low, horizontal shopping centers to the left. And there it is, with a skyline like New York City. Somebody must have gone mad, I thought. Why did people take the capital of Connecticut and transform it into New York or, for that matter, Omaha, Nebraska?

I didn't find out on Saturday night. I had dinner at the Sheraton, where I stayed. The Sheraton was partly filled with patrons of a Ricky Nelson concert at Constitution Plaza, next door. I couldn't believe it. People were walking around the small lobby of the Sheraton, wearing Ricky Nelson T-shirts. Not too many years ago when I came back to Hartford as an adult and stayed at the Statler—now remodeled and called the Hartford Hilton—men wore tweed sports jackets and rep ties and the women dressed in tweedy skirts with demure blouses with round pins—a gold circle over the heart.

The young women bought their clothes at Peck and Peck or at Lord and Taylor, which had just opened, and the men got their conservative clothes from Henry Miller or Stackpole, Moore, and Tryon. West Hartford, where everyone I knew lived, had the highest income per capita in the nation, and farther out in Farmington and Avon, you found miles of open land and quaint inns dating back to the Revolutionary War.

All that was only twenty-five years before 1983, and although in those days I thought Hartford was stuffy and full of very dull people, there was a good, orderly feeling to the city, and I always felt disarmed and relaxed when I made my way to the bar at the Bond or to the small cocktail lounge at the old Heublien Hotel or to one of the fine taverns in Simsbury or Farmington or Avon. Sometimes it was nice to be with well-dressed, comforting people even if they didn't know Freud from Fresno (the town in California), or Sibby Sisti (Boston Braves) from Lonny Frey (Cincinnati Reds), or demagogue from pedagogue, or, as old friends used to say, "Shit from Shinola." In essence, it was often consoling to be among Yale men and Smith or Vassar women, comfortable Ivy League people who were self-assured.

But now it was different. The city had changed, and where once on a Saturday night, downtown Hartford was as empty as Althea Gibson's East Orange, New Jersey, it was now abustle with consumers. Where they all got their money for their night on the town was beyond me. I could only guess that the massive insurance companies that long ago had turned Hartford into a white-collar industry town were flourishing, and perhaps all these people bundling into barrooms and hotel lobbies were the reason my insurance rates kept going up and up. I could have yelled to one and all: "Go home to Duluth!" but then I saw good old Stackpole, Moore, and Tryon still where it had always been and remembered when my father saw me in civilian clothes in 1955, having just been discharged and ready to return to Wesleyan University in Middletown, Connecticut. He said, "Go on up to Hartford and buy some nice things to wear. Get a good overcoat and a tuxedo. You will need them." So I went to Stackpole's and charged a cashmere polo coat to him, and a shawl-collar tuxedo and a few shirts. Stackpole's was a "gentleman's tailor" in those days. Yet on this Saturday night, I was surrounded by democracy-at-work and could not help feeling fondness for a time when class

99

lines were sneaky and wavering but nevertheless there, and a gentleman's tailor could spot even a renegade like me and see that somewhere back there, there had been a member of the old elite who had come from colonial times up through the Industrial Revolution that burgeoned during the midnineteenth century in New England. I would lie if I didn't say that I felt superior to everyone I saw and at the same time completely alone. I was lost in a crowd of fellow Americans who didn't look like me, think like me, or act like me. The city of my birth, where resided so much nostalgia, was now a strange land. I sidestepped the traffic and ventured into a few watering holes, only to be assaulted by rock and roll. The violins of the old Bond Hotel were probably gathering dust in some storage warehouse. Or maybe they had been broken and thrown away. Thank the good Lord for Shirley Fry Irvin. She was of my age, two years older, a woman to whom I could cling tomorrow.

When I saw her coming from her house, pausing to stand before the basketball hoop that was where it ought to be—attached to the top front of her garage—when I saw her thus portrayed, I knew that I was seeing once again the real woman athlete. She had those legs—strong calves, well-turned power stanchions that will move her about in any sport the way a Herschel Walker would move. And this is not to say that her legs were in any way a "problem" for an attractive woman. No, they were quite the opposite. They combined force and sensuality, which may be the same thing. What those calves really meant was that Shirley Fry Irvin had not gone to seed; she was still running, competing, playing sports. She was so healthy-looking that I thought of many other women of great health and longevity and power and of how a man of power and health would want to join himself to her, to combine the energy that was so manifest. Those were my thoughts.

Alas, I was not Jim Brown or Vic Seixas or Bob Mathias, the two-time decathlon winner of the Olympics. I was only me. I had the *gall* to involve myself with a woman who was surely my superior. We could run across fields full of wildflowers, but she would win. Every time. That is how my mind worked as I followed her to the Farmington Racquet Club, another warehouse for tennis.

Once, when I was twenty-four, I went out for dinner on a Saturday night and ended up at a place called the Tahitian Hut, which was near a new shopping center in Sacramento, California. I would have sold my soul for a Wellesley woman in those days or any young woman who even pretended to have read Hemingway and Fitzgerald. In Sacramento I was alone at the time of Honey Bear Warren, who was the governor's daughter—the daughter of the man who would become a hallowed Supreme Court justice, some thought rivaled only by John Marshall. But that was in 1954. Honey Bear and I never met. I drifted about the capital of California, trying to find *one* woman my

100

own age who might understand something along the order of what they were teaching back at Wesleyan, Swarthmore, or even Smith and Yale. God, I was lonely, and I so often ate alone.

I'd have two drinks at the bar, and if no one drifted into my shy world, I would go to eat and order a bottle of California wine—usually Almaden or Inglenook, neither of which was nationally known at the time, and then drift off into dreaming, and finally I'd go home. But on this night at the Tahitian Hut, a once-in-a-lifetime experience happened: a group of women athletes entered the place, and they took over the restaurant. I repeat, this was in 1954, and it marks the first time that I saw feminism in the raw. The women represented the ladies tour—the touring golf professionals from Louise Suggs through Jackie Pung to young Marlene Bauer. They commandeered tables, and they swore as Marines are supposed to swear in combat. I sat in total silence and in awe, watching these women jocks and listening to them converse. I think the occasion was called the Barbara Romack Invitational, and the whole gang had showed up for it. No one had brought along a male guest for dinner, and though I was consumed by flirtatious thoughts and vainly assumed some golfer would sense it, I was totally ignored. Looking back, I see myself as a good-looking young guy, but *no one cared.* And they all had those strong hard calves, and I wondered about them. Why didn't one of them signal to me? A group of male athletes from a similar tournament, devoid of females and seeing one lone woman at a table in an otherwise empty restaurant, would send an emissary and within minutes, if not seconds, the woman could opt for inclusion. But this was different. The women I was contemplating were consumed with their tournament. I heard the talk. I waited for a Marlene Bauer or a Barbara Romack, but no one came to my table. I was twenty-four years old and concluded that they were simply oblivious to my presence.

Is it possible to get sex out of the picture? I think not. So I wondered about Shirley Fry Irvin. I fantasized our competition; we would then lunch together, and maybe I'd glean an insight or two about "where she stood." On the drive home, I began to contemplate the tomboy in America. I searched for parallels in the male sex and could find none. The woman athlete: is she or isn't she? Why did I care? I think I cared because I wanted to be comforted by the kind of woman I'd always liked. As with many men of my generation, I admired women who would stick by as allies—laugh until dawn, travel to Timbucktu—but underneath I always wondered about their secret sexuality.

There is often a time in sports, and in this case in tennis, when a player can get on "a roll." This is when he begins to move the ball against his opponent, keeping the pressure on, keeping the other player on the defensive. On a roll, it appears that you have the feet of Hermes and can move quickly and at will to any spot on the court. You are always in position when the ball comes back, and then you apply the pressure some more, waiting for your opponent to crack.

And this is the way it was with Shirley Fry. In warming up, I fancied that we would have a close contest. I could not discern any power that would make me tremble. I saw only her ground strokes, which were adequate, and her lateral movement, which was smooth, almost as smooth as the glide I saw with Pauline Betz. But she was rugged, she hit hard, and she played nicely, and I said to myself, "6–4 either way." I had forgotten the roll.

And roll away it went. I was forever on my own baseline, wondering when the momentum would change and when I would be able to move to center position and start to volley and send Shirley sprawling. I was forever wondering why she always had to hit the line or come about two inches inside it. No matter what I tried, I couldn't break her command. In simple words, she just had me backed into a corner.

She took the first set 6–1, but I still had hopes. Her game was not strong, and once in a while I could pass her. I knew in my heart that I would turn the tables. Yet her accuracy was beyond my powers of belief. She just kept hitting inside the line or on the line, and for me to make a point, I had to exert myself, to take the net and put it away. Unfortunately I can't recall that I ever did that. I was always chasing down one of her deep placements. And the end of each point was the same: I'd reach the placement in a last-gasp sort of way and then flipper it back to the net, thumping like a dead fish.

The second set went 6–0. By now she knew I had no offensive backhand. All she had to do was send her shots into my backhand corner and watch me flail or block the ball or bloop it. Her shots were always right *in* the corner, and I was always on the run. Of course, I returned a few reasonably well, but that only prolonged the rally. She won the third set 6–2.

She played with a metal Head "Red Head" and had no serve to speak of, no net game, no volley that I could discern. What she had was lateral movement and placement. I blamed myself for staying up the previous night looking over the "new Hartford." I should have been in bed early, in training. I had forgotten once more that a champion can hit the lines, can go down the line, can manage a lethal crosscourt with little effort, can retrieve, and can move. It is second nature for a woman of fifty-six who had started playing competitively at nine years old. I had forgotten that for me to win, I would have to force the play. I think that on that Sunday, I was too tired to force the play. I think, quite honestly, that I have been playing defensive tennis for years. In a way, I've always been too tired to force the play. I count on other players' mistakes. With champions, you find few mistakes. I took some consolation in proposing a fourth set, and Shirley looked genuinely fatigued when she said, "Oh, no, I have had enough." I would find out later that she went all out against me, playing as well as she could. "I didn't want to let up for you. You wouldn't have wanted it that way, would you?" I said, no, I wouldn't have wanted that. I wanted her finest, and I got it. I got what women got at Forest Hills and Wimbledon and in Sydney and in France at Stade Roland Garros. Gardnar Mulloy had to play down for me, otherwise there would not have been a rally. Shirley played at her best, and we did have some good points. I had that somewhat mitigating factor in mind when I drove home. She had put me to shame, but at least she had done it playing all out.

We found a table at the Marriott Hotel in Farmington, where on Sunday an extensive brunch is served. As a result, the dining room was crowded with people consuming, spending, conversing: it was much like the previous evening. I placed my tape recorder on the table and ordered Shirley a Bloody Mary, and we began to talk. I had a copy of Gianni Clerici's *Ultimate Tennis Book*, which I showed to Shirley as a way of getting the conversation going. The work of Clerici's imagination appears in at least two books I am aware of and is an interesting mythical "draw." In the women's section, Clerici had listed almost every known woman champion through history, with Suzanne Lenglen of France seeded first and Maureen Connolly seeded second. Shirley Fry was unseeded but won her first match against Susan Partridge of Great Britain, 6–0, 8–6, an actual score from Wightman Cup play in 1952. However, in the next match, she plays Doris Hart, who beats her (as she did at Wimbledon in 1951 in the semifinals) 6–0, 6–1. I asked Shirley Fry about this rather lopsided score.

"Oh, yes, she beat me one and love on grass, but she couldn't do it on clay. That very year, I had beaten Doris in France for the French title and had beaten her in Egypt, as well as other places. But the grass at Wimbledon was very fast. That was the year Doris beat Maureen Connolly in the finals. We all wanted Doris to win. So did I, amazingly enough. But Doris and I traveled together. Everyone wanted it to be her year."

And it was, at least at Wimbledon, where Doris Hart won the singles, the women's doubles (with Shirley Fry), and the mixed doubles, playing with Frank Sedgman. At Forest Hills, however, Maureen Connolly, a junior champion, came back to beat Shirley 6–3, 1–6, 6–4 in one of the great women's matches of that period.

"It was the only tournament my parents had come to see me in, and Maureen had come in when I was at my peak. I should have never let her win that first year. She had beaten Doris in the semis, and we said she couldn't beat both of us, and she beat me by two points, you know, 136 to 134, two points in a three-set match. I really wanted to beat her, especially since I had beaten Doris in France, and Doris had beaten me at Wimbledon, and now Maureen Connolly, at sixteen, had come along . . . oh, well, she was *so* consistent. As a matter of fact, I had played her when she was only twelve, and it took three sets to win, and I was ranked in the top five then. I also played Maria Bueno in Brazil when *she* was only twelve, and again it took three sets to win.

"Maureen Connolly was taught to hit for the lines. She could be behind 1–4 and still go right for the line. She had pinpoint accuracy and could out-concentrate anybody. Champions make uncanny shots, and you could say that about Maureen."

I asked her who was the greatest woman player she had ever seen, and she answered Louise Brough. "There was a time in the 1940s when Louise had great confidence to go along with her great American twist serve. But then she lost her confidence. It lasted for one year, and I don't think anybody could beat her for that short period. And for three years, Maureen Connolly never lost a major tournament, I have to admit that.

"I remember when I had Maureen 5–2, 40-love at the Pacific Southwest in Los Angeles and lost. She made those same uncanny shots, but I said that I wouldn't let that happen to me again, and the next year I came out for the Southwest and I won.

"On *my* best day, I felt I could have beaten anybody in the world of tennis. *However*, if I were to play on my best day against another woman on her best day, that would not be the case. As an example, I couldn't have beaten Alice Marble at her best. I was always troubled by the big serve-and-volley players. I depended on placement and concentration, and that is why I was so upset when Maureen beat me at Forest Hills in 1951. She had been able to out-concentrate me. That is the difference when you talk baseline players. Who is out-thinking who?"

Still recalling Maureen Connolly at age sixteen, Shirley said, "I won the juniors in 1944 and 1945. Doris won it the two years before me, and Louise Brough the two years before Doris—that is how I can keep their ages straight. I go back to the seniors now, and I've played everybody somewhere along the line."

But in the shadow of Shirley Fry and others who still play the game, there is the memory of Maureen Connolly who died at thirty-five from cancer and who most probably would be out there with the other seniors, a division younger than Shirley Fry, but at the same club, part of the same tournament, one of a fellowship of women who can kid among themselves in the reflection of their early prowess and promise.

Shirley was born in Akron, Ohio, in 1927 and grew up as an athlete, "the youngest of four kids all of whom played sports." Her father was a track man and kept his children competing. She played tennis on pure clay ("almost white in color") and was often lucky enough to play on the private courts at the University Club of Akron, where her father had a membership.

She competed only against boys and men, and at the age of fourteen she gave up all other sports to concentrate solely on tennis. Already "having played in eighteen-and-under tournaments all my life," the idea of becoming a champion began to germinate in the mind of her father, if not in her own.

In those days, there were only two "name players" from the Midwest: Billy Talbert and later Tony Trabert. It was not a game that had the popularity it has now. "We grew up in an age when nobody except the English knew about tennis players. We were tennis bums. Until money came in, no one knew who we were. Tennis was a sissy game in this country, but it is *not* a sissy game. When there was money to be made, some athletes who might have taken up another sport took up tennis."

I mentioned Connors and McEnroe, both of whom I always thought could have been exceptional infielders—what a double play combination with that ability—and she said, "I feel really sorry for McEnroe. He is such a competitor. I admire him. He's so American, and he's liked off the court. He loves to play the Davis Cup. He's a true champion in both singles and doubles—Connors doesn't play doubles, Borg never even *learned* how to play doubles—McEnroe is an all-around player like Martina.

"As far as Martina goes . . . I just think she is awesome, just plain awesome. No one has ever been in such physical condition. I mean she's earned it, and she adds her condition to her great ability."

Shirley paused for a moment, and her earlier words sunk in: with money, some athletes who might have taken up another sport took up tennis. Indeed. I was thinking of the "awesome" Martina Navratilova, who could have done just about anything, and John McEnroe, a flanker back, a shortstop, a hockey star.

"But back in Akron," she was saying, "I learned to play by playing against men because there weren't any girls—I mean, there were hardly any girls. I started tennis at eight years old, and we were put in tournaments from the age of nine, and I traveled to them alone. My parents didn't have much money, and to be interested in sports you had to be independent, learn to go it alone. So by nine years old, I was given my first test, which was to go up to Cleveland to see the Exposition up there all by myself . . . take the train and all, stay with people, and then return. From then on, I was going to tournaments to compete."

Shirley's father was quite a believer in exercise. He originated the first walk around the town of Akron, a thirty-six-mile hike, and Shirley and her sister and two brothers (her brothers were swimmers, her sister also a tennis player) walked the thirty-six miles annually, starting as young children.

As a young child, she began to play in the under-eighteen tournaments. "In those days, I was always the dark horse. I was never expected to win. But I was beating sixteen- and eighteen-year-olds, and I think that was very beneficial to me. I had success at a very early age and avoided playing my peers. I was always playing up. There was no peer pressure that can upset someone. I excelled at badminton, and at fourteen I had won all the tournaments around and applied for the nationals, but they wouldn't let me play because I was too young. That's when my father said, 'Forget badminton and concentrate just on tennis.'

"So I had this idea at an early age that I had the potential to beat anyone. I knew I could run down anything on the court even if I didn't have the game that maybe Louise Brough had. Anyone is beatable once, so why couldn't I be the one to do it? My goal as a young child was to win the girls' championship at eighteen and Wimbledon the same year."

As it happened, she rushed matters. She won the girls' under-eighteen singles in 1943 at fifteen. She won again in 1944 and 1945, all ahead of schedule, but it was a few years before she won at Wimbledon—1951, in doubles with Doris Hart. Her schedule was askew by six years, much of which she spent playing at Rollins College. "I had met Pauline Betz and Dorothy Bundy on the tour, and they told me about Rollins, so I went there. I didn't have a scholarship or anything, but I think I got some help in my last three years. Of course, that was the college the country made fun of as a place where you could major in underwater basketweaving." Her older sister, meanwhile, had gone on to the University of California at Berkeley, where "some pro out there told her she didn't have the potential, so she left the sport. Years later I got her to enter a tournament with me out near San Francisco, right after the Pacific Southwest. I didn't have a doubles partner for that one, but she drove herself into condition, and we played. I think we lost in the first round, but it was a great joy playing. I would play with anyone who got a kick out of the game, and my sister, who had wonderful strokes as a kid, had been turned down by that professional, so we gave it a shot years later."

Listening to Shirley talk about her sister and her father, who had sent her out alone at nine years old, gave me an appreciation of a very loyal and trusting family and also a feeling for the days before the war when it was inconceivable that bad things could happen to anyone who wasn't, in effect, looking for them. Her brothers, for example, were sent hitchhiking across the nation when they were twelve and fourteen. They were told to make do, and they did, but imagine a father in 1984 encouraging such an adventure. He would be considered either a sadist or hopelessly naive.

She went on: "My greatest match was not my singles victory at Wimbledon. I won it in 1956 after a period of retirement from the tour. I'd been down in St. Petersburg, Florida, working as a copy girl for The St. Petersburg Times, and I did play a good deal with the local pro. But I had really resigned from formal competition. Then I was asked to play for the Wightman Cup, which was to be held that year in England. Well, you never pass up a free trip like that, so I went. I was barely able to win my singles, but I was encouraged and went on to Wimbledon. That was the year that Maureen Connolly was hurt. Doris Hart had turned professional, and Louise Brough couldn't even toss a ball in the air. Billie Jean had yet to come along, so you could say the ranks were thin. I remember thanking Beverly Baker Fleitz for getting pregnant. I beat both Louise Brough (sore arm and all) and Althea and then beat Angela Buxton (whom she had edged in Wightman Cup play) in the finals."

From there she won the United States clay court title and the United States championships at Forest Hills on grass. She had bypassed France, but a year later she won in Australia, all of this because she came out of retirement and a boring job for a free trip to England and one last crack at the tour. Yet she downplays it because "the ranks were thin."

"No, my best matches were with Maureen Connolly," she says. "Certainly the time she beat me when she was sixteen at Forest Hills by two points. Alison Danzig of *The Times* had totaled it up for us—that was my high point in singles."

In the doubles, she naturally mentions Doris Hart and gives her the credit for her success. "I was a singles player and was thrilled to death when Doris asked me to be her partner. We complemented each other because I could run down anything. She finally taught me how to play net, which I had been very inept at. In the early 1950s, we dominated women's doubles. All our matches with Louise Brough and Margaret Osborne duPont were close and tense, but you must remember that they had reached their peak and were going downhill by then. One match I remember as the best, but I can't recall whom we played. All I remember is that Doris and I won the tournament in the finals 6–0, 6–0, and yet *every point* was close. That was my greatest doubles match."

How different from Fred Perry, I thought. Here is a woman who lists her greatest singles match as the one that she lost. She says her best doubles game was against a team she can't remember in a tournament she'd forgotten. Truly, it appeared that for Shirley Fry, the game was the thing, not necessarily the outcome or the prestige that came with victory. She won the doubles title with Doris Hart three successive years in England and four successive years in *both* France and the United States, but as she spoke, I marveled at a person who extols a particular match she had all but forgotten but nevertheless ranks number one in her mind because it was so tough and the score so misleading and, probably, because it went unnoticed in the annals of the sport.

But back in 1957 when she and Althea were on tour in Australia and Shirley beat Althea for the Australian singles title, she having given up her job in St. Petersburg and living on expenses. ("I think it was $20 a day.") It was back then that she may have had the most rewarding days of her life. First

15. Shirley Fry in action

there were the Australian men. "I liked Frank Sedgman, who was just my age, and he and Rod Laver would carry Althea's and my suitcases when we traveled. The Australians were great then, and they were great champions. And after the match at Sydney when I beat Althea, I met my husband. He was the umpire who called the lines. He had been with J. Walter Thompson, an advertising man, and was in Australia working in advertising, and he asked me out to dinner. We got married the next month and then came the four children and the end of tennis.

"He had played at Northwestern and was a tennis fan, or buff as they are called, and had been calling the lines back in the States. So we were married, and we had our first child in Australia. We went back to the States in 1959, he back to New York, to J. Walter Thompson, and we lived in Darien, Connecticut. I knew Don McNeill. He tried to get me to play paddle tennis," she added, "and then we moved up to Hartford, and eight years ago my husband died. I have two boys who did not go to college and two daughters who did. I've lived in Hartford longer than anyplace in my life."

Shirley spoke with an autobiographical rush. I thought about St. Petersburg. Just suppose she had stayed on with the newspaper and not taken the offer to play for the Wightman Cup. Weeks earlier Gardnar Mulloy had told me that he was encouraging his assistant, Bonnie Smith, to play in any tournament anywhere. "Hell, you got to go out there and try," he had said. The point of it all was that people who pass up chances will never know what might have awaited them. If you volunteer for something, you will surely know what fate had in store, and there will be no lingering question marks to haunt your days. Shirley took the plunge and won her major titles as a result. She also had a merry tour of Australia, getting to know the great Australians, such as Sedgman, Hoad, Cooper, Laver, and Rosewall. Perhaps without knowing it, she and Althea Gibson became involved with Australian tennis at its zenith. And to top it off, she fell in love and was married to a fellow American.

Obviously Doris Hart was Shirley's favorite woman partner, but in the mixed doubles, she says, "I played with so many of them. Every time I got a good Australian, Louise [Brough] or Margaret [Osborne duPont] would take him away from me.

"I did play with Eric Sturgess from South Africa. We had the best mixed doubles match I ever played. We played Doris and Frank Sedgman." I asked if she had won. "No," she said, "we lost." Again I thought of Fred Perry and paraphrased him: the ego doesn't like defeat. But she continued, "The match was in France, and it was the finals of the French championships. I was outvolleying Doris Hart and Frank Sedgman, and we were all laughing . . . you see, we were such good friends. If you've ever played in a trance, I was in a trance. We won the first set and were up by three games in the second. I got a standing ovation, and I think that ovation woke me up.

"I played with Gardnar Mulloy and Billy Talbert and Ken McGregor, and I won with Vic Seixas. Doris Hart had turned pro, and I inherited him from her, and we won in 1956, beating Gardnar and Althea in the finals at Wimbledon. That was the time that Althea told Gardnar that she would take all overheads. Well, it didn't work out. After a few, she started to miss. In a way, that should be my best mixed doubles, but it was not the match that Eric and I had, yet it was the best, in a sense. We did win the big title at Wimbledon."

Shirley was full of feeling for those days of doubles, even though she had always considered herself a singles player. I could appreciate the workings of her memory as she recalled the pure fun of it: the laughter in France when she couldn't miss a volley. The travel. The palling around with Doris Hart, her friend and partner, who had taught her how to play net.

The Marriott was noisy, and we were in the middle of a large lunch from an endless buffet when I asked her about her heroes, the people she admired as a young woman and then later on in middle age, looking back in time. Immediately she said, "Alice Marble," and though I pushed her, she stuck with Alice Marble as the hero of her youth. As for this moment in late November of 1983, she said, unequivocally, that her parents were the two people she admired the most over the course of her life. Then with a laugh, she said, "And I suppose you could say Roosevelt. After all, he was the only president I ever knew about. He lasted so long. He dominated the country. I am being honest; he was a dominant person in my life. And royalty in England. You can't forget that. Here was I, little me from Ohio, and there was the Duchess of Kent presenting the Wimbledon trophy to me. We met Elizabeth and Margaret at the tea party they had for the American girls before Wimbledon. I remember that Prince Philip was there. You must remember, there I was, just little me from Ohio."

I asked her if she believed in God, a question I always ask because it intrigues me. Every politician I have ever heard speak evokes the Deity. It is always assumed that there is a life after death, a divine intervener to watch over us. I wondered about the great athletes who go one-on-one. Do they rely on themselves, or do they pray to the heavens for aid? Shirley Fry believes in God, but does not go to church. She is a lapsed Presbyterian. She was the seventh tennis star in a row who did not go to church, except on occasion. I was not sure it meant anything, but when I grew up, the church was like the public school system and freedom of the press. It was something you assumed to be of equal rank, but did anyone ever use it?

Shirley talked of her present life. She teaches tennis at Miss Porter's School in Farmington. She has no outside hobbies and is worried about this.

16. Shirley, after winning Wimbledon, and the Duchess of Kent

Suppose she should get arthritis. What then? What happens when tennis is gone and she, a widow and with four children grown and gone, what will she do?

I asked her about the great players of yesterday and how they compare to those of today. She said, "I think all the top players are equally good. Nobody will ever prove anything . . . right? I think that Maureen Connolly was as good as Suzanne Lenglen, and I think Margaret Court was as good as Helen Wills."

"But is there anybody as good as Martina Navratilova?"

"Well, she is awesome. Heck, I mean . . . well, she still has to prove she has the consistency."

"What about money under the table . . . back in your time?"

"I never got anything, but I think some of the big stars did. I am sure they paid Maureen Connolly."

"Was there anyone you did not like on the tour?"

"I didn't like Art Larsen. He expected so much. We toured together one year, and he showed no kindness nor sympathy . . . I mean, I was supposed to be his doubles partner, and I was never a good doubles player and, well, Art expected an awful lot from his partner."

"Forgetting Art Larsen for a moment, the record shows you were one of the best doubles players in history."

"I always picked good partners," she said.

Knowing her answer in advance, I asked her who was her closest friend on the tour.

"Doris Hart. After traveling alone for so many years and then having someone like Doris to ask me to be her doubles partner and to travel with her, that was quite wonderful to me."

"After traveling alone." I thought of her father, who had sent her off to Cleveland by herself at nine years of age to attend an exposition. I asked her about traveling by herself. "What was it like?"

"At first, when I was a kid, I went with a dollar a day. That was all my parents, who were not well off, could afford. That paid for breakfast and dinner. We always stayed in people's houses, both the boys and the girls. I remember I was ten when my father sent me off from Akron to Philadelphia for a tournament. From Philadelphia, once the tournament was over, I took the train up to New York City, changed over to the subway—by now it is midnight—and went on to Forest Hills, where I stayed at the old Forest Hills Inn. I saw the matches there and went to the World's Fair at Flushing Meadows and came home. All alone. That was part of our training; all the children."

As Shirley finished, I thought of how she always downplayed her doubles. She won fourteen major doubles titles in the four big tournaments that constitute the grand slam of tennis. She won thirteen with Doris Hart and one mixed doubles with Vic Seixas at Wimbledon. To keep winning as she did over a period of years simply undercuts her modesty, which implies she had been carried by others. Quite to the contrary, her doubles game may be among the best of all time, but for a woman who started out as an independent go-it-alone child, the singles game would always be the prize. And she *was* ranked in the top ten in the United States for more years than anyone else save Billie Jean King, Louise Brough, Nancy Richey, Margaret Osborne duPont, and Doris Hart. She'll hang her hat on that consistency in ranking, but the titles came in doubles, over and over again. Thinking of a child of ten taking a midnight subway out to Queens explains a lot. Who wants to be thought of as a partner when you have been doing it very well by yourself for a lifetime?

Shirley interrupted my speculations: "One year I decided I was going to play Wimbledon. It was 1948, and I was twenty-one and at Rollins. This was three years after my scrapbook should have showed me to be a winner at eighteen—remember, I wanted to be both girls' champion and a Wimbledon champion at the same time. So another player, Mary Arnold Prentiss, and I boarded the *Queen Mary* for Europe. We traveled tourist class with almost no money, and I got to the finals in France through a fluke. But, of course, I didn't get into the finals at Wimbledon, where Louise Brough beat Doris Hart 6–3, 8–6. As time went by, I always tried to travel by boat because it was such fun. The only trouble was that you got sea legs, and it took a while to get used to playing on land. But it *was* such fun. I never had any money back then, and my father was very supportive, but I didn't feel that I could ask him for money. To tell you the truth, I don't know how I managed in those days, but everything was so inexpensive. You just managed, that's all. I made do."

Outside in the parking lot, I got Shirley to pose near her car, and we kidded some. I told her that I was just getting warmed up after the third set, and she said that she was glad then that we had stopped. She said she could see I had been improving. I just started off making errors, that was all. "You

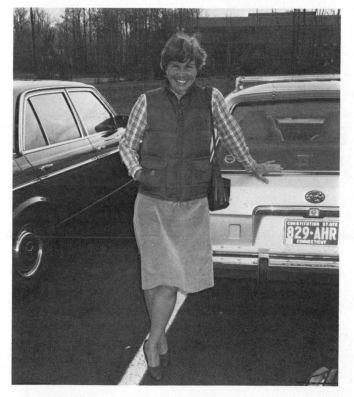

17. Shirley Fry

just made errors," she said. I would be a good doubles player, she added, and we talked about my latent abilities in that style of play. I then told her that I was going home to practice, and when I returned, I would beat her. "You can never beat me," she said smiling but with gravity in her voice. I thought that if she gets to be seventy and I am only sixty-eight, then, by George, I will beat her.

I said, "Suppose you are seventy, and I am only sixty-eight. You know I will win then."

"You will never beat me," she repeated.

"But I will work your backhand to death," I said.

"But, if you try that, I won't let you."

We shook hands. What a healthy, happy "peach of a girl." I was full from lunch and had played and lost to Shirley Fry, going all-out. I'd seen the old greatness at first hand. She always kept her eye on the ball, and I could never anticipate where it was going. She had twisted me like a pretzel and made me like it.

Back in grade school, I must have raced across a field full of wildflowers one time with a girl my own age and lost. Otherwise, how would I have recognized that old feeling that I got from being with Shirley Fry?

CHAPTER

8

Billy Talbert:

The River Club and the
Plateau Theory of Success

On January 4, 1984, I flew to New York to play tennis with Billy Talbert. Talbert had never won at Wimbledon and over an illustrious career had not won the U.S. singles title at Forest Hills, although he was ranked in the top ten for thirteen times from 1941 through 1954. He was runner-up twice, losing each time to Frank Parker. His forte was doubles, but as I found out, he was not above defending himself as a singles player. "I beat Pancho Gonzales more than he beat me," Talbert said later, standing before the lordly River Club where we had just concluded play.

But doubles was his game, and with Gardnar Mulloy and then Tony Trabert, Talbert was almost unstoppable. As an example, playing with Trabert, he won twenty-seven consecutive tournaments, which is probably a record. All through my youth, I had read his name in the papers and had rooted for him. He was a diabetic, and the press played up the disturbing reality of his disease, for which he had to self-administer insulin shots, and as the reporters would have it, he took his insulin the way Popeye took spinach: suddenly as a wan Talbert was on the edge of defeat, he would go to his insulin and then Pow! and there would be power in his system, the weakening illness would go into remission, and Billy Talbert would pull out the match. He was therefore a sentimental favorite, perhaps the first diabetic athlete to benefit from the development of injecting insulin, a hormone deficient in diabetics.

The technique was perfected in the nick of time for a man born over sixty-five years ago. Insulin treatment reached the world as Billy Talbert turned three years old.

I flew down in a small Cessna, sitting beside pop singer and celebrity Carly Simon. Behind me were the lovely Bramhall sisters and a beauty named Wendy Walker, all of Martha's Vineyard. It was 10:00 in the morning, and we were airborne. Carly was nervous, and I was telling her that no plane carrying her, the Bramhall women, and someone as good-looking as Wendy would dare to go down. Our local paper, *The Vineyard Gazette*, wouldn't be able to carry all the death notices.

And I was thinking of myself as well. What, indeed, would an obituary say about me? I had one novel behind me and a few articles for national magazines and a host of articles for *The Gazette*—and five children. No doubt my biggest claim to fame would rest in the mundane region of fatherhood, or so I thought. I badly wanted this book, *Once a Champion*, to work out. If the day ever came when I tumbled downward in a sputtering Cessna, I would want an obituary that would have a little more to say than that I was a "devoted Vineyarder who loved his children and enjoyed taking long walks on the beach." Sitting beside Carly, I realized that in this business of death notices, I would be an also-ran: *Carly Simon dies in plane crash. Along with her three friends, Emily and Nina Bramhall and Wendy Walker, Miss Simon plunged into the sea somewhere west of Block Island. Other passengers are identified as . . .*

I mention this because Carly Simon's nerves cracking beside me made me realize that I really did want to count for something before the end came. I assume people write for many reasons, but one of them must be a desire for a bit of immortality. The written word lives on. I thought of Roger Kahn and his book, *The Boys of Summer*, a book that helped trigger the very project I was working on. I had not heard of Roger Kahn recently—I had once interviewed him for *The Gazette*—but he would be remembered forever as the man who had gone out to find the baseball heroes of his early days on *The New York Herald Tribune*—the champion Brooklyn Dodgers of the 1950s—and his book soared to the top of the best-seller lists. Whatever might befall Roger Kahn, he had that book to his credit. I want the same thing, and surely wanting such a legacy was an ingredient working its way through my subconscious. Doubtless, sitting beside Carly Simon, gripped in a silent frenzy, prompted such thinking. But I also knew we would not go down and smiled at her constant grimace. There were too many of us with strong connections to the Vineyard. I was serious when I told her to relax, that *The Gazette* couldn't cope with all of us dying at once. It made her laugh, and I believed my own words. If death should come to me before my time, it will come when I am alone. I was positive it would not happen sitting next to Carly Simon.

It seems odd that I should start this chapter writing of fear. But fear was with me. I was afraid that my book might not make the grade. I shared with most writers that dreaded, generally supressed surmise that maybe I stank. Maybe I was investing my whole personality in a project that was doomed, not because of the nature of the enterprise, but because I was without talent or, at the very least, did not have enough talent to make the world care about a group of superb athletes who had once graced the great tennis courts of the world and had fired the imaginations of people everywhere. A Carly Simon record sold in the hundreds of thousands and sometimes over a million copies. Who would care about Pauline Betz and Billy Talbert in this time, in this world? I just had to pray that I would be good enough to bring everything together, my own fan's journey and the men and women I was finding, and, thinking thus, I said to myself, "If my thoughts are the thoughts of an ordinary man and made clear to the reader, then I will have to believe that as such they have value. John Updike could write about a Toyota car salesman and invest him with human characteristics of high interest. I could write about myself against a backdrop of people for whom the glitter had faded and hope I could make it work."

But back to Billy Talbert. I called him soon after arriving in New York. Although I had promised to pay for the match, to make everything as easy as possible for him to play at his convenience, at his time and place, he had taken on the responsibility of organizing the game. We would play at the River Club, where he is a member. I would bring my partner and he would bring his, and we would meet to talk at 9:00 sharp the next morning and play at 10:00. I called Dick Craven at once and alerted him to the time and locale of our match. Finally I would work my sidekick into a game. Dick Craven, whom I had contested in so many tennis games over the years, was a man who was instrumental in getting me back into shape. A friend, a wit, and a great athlete who had once been All-East in soccer at Harvard . . . together we would take on one of the four or five greatest doubles players the world had ever seen at an indoor tennis club of reknown.

Talbert had been the captain for America's Davis Cup teams for five years, and although no impresario like Jack Kramer, he was the closest thing to a Mr. Tennis there is in the East. He knew everyone, was beloved in the sport, and had always been a gentleman. He carried in his quiet demeanor the reverence due a fine, low-key sports figure. He was the Joe DiMaggio of tennis. A New Yorker for thirty-seven years, he is the kind of man who gets the right table at Twenty-One, who like DiMaggio knows his way around with sophistication. He is the type of man who never makes ripples. He had a reputation for being smooth. His style was without effort. All that had been told to me along the way from Pauline Betz to Shirley Fry.

I arose at 6:30. If we were to meet at 9:00 and play at 10:00, I wanted to be fully awake. Because of a slight case of arthritis, I had always hated running before lunch. I wanted to have the whole morning to get organized, to read the paper, to digest my breakfast, to stretch my legs. I was not a morning athlete, especially if I had been up late the night before. Craven, on the other hand, appeared impervious to time. At six-two he is a big man of fifty-five who had just missed All-American at Harvard. He has a large frame that is also very limber. He always slept soundly at night and hence looked well and was a cheery man who wrote television material for game shows and sitcoms and had for a long time been associated with Goodson-Todman, where he worked with Garry Moore on the old show, "To Tell the Truth." He, much like Talbert, had been around New York City for a lifetime and took it for granted. The only time I saw him rattled was after his car, parked on the streets of New York, was stolen for the second time. But even this did not dent his enthusiasm for the city. Dick Craven could walk from his apartment on Sixty-sixth Street down to the Harvard Club and smile all the way. I don't think he ever had a hangover. In many ways, he was my opposite.

As the son of the art historian Thomas Craven, he grew up staring at paintings by Thomas Hart Benton, a painter the elder Craven is credited with establishing in the higher levels of American art. His mother left his father somewhere back in time and married the writer Richard Harrity. People from the art world and the writing scene spilled across Dick Craven's youth like jewelry along a counter. Some were phonies, some were real. He was the kind of guy who took the real and the false with a wink and let the dice roll again. If the man ever worried much, I never knew about it.

As far as playing against Talbert at 10:00 in the morning, our time was his time. He would be there. I was pleased because I wanted him to go with me to New Orleans, where I thought I would find Vic Seixas. I wanted him to go to Chicago as well, where we could play Frankie Parker. I was tired of going it alone and ruminating. I liked allies. The passing of time had gotten matters confused in my life, and I was unsure if I had many friends left. Dick Craven was a friend, and now at last he would make his entrance into my book as a partner against a legend.

I arrived at the River Club ten minutes early and was idling about, not being sure where to go, when in came Billy Talbert, also early. He was wearing a tweedy overcoat and had an Irish cap on his head, but I recognized him at once. He was smiling, and we shook hands. "The trouble is," he said, "well, you may not believe this, but within the entire membership of this club, I can't find a fourth."

I assured him that the point was to hit the ball at each other, that the game was secondary, but underneath I was angry. I had Dick Craven already shaving in his apartment, grabbing some breakfast, looking forward to a match. Damn it all, we would just have to adjust some way. In the meantime, I followed Talbert down to the swimming pool, where there was a lounge where we could sit and have coffee. I placed my tape recorder on the table and began to ask him some questions. He was wearing a business suit and had on a light blue shirt with a white collar. I had seen such shirts advertised. I guessed that a benighted business associate had given him that shirt for Christmas. My mood was such that I thought his shirt made him look silly. My mind ran on: if he had taken me seriously, he would have found a partner. But Billy Talbert was so relaxed and pleasant that I couldn't stay irritated very long. I stared at the little white collar on his shirt and decided he looked like a minister: a kindly, nonpunitive cleric. But my big game with Dick Craven and Billy Talbert and a fourth . . . I had even imagined another sports legend, Hank Greenberg, who had taken to tennis being summoned . . . all that was regrettably gone with the wild hopes of a dream. I looked at the coffee and noticed that the cream had turned sour. There was a yellow crust forming on the surface of my coffee.

Talbert was born in Cincinnati and went through the public school system, including the University of Cincinnati. He was diagnosed as a diabetic at ten and wasn't allowed to do anything except, as he says, "sit in a chair, weigh my food, and take insulin two or three times a day. I lived that way for a couple of years, and because I was an avid sports fan and wanted to play something, my father spoke to the doctor, and the doctor finally said that we could take a chance on tennis and see how it went. So they handed me a tennis racquet, and that is how it began. I was a good athlete and at fourteen became the best *man* tennis player in Cincinnati. I was ranked ten in the country for the boys, and from there I just kept going. I played tennis in college for my last three years, and in my senior year I reached the semifinals of the National Intercollegiates at Merion, and that was the year that Don McNeill from Kenyon, another Ohio college, won it. It was 1939."*

Talbert took tennis very seriously right from the start. "For two reasons. One was that I was very poor, and tennis was leading me to places I had never known about. I was being invited into a new world. And two, I wanted to prove that being a diabetic, I could do the same things anyone else could do.

"There was a gradual progression in my emergence as a tournament competitor. It was one plateau after another. First, I became the best in Cincinnati and then the best in the Western Association. Once I made it to the big time, it was: could I move up from where I started? I was ranked twenty-one at the time. The next year, I moved up to sixteen, and the following year I was ranked number ten. By 1945 I was ranked second, and I think

* Memory lapses are to be expected when speaking of events that occurred over forty years ago; McNeill won the Intercollegiate in 1940. Frank Guernsey of Rice triumphed in 1939.

18. Billy Talbert: The Cincinnati Kid

that year I would have won the U.S. Championship, but I hurt my knee playing Segura, and I could hardly move the next day in the finals against Parker. I had won eleven straight tournaments that summer and, yes, that year was the time I thought I would win it, reach the top, and I had beaten Parker already that summer on grass.''

Frank Parker triumphed in 1945, beating Billy Talbert, who "could hardly move," 14–12, 6–1, 6–2. But in doubles, Talbert and Mulloy had won their second U.S. title, playing, of course, at the Longwood Cricket Club. He also won the mixed doubles playing with Margaret Osborne, with whom he had teamed for four consecutive mixed doubles titles from 1943 through 1946. And in the men's doubles, playing with Gardnar Mulloy, he won the title four times in a seven-year span, 1942 through 1948. Yet in 1945, when he had his best chance, he did not take the singles . . . a bum knee, the breaks of the game.

I asked Talbert what he would be remembered for as a player. "Well, I won almost every big singles championship in this country* but, well, yes, I guess I get credit for my doubles."

As for Wimbledon, Talbert said, "I only played it once, in 1950, and I was seeded two in the singles, one in the doubles and mixed doubles, but I had a terrible run. Not making excuses, but in my own mind I made the mistake of hurting whatever chances I had at Wimbledon by playing the French championships on the slow courts where I played all three events—I got to the semis in the singles and won the doubles with Trabert and then went on to Germany and played the German Championships, which I won. But those slow *en tout cas* courts just took too much out of me. I went up to Norway and Sweden and Denmark to play some exhibitions, and I was just shot. I knew it the moment I walked out on the court at Wimbledon. Usually I am raring to go, but that time I had a sagged-out feeling. I got to the quarterfinals and lost to Budge Patty, who won the tournament that year. In the doubles, Mulloy and I were beaten by Sedgman and McGregor in five sets. But we had to play earlier that day, so we had two matches in the same day because of rain, and the schedule had gotten backed up as it often happens at Wimbledon. But we were beaten by a better team."

"Who was the best player you ever saw play?"

"Budge at his best was the greatest. As far as comparing Budge against, say, McEnroe, that is an age-old question. But you put Budge at the same age with the same equipment, and he would be the best."

I thought: there he is again, Don Budge. Don McNeill had said that he was lucky as a boy to have had two idols such as Bill Tilden and Don Budge. My father always rooted for Budge, preferring him to anyone else. To my father, Don Budge was the Gene Tunney of tennis, while Tilden was Dempsey, and when Don Budge beat Baron von Cramm in the Davis Cup interzone finals at Wimbledon in 1937, it was like the Fourth of July in my home. Budge was a great American athlete who had played baseball as a kid and who had won what a panel of experts selected by *Tennis* magazine calls "The Greatest

---

* He won the National Indoor Singles Championship in 1948 and 1951. His name occurs twice amidst a trio of great singles champions: Kramer, Gonzales, and Don McNeill.

Match Ever Played," beating the aristocratic German, von Cramm. Surely von Cramm was still a "Hun" in my father's eyes, the old machine-gunner mind inevitably drawn to the trenches of World War I. Now talking with Talbert about Budge was like sitting with the once great Red Sox second baseman Bobby Doerr, talking about Ted Williams. As a boy, I loved to read about Bobby Doerr, but I idolized Williams. Here we were, Talbert, a great champion himself, discussing his greatest player, his voice touched with feeling. I liked being with one of the best talking about someone even better.

I mentioned Bill Tilden. "Oh, I saw Tilden. But you have to remember that the kind of competition Tilden faced—I don't mean at the top—but the players he played on Monday, Tuesday, Wednesday, Thursday were nothing like the players you play today. *Now,* if you walk out on the court on a Monday, you better be ready to play, because you can meet a really good player. I mean that the depth of good players is so much greater now than it was in those days.

"I don't think at the top they are necessarily better, the proof of that is Gardnar Mulloy, how well he played fifteen years ago [at fifty-five], and Kenny Rosewall who never won Wimbledon, yet at forty-two he was still playing against the guys of today."

I made note of Rosewall. Ken Rosewall had won the Australian singles championship in 1953 and again in 1972, a span covering twenty years.

We paused for a moment as I drank from my speckled coffee and eyed a lovely young woman in a one-piece bathing suit who had just walked onto the cement apron of the pool. At first I thought she was an errant intruder in a men's locker room, my mind so set in the past with the male stars, and I watched to see Billy Talbert's expression. If he noticed her, he didn't show it. She stood near us, a spectacular beauty, and Talbert's mind was still on tennis, letting his argument sink in: you couldn't say for sure how Tilden or Budge would do in today's highly charged, big-money world of tennis, but his educated hunch was the same as the others I had spoken with. Great players are great players. The game itself had not changed enough, and with some men, such as Mulloy and Rosewall, there had been a crossover in generations. He was sure that Don Budge, if not a few others, could take the center court at Wimbledon in 1984, given a time warp that would present him on any given date at his best from yesteryear.

When asked who his favorite doubles partner was, Talbert answered, "Well, Mulloy would certainly be . . . well, our record was certainly exceptional. And only Trabert, whom I trained and brought along . . . I believe I took him to Europe when he was nineteen, and we won every tournament we played in. We won twenty-seven tournaments without a loss, including some big ones: the National Indoor, the Italian Championships, the French, Monte Carlo."

"If you had to take your choice between Trabert and Mulloy, whom would you take?"

"They were two different types. One I taught and the other, we just teamed. We had an incredible record. If you look at the number of tournaments Gardnar and I played and the number of tournaments we won, nobody even comes close. We won the national doubles title four times and the seniors four times. There was a long spell when we didn't play together, but when we came back, we won again, all on grass."

"What was your greatest singles match?" I asked.

"That's a hard question. I won Newport, Southampton, Seabright, Rye, Orange—major grass court championships, but I suppose it was the time when I beat Segura in straight sets in the semifinals at Forest Hills in the National Championships. That was the year I had won eleven straight tournaments, and though I had beaten him the year before, it had taken me five sets. To take Segura in three straight would be my best singles victory."

"How about doubles?"

"I guess the match against McNeill and Guernsey," Talbert answered. This was the match I recalled from talking with both Mulloy and McNeill. It was won by Talbert hitting the baseline after coming back from eight break points on his serve. Mulloy saw the chalk dust fly, McNeill said Frank Guernsey saw it as out, and Billy Talbert sticks by the decision of the linesman, the net court judge, and the umpire. "I had come in and hit a midcourt volley. I thought it was good."

As for heroes of his youth, he readily admitted that most of them were baseball players. Sunny Jim Bottomley. Babe Ruth and Curt Walker came to mind. "Ruth, of course, played for the Yankees, but he got a lot of ink and anyway, I was a big Yankee fan as well as a Cincinnati fan, and I haven't changed."

"Did you idolize anyone other than a sports figure as you grew up?"

"No, I don't think so. I can't think of anyone. I remember the Depression and the steps that Roosevelt took, and I remember the first time I voted in 1940. I walked into the voting booth with my father, and when we came out, he, a Democrat, said he voted for Roosevelt. But I said I voted for Wendell Willkie. He asked why. I told him that by traveling around playing tennis and staying with the people I would stay with and hearing them talk, I thought Willkie was better."

I asked Talbert about his father.

"My father was in the livestock business, Talbert and MacDonald, and he liked the horse races, and things changed in the livestock business, but he didn't change with them, and everything sort of collapsed."

With no money behind him, Talbert started working at fourteen years old and later worked his way through college.

"I was a janitor in a bank and used to go to work at 5:00 and work to 11:00 at night, cleaning offices and scrubbing floors and things like that. I also worked for a clothing store, Dunlop Clothing Store, and I could work there whenever I wanted to. I liked clothes, and the people at Dunlop's liked me. And then they had those government jobs back then, but I can't remember what they were called. But I worked at those, too, and as it turned out, I had a lot of jobs while I was in college."

An only child, Talbert was close to his parents. He looked up to his father, who was a good athlete and who introduced him to tennis.

"He was always available to me. My mother is still alive at ninety and drives her own car, lives in Cincinnati, and goes to the horse races. My father died at age sixty-one in 1951."

I noticed that so many of the people I interviewed had an aged parent still alive somewhere, often a mother, usually in her nineties. (In McNeill's case, his mother was one hundred.) I wondered if latent longevity in a parent indicated a certain tenacity that was passed on to a child.

We talked about Fred Perry, who had referred to singles as "one-on-one" and implied a comparison to boxing. I mentioned Jack Dempsey, Pauline Betz's old boyfriend and everyone's hero.

"Well, I always liked Tunney," Talbert replied. "My father saw the two Dempsey-Tunney fights, and I was always for Tunney, but I don't know why. Later I had the opportunity of meeting both men, and Jack was just an absolutely super guy, and Tunney was a kind of held-back social type who lived down at Hobe Sound, Florida. I knew Jack. I would go to his place, his restaurant, and I saw Tunney down in Florida, you know, social chatter, but what has that to do with anything?"

Getting back to Fred Perry's one-on-one, I suggested that above a certain level, there is a similarity between boxer and tennis player.

"Yes," Talbert answered. "The killer instinct."

And then I remembered Althea Gibson, who said she would drive a tennis ball at a person regardless of where on the anatomy it might strike in order to win a point. She admitted to being ruthless. It was hard to believe that Billy Talbert could ever be ruthless. But I knew he was or had been. To get where he got, he had to possess the instinct to slap you apart with driving shots. His mother at ninety went to the race track. There is a tough strain in such people, Billy Talbert's silly white collar notwithstanding. I wondered whom he admired now, at sixty-five, looking back over the course of his life.

The first name that came to his mind was that of a late senator from Ohio. "I was a big fan of Bob Taft," he said. "Also, Joe DiMaggio and Gary Cooper. These were all people I knew. I had a great time with Errol Flynn. I admired them in different ways. Taft, I liked his philosophy; DiMaggio, I liked his approach to baseball. Flynn for his flair. I went to Acapulco with Er-

19. William Talbert in 1954

rol Flynn way back, and he was a colorful, fun person. I don't know if I would want to lead his life-style, but for two weeks it wasn't bad."

"You wouldn't pick any spiritual leaders, say Mahatma Gandhi, as someone to admire?"

"No. I liked Bob Menzies, prime minister of Australia. I thought he was a tremendous man. I liked General George Patton. I liked his style."

"Style—going back to your days at Dunlop Clothing—obviously means a good deal to you."

"Yes. My parents taught me good manners, and tennis taught me a lot of how I should look if I wanted to travel in that world."

And into that world he did, indeed, travel. But what a world! It was 1939, and Joe DiMaggio batted .381 and was named most valuable player for the American League. A skinny youth called "The Kid" broke into the starting lineup with the Red Sox, and in 1939, his rookie year, led the league in runs batted in with 145. Ted Williams also batted .327 and hit 31 home runs. Lou Gehrig played his last game in 1939 and within a year was elected into the Baseball Hall of Fame. Tommy Harmon made All-American for the University of Michigan, and golfer Byron Nelson won the U.S. Open. Joe Louis, the "Brown Bomber," was the undisputed king of boxing.

And towering above such titans of sport rose the overwhelming presence of Winston Churchill, who in 1939 became prime minister of Great Britain, again at war with Germany. It was a year of charisma, a year when the great personalities and abilities of men of action took the newsprint of a free press and made it their own. Into such a world entered a young college graduate from Ohio, Billy Talbert, who could look about him and feel human greatness in the air.

But it was 1984 when we talked. I could not help noticing the difference. George Orwell had found 1984 in his mind, and true to his vision, there were no personalities, a noticeable lack of individual excitement. Nineteen thirty-nine was chockablock full with personality. The tawdry days of celebrity-tainted 1984 had heroes the way Reggie Jackson had humility or John McEnroe had manners. Looking back to 1939, I could feel my flesh tingle.

"How do you value athletics as an ingredient in a good life?"

"It is important to me because I've had diabetes fifty-five years, and it is the third top killer, the leading cause of blindness, and I have to believe that the exercise I have taken every day is the reason why I have lasted so long. But you have to have sports properly proportioned in an equation. There are too many ingredients in life. In that equation, you can't have one ingredient knocking the hell out of the others. You can't overweigh sports. I have my diabetes, my family, my business, my sport . . . all of it keeps me well and happy and lets me sleep at night and makes me want to get up in the morning and want to go."

"Is there any special factor that goes into the making of a champion? Taking a group of otherwise equal athletes, why does one get to the top while others slip back and don't make it?"

"I was asked this same question in 1950 by *Time* magazine, and the answer I gave then is the same I will give you. It's X. I don't know what it is. I had some players on the Davis Cup team who were good athletes, who worked their butts off, who seemed to have all the equipment in the world, and who didn't make it. I guess my greatest prediction of someone I felt would be a super tennis player was McEnroe when I saw him play the junior Davis Cup down in Miami Beach. I told Bud Collins, with whom I was doing the television. I said, 'Bud, that is the best tennis player I have ever seen in this competition. I've got to believe that he will cut the mustard.' And that June he went to the semifinals at Wimbledon. Even then in Miami Beach, McEnroe had a sense of what a tennis court was all about, how it should be used, when to apply the pressure better than anyone I had ever seen."

"Has diabetes been a real handicap?"

"I don't think it's been a handicap at all. I think that I have been very fortunate to manage to get along as well as I have. In a match, sure I have had a few problems, but they were mostly of my own doing—not preparing properly. No, I don't think it was a handicap. I think the converse is the truth: that when I found I had diabetes, I felt I had to prove something. Without diabetes I don't know what I might have become, but most likely not a tennis player."

I wanted Talbert to rank the great players, and he mentioned Kramer, Gonzales, and Budge, and he used Rosewall as a yardstick to show that the old-timers would do very well in today's tennis world. We had been over that before, but I was still curious about who was the best. He said, "I never had a more helpless feeling against any tennis player, and I played them all. I started in 1936 with the men's and played through 1958, a pretty long run. I never felt so helpless as I did against Don Budge. If Budge in his prime should play McEnroe, let's leave it like this: I'd like to see the match. And ground strokes. Ground strokes are such an important part of the game. Why is Jimmy Connors so good? His return of serve. Budge's return of serve was spectacular."

"Does all the money now being made bother you at all?"

"It doesn't bother me, but I think it brings an unattractive quality to the game. The money tennis players make for wearing certain types of clothes as an example. If I were a clothing manufacturer, I would pay them *not* to wear my clothes because of the way they looked. I mean, elegance has left tennis. When you think of a Fred Perry or Budge or a von Cramm, the way they walked to center court . . . now you look at the men in warm-up suits. They look like a bunch of basketball players.

"But you know, I have two heroes among today's group. Chrissie Evert and Jimmy Connors. Jimmy does things I don't approve of, and I tell him so, but I admire anyone who goes out and gives 110 percent. I agree that you lose a great deal to television. You don't have the old heroes for whom you used your imagination, but with Chrissie and Jimmy, I have a sense of being a fan."

"At your best, could you have beaten anyone?"

"I beat Kramer many times. I beat Gonzales. He says I am the only one he hasn't outdistanced."

"How about McEnroe?"

"I think I could have given him a hell of a match. Could I beat McEnroe? I think my best game was a reasonable game. I had a sense of how to play people. I think I would have found areas where I could hurt him."

We paused for a moment while a man with a floor buffer went to work several yards behind us. I wanted to change the subject for a moment, so I asked him if he believed in God.

"Yes," he said thoughtfully. "I believe in God, yeah. I think it is an individual thing, and it helps me when things get down to a difficult time. He's someone to relate to."

"Do you go to church?"

"No."

"Where do you work, and did your work keep you from going to Wimbledon more often?"

"For the U.S. Bank Note Company. I went to work for them in 1947. I came back from Australia, where I'd been on the Davis Cup team, and then I went to South America, and I came back from there and went to visit my parents, who were in Florida. I was talking with my Dad about the great life. Playing in the pool with the pretty girls, a little tennis, and parties all night. He said, 'I can see you enjoy it, you enjoy living that way, but obviously I am not going to leave that kind of life to you. Have you figured how you're going to pay for it, if that is the way you're going to live?'

"So the next day, I was taking this girl to dinner, and I thought about what my father said, and I said to myself, 'Yes, I do like that life-style.' So I took this girl to dinner at Twenty-One, and we were seated next to this guy whom I had known for years from Southampton, Palm Beach, and Newport, and he said, 'Billy, how you doing?' and I said, 'Fine, but I'm looking for a job,' and he said, 'You got one. Come to my office in the morning.'

"So the next day, I went down to 52 Wall Street to the Bank Note Company, and I was in his office when he got a phone call. He was talking about an issue of bonds for the Delaware Memorial Bridge. From the tone of the conversation, I could tell that things weren't going well. When he was finished, he said, 'Well, I know we are not going to get that one.' I said, 'I don't know what you were talking about, but that guy you mentioned on the phone . . . he's a good friend of mine.' He said, 'Really? Will you call him and see if he can help us?' I said, 'Sure, just tell me what to say.' So I called this man I knew, and when I called into his office, he said, 'We got the deal, and you just earned yourself $4,800.'

"I was lucky. It enabled me to begin work and live the way I wanted to live, and in thirty-seven years, I have never had a salary, never had a draw. They pay me when I sell, and from that first day, there hasn't been a day when they haven't owed me money.

"I can do what I want to do. And to answer your question about Wimbledon, no, work never kept me from Wimbledon. I had a new son . . . I really don't know why I didn't go back."

I then asked Talbert if he had any wisdom to impart. How would he like to see the world run?

"I'd like to see people work. Not be on welfare with nothing to do. Whatever you do, do well. You should do the best you can. I don't think too many people in the world do that. As for Russia and the United States—you need communication. I don't think because of the way they run things in Russia there is . . . well, unless there is communication, you won't find a common ground on which you can exist."

"When you were playing at Palm Beach, Southampton, and Newport, how did you support yourself? Did you get money under the table?"

"No, I was put up in houses. I stayed with Henry Ford and Dan Topping and Jock MacLean, and I believe my manners were good, and I wrote my thank-you notes, and I was invited back. No, I didn't get money under the table. Look, in 1954 the Davis Cup players got $20 a day to live on. I would work hard all winter so I could go off in the summer, and I would play in Kansas City, Indianapolis, Chicago, Louisville, and I would get my expenses and, well, I didn't need a lot of money. When I went to my first grass court tournament in Seabright I was put up by a family, the Haskells, and then I went to Southampton and was put up . . . I paid my way to those tournaments and things took care of themselves."

I mentioned that Gardnar Mulloy had said that he was paid under the table.

"When Mulloy says he got money under the table, I would like him to explain it to me. He says a lot of things that I should double-check. Particularly his Davis Cup reminiscences. I mean he was so wonderful to me and I had a great time with him, but I am not sure of his memory. Gardnar says a lot of things for effect. He will say a lot of things that will open people's eyes to make them pay attention whether they are true or not true."

"Was there anyone on the tour whom you didn't like?"

"Oh, you know, we all had to exist. There were a lot of them whom I didn't hang around with. There weren't many whom I *did* hang around with once the tennis day was over. They would talk tennis, and it was more fun to listen to Henry Ford or Dan Topping, who owned the Yankees. I liked hearing about the business world which I was in. I was in selling, and I thought I could learn from such people. Tennis players will talk tennis morning, noon, and night."

"Gardnar said he didn't like Ted Schroeder."

"Well, I think we would all buy that one. If I had to put my finger on one guy . . . Ted Schroeder was not easy to get along with."

"Going back to work. Work is the answer to a good life?"

"Work and use your skills intelligently."

"How does that handle the problem of those who are not gifted, who may be dumb?"

"That's the way the world is, isn't it?"

"Well, what do you say to such people, those who are weak or without ability?"

"They will find their niche. There is a plateau you can work on. For everything."

"You live in Manhattan; you have for thirty-seven years now."

"Yes. And we take a place in the country, and I own a house now in Palm Beach. Life has been good. If I hear we are going to have twenty inches of snow tomorrow, I tell my secretary to get me on a plane to Palm Beach. My wife socializes, has two terraces and a lot of greenery, and we live a comfortable life.

"We have two sons, thirty-four and thirty-two. The older one, Pike, got out of Harvard Business School about three years ago and is now with Morgan Stanley in the investment banking business and has just been made a vice-president. The other one, Peter, is a free spirit. He is one of the best squash players in the world and is on the circuit. He is a writer. He's associate editor of *Racquet Quarterly*, has had two books published, and is right now in Toronto playing with the Khans and the Talbotts and the rest of the pros."

"Would you say that all of this comfortable life and family success comes from playing tennis?"

"Oh, sure. Were it not for tennis, I could still be selling ties in Dunlop's in Cincinnati. Tennis, diabetes, the whole combination. Gee, I am a great believer that in whatever you are given in your life, there is an equation that is going to work for what you want and the way you want it to come out. I have been lucky . . . it happened for me."

We were standing in the locker room. I wanted to hear about the Davis Cup and turned on the tape recorder to get some offhand remarks by Talbert. I had the official 1983 Tennis Yearbook with me and was shuffling through the pages trying to find important data. He had been on the squad for many years starting right after World War II playing on the somewhat factious team that traveled to Australia in 1946 for the challenge round, which the United States won, 5–0.

"The squad consisted of Kramer, Mulloy, Schroeder, Parker, and me. Schroeder would only play if he could play both singles and doubles. I didn't get to play, nor did Parker. Parker, once back in the States, blasted the team captain, Walter Pate. Mulloy and I stayed six weeks after the matches were over, and we played every country town there was in Australia. We then went to New Zealand and played there."

I said, "But Gardnar told me that you had other commitments."

"No. I was not playing well, and I said to Gardnar, 'You and Parker are a good team. You've played some together. Why don't you have a run at it?' And they did and it looked like Parker and Mulloy were the best team because they were beating Kramer and Schroeder. But a deal had been made by Perry Jones that Schroeder would play both singles and doubles."

"Is there any reason that Ted Schroeder was the fair-haired boy?"

"No. He was the fair-haired boy with Perry Jones out in southern California, and he was a good competitor. And part of it was that Parker had lost so badly to Bromwich in 1939 that everybody thought Bromwich had his number. Maybe he did and maybe he didn't—seven years later."

"In 1948 you did play Davis Cup with Mulloy and won. But in 1949 you lost with Mulloy. How come?"

"We should have won. We took the first two sets (from Sidwell and Bromwich) and then lost the last three 10–8, 9–7, 9–7. We had a break in the third set on Mulloy's serve. I remember that match very well because I didn't lose my serve once in five sets."

Later Talbert became captain of the Davis Cup team and amassed a 12–0 record in zone matches but was 1–4 in the challenge rounds. By 1957 it was frustrating because of the paucity of good players.

"By then [1957] I was groping for players to represent us for the cup. I had Seixas, who played all five years for me. [Actually, according to the record book, Billy Talbert was a Davis Cup captain for part of 1952—a sixth year—but I kept my mouth shut. Earlier I had questioned his memory, and I was wrong with my information, and he snapped, "Get your facts straight."] Other than that, I had Herbie Flam, who was having a nervous breakdown of some kind, and Barry MacKay and Ron Holmberg, both out of college. I also had Mike Green, who had been around but just couldn't cut it. I also had Gardnar Mulloy, who was forty-three years old and who played doubles with Seixas. We were playing Belgium in the interzone finals, and I was going to play Gardnar instead of Flam, but I went with Flam instead of forty-three-year-old Gardnar, and Flam lost."

"Forgetting the niggling problems and the stresses, it must have been a great honor to be captain of the Davis Cup team."

"I was flattered to be chosen as captain. To represent your country is a big thrill. Except for the Billie Jean King-Bobby Riggs match, we played in front of the largest crowd in tennis history—26,000 spectators at White Stadium in Sydney in 1954. You take center court for your country . . . it's a big thrill."

That was the year that Seixas beat Rosewall and Trabert beat Hoad, and then they teamed up to win the deciding doubles matches, beating Hoad and Rosewall 6–2, 4–6, 6–2, 10–8. I could imagine Billy Talbert's pride in his players and in his own role as captain.

Later on I asked Talbert about his social life. I was still struck by his demeanor that brooked no foolishness. He was kindly and courteous, yet he almost made me feel like an employee with him as the president, and though I could kid around, he could always call for my resignation whenever he felt like it.

"Look, I don't like to name-drop," he said, "but when you stay with business leaders, people who are now my friends—Henry Ford and I have exchanged Christmas cards for years, that sort of thing—when you socialize with people of substance who discuss interesting subjects and not just tennis, you learn from them."

Shirley Fry had said that in the old days traveling the circuit, she was a tennis bum. I rather doubted that Billy Talbert thought of himself that way. A poor boy from Cincinnati, he had learned quickly. On the tennis court, I would call him "Billy." Off the court, I rather suspected that "Mr. Talbert" might be a better choice. Billy Talbert had transcended the game of tennis. "Get your facts straight," he had told me. It was an order.

The River Club suggests the great polo player of yesteryear, Tommy Hitchcock, or the ghost of Hobie Baker, Princeton's priceless hockey and football star at the time of F. Scott Fitzgerald. I do not know how old the club is, but it reeks of what C. Wright Mills called "the power elite." One thinks of boarding school and success, privilege and power. I thought of old New York money as I stood under the metal awning at the entrance of the club. The awning is painted Gulf Stream blue and is a sure reminder of great sailing yachts and blue blazers and hearty Anglo-Saxon faces reassessing ocean races.

When Billy Talbert told me where we were to play, I said, "Oh, I know where the River Club is. I've been by it."

"No, you haven't," he said, and then he paused for a second and explained. "It is at the very *end* of Fifty-second Street overlooking the East River."

But I had been by it several times on my schooner. Going south, I always waited for the tide to change at Hell Gate and then would seemingly fly down-current right by the River House and the United Nations building and other structures I recognized. As a matter of fact, I had been to the River House back in the 1950s, invited there by a young lady whom I sat beside on an airplane flying up from Palm Beach. The River House is the mother building for the club that takes up at least four floors at the end of the street. It was very fashionable to have an apartment in the River House and doubtless it still is.

I remember one time going by the River House under full sail—even the fisherman's staysail flying. A boat from the New York Harbor Patrol came out to pull us over for sailing the river. I pointed to the exhaust that was coming from our stern, and they went away. Sailing the river without power was illegal. It was too treacherous, but we could not resist raising everything we had in order to make a spectacular entrance to the city. Billy Talbert probably thought he was being clever and his tone suggested I was a rube when he said I had never been by the River Club. I had been by it with flags flying.

Yet though I had had cocktails with a long-forgotten woman high over the East River, that is not to say I had ever played tennis on the illustrious courts where Sidney Wood and Huntington Hartford and Stuart Symington and Billy Talbert had their names on the winner boards, old wooden plaques carrying the names of club tennis champions. And I had not stepped into the locker room, where the lockers were made of dark wood and had brass keyholes and the shower stalls had doors. If I had started playing tennis right after the Korean War in the Air Force, changing on cement floors with one open shower to cram into with naked men looking like slabs of beef, I was now in a rarefied, genteel "old boy" dressing room fit for a prince. I changed along with Dick Craven and Billy Talbert, talking mindlessly as I cast my eyes about.

We entered the court, a court isolated from any other, the surface clay-based with a dusty cover and plenty of room for running under deep topspin lobs. Dick and Billy went over to one side of the court, and I hit against them for a while and then suggested Canadian doubles.

Now, Canadian doubles is an ersatz tennis game and is eschewed at all costs. But I couldn't tell Dick to go home, and I certainly wasn't going to sit by and watch Dick and Billy play singles. Anyway, Talbert said singles was out. In tennis shorts at sixty-five, he looked his age. His legs are not strong as were Gardnar Mulloy's, and he moved with hesitation. So I said, "Let's play Canadian doubles," and Talbert agreed, even though as time would show, he did not know what he would be playing. Then, too, to ask Billy Talbert to play Canadian doubles would be like asking the Duchess of Kent to lunch at Burger King. But I had little choice.

In any case, we began playing, with Craven and Talbert against me, and as the game progressed, we all rotated around the court, each taking his turn at the singles, playing into a doubles team. The scoring system is laborious to delineate, so let me just say that the idea is to win when you are on the singles side of the court and amass points. The first player to reach eleven points wins. So, in a way, Billy Talbert was playing singles whether he liked it or not. He had to take his turn.

Talbert's game is no longer strong and for once I had met a man who acted his age and affirmed my original supposition that in tennis I could catch up to a champion who is older than I.* I noticed that he does not run with alacrity, that he misses his volleys, and can err on a ground stroke as well. I also noticed that he aced me twice in a row and once in a while hit deep winners down the line. He also used a champion's drop shot one time against Dick Craven, who started to run but saw the ball wasn't going to bounce high enough to reach and then gave up. I suppose if Billy Talbert were serious he could have repeated his drop shots, kept up his accurate serving, and showed off for us. But he gave me just a taste of what he had been and what he could do if he had to. However, certain shots notwithstanding, his movements were slow and appeared almost torturous as though he had a pain in his back and his legs hurt. Without agility, his timing was off, and, as a result, the equalizer of age came into play, and we played away almost even in the scoring.

I hit one backhand winner down the middle against Talbert and Craven and the ball had a real sting to it, and Billy said, "Nice shot." He then repeated himself, looking across at me. "Nice shot!" he said again so I would know he meant it. On another occasion when I had the singles court, I got into a duel with Billy, who was playing the deuce court with Dick on his left. We exchanged a series of ground strokes, and finally I took midcourt and hit an off-speed volley that left him dead in his tracks back in his corner where he had been stroking the ball toward me, corner to corner. I, a lousy B player, had pulled off a good one, but I almost suspected that Billy had let me do it. He was not hitting forcing shots, just returning my ground strokes. Gardnar Mulloy, on the other hand, would have been on the move, taken my off-speed volley and put it away. Cutting through my euphoria over making a winning point was the sure knowledge that I was playing a gentleman who had taken time from work and was trying to give me some fun. When Dick Craven finally took his eleventh point and won the game, we stopped, and Billy said, "Keep on playing. You have fifteen minutes to go before we give up the court. I'll see you in the locker room," and then he walked away.

---

* In a subsequent phone conversation I asked him, "With age, what are the first things to go?" He said, "With me it was my eyesight, then the legs." Later I talked with a doctor who was amazed that a man who had diabetes as a child could play *any* tennis in his sixties.

20. William Talbert today

We had played for forty-five minutes, and, to be sure, I had lived my fan's dream. Had we a fourth, the game would have been different. No doubt Talbert never did understand our crazy Martha's Vineyard scoring of what Dick and I assumed was truly a Canadian game. Once when I mentioned the score and was going to caution him to try harder, he said, "I don't care what the score is," and shook his head as though he had been caught up with two mutants who had invented something to suit their odd natures.

In the locker room, Talbert asked if we wanted a beer or anything to drink. It was 11:00 in the morning and too early for imbibing. Both of us had work to do as did, I was sure, Billy Talbert. Again he was being as courteous as he had been when he kept stroking the ball toward me, letting me finally make my move. We showered and dressed, and I walked with Billy out to the dead end of Fifty-second Street, where you can look down on the East River. I thought of Bobby Jordan, Leo Gorcey, and Huntz Hall and other "Dead End Kids" of the movies from the 1930s and 1940s.

Billy Talbert posed for a couple of pictures, and then he was gone. I went back into the club to retrieve my raincoat and found Dick Craven smiling at me.

135

9

Don Budge:

"What's good enough for George Bernard Shaw
is good enough for me."

A week after seeing Billy Talbert, I was back in New York City to see J. Donald Budge. I had called Budge's home all through the month of November, to no avail. Once I got his cleaning lady, who told me he was in California visiting Gene Mako, his old doubles partner. I fired a letter off to him, in care of Mako, saying I would fly out "at the drop of a hat" if I could see him and Mako—"for only an hour or so." I did not get an answer. By then I was growing too timid to call. I had telephoned so many times that I was becoming afraid that he might answer. I wrote an impetuous letter instead.

I had confided to both Sarah Palfrey and Billy Talbert that I felt Budge was being "elusive." Without him, my book was doomed. By January I was quietly panicking, and I grabbed the phone and called his home in Dingmans Ferry, Pennsylvania, for the last time. I got his wife. They would be in New York the next Thursday. Surely, she said, Don would see me. All I had to do was call on the morning of that day. Budge, himself, was not at home—I wondered if he ever *was* at home, but his wife sounded wonderful. I believed her.

So I was back in town the night before our meeting, and when I called the Essex House about 10:00 in the morning, it was Don Budge who answered. He would meet me at 4:00 that afternoon in the lobby of the hotel. He sounded very pleasant on the telephone. Everyone whom I had met liked Don Budge. The word "gentleman" was a constant accolade of description.

Now, finally, I had him locked into a time and a place and he sounded . . . like a gentleman. I was whooping it up alone in my hotel room. That afternoon I was meeting Don Budge. I'm fifty-four, and I'm looking into the mirror, straightening my tie, and saying, "Hot damn!"

I had several hours to think about the man. Along with Joe DiMaggio, Ted Williams, Ben Hogan, Sam Snead, Sugar Ray Robinson . . . the list ran on . . . Budge stood like a giant in my mind. I thought once more of my father and how much he had admired Budge. I thought, of course, of Gene Tunney, always in the shadow of Dempsey, the way Budge had followed "Big Bill" Tilden. Yet Tunney had beaten Dempsey twice, and Budge had overwhelmed Tilden on the pro tour. In terms of celebrity, Tunney and Budge were runners-up: much like Sam Snead to Ben Hogan, although Snead's record is superior. "Like Billy to Jack Armstrong," I said to myself. And, yes, back in the 1930s, listening to the radio, to the Hudson High Boys, I had always sided with Billy, Jack Armstrong's sidekick and pal. I liked number two. I liked Avis. I liked little Albie Booth against a big Army team. I had placed a good-sized bet one time on Adlai Stevenson against Eisenhower in 1956. It was very stupid to do so, but the underdog had my heart. I remembered once when I was in the second or third grade, when my mother had told me that Lincoln was a greater man than the "Father of Our Country," George Washington, and I went with that all of my life.

But all that said and pondered, the fact was that Tilden was dead, having died alone and in disgrace and poor. Don Budge now had the stage all to himself, as it should have been all along. The greatest tennis player of all time was upstairs in his room at the Essex House, and though Fred Perry would dispute me, I believed the implication in Billy Talbert's remark when he said that against Don Budge, he was helpless. I knew that number two had probably been number one all along.

As a fan, I could be seeing Joe DiMaggio, Ted Williams, or Sugar Ray Robinson when I saw Don Budge. They cohabited a room somewhere up in the stratosphere, where reverence and respect are their just desserts. Oh, yes, I loved it all. Once a champion, always a champion. And among champions, there are layers. Don Budge and a handful of others were upper deck.

I saw him coming down the hall. He walked on the balls of his feet, giving a spring to his step. He walked quickly. He saw me at once, and we shook hands. Budge is tall, around six-two, and his blond hair is thinning, and he has a touch of a jowl under his chin. He doesn't look sixty-eight, but he doesn't look fifty either, the way Gardnar Mulloy looks. He appeared to be in his middle sixties, a man in more than reasonably good shape and full of spirit. He smiled on meeting and suggested we find a good place to talk. He has broad shoulders and a full chest. I thought of that backhand of his, crossing a strong upper torso.

We ended up in the bar, sitting at a small table, and I placed my tape recorder next to his teacup and lit a cigarette. At once I thought, "Oh, oh, no smoking around this fellow." So I asked him if it was all right. He said it was okay so long as I kept the smoke away from him. Within two minutes, he asked if I would mind putting out my cigarette. The man did not smoke and had never touched a drop of liquor through all of his playing years. Way back as a kid in Oakland, California, Budge knew enough to stay away from what he considered to be poison to an athlete. His jaunty manner at sixty-eight gave evidence that it had paid off. He was wearing an expensive tweed sports coat with a leather band on the edge of his breast pocket. He could have been a country squire, which in a way he is. He smiled at me and said, "Okay, let's go." The interview would begin.

Budge asked me about my book, how it was going, whether I was pleased about it. "Are you doing the George Plimpton thing and going around playing everybody?"

"Whenever I can, yes. I played Shirley Fry, who just took me apart. I mean, I found that there is no way that a B-level club player such as I can even come close to a world-class ex-champion, regardless of age or sex . . . or so it seems."

"Well, I have to disagree with you," he said. "I know that there are at least one hundred good club players who can beat Martina Navratilova. Roy Emerson practices with her and beats her steadily."

"But I am not Roy Emerson," I said, confused by his remark. What did Roy Emerson have to do with "club players?"

"I know that," Budge said flatly, and when he said that I was somewhat at a loss. I knew he was right . . . that there were many men who had played in college, gone to work, and kept at their games and could beat an existing woman champion because of their strength. I thought of a man who summers on Martha's Vineyard named Terry Robinson. The trouble was that here at the very start, Budge had refuted one of my generalizations, and I realized that he could be contentious and that from now on I had better be sure to qualify what I was saying. But to bring Roy Emerson into the conversation was a bit offsetting. Hell, Emerson could beat 99.9 percent of the people in the world. But, then, Budge had a point of sorts. I'm sure I can beat Billy Talbert. I concluded there were too many variables and dropped the subject.

Budge was born in Oakland, California, and graduated from University High and went on to the University of California at Berkeley. "I dropped out, though, because I had a chance to play on the Davis Cup team as an auxiliary member. I thought, well, it would be great to go over to England and play at

Wimbledon and then I would go back to school. But as luck had it for me, I made the team and never did go back to college.''

Budge was the national champion for boys eighteen-and-under in 1933, two years before going to England. Years later he met Joe DiMaggio, who confessed that he always wanted to play tennis, and Don Budge, a good high school baseball player, admitted that he had always wanted to play big league baseball. It was almost as though they were sorry they had not switched sports. "We both wound up in the opposite sports, and I guess we were lucky, because when you think of DiMaggio—who could have been better at baseball than he was?''

I pondered the image of DiMaggio at Wimbledon and Budge playing for the Yankees. There was something in the manner of his speech that told me that it could have been possible. They had been good enough as kids to go either way.

Reading my thoughts, he said, "This year I played in the Joe DiMaggio-Jim Brown Hall of Fame Golf Tournament at the Riviera Hotel in Las Vegas. The first year I played, Mickey Mantle was my partner, and we came in third and each won $6,000. This year I played with Ernie Banks, and we finished fourth, out of the prize money.''

I asked Budge about his parents.

"My father came from Scotland. He was a soccer player, and in a practice game he got knocked out. His brother, Donald Bruce Budge, whom I was named after, finally went back and found my father still unconscious, lying in the snow. He developed pneumonia from that and came to California for his health. That's how he got over here, but my folks and I were very close. My mother was great and a great influence on me, and one time I was playing in a junior tournament, and I had my opponent match point, but I lost the match. I came home and she said, 'How did you do, Don?' and I said, 'The damn guy was lucky. I had him at match point.' She said, 'What did you say?' I said, 'The damn guy was lucky . . .' She said, 'Look, you're representing the Budge family. Don't you even think like that or you won't play anymore.' My mother lived until she was eighty-nine, and my father eventually died of tuberculosis at around seventy-six.''

"Between 1933, when you won your boys eighteen-and-under championship"—on this he corrected me.

"*Juniors*, not boys," he said. "Juniors play through eighteen, and boys is fifteen-and-under.''

The *Tennis Yearbook* used the word "boys," and for a second, I was going to do battle over this point but gave up at once and wondered what the hell was wrong with me? It must be nerves. Don Budge was making me nervous. I began again. "Between 1933, when you won the juniors, and 1939, when you turned pro, how did you support yourself?''

"Well, I won a few local tournaments in California, and the Northern Tennis Association sent me back east to compete in eastern tournaments, and so they paid my expenses. We had a dollar and a half a week for laundry and a dollar a week for spending money. We were either put up in hotels or in homes so that our expenses were taken care of. Then when we got on the Davis Cup team, the Davis Cup put up our expenses. I think we got $15 a day, and we thought we were stealing the money."

At that moment, his wife of nine years, Loriel, joined us. She is younger than Budge, close to my age, I would assume. She was wearing a full-length mink coat and had just come from having her hair done. She ordered tea, and we sat crammed together at a small table in the bar. She has dark brown hair that is shoulder-length, and her good looks lie in that area between attractive and nifty. You wouldn't expect her to stop traffic on the corner of Hollywood and Vine, but she'd fit nicely in Billy Talbert's River Club. She has a familiar way that made me like her at once and felt we were all old friends, meeting overseas, crowding into a bar, reuniting, a familiar trio. Loriel had that effect, and I could see Don Budge beam at her. She took the edge off the tenseness of our interview.

"Going back to your expenses and how you lived . . ."

"When we went down to Australia, as an example, the Australian Tennis Association would invite Gene Mako and myself to go down there to help them with their tournament, and they paid our way."

"First class?"

"Well, we went by boat."

"I mean first class on the boat."

"Oh, yes. It was great fun. Twenty-three days one way and twenty-one the other way."

"Gardnar Mulloy said he was paid under the table."

"I never was. I never made a dime out of amateur tennis."

I asked Budge about his book, *A Tennis Memoir*, which is now out of print. I had read two excellent excerpts from it in a recent publication called *The Tennis Book*. One of the excerpts dealt with "The Greatest Match Ever Played," which was his match in the interzone finals at Wimbledon against Baron Gottfried von Cramm. I asked if he had written his book himself or had had a ghost writer. He said that there had been no ghostwriter, no collaborator.

"Well, you write better than I do," I said, and I meant it because both excerpts were splendid examples of sports writing and memoir.

"You're wrong," Budge said, contradicting me again. "You're wrong because I dictated it over a tape recorder. I can talk better than I can write."

I sensed another confrontation, but plunged ahead anyway and told him

140

that I couldn't see any difference between dictating your thoughts or writing them down. Winston Churchill dictated his books after the war.

"Well, all right," Budge said and went on. "Cramm was one of the highest class fellows you could ever meet. There might be someone who is as good a tennis player, but no one was a better sport than he was, and it was a thrill just to be on the same court with him. I don't know what he would do if he played some of the players today who behave the way you wouldn't want your son to behave."

"What would *you* do?"

"I would take a rest period. I would say to myself, 'If someone wants to make a big issue out of a point, I'm just going to sit down, just relax, and let him get it out of his system.' "

I mentioned that Fred Perry said that Bill Tilden would not tolerate bad behavior.

"That's right. He would have done something to steal the scene from the player who was making the issue. He was something else. Bill was a great student of the game, and I played on the tour with him, 76 matches after I played Vines and Perry, and every night something would happen, and you'd sit back and say, 'I wonder how he's going to get out of this?' "

"How did you do against Tilden?"

"Well, he was past his prime, and I was at my best. I won 68 matches and lost 8."

"How do you think you would have done had you met him at his prime?"

"I don't know. I only know that they had a computer tournament about ten years ago that IBM did. They had me beating Laver in the quarterfinals, me beating Kramer in the semis in five sets, and then beating Tilden in the finals in five sets. They fed everything into that computer—all our wins and losses and so forth, so I have to believe it was right."

"Billy Talbert told me that you were the only player who ever made him feel helpless."

"He told me that, too. And others have said that against me, they never felt they were in the game. It's fun to believe them."

I asked him what was his greatest doubles game—I let the singles game go for the moment because I knew the details of that match with von Cramm, and so did most tennis fans. Later I would briefly recapitulate it for my book. But in the doubles?

"That's a hard question. There was one match, the most important match that Gene Mako and I won was a match where I didn't play my best, but Mako took over and actually held us up as a team. My overhead had gone off a little, so I said to Gene, 'Look, any time a lob is coming my direction, you holler *mine*, and I'll get out of the way.' The game was against von Cramm

21. Don Budge and Gene Mako: A pair of youngsters the world would never forget

and Henkel in the same interzone at Wimbledon, which our Davis Cup team won 3–2. It was the day before I played that fairly well-known game with von Cramm."

"Now, to continue the tennis questions before we get to more interesting ones."

"Oh, tennis isn't interesting?" he said.

"Yes, yes!" I answered. "But I can probably get most of the tennis information by reading your book, if I could ever find it. I can't get it where I live."

"Nobody can. They sold the first edition out fast, and it never went back to press. I don't know why."

I didn't know why either and I comically repeated the old clichés from the publishing world: "The economics of publishing make it impossible to continue printing your book in today's market, etc., etc." Back when I was in the publishing business I heard that line often, and I let the familiar but still dismal news of a good book gone out of print go out of my mind. I asked him about mixed doubles.

"I had a real good partner in Alice Marble. She was more like a boy, the way she played. She was feminine and all of that, but she was a great athlete. In fact, Joe DiMaggio told me how she would shag balls with the San Francisco Seals baseball team when DiMaggio played for them before coming up to the Yankees. She was the only girl he had ever seen who could throw a ball in from deep center field to home plate on one bounce. I mean, she shagged flies with Joe!"

"Can you think of a single match with Alice Marble that stands out?"

"No, not really, because Alice and I won our matches so easily that we were never in trouble. In fact, mixed doubles was what I liked best. I would win my singles match and then play the men's doubles and then to play with Alice was a lark because she played like another guy and we would waltz through those people, 6–1, 6–3."

"If you had to rank tennis players, forgetting yourself and Bill Tilden, could you possibly name the top five players below you and Tilden?"

"Forget Bill Tilden! Why forget Bill?"

"Well, the argument of who is better between you and Bill Tilden could go on for years. I am assuming your modesty is telling me to leave the argument alone."

"I don't think you should limit me to saying that Bill Tilden and I are equal. He might have been a lot better—who knows? But I might have been better, also. But I would say the best player on his day was Ellsworth Vines. He had the best serve of anyone who has ever played. If I had to take three hundred and sixty-five days out of the year, I would take Jack Kramer."

"What about Gonzales?"

"No, I wouldn't include him. I will tell you why. First of all, Gonzales after he won the national championships *twice* . . . he and I were practicing out in California, and he couldn't win a set from me, and I was over the hill at that point. Meanwhile, I was winning an occasional set from Jack Kramer. And Gonzales wanted to turn pro, and I said, 'Pancho, you can't even beat me now. How in hell are you going to beat Jack [already a pro]?' To make a short story shorter, Pancho turned professional and played Kramer, and Kramer murdered him.

"My number three would be Laver. I wouldn't put Tilden in the first five. He couldn't play net very well. He had a great deceptive serve, and his ground strokes were marvelous, but at the net he was kind of lost. And Fred Perry was a super player. And so was von Cramm. I would like to see Laver and Gonzales and some of those guys play von Cramm . . . Wait a minute. Ahead of Laver I would take Lew Hoad."

"How would you compare McEnroe to others in their prime?"

"I would take Kramer and Gonzales and Laver over McEnroe. I'll tell you why. Kramer, Vines, me . . . Fred Perry said he *never* practiced, but that is a lot of baloney . . . if we had a weakness, we would take time off and practice like hell to correct it. Players today don't do that. Connors had three weaknesses, and he did correct one by standing in closer to return serve, but he still has a faulty first serve, and he makes errors approaching the net with his forehand when he makes that undercut shot. If any of us [Vines, Perry, or Kramer] had a weakness, we would have worked like hell over the winter to correct it."

Of course, Connors isn't McEnroe, but I think Budge used Connors as an illustration of today's top players.

"When you were a little kid out there in Oakland, who were your heroes?"

"Ellsworth Vines, Ed 'Bud' Chandler [an intercollegiate champion from the University of California in both 1925 and 1926], and Babe Ruth, who was my idol in baseball. But Chandler in particular. He won the national intercollegiate doubles with a fellow who helped me a lot, Tom Stow. Bud Chandler was a real high-class fellow."

"In other words, when you were a kid and if I went into your home, and I said, 'Don, who are your heroes?' you wouldn't say Abraham Lincoln?"

"I thought you were limiting it to sports. I would say Albert Einstein, whom I admired very much, and I would say Abraham Lincoln, whom I liked to read about. But Einstein to me made so much sense. I think you'd have to be kind of stupid not to appreciate what he represented."

I told Budge that if someone had asked me about heroes at ten years old, I would have said Tommy Harmon.

"Tommy Harmon over DiMaggio!"

Harmon had made All-American for the second year in a row when I was

22. John McEnroe meets the master, Mr. J. Donald Budge

ten. "Yes. And as a matter of fact, I liked Williams more than DiMaggio but hell, they were all my heroes."

Budge smiled at me, and his wife, Loriel, looked over at the two of us who were remembering what it was like to follow the sports pages to concoct great visions, to visualize in your mind the dash of Tommy Harmon, the swing of Babe Ruth. But we left the battle of who was better—DiMaggio or Williams—alone. It was clear that Budge would vote for his friend DiMaggio.

Now at sixty-eight, looking back over an illustrious career as a world figure, he said that one of the people he admired most was Mahatma Gandhi and the actor William Powell, who "is still alive, a marvelous man, very bright, and I really loved the guy, and he is a good friend. I liked Errol Flynn very much . . ."

"You're the third person to mention Errol Flynn," I said. I could not help interrupting him. Fred Perry, Billy Talbert, and now Don Budge all had the highest regard for a man known to the world as a rogue, perhaps a cad. Errol Flynn had died in disgrace with a teenager in the state of Washington under very cloudy circumstances. He was a man who had dodged World War II—or so it was thought.

"Errol was a heck of a guy, and the nice thing about Errol was that any time there was a woman in the company, he was a gentleman and never did anything you could criticize.

"Another man whom I admired would be Groucho Marx. I knew all of the Marx brothers, but Groucho was a great tennis fan, and we had a lot of fun together."

"How about world leaders, such as Churchill?"

"Oh, yes, Churchill was a fine speaker, and so was Roosevelt. I admired them, but I would stick Edward "Bud" Chandler on the list. He was a great influence on me back when I was in junior tennis, and he is an Abraham Lincoln kind of guy, as far as I am concerned. He was a lawyer and an intercollegiate champion and for a while was ranked fifth in the country. He beat Vines a few times, so you know he was a good player."

"How does Gandhi fit into this?" I asked.

"In later life, I learned more about him, and even Einstein said that Gandhi was one of the super people he had ever met. And after seeing the movie and knowing more about Gandhi, I think what he did was terrific.

"And there is one more. Pablo Casals, the great cellist. He gave me a private concert in Paris after I won the French championship. We were having tea after the match and he said, 'Don, you have given me so much happiness by playing tennis, I would like you to come to my house for dinner, and I will play for you.' So I got a private concert, and I mentioned that to Benny Goodman, and he said, 'You lucky stiff. I know a hundred people who would pay $50,000 for a concert like that.'"

"If you had your life to live over again, is there anything you would change in it?"

"Yes, I would like to win the grand slam in doubles, as well as in the singles. I didn't even think about it at the time. I assumed we were going to do it, but Gene and I won two and lost two. In a monetary way, I am kind of sorry I wasn't born later, but had I been, I wouldn't have met my wife, and so I guess I really would not want to change anything."

"On a national or world level, would you change anything? In hindsight, would you have handled the Russians differently right after the war?"

"I don't think I am qualified to talk on that. I know that Roosevelt said, 'Leave everything to me. I will handle Stalin when the times comes,' but when the time came, he couldn't do it."

"What about war? Were you in the service?"

"Yes, I was in the Army Air Corps. Just as I was at the top of my game, I went off to the Air Corps. It was kind of tough to while away time when no one could beat you."

Budge was in special services and then a tactical officer and, "I did everything except fly. First, I was in Hawaii and then Guam and Saipan and Tinian—out in the Pacific."

Budge went back to the topic of tennis. "Now look at Borg. He had nine tries at the U.S. Championship and didn't win once. So as good as he was, there was something lacking in his game. Today there are four grand slam events, and you have a different winner in each one. There is something wrong with some of these fellows that they can't win all of them.

"There was a great player, Jack Crawford, back in my day, who had three legs on the grand slam and had Fred Perry two sets to one. Crawford was one set away from winning the grand slam at the U.S. Championships, and he used to take a sip of brandy whenever he had asthma attacks, and Fred beat him one and love to win the last two sets and the match because Jack Crawford got high. Hoad was two sets away from winning the grand slam. What is wrong with these later guys? Borg won two out of four in any given year, the French and Wimbledon, but he couldn't win in Australia and the United States."

I said I understood that Jack Crawford was a recluse, living in Australia, and would not see anybody.

"Well, his wife, Marge, had been ill for a long time, and she had stuck by him when he was traveling around, and so he took care of her once she was sick. Now that she has died, I think Jack is getting around a little bit. If he is invited to some of these tennis events, he would go. He was a marvelous fellow and a marvelous player—one of the prettiest players I have ever seen."

"Helen Wills, I guess, is *really* a recluse. Nobody can get to her."

"Yes, but I was inducted into the Bay Area Hall of Fame in San

Francisco two years ago, and Helen Wills did the voice-over on my film, and the fellow who promoted the affair said, 'Don, why don't you call Helen?'

"I said, 'I don't think she wants to talk with me,' but he repeated that I should call her. So I did call her, and we talked for an hour on the phone. She didn't want to get off. We had played in a few doubles tournaments together after she had passed her prime, and she was a nice lady as far as I knew."

"Who was the best woman player you have seen play?"

"I think Maureen Connolly could have handled these girls today. She could do everything Chris Evert can do, but she could run better. She could hit the ball harder . . .''

"Could she beat Martina Navratilova?"

"I think so. Helen Wills was a strong player. She was tough. It's hard to know, but Alice Marble, for instance, played like the guys, and she probably would have done better against Navratilova. It's hard to know."

At that moment, I began coughing, and Don Budge said, "It's those damn cigarettes you smoke."

I said, "No, no, it's the peanuts I am eating."

"Look at her," he said, pointing to his wife. "She quit."

Loriel Budge smiled at me and said, "Read today's *Times*. The editorial page. Read that, and you'll quit."

"So easy," I said. "Hell, you have more willpower than I. I'm an aesthete, not exactly famous for great self-control."

They both grinned and shook their heads.

I went back to Budge. "If you were asked to speak to the graduating class of Oakland High School, what advice would you give to the young of today?"

"First, you have to decide what you want to become in life, and if you can come to that conclusion at that point, you go out and work like the dickens at it. Be an expert in something rather than be a jack-of-all-trades. I think a lot of people are in that boat. I didn't make up my mind that I wanted to play tennis until I went over with the Davis Cup team, and then I thought, gee, maybe I can be the best player in the world—at least I am knocking on the door now."

"So it was really the Davis Cup experience where you said, 'I can go all the way with this thing.' Rather than be a college boy who played tennis, you could be the best in the world and say farewell to college."

"Yes. But it was a gamble, but life is a gamble. My hope was to win the big tournaments, turn pro, and play Vines. He was my idol."

"But the idea of a touring pro wasn't so lucrative then, was it? The idea would be to tour, but be a club pro and give lessons and such, wouldn't it?"

"No, not really. When I joined up, there were only two guys making appreciable money. The others weren't making nearly what the guys make today. There are a hundred players now making better than $100,000 a year. Vines and I were making big money. In my first year, I made $148,000, and I paid $2,080 in taxes. Gasoline was ten cents a gallon. A good steak was $2, and a good room was $6 a night. So I was able to invest a lot of that money when the dollar was worth six times what it is today. With the help of Bud Chandler . . . I was lucky there. I figure I would have to gross about $800,000 today, and I still wouldn't have cleared as much as I did then."

"How do you think a guy like Karel Kozeluh did?"

"Oh, he made a little, but nowhere as much as Tilden. But Tilden lived like Howard Hughes, as far as spending money was concerned. One day I said, 'Bill, what will you do when you can no longer play tennis?' You know what his answer was? 'Kill myself.' That's just what he said, 'Kill myself.' He loved it more than life itself."

Loriel rose from the table at that point. She had to get ready because they were due to leave in a half hour. I said, "It is nice to meet you," and she responded in kind, and added, "Good luck with your book. It sounds like a winner." Don Budge looked at her and said, "It was nice to meet you," and she stared back with a look that said, "Oh, yes." He then said, "I'll see you upstairs in a few minutes."

I paused for a moment, thinking about love over sixty-five and realized again how much staying in shape meant. Don Budge looked like a millionaire, which I am sure he is. He was smiling all the time now and seemed to enjoy talking with me. He was getting a kick out of the crazy little bar that had a nautical motif and a brass funnel that rose up behind his head. We almost got into another argument about how much Babe Ruth got paid by the Yankees. I said his top salary was $80,000 and Budge said $90,000, and the verbal jousting seemed to bring us closer together. Loriel had been a catalyst in all of this.

I asked him if he believed in God.

"I believe in a supreme force," he said, "but I don't believe in any formalized religion. Einstein said, 'God doesn't play dice with people.' Heinrich Heine, the German poet, was blaspheming against religion, and someone said, 'You'll be chastised,' and Heine said, 'God will forgive me because that's his business.'

"I believe that if you don't hurt anyone and pay your bills and you're a decent person, you're as religious as, say, a Catholic who can go out and screw the town and then go to confession, and he's okay.

"If there is a life after death, then that's fine. All I know is that I want to enjoy life to the utmost while I am here. I like to look at a pretty girl. I like to laugh. I don't want to ever hurt anyone. My mother instilled in me the thought that when you go traveling the world, if you don't have anything good to say about someone, don't say anything."

"Speaking of liking girls—I've never asked anyone this because it seemed too touchy—but when Tilden [an obsessive homosexual] was around, did he make you guys uneasy?"

"Well, wait a minute. He used to embarrass us. Often in England when I was traveling with Vines and Tilden and Lester Stoefen, and we'd be playing and the match would be interrupted by rain, let's say, and we would go into the locker room, and they would have two or three ball boys hanging around, and Tilden would get his eye on one of the ball boys, the way you would be looking at Elizabeth Taylor, let's say, and we couldn't look at it, you know. We'd turn our heads."

"Apparently he was obsessed with young boys. He couldn't help himself."

"That's right. How can you fight an imbalance of genes. You have a man's body with female hormones. It's going to govern your life. One time—oh, we all knew about Bill—but one time he and I were alone and he said, 'You know that I am different from the rest of you.' I said that I did. He then said, 'I guess you have a date tonight with a woman,' and, as a matter of fact, I had. Then he said, 'Well, Dickie Boy is coming over, and he's about the grandest thing that ever happened,' and I thought, 'God! Who wants to hear this?' "

Just talking about Tilden's "other life" made Budge ill at ease. I switched the subject.

"Lately I've been thinking about style. Billy Talbert believes in dressing well. Does style go with tennis?"

"I think so. You think of Fred Perry and Jack Crawford and von Cramm and me . . . we all dressed well. And in our tennis camp, which we just sold, the Don Budge Tennis Camp in Baltimore, we noticed that when the kids dressed up for dinner, they had better manners than when they came in with their shirttails hanging out. I think that players who dress better perform better. Sloppy dressers are apt to be sloppy in their approach to the game. The girls dress a lot better than the boys do, but it's not up to me to go around telling young men to shape up."

"When I talked with you on the phone back in October, you said that Sidney Wood helped you with your backhand."

"No. He helped me with my forehand. I had a western grip, and he told me to change to an eastern grip because I was having trouble digging low balls out of the grass. My backhand came from playing baseball. I was a left-handed batter and threw righty. There was a time when I was starting out, and a few of the older players who were better than I tried to get me to change my grip. After several tries at it without success, I went back to my original grip. That was one stroke that was as natural to me as eating when you're hungry."

"What goes into making a champion?"

"Discipline."

"What about a killer instinct?"

"If beating someone as badly and as quickly as I could is having a killer instinct, then, okay, you can call it that. But it takes discipline. For instance, if you stay up late before a match having a good time—and the ladies can be enticing around a tournament, parties, and so forth—well, you don't do that. You have to have the discipline to go to bed early."

"Whitney Reed, who was ranked number one in the country for one year back in the late 1950s, I saw at a tournament, and his training system was unusual, to say the least. I don't think he ever went to bed."

"Then [if that were true] Reed stands for the opposite of what I am talking about."

"What do you think of the world today? Someone said there are forty-two wars going on simultaneously."

"I think it's awesome. There is so much to be thankful for. Think of all the money spent on blowing each other up that could go toward cancer re-

23. Budge at work. No one ever did a better job

search, finding cures for diseases. Think of all the money that is wasted on developing weapons that are obsolete as soon as they are built. I think it is crazy, myself."

"Do you have a remedy for this?"

"No. Well, yes, I do. I believe what George Bernard Shaw said. Do you know what that was?"

"No."

"He said that there would never be another war if you let the guys forty-and-over fight it. What's good enough for George Bernard Shaw is good enough for me."

"What are you doing now with your tennis camp sold? Are you totally retired?"

"I sold the tennis camp in Baltimore, but I am with the Prince Racquet Company. I am on the board of advisors and do a certain amount of promotional work for them, and I am on the committee to pick the world's champion each year, and I can't get out of tennis even if I wanted to.

"I've now put my name up before the Davis Cup selection committee for the captaincy. I'd like to do it. I have the time now, and I've invested my money well, and I sort of think that I am qualified. I think my record is pretty good."

Budge said that with a straight face, and I think he meant it to be taken in a straightforward way. But what a modest man. His record? He "invented" the grand slam, winning the French, the All-England (Wimbledon), the U.S., and the Australian championships in the same year. This was in 1938. Fifteen years later, he was followed by Maureen Connolly and then by Rod Laver twice (1962 and 1969) and by Margaret Smith Court in 1970. In 1936, 1937, and 1938, he was ranked first in the United States and during those years, he won Wimbledon twice and Forest Hills twice. He took the doubles twice in a row at Wimbledon, playing with Gene Mako. He led the U.S. Davis Cup to victory over Great Britain and brought the cup back to the United States after ten years. In all of his Davis Cup play, his record stands at 25 wins and 4 losses. His record as a professional was amazing and would have been miraculous had not the war interrupted his career. His mixed doubles play with Alice Marble was lopsided. Overall, no man had done so well in so short a time as Don Budge: from high school athlete to professional superstar took him six years. He beat everybody and, at the end, knew no peer. No doubt all his trophies, if stacked in a pile, would fill up the very bar where we were talking.

And, of course, the von Cramm match. Don Budge had to win, or else it was curtains for the United States. It was the last step to the challenge round against Great Britain. Bryan "Bitsy" Grant had lost to von Cramm, and Grant had also been beaten by Henner Henkel. It all boiled down to the final singles match because Budge and Mako won the doubles. Now Budge was playing von Cramm for all the marbles. Remember, it was 1937, and war clouds were everywhere. Nations were rising to their feet. The United States wanted to win this match against Germany, get on to the English team, and take home the cup after ten years. When it was over, Bill Tilden called it "the greatest tennis match ever played." *The London Times* correspondent wrote: "Certainly I have never seen a match that came nearer the heroic in its courage, as in its strokes, as this."

Serving at match point for the fifth time in the fifth set, Budge recalls in his book, *A Tennis Memoir**, what happened:

So once more I served. It was the 175th time that day that I had made a first serve. Gottfried made a beautiful long return that kept me far back in the court. All I could do was trade long ground strokes with him.

[Eventually] he caught a good backhand with his forehand and hit it crosscourt. I had to move from my own lefthand side of the court toward the center. Now, however, when I saw Cramm place the ball so far over, I had to break into a dead run. In fact, as I neared the ball, just as it bounced in, I realized that my speed had brought my body too far forward. There was suddenly no way I could keep from falling.

Going at full speed, I just took a swipe at the ball. Then immediately after I swung I dived for the ground. The ball whipped down the line past Cramm's outstretched racket. He had come up fast and could cover all but two feet of the net. I had been forced to try for a shot right down the line.

I was flat on the ground, and I waited for the call, and then suddenly, even before the linesman could begin to flatten his hands in the "safe" sign, I could hear the cheers begin to swell.

But now the roars were greater and more excited, and here I was still lying flat out on the ground. Gottfried, the noble loser, had to stand at the net waiting patiently for me. I rose finally and rushed toward him. "Don," he said, evenly and with remarkable composure, "this was absolutely the finest match I have ever played in my life."

I suppose it was an hour or so after the match before I was at last able to dress and leave the locker room. I think it was almost nine o'clock by this time, but the midsummer sun wasn't down. I walked out and glanced up into the stands, and I was shocked because there were still thousands of people there, clustered together all over the stadium. I've never seen anything like that, before or since, just all those people remembering long after I had dressed and gone.

Walter Pate, the team captain, said, "No man, living or dead, could have beaten either man that day."

I knew Budge had to leave. His wife was ready by now, and they had a date. Fred Perry and Lew Hoad were coming into town, and the three of them had to select the best player in the world for the year 1983. The Volvo Masters Tournament was going on at Madison Square Garden, and there was that to watch. He'd driven up—"it only takes seventy-five minutes"—from Dingmans Ferry in the Poconos in Pennsylvania, and there were so many friends to see.

He was talking to me as I walked him out to the lobby. He was recalling the old Hollywood days. "You know," he said, "the movie people looked up to us as much as we did to them. A guy like Errol Flynn, as an example—he was the best tennis player in the movie colony. He was always well-mannered around us. Except for that time when he got into my mother-in-law's absinthe. He was perfectly polite, mind you, but three days later, he found me calling the lines for a game between Bobby Riggs and Ted Schroeder, and there was some money on the match, and they asked me to referee it, and I did. Well, Flynn came over and kept calling at me, and finally I had to go over and see him. He looked like a train had run over him. He said, 'My God, that absinthe. It's done something to me. I can't stop with the women. I am going crazy. I'm exhausted.' "

Budge laughed at the remembrance of Flynn, a good athlete himself who, before too long, went to seed. Those were Budge's salad days, a time of innocence and youth and his first marriage with two growing boys. He said that his first wife and he drifted apart, but one son grew up to become an architect and the other is in public relations. There appeared to be no remorse over a marriage that finally didn't work out, and, instead, you could sense a nostalgia for the time when the movie people came around looking for a game, and in a growing America, his investments, supervised by Ed "Bud" Chandler, swelled with the corporate growth of a free country. If the Great Depression was dampening spirits and destroying lives, it was also a period when athletes and movie actors could seize the day, find opportunity, and look across a land where there was no horizon. When Don Budge made $148,000 a year, there were soup kitchens in my hometown of New Britain, Connecticut. In the 1940s and 1950s when the nation was rolling ever upward, ex-Air Force officer Don Budge was the star of the show. He had laid his groundwork at a time when the rest of us looked for heroes to give us a lift. As he said, he "had been lucky."

"Fit as a fiddle and ready for love" was a line from a song in the 1930s. It came to my mind as he walked off. Then he turned and said, "You know, I am

154

sorry we didn't get to play. I guess I could have played, but it isn't something I really like to do anymore."

Don Budge was apologizing to me, but he didn't have a thing to apologize about. To me, he was the best tennis player the world had ever known, and hell! I had even met his wife. I sprang out of the Essex House with Jack Kramer's phone number in my hand. Don Budge had said, "Give Jack a call."

I told Jack Kramer that I had just been with Don Budge.

"Well, then you have just been with one great person," he said.

I knew that. Number two had been number one all along. Big Bill Tilden had had his fan club. Don Budge had the world.

10
Frank Parker:

The Quiet Man
from Milwaukee

Between seeing Don Budge and leaving Martha's Vineyard for my flight to Chicago for my meeting with Frank Parker, I had given myself too much time. I had allowed myself three weeks to write my Budge interview and to wait for Frank Parker to have a birthday, on which day we would play tennis. Playing Parker on his sixty-eighth birthday was an opportunity I did not want to miss. So I waited around the Vineyard in the raw winter with plunging temperatures and caught a respiratory infection that began to wear me down. By the time I was to leave for Chicago, I felt weak and drawn. I had tried Vicks' 44, Robitussin PE, Coricidin 'D,' and Nyquil, with not much success. They managed to put me to sleep but had sapped my strength.

I looked over Parker's record and realized that strength was an ingredient I would need if I was going to play at all well. Frank Parker had been ranked in the top ten in the United States for seventeen years. In this matter, he was second to Bill Larned, who played tennis over eighty years ago. Behind Parker came Arthur Ashe and Gardnar Mulloy. His career spanned the Ellsworth Vines era, the Fred Perry era, and the time of Don Budge, as well as the great days of Jack Kramer. He arrived in the top ten in 1933 when Jack Crawford beat Vines at Wimbledon. He was ranked number four in 1949 when Pancho Gonzales was supreme in amateur tennis and Jack Kramer had already turned professional. To have played with Vines and Budge and Perry and Kramer at their respective peaks, not to mention Bobby Riggs, and to keep on playing, and to keep on being ranked right up to the days of Frank Sedgman and Vic Seixas was something to ponder.

On the phone, Parker told me he could beat Gardnar Mulloy *now!* Mulloy, of course, had crushed me, the wily and graceful Gardnar who had won the public courts championship in singles in 1961 at forty-seven years old. Well, I knew that Gardnar Mulloy had found the fountain of youth in south Florida, and if Frank Parker was correct, there was another fountain of youth in Chicago. My insistent bronchial condition told me that I had found the drain of age here on the Vineyard. I was getting tired of losing to older men and women. At least I should be able to play at my best. Sick as I was, I knew I would not die out there in Chicago, but I would not be worth a damn on the tennis court, either. Yet I wanted to play Frank Parker on his birthday, so off I went.

Frank Parker won Wimbledon once, playing doubles with Pancho Gonzales in 1949. But in the United States, he was a winner everywhere. He took the singles at Forest Hills in 1944 and 1945 and was runner-up to Ted Schroeder in 1942 and to Jack Kramer in 1947. He won the doubles at Longwood in 1943, playing with Kramer. He won the indoor title twice: in 1937 he had triumphed in the singles competition and had won the doubles with a player lost to my memory named Greg Mangin. In the U.S. Clay Court Championships, he accrued a record second only to that of Bill Tilden. He won the singles five times between the years 1933 (he was only seventeen) and 1947. In 1932, at sixteen, he took the juniors, one year ahead of Don Budge. All of these dates made me remember that Parker had been a star for years and that it was now 1984, fifty-two years since the precocious sixteen-year-old conquered in the eighteen-and-under category and found his name in newspapers from San Francisco to Boston.

I wondered about 1932. Lon Warneke won 22 games that year, and Jimmy Foxx hit 58 home runs. Jimmy Foxx had died years ago, and I fancied Lon Warneke residing in obscurity somewhere, another "boy of summer," now lost to the world. In a way, such was the fate of Frank Parker. Who had last heard of him? He eschewed the senior circuit. His name did not pop up alongside those of Mulloy or Riggs in the record books. Did he ever come east? The Hall of Fame in Newport had given me an old address. When Parker finally answered my letter, he said he was director of tennis at the McClurg Court Sports Center in Chicago and replied, "Just call, and we'll set up a game." I did not know what I would find, but it would not be Lon Warneke. The man wanted to play, and if Warneke is still living, as I hope he is, it is doubtful he would like to throw a few fastballs my way just so that I could test his arm. Frank Parker, director of tennis, was ready and willing for any test that might come from the likes of me.

Tennis, at its best, is pure combat. I thought of this as I remembered somber mornings years ago—in the late 1930s when my father would eat his breakfast oatmeal in silence, reading *The Hartford Courant*, which a paperboy would whack against the kitchen door around 7:00 every morning. My father was a silent man, and at breakfast he would read his section of the paper and then exchange it for mine. When he got to the sports pages, he would mention something: a name, a phrase. I can remember him saying, "Good for Frankie Parker. Budge just beat Tilden again, but Parker's the man to watch. A swell guy, that Frank Parker." I think, he, a silent man of the trenches, appreciated a man whom the press had dubbed to be a "tennis robot." Parker was like a machine gun: efficient, no monkey business. He was a swell guy.

But to many, Frank Parker had not always been a swell guy. At twenty-one he married the wife of his benefactor and tennis coach, Mercer Beasley. By then Audrey Beasley was "near forty," and they had been seeing each other for two years prior to that. He describes it now as a "secret romance." Standing in the locker room, he admitted that had Audrey Beasley wanted to sue for alimony, there would have been a scandal second only to that which attended the life and times of Wallis Simpson. Instead she asked for nothing and remarried the young Frank Parker and became his coach and manager. Under her guidance, his forehand was rebuilt, a new life came into his mechanical though effective game, and a champion was born.

Frank Parker came as close to greatness as one can get, always in the backswing of Budge and Bobby Riggs, until Budge was, in his own words, "over the hill" after World War II and Frank was still in stride and still an amateur. Riggs, however, kept on rolling as a professional and hence was no impediment to Frank Parker.

Parker was a veteran of the great U.S. Davis Cup team that brought the cup back from England in 1937. He won a crucial singles match against Charles Hare in the challenge round. Budge, of course, had taken von Cramm in the interzone finals in "the greatest match ever played," and so, in a way Parker's feat of winning is often overlooked. But think of that 1937 squad: Budge and Parker and Gene Mako and Bitsy Grant. Then think later to 1948 when Parker, ranked third in the nation, won both his matches, against William Sidwell and Adrian Quist, and America withstood the Australian challenge.

Parker was a Davis Cup winner, spanning eleven years. If there is an endurance test for tennis, that feat must stand up with the best of them. Unlike Talbert and Mulloy and Schroeder, you will not find his name in any list of major tournaments after 1949. When open tennis finally arrived, he was still noted by his absence. For all intents and purposes, the man who had dominated clay court tennis, who had won a crucial match against England and brought home the Davis Cup after ten years, and who had gone on to succes-

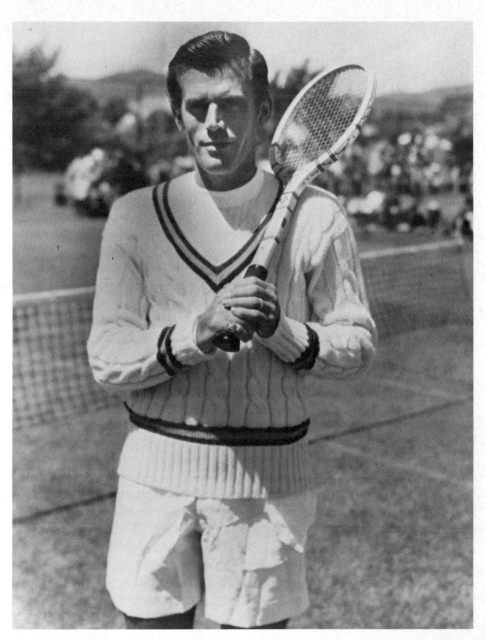

24. Frankie Parker: Placid . . . for the moment

sive victories against the Australians in 1948—for reasons unknown—had slipped away. There was no more Frankie Parker to cheer for. Instead there was the estimable Vic Seixas, but Seixas—as good as he was (and is)—had not cut a swath through the likes of Ellsworth Vines, Don Budge, Fred Perry, Bobby Riggs, and Jack Kramer and taken Wimbledon with the charismatic Richard "Pancho" Gonzales. For thirty-five years, there had been silence. Frankie's guns were stilled.

Or so I thought, and I was wrong.

Frank Parker was born Franciszek Andrezej Paikowski in Milwaukee. His father left home when Frank was one year old, and he and his mother, three brothers, and a sister lived in what he called "the low, low class. My mother took in washing. I worked as a ball boy for the Town Club in Milwaukee and would make a dollar a week at five cents a set. Mercer Beasley, who was the pro at the club, allowed me to hit with some of his pupils and he saw something in me that made him think I might become a champion and things went on from there."

The Beasleys moved to New Orleans and Frank Parker was taken with them. Mercer Beasley became coach at Tulane and then later at the exclusive prep school in New Jersey, Lawrenceville. The Beasleys wanted to adopt the boy, but his mother said no. She did allow them to take him along, however, "the economics of the situation back home being what they were."

At Lawrenceville, Frank Parker developed his game, and at fifteen won the U.S. Boys' Championship. By eighteen he was in love with Audrey Beasley, his secret romance aflame in what he now refers to as "a love match." It was not something elaborated on, but one can imagine the conflict in loyalties, the passion of a woman in her late thirties, the incredible, always startling libido of a teenage boy.* Of course, Mercer Beasley had been like a father to the youngster, and Audrey could easily have been called his foster mother. Indeed, had Mrs. Paikowski given her assent to the offer of adoption, what eventually transpired could have been thought of as incestuous. And what of Mercer? Why would a divorce suit bring forth such a scandal in his life? I did not ask Frank Parker, and I will never know. By twenty-one Frank Parker and Audrey Beasley were husband and wife. Frank says that Audrey was the love of his life, and now that she is dead he gives no evidence of having found a successor. It was probably the tennis love affair of the century, an ineluctable compulsion. The boy had moved in on the man who had been his mentor, his benefactor, his coach, and his "father." For Audrey's part, she

* In a letter to me, Frank explained: "I had nothing to do with the Beasleys' divorce. It had been brewing long before I entered the picture. They had agreed to disagree, to paraphrase a phrase."

had dropped her husband, carried on with a youth in her husband's home, and as Frank said, had she sued for divorce, the contents of the scandal would have rivaled the predatory obsession of Wallis Simpson. Edward VIII had met Oedipus Rex. Though love is blind and the ensuing momentum was out of control, Audrey Beasley nevertheless supposedly had the goods on her husband, which gave her an edge. What had Mercer Beasley done? I did not invade Frank Parker's privacy.

McClurg's is attached to the Holiday Inn and is located on West Ontario Street in the heart of the city. When you play there, you play on a carpet that had not been replaced in many years. It is the color of the top of a pool table, and when the ball strikes its surface, it flies for a split second so that if you are there for the first time you have to adjust. But this is not difficult. I have never played on grass, which I am sure would be hard for a man who is unfamiliar with the speed that grass engenders. But the carpet at McClurg's was ideal for my game, and the lighting is superb.

Parker was wearing running pants and a quasi-polo shirt that showed his broad shoulders and his tight upper torso. His hair is silver and cut like Bruce Jenner's. He is handsome and at five-ten is not an overpowering presence. He has kind eyes and a soft, precise manner of speech. I thought briefly of Pauline Betz and how I said that it was impossible not to like her. I liked Frank Parker at once.

I arrived in the afternoon, just in time to join in on an hour lesson he was giving to a hard-hitting eleven-year-old Lebanese boy who hit forehands with a grunt that reminded me of Connors or McEnroe. He thought I would like the experience of assisting in a lesson, and I did . . . immensely.

For one thing, the boy was a real enthusiast and would chase down all of Frank's long, looping ground strokes. The boy's name was Wally Tamari, and every now and then he would slam one at me, and I, unlike Frank, would sting one back, hoping for a winner. Frank, on the other hand, was content to keep the ball in play. It was, after all, a lesson, and the great pro would hold the baseline, taking "out balls" on the volley and returning them effortlessly with his smooth looping shot that gave the lad plenty of time to reach his return.

We rallied thus for about fifteen minutes and then switched to Canadian doubles, and each of us took our turn at serving. We went around the court amassing points until Frank changed the rules. Now we would only take crosscourts, which is to say that if Wally was serving and Frank was receiving, they would have to keep the ball on the diagonal, back and forth, usually forehand to forehand. Conversely, when Wally served to me, Frank would step aside, and we would angle each other until one of us failed. We still rotated serves, however, and once, when Frank was serving to me in the deuce court, we got into a long exchange. I hit a deep one to the champion's forehand and then quickly stepped to midcourt. Frank, not seeing me, arced his return, and

I caught it with an overhead smash that hit the chalk. It was a good overhead, with a great deal of sting. I could see a split second of fire in Frank Parker's eyes. I had caught him unaware and won a point, and he gave me his respect with "nice shot" or something akin to that. As the game progressed with every shot hit on the diagonal—if it landed on the other side of the center service line or an imaginary extension of the center service line, it was the opponent's point—I began to understand the value of such training. Obviously, what Fred Perry called "the late hit" would be a loser. You had to time your return. You could not just swing and hope that the ball might spin off in some surprising way, thus giving you a point on a fluke.

Toward the end of our hour lesson, Wally Tamari's father showed up, and when the time came to stop, he shook my hand. He said, "You have a great love of the game. You are marvelous fun to watch, and you gave my son much pleasure." He was speaking to me, not to the coach, and I was more than pleased. The youth and I had become friends and had slammed at each other while the mechanical Parker was simply returning everything (other than my overhead) to keep the ball in play, to watch his pupil move. Later Frank said that Wally Tamari had the potential. At eleven, the boy loved tennis the way a young Frank Parker might have loved it when he was ball boy playing with Mercer Beasley's clients.

But I was now looking for singles with Frank Parker. Thus far, during the lesson, he had showed no power, no serve to speak of, and no overhead. All I could tell about him was that he had flawless strokes and could run from corner to corner without taking a breath. He was in superb condition. His silver hair fell over his ears like shreds of shined steel from a Swiss army knife. He would cut me to ribbons, but if I could force him a bit, I might get a few games. If my reverse spin serve to his backhand began to go in, I'd get him off the court. I had my hopes.

But I could forget about my hopes.

He aced me at will. He covered his baseline like an ocelot, and he could hit the lines; the only points I won were with what I call my "slither shot," or slipshot, which comes off my forehand and spins away to my opponent's left. Of course, this is exactly the kind of shot Frank's diagonal tennis is designed to eliminate. I took a few points that way, and then I drop-shot him once for a point. Finally I drove one deep to his forehand that caught the back of the line, and he muffed his return. Otherwise it was bang, bang, good-bye Stan.

We played three games and then broke for our interview. There was no point in continuing and time was becoming a problem. I wanted him alone and on tape for an hour. Parker just smiled at me, and we walked off the court. He had turned sixty-eight and much like Gardnar Mulloy had that easy grace that could rise to the occasion. Otherwise, he just flowed, and it was beautiful to observe him. Others were watching us, and a photographer from *World*

Tennis was taking pictures. This would be as close to "doing my George Plimpton thing," as Don Budge called it, as I would get.

I hated to admit it, but I knew that Frank Parker would rather talk to me than play against me. As I found out, he has 20/90 vision and with me he didn't even bother to wear his glasses. No wonder I caught him napping on my slipshots—my famed slither. But no contact lenses would have aided him with my overhead put-away and my deep back-of-the-baseline ground stroke, which was as good as they come. I had those two shots to remember Frank Parker by and, of course, the thrill of a lesson and the praise from Wally Tamari's father.

We sat in the lounge, and he started to tell me the story of his life. The early part and the Mercer Beasley part I have already alluded to, and yet I will go back once more to Lawrenceville. At Lawrenceville, Frank Parker became team captain and captain of Cleve House. I have never been a member of the prep school world, having gone to a Southern military academy, but I can imagine the snobbery back in the 1930s and the underlining name, Paikowski, and the beginnings of another account of the American Dream of a poor boy becoming captain of a sport and a social leader as well. Has anyone from Cleve House done better than Frank Parker? Would anyone at sixty-eight give away a directorship, his money now, *this day,* if he could look like Frank, sense his youth and achieve his everlasting fame? I wondered about that. A kid from the "low, low life of Milwaukee" as head of Cleve House. How many men from Frank's class would stand in awe if they could see him, and how many suspected when they voted him their leader that this was the way it would turn out, even though he was already a junior champion as a schoolboy and national clay court champion at seventeen? A poor boy making good in a free society has an American touch. For all I knew, Frank Parker in 1984 was barely making it economically (but I doubt that), yet how grand he seemed. How fit. I do not want to overemphasize the obvious: except for Sarah Palfrey, every champion I had interviewed had overcome layers upon layers of American class strata, and now they stand at or near the top, not just as athletes but as people. Listening to Frank Parker talk about Lawrenceville was like seeing an old Hollywood movie. He could be Jimmy Stewart or Henry Fonda or Robert Montgomery. He echoed the story lines that movie moguls would peruse beside swimming pools in the glorious California sunshine. I felt I was listening to a miracle, but the kind of miracle we all believe in.

Parker is the only man now living who has won the boys, the juniors, and the national championships. Budge and others had won the juniors and then won at Forest Hills. Frank won the boys at fifteen. He does not want people to forget that. It was a time in his life when the name Parker was already absorbing Paikowski. He had to change his name because umpires calling points from their chairs couldn't pronounce it. He won the juniors again at sixteen and was in the top ten at seventeen years old.

So I plunged: "How would you do against McEnroe in your prime?"

He dodged the question. "Oh, that's difficult to say. I would love to have played him. I don't see where he would force me off the court. I'm sure that we would have had long rallies. He's no different than other great men I have played with in my era. We had Johnny Doeg, who had the best serve I have ever witnessed . . . the ball would come egg-shaped."

"Doeg?"

"Johnny Doeg was runner-up to Tilden at Forest Hills. Doeg also won the doubles twice, playing with George Lott."

"How about Vines?"

"I played against Vines in Pasadena. I worked out with him just before he went on tour with Fred Perry."

"How did you do?"

"I was sixteen then. Oh, he hit the ball hard, and on a given day he was hard . . . he had a low trajectory over the net. But when that wasn't working, anybody could beat him straight sets. When he was off, people beat him who never should have beaten him."

"When you were a kid growing up in Milwaukee and then in New Orleans, who were your heroes?"

"Tilden. We played when I was a junior and he was past his prime, and then we played during the war. To me, he was the greatest player of all time."

"Outside of tennis, were there other heroes?"

"Bobby Jones, the golfer. I play golf some. And Babe Ruth."

"I mean outside of sports. Say, if I came in your house when you were a kid and asked you that question, you wouldn't say Abraham Lincoln?"

"No. All sports figures. No, not Lincoln. I didn't know Abraham Lincoln. He was before my time."

"What was your greatest singles victory?"

"Winning at Forest Hills against Billy Talbert. I had strived for that victory for seventeen years. I had reached the finals four times. I lost to Ted Schroeder, won it twice against Billy, and lost to Jack Kramer when I had taken the first two sets. You see, in 1944 when I first beat Billy Talbert, I had been out on Guam all year in the Army. I don't think I'd played a match all year. So when I got leave to go to Forest Hills and won it, that was my biggest moment in tennis."

"Who was your favorite doubles partner?"

"Segura. We didn't play that often, but when we did play in tournaments, we won most of them. Then Gonzales. We hit it off awfully well. We won Wimbledon in 1949 against Mulloy and Schroeder. Gonzales and I played seven times and won six championships. Then we both turned pro. After Wimbledon in 1949, Gonzales, Segura, Kramer, and I went on tour and toured ninety-one cities."

"On that tour, the big match was Kramer versus Gonzales. You and Segura were second tier, I would suppose."

"Yes, and Segura killed me indoors. I had always beaten him outdoors, but indoors he just killed me."

I thought, so he didn't just vanish after 1949. He toured as a pro but had fared poorly. Parker was still firing away, but nobody was feeling his shots.

"Do you think the Army messed up your career?"

"No. We were all in it. It would have been nice if there had been no war. But, no, we were in it together. It hurt Kramer and Mulloy and Budge. It hurt all of us but . . . no. You take that sort of thing. Look at Ted Williams. He lost at least three years."

At the mention of Jack Kramer, my mind flew off track for a moment, and I could not resist asking Frank Parker for his version of the disputatious 1946 Davis Cup match against Australia. I wanted to check out Mulloy's story. Gardnar had said that Frankie Parker was the only member allowed to bring his wife, that he had been assured a singles berth. Talbert and Mulloy would play the doubles. The other obvious singles player was Jack Kramer, the best in the world at the time.

"Yes. I told Pate, the captain, that if my wife didn't go, I wouldn't."

"You loved your wife?"

"I loved her very much. We were married thirty-two years before she passed away twelve years ago. I never remarried. We had no children," he added.

"So you went down there, and what happened?"

"Jack Kramer brought along his friend, Ted Schroeder. Now Ted had not won a tournament all year. He had no record whatever.* In the doubles (after Talbert dropped out because as he had said, his game was "off"), Gardnar and I played Kramer and Schroeder and beat them every time. In the singles, in the practice for the challenge round, I beat Ted Schroeder all of the time."

"So how did Ted Schroeder get to play?"

"Well, Perry Jones controlled the Southern California Tennis Association, and in so doing he controlled Kramer and Schroeder. And he wanted them to play."

"I still don't understand why you didn't play the doubles, accepting for

* Not quite. Ted Schroeder and Jack Kramer teamed to win the Pacific Southwest doubles in 1946.

the moment about Schroeder being given the singles slot because of Perry Jones' influence."

"When I didn't get the singles, I refused to play the doubles. I said, 'No thank you.' "

"When you returned to the States, Billy Talbert said that you 'lambasted' the team captain, Walter Pate, for giving into Perry Jones."

"Yes, I called it the 'fickle finger of Pate.' "

"When I get to California, I am going to ask why a national team should be manipulated so much by one man, a man like Perry Jones."

"I think you will find that the Davis Cup has a history of Davis Cup captains choosing the wrong men at the right time. It happened with Vines, and it happened with others. For instance, they tried to split up a great doubles team, Allison and Van Ryn, at Davis Cup level. It was ridiculous. Favoritism plays a role in this."

"In your personal history of the great moments in playing tennis, how would you rate Davis Cup play?"

"In my time, if you didn't play Davis Cup, you were nobody. It was the tops."

"Now, looking back over your life—you are a widower, you live alone— you must think about things . . . what people do you respect the most?"

"Eisenhower was a great leader. Churchill. Then you get into entertainment. I went to work for MGM as an assistant director in special effects. Gary Cooper got me my job. I played tennis with Robert Taylor and Errol Flynn. I got to know Garbo."

"Flynn keeps coming up. I guess he was the best in the Hollywood crowd."

"Yes, he was."

"But getting back to MGM. Was that a flashy life? Did you get caught up in Hollywood and the hoopla?"

"No. I was married at the time and had to support myself. It was before the war, and I was ranked and played in the tournaments, but I had to work. I started out riding a bicycle around the MGM lot, delivering blueprints. Finally I got into special effects. I sold tickets at the Santa Anita Racetrack. I did a lot of things to keep going."

"Did you ever get any money under the table?"

"That is a good question. I would tell people to handle it with my wife, Audrey. So when people ask me, I can say no, I never received any money. But she did. My wife took the money."

"Gardnar Mulloy was clear on that point, that he did get paid."

"We all did."

"Others say they never made a nickel."

"I would disagree. I had to borrow money to play tennis. I went into hock. You couldn't do it unless you were a rich person."

"Now, going up to the postwar time when you were a pro and playing with Segura and Kramer and Gonzales, how did you do financially?"

"Not well. I signed on for $16,000 or $18,000, but I had to leave the tour. [As mentioned earlier, his record indoors was dismal.] I then went into

25. Frank Parker

the corrugated box business. A fellow had seen me play tennis and asked me what I was going to do after the tour ended. I said I didn't know. So he said, 'How would you like to sell boxes?' So I did. I sold for thirty years and then retired from the Champion Paper Company. I had a friend here at McClurg's, and now I am the director of tennis. It was a chance for me to keep on working, and I am glad I took it. At my age . . ."

"You look at least twenty years younger than your age. Do you attribute that to tennis?"

"Yes. I always took care of myself. I never had a cigarette in my life. Until I was forty, I never took a drink. In California, when you say Vines and Perry were running their Beverly Hills Tennis Club, I was living a quiet life and kept to myself. I didn't have the means to join in. I wasn't wealthy."

"If you had to rank the top five tennis players in the world, who would you pick?"

"I'd say Tilden, Budge, Vines, Perry, and Jack Crawford."

"You'd put all of those above McEnroe?"

"I'd say that Gonzales, Kramer, and Laver could take care of McEnroe."

"And they are not in your top five?"

"No."

For a moment, Frank began to talk about the composition of the carpet we had played on. He said it was called Bolltex, and all you had to do was wash it and vacuum it, and they'd had the same carpet for thirteen years. But as he was talking, I was thinking of a subtle magnanimity in his character. Earlier on he told me that he admired Sarah Palfrey, the only Wimbledon champion whom I had met who had been born into a family with money. He said that she should get a lot of credit. She would have distractions that he and the others did not have. In effect, it would have taken more fortitude for her than for him to make it to the top. For him, tennis was the way you fought your way up—a phrase that was almost identical to what Pauline Betz had used. He also had said that when Billy Talbert was in Australia for that first Davis Cup match after the war in 1946, he had diabetic episodes. Talbert had not told me that. Talbert had simply said that he was off his game. Frank told me that Tom Brown, Jr., who was also on the squad, had been sick. Nobody thus far had mentioned that. It seemed to me that Frank Parker was trying to give credit where credit was due, even including a salute to a society woman, coming, as it were, from a poor Polish immigrant's kid. The man was uncommonly fair. No wonder Billy Talbert did not play the doubles. No wonder Tom Brown had little chance. And bless Sarah Palfrey for her determination in spite of conflicting opportunities.

"If you could live your life all over again, what would you do to change it?"

168

"In my personal life, I would like to live it over again as it was. I had a wonderful life."

"How about the larger world, the world outside yourself?"

"I'd like to eliminate hunger."

"Would you part with some of your own money if it would go to a worthy cause toward that end?"

"Yes. If it would help a worthy family, yes."

"Your father died when you were one, so your mother must have been a strong influence on your life."

"Yes. But so was Mercer Beasley."

"If you hadn't met him, being a Polish kid from Milwaukee, might you have ended up in a factory or working in a saloon?"

"Absolutely. I could have been building cars in a plant, working . . ."

"So, in effect, you would say you owe everything to Beasley and tennis and then to Beasley's wife."

"Yes. She was a great woman. Ellsworth Vines was coached by Mercer Beasley. Bitsy Grant was coached by Mercer Beasley."

"Why don't you ever enter any of these senior tournaments? I have a record book here . . ."

"Number one, I had pleurisy and pneumonia and my breathing got shallow. Then I had a herniated disc operation that has pretty much healed. But I said, 'What for? Why should I knock myself out?' I did play in the Grand Masters for about six years with Torben Ulrich, Tom Brown, Frank Sedgman, Gardnar Mulloy . . . there were eight of us. I would always meet Ulrich or Frank Sedgman, who are ten years younger than I am, and get waxed. Mulloy and I would always say, 'Give us someone else we can beat.' "

"Was there anyone over the seventeen years that you were ranked whom you didn't like, wouldn't want to sit beside, that sort of thing?"

"I didn't mingle with the players. My wife and I would go to the movies or to the hotel room to read. After the locker change, I'd get the hell out of there."

"One thing that keeps coming across is your quiet life. Other players have told me that they got contacts in the business world. You had to scrape for everything. Didn't you ever meet some wealthy guy who would kind of back you so that you could get out of, say, riding a bicycle around the lot at MGM?"

"No, not really. Once I got to know Huntington Hartford. We played together out in California, and I asked him for a loan of $2,000 so that I could go east and play some tournaments. He gave me the money, and I paid him back, every cent."

"Well, I guess what I am getting at is your image. Jack Kramer could walk down the street and everybody would say, 'Hey, there goes Jack Kramer.' But if you went down the street you would go unnoticed."

"Jack Kramer was smarter than I was. Or maybe more lucky."

"You know there is something in you that I have always liked. It is the quiet Gary Cooper style. You're the kind of guy who underplays himself and in the end gets the girl. Do you see that in yourself?"

"Yes," he laughed. "I can see it."

Once I was home on Martha's Vineyard, I called Frank Parker. I asked him what racquet he used and he said a Wilson, Jack Kramer, which, by the way, is a racquet many players used. I told him that there should be a round robin tournament between Frank Parker, Bobby Riggs, and Gardnar Mulloy. I asked, "Who would win it?"

"I spot Bobby three games for every set. The last time I played Mulloy was at the Evergreen Club in Chicago four or five years ago for $1,000 dollars. I beat him 6–2, 6–3."

"Well, I guess that promoter's dream went up in smoke." I laughed. He laughed along with me. No contest.*

As I finish this tribute to the quiet man of tennis, I think of him in the locker room. We had showered and were drying off. I looked at his torso. He was sixty-eight that day, and he looked like a Marine sergeant ready for battle. If looks mean anything in old age, Frankie Parker may have won another tournament. But he held titles ever since he was fifteen. As my father surmised, he is a swell guy, and to top it off, he looks it. In his birthday suit, on his birthday, I saw the kind of man I'd like to have been ten years ago. As for his personality, we were talking about his pupil, Wally Tamari: "I could almost see myself at his age as a ball boy in Milwaukee. I wanted him to love tennis the way I did. I could see myself in that boy."

Amen to that.

---

* From Frank Parker's point of view. In recent years both Mulloy and Riggs have been active playing senior *tournaments*. I think I'd bet on Mulloy because of his activity in ongoing competition. I also think Mulloy could now beat Riggs, five years his junior. In any case I'd still like to see the three of them play for money.

CHAPTER

11

George Lott:

They Broke
the Mold

Frank Parker waved good-bye, and I walked out into the cold chill of Chicago. He had said that it was a pleasure to have met me and that I clearly loved the game. I told him that it was a treat for me. The last minutes of our talk had been full of good-natured bantering, and then at the end he gave me a tip. He said, "Why don't you get a hold of George Lott?" George Lott? I knew of George Lott and had thought that he had passed away—gone to the grass of Wimbledon-in-the sky. But no. He was alive and right in Chicago and still played tennis. "He's quite a character," Frank said.*

I called George that night on a phone number supplied by Frank. He is still unlisted after all of these years. He sounded gruff, if not rough, on the

---

* Frank Parker and George Lott have a relationship that goes back many decades. Both from the Midwest (the shores of Lake Michigan), their competition has not been without humor. Maitland Edey, a writer of distinction, tells a story about the two men. "I was at Forest Hills, watching the national championships, and George Lott was playing Frankie Parker. I believe Parker was ahead and was taking matters lightly as George Lott became increasingly irritated. Parker was serving and wanted 'a lucky ball' and began searching around the court for it—he wanted to serve with it and end the match. Lott, finally filled with fury, picked up a ball over in the corner of his court and yelled across at Parker, 'Is this it, Frank?' 'Yes,' answered Parker, at which point Lott whacked the ball high in the air and out of the stadium."

171

26. George Lott and Harry Hopman

phone and agreed to meet the next morning at 10:30. We'd play at the Midtown Tennis Club and then eat lunch, and he would drive me to the airport. He didn't know where my hotel was—the Talbott—had "never heard of it," he said. But he'd be there.

So it was to be that I would meet one of the truly great sport personalities who still pace a playing surface. Indeed, George Lott is what you might call "a hot ticket" or "a pistol." He is part curmudgeon, part grandfather with a heart of gold, part ruffian, surely a rascal; but then maybe a sweetheart. All of these descriptive words come to mind when I think of George.

If you should meet George Lott in midtown Chicago in the dead of winter, huddled in the front seat of his car under an overcoat, his large face lined with memory and his broad shoulders made broader by his clothing, you could not help thinking of Carl Sandburg. *The city of the big shoulders. Hog butcher to the world. Player with the nation's railroads.* Such lines we learned in school sprung to my mind as I looked at George Lott. He could be down at the stockyards. He could be a police lieutenant or a tackle for the Chicago Bears, circa 1927. He could play with a railroad or butcher a hog. He had big shoulders, and he was Chicago as much as was Wrigley Field. He was from the movie age of Barton MacClane and Edward G. Robinson. I could see him snarl. I could see him laugh. I thought, "Holy Moses, what is this guy?"

We hurried over to the Midtown Tennis Club, and when we got to the locker room, I found myself crowded in with men who looked like chunky linebackers, bumping into each other within the aroma of sweat that pervaded the dressing area. Lott knew everyone, and I found that he used the club to train the De Paul tennis team. He was the tennis coach at a university famous for basketball. I saw his huge hands and thought of first basemen Gil Hodges and Ted Kluzewski. Although only six feet tall, he appeared much taller, and his weight at 225 pounds made him look like a man who had spent a lifetime as a bouncer.

Yet I was sure that for once I was going to beat a former Wimbledon champion. I didn't know his age, but I knew he was as out of shape as I was, and I suspected that he didn't give a hoot about training habits. He took charge of the locker room with a great enthusiasm. If Frank Parker thought I liked tennis, this hulk of a man adored it. I recalled that in 1926, Lott was in the top ten. That was fifty-eight years ago. I was four years away from being born. That alone made me realize that at last a Wimbledon winner would fall like a giant oak.

When George Lott takes the court, he goes out there in whites. He doesn't wear running pants like Frank Parker; he doesn't dress like a basketball player, as Billy Talbert put it. He won the juniors in 1923 and 1924 and the U.S. Clay Court Singles Championship in 1932, a year after Ellsworth Vines, a year before Frank Parker. As with Billy Talbert, I knew Lott's reputation rested in his doubles, but he wasn't ranked in the top ten for seven times for a weak singles game. Alas, I had noted that he got to second place in the rankings in 1931, again following Ellsworth Vines. But as I saw him test me with his ground strokes, I knew what transpired fifty years ago would not matter today.

The only trouble was . . .

I guess you could call it tenacity. Surely you could call it ball control. In any case, this is what happened. When we started play, I knew that I would win my serve as he was unable to get my reverse twist to his backhand in his backhand court. And my serve to the deuce court went in just fine. For once, my serve appeared flawless. I had been up late the night before and had a bad case of what was later diagnosed as severe bronchitis. Maybe this negative combination had done something positive for my serve. So I had him every other game. My problem then was how to break his serve and take the set. George can't move quickly anymore, so you would think that all I had to do was to hit the ball away from him. This I tried to do, but he kept his shots strong and deep and often down the line, and I couldn't get any momentum going. And his serve is indeed a miracle. He started to serve underhanded with such a spin that the ball bounced away at a ninety-degree angle. In order to retrieve this soft spin-away, I would lunge and then my racquet would get entangled in the net that separated one court from the other. If I moved way up on the underhand serve to get to it before it could spin too far away, he would sting me with a surprise overhand serve and get the point.

So Lott won his serve, and I won mine, and it went on until it was four–all, and I broke him. I broke him by getting to his blasted spin before my racquet could get snarled up in the net, and I'd tap it back. Because he could not run well, my tap would be a point. It worked for one game, which was enough for me to break him, and I took the set.

Set two was identical to set one. Finally at four-all, I broke through and held my serve to win. The giant oak had finally fallen, and we shook hands at the net, and I felt like Bill Tilden. I was back in the 1920s in a city famous during that time. We'd played about an hour of hard singles, and I had beaten a Wimbledon winner.

I celebrated at the bar by buying gleeful midwestern fellows drinks, and I loudly proclaimed that my life's ambition had been fulfilled. George Lott peered in at me and thought I was crazy as a June bug and departed. I saw him leave and paid my bill and caught up to him. He huffed and gruffed a bit, and then we went to his car.

The weather had changed. At noon Chicago was a surprisingly warm 50 degrees. I was sweating inside my heavy 1956 Rogers Peet overcoat, and my cough seemed to have worsened. George drove and we talked, and somewhere near O'Hare Airport, we found a Ramada Inn with a restaurant called Ferenci's. I knew as we entered the dining room that the customary interview was off. I had mixed patent cough medicines, wine, a couple of drinks at the bar with a wild change in temperature. In fact, I felt tipsy. Words, feelings, and nostalgia would rule my intellect, and typically our first topic of talk was about baseball.

"Who won the 1941 National League batting title?" he asked.

I was stymied. It was a question for which I would have had the answer in a second had it not been for the condition of my mind. I groped and finally offered, "Musial?"

"Yeah," he said. "I think it might have been Musial." He didn't know the answer either. (It was Pete Reiser.)

So I said, "How old are you, George?"

"What was Red Grange's number?" he replied.

Again the brain went empty. I didn't know. I said, "I can't remember, George."

"Seventy-seven," he answered and stared at me as he would stare at a dummy. He also looked proud. Three years shy of eighty, he could still play a good game of tennis. He looked hell-bent-for-leather and emitted a personality that would admit a wide latitude. I didn't mind being stupid with him, and it didn't worry me much that I might slur my words. He'd seen it all, and if I was losing control of my interview, I didn't care.

"Of course, I knew that," I said, referring to Red Grange's number. Meanwhile, I was thinking of the Brooklyn Dodgers but couldn't get a handle on the name Reiser, an idol of my youth.

And that was how it started off. I had a few and he had a few, and I had some sandwich with cheese in it, but I never finished it. Laughing and talking with George Lott, sometimes letting him finish an anecdote, then butting in, throwing my personality at him, knowing that within an hour or so I would be inside O'Hare waiting for my flight home, I flowed through lunch.

Luckily, however, I had my tape recorder on, and the conversation went something like this.

"I can't believe that you and Barnes beat Vines and Perry on the tour."

"Night after night."

"Night after night, you sure?"

"I said, 'Night after night.' "

"And what about you and Lester Stoefen against Vines and Tilden? Also night after night?"

"No, no, that was abbreviated. We beat them eleven to nine. But I wouldn't want to bet on that. It was damn close. Vines could play good doubles. He was the controlling factor. You know that Ellie beat me in the finals of the National singles the year I had beaten him three times. That was 1931. I had won the first set and had him 5–3 in the third set with a service break coming [it was 15–40], and he won. I had him in the fourth set at 5–3, and he won that one, too. It wasn't because I was playing bad. It was because Ellie could raise his game to unbelievable heights. He hit the ball so damn hard and close to the lines that there was nothing you could do about it."

"That's what Don Budge said. He told me that when Vines was hot, there was little you could do."

"I agree with Don, but when Donald says he didn't make any money from amateur tennis, that is a lot of bullshit. 'Course I don't know about Walter Pate [Budge's Davis Cup team captain], but when I played Davis Cup, our captains were extremely wealthy men."

"In other words, if you ran short of cash, they'd bail you out?"

"Yes."

I was groping. I hadn't realized that the old topic of money under the table had arisen in our drive in his Chevy station wagon, somewhere along the way.

Lott had played on the Davis Cup, starting in 1928. He was on a squad with Bill Tilden, John Hennessy, and Francis Hunter. In 1929 he lost both his singles matches in the challenge round with France: first to Borotra and then to Cochet, tennis immortals. His team captains were Joseph Wear, then Fitz-

Eugene Dixon, and in 1934 when Lott was playing doubles with Lester Stoefen and won, the team captain was R. Norris Williams.

"But the point, as I think Don Budge, in deference to him, would say, is that no one got paid outright on amateur tennis."

"That's true. We would just chisel."

I thought with that remark that the old buzzard was going to stick to his guns on this, and like Gardnar Mulloy, he was going to make a point of it. He said they chiseled in order to survive the tour. Rich men, team captains, helped them along. I let it ride. I kept to my position that being given money by rich friends was not exactly professionalism. It lay somewhere in the middle ground, and in any event with open tennis, it was all over.

This had become a running argument ever since I saw Gardnar Mulloy back in October. And though it was becoming a matter of some tedium—what with the great men of the game apparently disagreeing over a matter of expenses, largesse, or outright payment—there was a point to it. The underlying point is that there had been a time when the Davis Cup meant very much to the game of tennis. It was a romantic time when, as Fred Perry had said, "We would carry the flag. We always went first class." Just making the squad was everything, and failing meant more practice and still more practice. *Of course* there was money around supplied by wealthy benefactors who loved the game of tennis, who loved national competition. And, too, there would be the perquisites, the first-class tickets, the parties, the blazers, and maybe the money if you needed it—and who did not? And remember tennis is not included in the Olympics. The Davis Cup was and is the Olympics of tennis. When you took an ocean liner to England, no one expected you to eat grilled cheese sandwiches.

And speaking of practice and more practice, George Lott talked about the great von Cramm. I told Lott how he had helped Don McNeill, and indeed it was through von Cramm's care and training that McNeill won the French championships in 1939. "You know, I played von Cramm in France in 1930," he said. "I beat him 6–0, 6–0. If he was so good by 1939 to help McNeill, that shows how practice pays off." (At the time, I did not check my record book, but von Cramm had improved long before 1939. He won the French singles in 1934 and 1936.)

And thus our conversation ran. George listened to me talk about Don McNeill for a while, somewhat confused by it all—he had forgotten the ordeal of von Cramm's going to jail on a trumped-up charge of homosexuality on orders from Hitler—the aristocratic von Cramm would not support the Nazis—George thought he had been in jail during the war. But McNeill had played him *prior* to the 1939 championships when he had already been released. We rehashed this, and suddenly George said, "Don't say anything that isn't true because I have record books at home, too, and I will catch you."

176

Then he said, "You know Frank Shields? He was a hell of a guy. He and I would pal around together. I would get the girls that he didn't want. He was big and handsome . . . he was really something. We were in Paris one time with Lester Stoefen (he was a tall, blond guy) and Shields (now he's on the dark side) and they had the women in a parade after these two guys." Lott was chewing his food and talking, and I was chewing and talking, and the garbled tape reflected more mastication than cerebration as I knew it would when I sat down to eat.

"Who was the best player you ever saw play?"

"Tilden."

"Tilden could have handled Vines?"

"No doubt about it. On Vines' best day, Tilden would have broken it up. The same thing would have happened to Vines that *did* happen to Lacoste. Tilden would have upset his game."

"To view the women players. Just for fun, how do you think Alice Marble might do against Martina Navratilova?"

"Not too bad. I get the impression, and I may be wrong, that Martina doesn't like to be pressed. She's a little like Lendl that way. She doesn't have that real definite fighting spirit. Alice Marble might be able to apply that pressure. I think Billie Jean King might have been able to press her, too, but I don't think Helen Wills would have, as much as I like Helen."

"How about Helen Jacobs?"

"No way!"

Then he went back to Tilden. "One thing about Tilden, he would raise hell with a linesman, but he would never take a point that didn't belong to him. He was the fairest player I ever knew."

Tilden could wait. I wanted to go on about George Lott. He was born in Springfield, Illinois, from well-to-do parents. He was an only child and at about five years old moved to Chicago. He had been married and was still friendly with his first wife. He married again for a year. He lived alone but had "a lot of interests." He has a daughter, "who must be damn near forty by now." As he chewed his food and I slurped on coffee (and then before I could say, "Tennis anyone?"), he was back in the 1931 Davis Cup playing against Britain.

"We should have won the cup that year. We had Sidney Wood and Frank Shields, who were winner and runner-up at Wimbledon. And Van Ryn and I, well, no one came close to us in doubles anywhere. Frank beat Perry (10–8, 6–4, 6–2), but Sidney lost both his matches, and Austin beat Shields. We won the doubles, and it was 3–2 for Great Britain."

I was wondering why they had lost.

"What was your social life like over there? Did Frank Shields monopolize everything, lead the team astray?"

"No. Frank never monopolized anything. He was a hell of a guy."

"Did you go out at night?"

"No, we trained until the match was over. By that I mean we played tennis during the day, went to bed early, and ate three meals a day. We didn't do any running or take exercise. Then, after the matches, we went out. The Davis Cup was everything. I never forget when I made it. The first year that I made it, man, was I happy! My father came down to see me off on the *Twentieth Century* in Chicago, and he gave me $1,500, which I didn't need. He wanted me to have it as a present. One thing I regret in my life is why I didn't put that $1,500 away and give it back when I returned. Instead I threw it around. I regret that, and when I think of my father, I regret the things that I did."

As Lott spoke, I thought of my own father and how he would give me money and, true to form, I would blow it. And then one day he died, and it was too late to really say "thank you" and too late to give something back. It was too late to repay him for what he had given me.

Looking at George, robust at seventy-seven, I thought of my five children. The greatest thing they can do for me is to place a premium on exercise. If exercise (preferably some sport) comes first in your life, then the inevitable vices will always be minor and in control. You can't do well and be drugged. You can't do well and be fat. You must stay healthy to be able to exercise, or so I was thinking watching George Lott, and staying healthy made everything else work. I remembered Billy Talbert's use of the word "equation." Sport is part of that equation that controls your life. Money means nothing when you compare it to good health. Frank Parker and now George Lott had confirmed in Chicago what all the other champions had been confirming along the trail.

I asked George how he could almost beat me at seventy-seven, "when most people are already buried."

"Contrary to what people may think, I have always taken care of myself. I may go to a cocktail party and get loaded like everybody else, but then I might not take another drink for three weeks. Alcohol doesn't mean anything to me one way or the other. Hell, I like sports too much to let alcohol interfere with me. I go to basketball games, football games . . . I used to play baseball for the University of Chicago. I played shortstop and could have been a big leaguer, so Connie Mack told me, anyhow."

He went on. "I played tennis for three years at Chicago, going south every spring, and that meant I couldn't play baseball. Then in my last year, I said the hell with this, and our coach was Fritz Crisler—the great Princeton, Michigan, and Minnesota football coach—he was at Chicago coaching baseball, and he said, 'Come out for the baseball team.' So I played shortstop instead of going south for tennis and hit .380."

Now he, George Lott, is a coach, and he began to complain about the players on his tennis team. "I can't get them to think ahead. I don't know why you can't teach them strategy. *I* always had a plan. Remember Jacques Brugnon? A damn good Frenchman. Well, we would play doubles, and I would press up near the net and beg him to lob over me. For three years, he would lob, and for three years I would see it coming and step back and hit an overhead smash to put it away. I'd open the door and suck him in, and then I would close the door."

On this subject of strategy, I mentioned Fred Perry's "fiddle shot," how Fred would move up on a hard serve and "fiddle it back" on a short angle, drawing the server in and then pass him on the next shot. George interrupted me, "If Fred says he beat Vines on that tour, he's crazy. He didn't beat Vines. I was there."

(Earlier I'd mentioned Perry's supremacy over Vines. The facts backed George Lott. Vines won 86 matches to Perry's 71 in direct competition on the pro tour. Incidentally, the only player to have an edge on Vines was Don Budge, who won 22 out of 39 matches.)

And again George became contentious. I was talking about Frank Parker's great health and his amazing body at sixty-eight. "All he ever did was play tennis," said George. "He never drank and didn't chase around with broads. Hell, he didn't even play mixed doubles because his wife wouldn't let him."

Wallis Simpson strikes again, I thought, and remembered how Frank had said that he didn't care for mixed doubles and avoided it at tournaments. My mind drifted off: what was Audrey Beasley Parker like?

George brought me back to the moment, however. He mentioned Hartford and one of the first tournaments he had entered, and I told him about my two great uncles, Max and Ed Hart, who I was told were consistent winners in doubles for the state championship held in Hartford. We talked on about tennis in the old days and how it had "class."

I said, "There is etiquette. You would not call a ball out against your opponent unless you saw it out. If you didn't see it go out, you gave the other fellow the benefit of the doubt."

And George said, "I'll tell you something. I was in the semifinals at Forest Hills—now this is a big deal. It means I am one of the four best in the world. I'm playing Frank Hunter, Tilden's doubles partner. I won the first set, and we are at 4–4 the second set, and Hunter is serving at break point. We rally a while, and then I hit a backhand down the line that lands right on the chalk, and I can see it where it landed, and the chalk flew. And the linesman calls it in—well, Frank throws his racquet up in the air and implores the good Lord to witness this atrocity. So I (knowing that Frank thought the ball was out when it was in and the call was correct) threw the next two points. I had to respect my friend, Frank. Then when I tried to get back in, it was too late. I lost the game and the match."

"In other words, tennis has to be a gentleman's game or it won't work?"

"If you have a friend across the net and he goes into gyrations, you have to believe him, even though you know he is wrong. You have to believe him because he *thinks* he is right."

"It's a question of character, isn't it? Men of your age often compare tennis to boxing. You take the ring or center court, and you stand up and be counted."

"I'll tell you something. I am glad I'm a tennis player and not a boxer. I care nothing for getting hit on the nose."

I then went on to my familiar question. I asked him who were the top five players in his lifetime.

"Tilden, Budge, Kramer, Laver, and Vines," he said, without a moment's hesitation.

"Who was your favorite mixed doubles partner?"

"Betty Nuthall, who just died recently. We won the national mixed doubles twice. Her return of service made it easy for us."

I omitted asking him who his favorite partner was in the men's doubles. The record book showed that George won the U.S. title five times, winning first with John Hennessey, then twice with John Doeg, and twice with Lester Stoefen. He took Wimbledon two times, once with John Van Ryn and once with Stoefen. He won the French with Van Ryn. Something must have told me not to pin him down. But, as I have said, it was a freewheeling talk, and I was rolling along without giving much care to my questions, and he gave me the answer I wanted anyway. George said that he and John Van Ryn had never been defeated, never lost a match, but then he paused for a moment (I knew that Van Ryn for the most part played with Wilmer Allison, not George), and after that short pause, he reconsidered and said, "But Lester Stoefen was my favorite partner. We retired undefeated and went professional at the same time in late 1934. [That year they won Wimbledon against Borotra and Brugum and beat Allison and Van Ryn in the finals at Forest Hills.] That was when we went on tour against Tilden and Vines. We were ahead [11–9, he thinks], and Lester came down with a dose [venereal disease] and the tour ended."

"If you had your life to live over again, is there anything you would want to change?"

"Oh, I don't know."

"Across the board, I mean. In world affairs as well as your personal life."

"I think in 1931 after John Van Ryn and I won both Wimbledon and the French Championship, I should have quit tennis and gone to work."

"What *did* you do?"

"I kept playing through Forest Hills 1934, and then I turned pro for three years. Then I went to Bermuda as the head pro down there. Then I got drafted into the Army. After the war, I went back to teaching tennis again. It was the easiest thing to do."

"When you were a little kid, who were your heroes?"

"Ty Cobb. Later, Babe Ruth. Bobby Jones."

"Now that you look back from seventy-seven years, whom do you respect the most?"

"I respected my father the most. But you mean whom do I *admire* the most, but now you're getting into another thing. I can't understand why Congress voted a holiday for Martin Luther King, Jr. There are a lot of Americans who contributed more to this country than Martin Luther King, Jr. King helped the black people, and that was good, but they are a minority. How about Franklin Delano Roosevelt? How about Dwight Eisenhower or Harry Truman? I can think of dozens of people who contributed to the whole country."

"Do you believe in God?"

"I don't believe in a personal God. My mother was a Christian Scientist."

"Do you go to church?"

"No. I don't go."

"Do you believe that there is a supreme power somewhere?"

"No. I believe that the word 'God' means to love your neighbors and your friends."

"If you had some wisdom to impart to a young man growing up, what would you tell him?"

"Never take a called third strike. You know, you can translate that into a lot of things."

Of course, I knew what he meant. So much a man of action, the term "laid back" would be anathema to him. You move in, take advantage of the openings, don't let an opportunity pass you by. He's sorry that he didn't go to work—to real work after winning Wimbledon and the French championships.

I asked him about love.

"Do unto others," he said. "If everyone did that, we would have a better world."

It is conventional wisdom from an unconventional man. I recognized, as a fan, that this facet of my interviews continued to amaze me. I wanted something special from special people. As he talked about the Golden Rule, I realized that special people are the same as I am, only a little bit better at whatever it is that makes them special. It was as simple as that. Yet Lott had a flavor I was trying to capture.

"Look," he was saying, "there is no way you can believe in God. If you did, you'd have to believe that he created this whole mess." (As we talked, U.S. Marines were in Lebanon, and the Middle East was about to erupt again, and Lebanon was being ripped asunder by conflict.) He didn't like the space program. "If there were a God, our going up into space would be an interference." He stuck with his Golden Rule theory.

I asked him about monogamy. "Would you tell a young man or woman to find one person to love and stick with that person?" I was angling after my "solid home theory," which I suspected was important in creating confidence.

"No. The Golden Rule," he repeated. "I told you that already."

"But what price would you place on love? I mean human love. Is it a lot of junk?"

"No. I don't think that there is anything greater than being happily married. You know you have one person who is with you and by the same token, you are with her."

Like teammates.

George Lott was married for the first time for fifteen years to "a girl from Philadelphia," where he was working in the brokerage business. This job was his attempt at respectability after quitting the amateur circuit, before he went back to what he does not consider real work, to tennis. He worked for his Davis Cup captain, Fitz-Eugene Dixon, who was connected with Smith, Barney and had his own business in Philadelphia.

"He put me and Van Ryn both to work there. So I married a girl there, and it was all right. We are still friends. I wanted to quit and play tennis, and she wanted me to keep working, and she was right and I was wrong."

By now the waitress was trying to clear the table, and George was warming up. The waitress was going off duty. I tipped her, and we stayed on having coffee.

He told me about Shields. "Frank was one of my best friends [as he had said], but he wasn't one of the great players. His backhand was weak. He was my doubles partner in the national doubles, and it was one of the few times I ever lost. We should have had that match."

And Tilden. I had been waiting for this story because it illuminates both George and the immortal Bill Tilden. He had broached the subject earlier in the car.

George was playing Tilden in singles on the tour. They were in Cleveland, and George had won the first set. He was ahead 5–1 and 30–15 in the second set, with the match more or less wrapped up. But George erred badly. He quick-served Tilden to make it 40–15. Tilden complained and "was justified" and then "went to work." He took George apart, won the uphill set, and then took the next one to win the match.

"Tilden was so much better than anyone else that we would do anything to get his goat. We figured that anything we could slip by him was okay. No one could touch Tilden until 1928, and even then he came back and won Wimbledon in 1930, ten years after he first won it in 1920." (He won Wimbledon three times. Oddly and symbolically, Bill Tilden was never a runner-up.)

And much like the quick-serve, there was the time when George, in his zeal for an upset, again tried to slip one by on Bill Tilden. He was far ahead and had the match, and he called across at Big Bill and yelled, "Okay, Tillie," and Bill Tilden, whom everyone knew was a homosexual, heard "Tillie" and rolled up his long white sleeves and once more went to work. He took every game from then on, and George once more had pressed his luck too far. He had trespassed on the man's pride as before he had trespassed on the man's instinctive sense of fairness. "Tillie" had made him angry. A quick-serve had wounded him. By all accounts, a wounded Tilden was a dangerous man. Along with Bobby Jones, Red Grange, and Jack Dempsey, Bill Tilden ruled the 1920s, one quarter of a royal quartet.

"When Bill Tilden entered a room it was like a bolt of electricity hit the joint," said George Lott.

"At breakfast he would call 'Captain! My heavy cream.' He didn't want ordinary cream on his oatmeal. Boy, did the captains jump to attention and . . ." At that we were interrupted. George had imitated Tilden to such a degree that a new waitress came scurrying. "Heavy cream?" she asked.

"No, no," said George and waved her off.

But back to Tilden. "He would never show himself going into or out of a shower."

I asked why.

"I never figured it out," said George. And then he said, "Here's the thing about Tilden. He never fooled around with the kids he was genuinely trying to help, youngsters who traveled with him, kids he'd give lessons to. Where he got in trouble was when he tried to pick up ball boys and kids selling newspapers. He was a guy who had ascended the heights of society and was like some guy who could not lay a broad who was his equal. He had to go lower [to the newsboys]. I don't know if you can draw an analogy with that."

I thought I could. I had just read the biography of Dashiell Hammett who, as they say, had women coming at him from all directions, but preferred to go to Harlem for adventure in a whorehouse.

I had told George that Don Budge did not place Bill Tilden in his top five players of all time.

"I think Don is a bit off base there," he replied.

"Budge said that Tilden had no net game."

"He had one when he needed it. He seldom needed it. But let me tell you about the greatest I ever saw Tilden play. It was in France. Mind you, it was 1928 against René Lacoste. Now the year before, in 1927, when the

French won the Davis Cup, they began to feel that they had mastered Tilden. They had been trying to win for two or three years. Finally they got to him. So in 1928, the challenge round came around, and Tilden played Lacoste in the first match. He gave an exhibition of tennis that has never been equaled. Tilden used every shot in the game—topspin forehand, flat forehand, slice, chops, lobs, drop shots . . . even Lacoste after the match said—and he was the great baseliner of his day, much like Borg was in *his* day—he said, 'I completely lost my timing. I couldn't do anything.' " (Tilden won the match in typically dramatic fashion, 1–6, 6–4, 6–4, 2–6—he rolls up his sleeves—and finally, 6–3.)

Thinking of the 1–6 score in the opening set, I said, "Tilden was famous for letting people get way ahead and then catching up, to make good drama out of it."

"He did that," answered George, "but one time he was playing Cochet and had him two sets to one, and 5–1 at Wimbledon, and King Alfonso of Spain hadn't filled up his royal box yet, so Tilden decided to drag it out a bit, and the first thing you knew, his ass was out."

"In other words, Cochet beat him?"

"Yes."

"Now, on Vines," I said. "Most people seem to think that at his best, Vines was the greatest."

"*At his best*, he was as good as anyone, even Tilden."

"But he couldn't *beat* Tilden. You said Tilden would find a way to break up Vines' game."

"Yes, he would."

We let our dream match rest for a moment. Lott would no doubt agree that Tilden in top form was supreme. Vines in top form was also supreme. I let George stick to his first opinion that Tilden would find a way to win, all other factors being equal.

I told George what I had told others—I recalled a long talk with Pauline Betz on the subject. I said that I always thought that when Vines gave up tennis and switched to golf and then beat Ben Hogan in a playoff at the Tam O'Shanter in Chicago—that that was the greatest sports feat ever accomplished.

"Let me tell you about Vines and golf. On the Vines-Perry tour, Bruce Barnes and I were with them, and we played at night. [He'd already mentioned that in doubles, he and Barnes won consistently.] So we played golf in the daytime. At that time, I used to take $16 a day from Vines playing Nassau, and if you knew Vines, you'd know that he would walk up and down the street before going to the movies to see what movie cost less, no matter what was playing. Well, he went back to California after that tour, and he practiced his golf from sunup to sundown. All right, he got pretty good after that. I was living in Pittsburgh at the time, where they had the PGA that year. So Vines comes in and gets to the semifinals, which is pretty good. You know, all the golfers are playing. Well, I go to the locker room to commiserate with him, and he says, 'You want to play some golf?' I say, 'Sure,' and he says, 'Be here at 9:00 in the morning. I want to get my money back.' I said, 'Nothing doing.'"

27. George Lott: Hollywood, George?

Time was passing and the restaurant was empty. We were in that odd twilight time between meals that reminded me of long, long lunches back when I was in the publishing world. Sometimes we would keep talking and drinking coffee after lunch, and then we would look up in the gloom of cigarette smoke and see the cocktail crowd coming in, all dressed and ready for the evening, and we'd have a cocktail and keep on going. Phone calls would go unanswered in the office, an anxious secretary would be covering for Mr. Hart. If away, I would miss my plane home. Yet it was always (and perhaps perversely) thrilling to have that power to tell time to take a vacation. And that was what George and I were doing as he reminisced. He mentioned his friend Pola Negri. He talked of the golfer Bobby Jones. Then he said he spent two weeks as Charlie Chaplin's guest. Great names from the older generation rolled from his lips, and I could imagine a young George Lott back in the 1920s—Jones himself, were he alive, would be only five years older than George. And through it all, I had to keep reminding myself that he and I had just played tennis and that he had almost won. He'd taken me from the playing surface back to the days of my parents and to people whose names would live as long as the human race. I wondered what it would be like to live with Charlie Chaplin for two weeks, to pal around with Bill Tilden, to play golf with Bobby Jones. To me, there was no generation gap, as it is now called. George and his times began to blend into my world as a continuum. The essence of it was that I cared for the people he was talking about. Would my children grow up wondering what the writer Bill Styron was like, or the playwright Lillian Hellman, both of whom I know or knew? Did people under thirty give a damn about some of my contemporaries as I did about George's? Of course, the link that made my caring real was my father. My father passed on his enthusiasms, and I caught them. Here in Chicago, George was bringing up the same names, the same feelings I would have received far back in the 1930s and during the war, when my father and mother would sit with their cocktails and recall the good old days. There was no generation gap in my youth. We just went on with the same old show. Babe Ruth gave way to Ted Williams, and Vincent Lopez gave way to Glenn Miller; that was the difference. There really was no difference.

George was going on about Fred Perry. "Fred and I are great friends. Once I wrote an article about Fred beating Jack Crawford at Wimbledon [1934], and I said he was the greatest athlete I ever saw. Fred liked that, so every time we get together, he plays that tournament for me, match by match—year after year! And I'll come and sit down and I'll say, 'Okay, Fred, now get it over with . . .' You know he was great on discipline. He was a combination of a stone wall and a rabbit."

I steered the two-time Wimbledon winner and five-time U.S. champion back to doubles. I asked him who was the best doubles player he had ever seen.

He answered, "Jack Kramer. He had a great second serve. He put it within a foot of the line, and you don't run around those kinds. My philosophy of doubles is that you hold your own serve, and you do that by following the basic fundamentals. In terms of winning, you are only concerned with getting one break. You can do this two ways—with consistency or with speed. You take chances when you are receiving. You do *not* take chances when you are serving."

I interrupted him and repeated mention of Fred Perry's "fiddle shot," a term that amused me. I asked Lott if he ever moved up on a serve and kind of fiddled it back. I inadvertently mentioned Ellsworth Vines who would serve bullets and suggested that Fred Perry would fiddle them back.

"Look," said George. "The first match of the ninety-day tour, and I was on it with Barnes, I placed a bet at the Algonquin Hotel with Franklin P. Adams for $100. I bet on Vines. Well, Vines shows up with a temperature of 104 and doesn't tell anybody. Perry wins, and I lose my bet. After a few matches when Vines got well, he killed Perry. Just killed him."

We were repeating ourselves, but I went on. "It's funny," I said. "When I saw Fred Perry, he was under the impression that he had the edge on Vines. I guess as you get older, the memory plays tricks."

"The memory is like wine. It gets better as you get older."

And perhaps so does George Lott. He could have gone on forever, and I enjoyed two more anecdotes. The first one concerned the Davis Cup selection committees. "You want to hear about those committees? Go back to my time. In 1929 they selected me to play singles, and Tilden and Hunter to play doubles. Johnny Hennessy and I beat Tilden and Hunter every day for three weeks at five bucks a set. Hunter had beaten Borotra in Holland just before the challenge round. We had three weeks to practice in Paris, and Hunter was the logical man to play singles, and Hennessey and I were the logical team to play doubles. So the Davis Cup committee at 120 Broadway made me play singles, and Tilden and Hunter play doubles. We played, and I lost two singles, and Tilden and Hunter lost the doubles."

Another anecdote: "I picked Lester Stoefen out. He was from California and is now six feet under the ground, and I sent a telegram to the Davis Cup chairman, telling him to order me to play with Stoefen at Newport. The order came through, and we won, and then the next week we won the national doubles at Longwood, and the Davis Cup chairman is taking all the credit for selecting Stoefen."

I asked him to describe his greatest doubles match.

George said, "Johnny Doeg and I had a five-set match at the finals at the Longwood Cricket Club for the national championship. We were playing Allison and Van Ryn, a damn fine doubles team, and we got to 5–4 in the fifth set in our favor, and Doeg's serve. There were new balls coming up [requested by their opponents], and I was going around the net, and Johnny

28. From left to right: Perry, Bartzen, Seixas, Larsen, Trabert, Budge, Parker, and
Lott—champions all

comes up and says, 'Give me those blankety-blank balls!' and [George
laughs—heh, heh] three aces and one unreturnable serve. Boom, boom,
boom, boom. That kind of sticks out in my mind.

"You see, I had been thinking that maybe Johnny's serve might be short,
even though he had one of the best serves of all time, and I said to myself, 'I'll
just slip over and cut off the return.' But I didn't have to. Just boom, boom,
boom, boom."

After that we walked into the late afternoon. George drove me to the
airport, and we kept on talking. Were it not for my flight home, I would
have sat in that restaurant much longer, putting in my two cents' worth,
butting in on his stories, correcting him if I could. (For instance, he was
wrong about 1929. Tilden did not play doubles with Frank Hunter in the
Davis Cup against France. John Van Ryn and Wilmer Allison played the
doubles and won. It is true that George *did* play singles and lost both times.
Tilden split his singles, and Frank Hunter did not play at all.) What I
wanted was what I got: I was part of a real exchange that combined facts,
supposition, horse manure, all a grand overlay to the pleasure that comes
from being a sports fan.

I do not recall what we said as we parted. I have a feeling that we were arguing about baseball. That was the way it began, and no doubt in a way that was how it went. Previously, George had said that he couldn't believe that Frank Parker and Gardnar Mulloy had beaten Ted Schroeder and Jack Kramer in Australia as they practiced for the 1946 Davis Cup. I insisted that they had. I think he was trying to get a rise out of me. I love that kind of thing, and after ten interviews in which I was somewhat restrained, I had found in George Lott the kind of guy who didn't mind letting his opinions fly. Soon after leaving his car, I was flying, and I was thinking, not for the first time, that I was sorry to be born too late. Imagine playing with Tilden and Vines. Imagine being told by Connie Mack that you could be a big leaguer. I was empathizing with George Lott.

In the 1930s, when I used to buy baseball cards, there was cheap gum in the package that tasted a little like spearmint but had its own particular flavor. My mother wouldn't let me chew it because she thought it would rot my teeth. I chewed it anyway, and I could *taste* it as I sat strapped into my seat in a jumbo jet.

And, incidentally, George thinks I beat him 6–4, 6–1. My notes say 6–4, 6–4. Who knows? Even our recent match has blended into the mishmash of memory.

I called George Lott after I got home to thank him. He said, "Come back and we'll play again. Only this time, for money."

"Typical," I thought, and then later I said to myself, "Well, why not?"

PART TWO

The Wild West

CHAPTER

⌇*12*

Gertrude "Gussie" Moran:

"Winning never turned me
on all that much."

Back in the 1950s and 1960s, my father rented a small cottage in Palm Springs at a very conservative dude ranch called the Smoke Tree Ranch. There he and my mother, who by then was very incapacitated from multiple sclerosis, spent their winters. My father rode horseback every day and lawn bowled and looked after my mother, and in the evenings they had their drinks and watched television and reminisced. Once a winter, I would visit them.

But now it was 1984. I was going back to Palm Springs, and I could feel the same sadness and the odd, quirky loneliness of my father who, in late middle age, had still been an attractive man, and always a loyal husband and a devoted nurse to his wife. As compensation, he had his riding and his lawn bowling, but if he was late for a meal, late coming back from the stable, my mother attacked him with verbal viciousness.

I was filled with such thoughts: my parents, the ranch, the chance meeting with movie people who came to ride or live there. Walt Disney had his home at the ranch, and so did song-and-dance man George Murphy, who later became a U.S. senator. It was a Republican hangout, and probably my father, who had money but never thought of himself as being rich, was the poorest "dude" on the ranch. With a big grin, he would meet me at the airport or at the old train station, and I would hang about, playing some tennis and dating the young women who worked in the office. It was a time to be

193

close to my parents, but it was sad because I knew they were not happy. They were just there—my father wheeling my ill, enfeebled mother into the dining room at night and then back for their TV. Walt Disney never dropped by for cocktails. The older members of the staff did. I suspect that, because of my mother's drinking, their only real friends on the ranch were the employees.

I arrived in Los Angeles full of fire, which overlapped the foreboding I held deep inside of me. First I would see Jack Kramer and then go on to Palm Springs. Interviewing Jack Kramer and playing with him was foremost on my mind. As it happened, a friend from Martha's Vineyard, Lennie Baker, who is a star for the rock group Sha Na Na, had taken a small apartment on Hollywood Boulevard, and I was to stay with him while I visited Jack Kramer. I went directly to Lennie's place, and we went out to dine in what he described as "a restaurant where screenwriters ate." It was very casual, and the food was adequate, but who could tell a screenwriter from a car salesman? I surely couldn't, nor could Lennie, so we just ate and talked and went home to sleep. For all I knew, the greatest wits in show business could have been at the next table. I felt let down. Where was Jimmy Durante, who had once joined me at the Brown Derby in 1960? Where was Ginger Rogers, whom I met at a piano bar in Lake Tahoe? Where was Bob Mitchum and Ava Gardner, whom I got drunk with in New York in 1949? Where was Prince Mike Romanoff, whom I dined with in New York? All were either dead or old and settled, and in any case they didn't write screenplays. To make the point clear, the joint was without glamour. But it was good to be with Lennie, and I slept like a dog in the sun, on a couch in his apartment, while the rather rotund Baker slept in a bed big enough for the four Marx brothers.

The next morning, I called Jack Kramer and got a rather frantic wife. Jack was sick with the flu and so was she and so, she guessed, was everyone else in Los Angeles. "Where did it come from?" she wondered. I told her I didn't know, but I had had the flu already, back East. "Probably from the Mexicans," she opined, and I suggested that the Russians were sending it down from a satellite. She paused for a second and suggested, "Come back in a week. Jack will be better then but *no tennis*. That is out of the question," said Mrs. Kramer.

I looked at Lennie and he at me, and we both said, "Now what?"

"Gussie Moran," I said. "I bet I can get to see her. She still lives in Santa Monica, and we can drive down there. She'll play tennis with me. Gorgeous Gussie Moran."

Lennie had not heard of Gorgeous Gussie, who was before his time, but when I reached her on the phone, and she said, "Come on down," he was glad to drive me.

Lennie had been lent a huge blue Mercedes, and we slipped out of the garage that went with the apartment building and was kept under heavy security. I told one of the watchmen that he looked like Nat King Cole, and he beamed. Lennie asked him to sing, but he demurred.

Like two kids, we tooled down the various highways and roadways that are familiar to movie fans and finally found Gussie's house. She lives on Ocean Avenue in a Victorian structure wedged in among a row of condominiums. It was an eccentric setting, but we both loved it—at least one person had the guts to save a home from the developers. There was a small green front lawn, fragrant with shrubbery, and on the top right of her house was a turret so that you could go up there and stare out at the Pacific and watch the great sailing ships of a bygone era sail by. I suppose no one had been up there in years, but I fancied that, when the house was built, you would have seen square-rigged whaling ships of the seven seas and trading schooners working their way north toward Alaska or south with seal skins. It was a most romantic setting, and Gussie Moran lived there alone with her memories.

Now, Gussie Moran is not one of the great champions. In a way, she does not belong in this book along with the immortals of the game. Yet I remembered Pauline Betz telling me that Gussie was a lot better than people thought. The trouble had always been that designer Ted Tinling had fashioned for her a tennis outfit that was somewhat sensational. For Wimbledon she wore lace panties that became the talk of the world—not just the tennis world. Sex had entered the hallowed grounds. But Gertrude Moran was indeed a champion. In 1949 she won the ladies' indoor singles and the ladies' indoor doubles. I do not know how many local tournaments she has won, but

29. Gussie Moran

she was good enough to go on the pro tour with Pauline Betz and Bobby Riggs. And what was important to me was that she had a name. I am a fan, and fans like famous people, even though they do not necessarily get into the Hall of Fame.

Gussie met me with a smile. Her figure is still trim, and she wears her hair in a manner I would describe as Jennifer Jones Oriental. It is the color of india ink and is straight, and if you wanted to see a Caucasian (Jennifer Jones in *Love is a Many Splendored Thing*) trying to look Asian, you can get the picture I have of Gussie. She wore a touch of makeup and a bit of eye shadow. She led me to a round table where I could place my tape recorder and offered me a choice of Sanka or near beer. I chose Sanka. Lennie, who had a date with an oculist, was gone, leaving us alone in a house that should have been on the New England coast, dark paneled and somewhat spooky, with ancient secrets and family ties. Indeed, it was her parents' home, and she had retained it. It was hers, and she was not selling.

Over the years, I had seen many houses like Gussie's, domiciles that belonged to family. I had been to Hawaii at a house high on a mountain, owned by a man named Montague Richards, and it too was strewn with the haunt of older generations, and it too was a family house. Like Gussie's, it offered a pervasive sense of the sea, of a vast ocean and bravery. People move about in our country, and you find modern art and modern furniture and fancy bathrooms with sunken tubs, and a strewn transiency. With Gussie, I found the old days. I loved that feeling and settled in, her gracious ways and winning smile entrancing me. Gone was the razzmatazz, but like the woodwork, she appeared genuine. It had been thirty-five years since her last major victory. The young brunette with the lace panties and the pretty figure had transformed herself. As I would find out, Gussie Moran is a serious adult and has had her share of troubles and her share of growing up. She did not hang on to tennis—forever suntanned, forever stroking a ball at some club. She had turned herself around and inside out and came out someone other than what she had been or what everyone thought she had been. Pauline Betz and Shirley Fry were still Pauline and Shirley. Gussie Moran could pick another name, if she chose. My hunch was that I was with a person who had altered herself dramatically. The past had not worked for her, so why keep it going?

We started out talking about how hard it was to get back into competitive tennis once you have left it. Gussie brought up the case of Maria Bueno. Maria, who had won the singles at Wimbledon three times and had taken the U.S. singles title three times, had dropped from competition, and then decided she wanted to come back to the big time. The tournament she chose for her return was closed to her unless some entry should default, and then she would be able to fill that slot—provided, of course, that it was not seeded. To get into the tournament any other way, she would have to qualify—that is, to play in some smaller, insignificant events and prove herself. Now this is like telling Marlon Brando, who has not made a movie lately, that he has to go out and do summer stock for a while so that those in charge can be sure he still has his touch.

And those in charge were, said Gussie, Billie Jean King and her group. Of course, this was what Althea Gibson had suggested when she recalled wanting to return at forty-five. She said they told her to qualify. I mentioned this aspect of the Althea story to Gussie, and she replied, "Althea represented something. She represented an ideal. She was the first black to open it up for all of them. For her to qualify, in order to play on those stinking asphalt courts at Forest Hills—I hope she didn't play."

Gussie, who preceded Althea Gibson by almost a decade, tells of how they had met at the Town Tennis Club in New York when Gussie was married to a man named Eddie Hand and was working at a New York radio station. They had been playing tennis, and she invited Althea and her manager to her apartment, where she cooked a meatloaf and Eddie, her husband, poured cocktails. They stayed up until 3:00 in the morning, and Althea was singing into a recording machine, and finally the management called to tell them to cut out the noise.

"She had a great sense of humor," Gussie said. She recalled the time when Althea was the best woman player in the world and was walking back from a victory at Forest Hills. "She spotted me sitting by the tea garden, or whatever it was, and she started to come over. The trouble was, she had to get over a fairly high hedge, and rather than just walk around it, she started to lift one long leg over the hedge and jump it, and at the last moment realized how unladylike it would look, and she stopped and came around through an opening."

Once again going back to Maria Bueno having to qualify, Gussie said, "It was degrading." But then she gave an example of the politics involved in tournament play. "In 1971 I was doing freelance work for Kodel, a branch of Eastman Kodak, and teaching tennis here at the marina. Now Kodel is a manmade fiber that they used in tennis clothes, and I was sent East to promote it, to do television and radio interviews, that sort of thing and to get into the tournament at Forest Hills. Well, I got in without any problem.

"Now there were a lot of young girls who were ranked in the East, and they were irate. I think they had a right to be because after all, I wasn't any Maria or Althea. Also, I had not played in a tournament for twenty years. But because Kodel was one of the sponsors of the tournament, Billy Talbert put me right in. Of course, I was beaten in the first round, but it wasn't because I wasn't playing well that year. I had been playing hard at the marina. It was just that I didn't even know what I was doing. It had been twenty years since my last tournament. There was a lot of complaining after that—not to my face, but, you know . . ."

In 1949 when Gussie won the indoors, she was playing on a gymnasium floor. It was very fast, and by playing on wood, she learned to like grass. "What I liked about grass was that if you made a slice or a drop shot, it was a slice and a drop shot. As Bill Tilden said, 'If you hit it correctly, you could count on it working when you played on grass.' "

I asked her about the great Tilden. I said, "In the men's group, who would you say was the greatest?"

"For sentimentality's sake, I would say Tilden. I only saw him when he was over the hill, but he could still take a set from Kramer or Budge or Gene Mako [Budge's outstanding doubles partner]. I loved Bill. Toward the end, he was sort of like a mother hen. He was bitchy and kind of chirping like a bird, but I loved Bill. I had some very happy moments with that man. But I suppose when you rank them, you say Tilden, Budge or Budge, Tilden. But I am not really qualified to answer your question."

"How about the Frenchmen whom Tilden battled against?"

"I got to know some of them. I knew Borotra and Cochet, and I loved Brugnon. You know, when I was playing against these men, they must have thought it was funny. Here they were, men who had forgotten more about the game than we would ever learn and, well, we must have looked like a bunch of little snots to them, walking around asking for extra this and extra that, demanding things."

At that moment, Lennie Baker returned, and we talked about her house, which she said had been built around 1890. I could tell that she was pleased to meet a member of Sha Na Na. As it happened, it was a group she liked and watched with pleasure on television.

But I pressed on, Lennie staring at the anomaly of a home amidst the concrete beachfront of Santa Monica.

"If it had not been for tennis, how do you think your life would have come out?"

"Well, I always wanted to become famous, and at about eleven, I took up tennis as a way to become famous. I thought, wow! if I could beat Helen Wills Moody, I'd be famous. Why I wanted fame so much, I don't know. When I was in elementary school, I was a puppeteer. In high school, I wanted to be an actress. Later on when I was nineteen, I fell in love with a man, and really then all I wanted was to be married and have children."

"Do you have any children?"

"No. I wouldn't want any now particularly, but I guess I wouldn't mind a couple running around the house, however."

"How many times were you married?"

30. Gussie and her panties

"Two and a half times."

"What do you mean?"

"One was an annulment."

"Who was that with?"

"My first husband, Tom Corblly, an ex-RAF pilot and later an architect on the nuclear submarine *Nautilus*."

"How do you get annulled after you had been in bed together?"

"You lie. There were awful emotional problems."

"Did Mr. Corblly have them from the war?"

"No. I did."

"Who were your other husbands?"

"Eddie Hand and Bing Simpson."

"You asked Lennie if he wanted a near beer. Does that mean that you don't drink?"

"No, I love to drink. I'm on the wagon now, trying to be good to myself."

"When you were on the tour, did you drink and smoke?"

"Well, I didn't smoke, but I carried them with me and, yes, I always had cigarettes in the apartment. Eddie [Hand] smoked."

"Back to those emotional problems—have you been in therapy, say for years and years?"

"No, not years and years, but from time to time. I enjoyed it."

And then, without stopping, Gussie looked over at Lennie and said, "I just loved your show [now off the air]. I just think it is my favorite."

I told her that "Sha Na Na" was without doubt the world's worst television show, just to get a rise out of Lennie. But he beamed at Gussie, suddenly in heaven. I thought, here we were talking about emotional problems, the irritation of Maria Bueno, who could not make a comeback when the comeback is the apex of sport, listening to a rundown of marriages, and now suddenly we were talking about "Sha Na Na." It was good fun. I realized that for a moment I had entered her life and was a buddy who could josh and horse around and could open up, and I felt that we had known each other for years. Not just Gussie and I, but Lennie as well. It was homey in that house—a feeling now further affirmed as she kept complimenting Lennie, and Lennie, the large rock-and-roll sax player, smiled like a kid at a candy counter.

"What would you say was the best time in your life? What I liked was when you were on that radio program with Marty Glickman, the one that came after the Brooklyn Dodger baseball games when the Dodgers played night games."

"That was one of my best jobs. I liked that a lot. But I'll tell you, the best job I had was when I put my own dough into it and had my own manufacturing business and sold my own tennis clothes. I lost my shirt on it, but it was a great time.

"As far as the best time in my life, I think I am looking forward to it."

"What about the 'Gorgeous Gussie' period? Wasn't that a great time for you?"

"No. It was more of an embarrassment. Although I was twenty-seven when the lace panties thing appeared, I was emotionally unstable and couldn't handle it. I was reacting to it like a seventeen-year-old girl. I was reacting to my love life like a seventeen-year-old girl, too. I had not matured."

"Were the other women tennis players jealous of you during your 'Gorgeous' period?"

"No, I wasn't aware of it. But I got some trouble from men. I ran into some really nasty men who would really take off at me."

"Now that you have matured, are you a feminist?"

"No, not really. I am for the causes, and I respect women's rights, but I'm not political."

"Do you go out with men, meaning you haven't given up on them?"

"Of course I go out with men. But if a girl friend comes to town, I will go out with her for dinner and stuff, and I'll have her as a houseguest, but *of course* I go out with men, if I choose to go out. I go out with girls, too."

"If you had your life to live over again, is there anything you would want to change?"

"I am very happy that I was born."

"And the way things progressed?"

"I think we create our own pits."

"You wouldn't say, 'Gee, I wish I were born with a million dollars and a silver spoon in my mouth'?"

"Oh, it would be nice to have money, but I wouldn't swap a million dollars for my parents."

"How about heroes and heroines?"

"Amelia Earhart. Let's see . . . my mother cut out current events from the newspapers and kept them in a book, and I was very aware of Charles Lindbergh, Mahatma Gandhi, and Al Smith who ran against Hoover."

"Now that you are your age . . ."

"I'm sixty."

" . . . whom do you admire the most, looking back over your life?"

"I always admired Clare Boothe Luce. I respected Eleanor Roosevelt; Marie Curie for her work on radium . . ."

"It's odd you don't mention any athletes."

"No . . . Well, I admired Babe Didrikson, but no . . . I really respected Eleanor Roosevelt. In fact, I enjoyed reading the Roosevelt books by Joe Lash so much [Eleanor and Franklin; Eleanor: The Years Alone]. Just to think of the matriarch Roosevelt woman, Franklin's mother. We always thought that Eleanor was so strong. But when you think of her mother-in-law! Franklin was lucky he had Eleanor. A weaker woman would have crumbled."

"Do you believe in God?"

"Yes."

"Do you ever go to church?"

"No, but I'm thinking about it. My father was Irish, and my mother was German, and I was first brought up as a Christian Scientist, but they had to get me out of there because they said I didn't hurt when I did hurt, and I was really brought up Presbyterian."

"How would you define God?"

"God is something that hears you when you talk."

"You mentioned earlier about emotional upheaval. Can you explain that?"

"My emotional upheavals came strictly from my involvement with men. But when I say men, I mean a man. It wasn't that men came like a box of chocolates."

"Would that detract from your training as a tennis player—hold you back?"

"It didn't decrease it. It confused it. A man could be three thousand miles away, and I would be entered in a tournament, and just a phone call would strike me and make me sort of volatile. It would divert my psyche from tennis into an emotion that was really unnecessary. I should have gotten married and forgotten tennis or played tennis and forgotten the guys. The two just didn't go together. To get a transatlantic call just before you are to go on the court, when the caller wants to hear endearing things, is just too distracting."

Gussie paused for a moment, and then we rehashed the familiar story of Hitler's phone call to Baron von Cramm a minute or so before his great match with Don Budge. Such a call could be ruinous. Gussie then went on about several transcripts that she had read of that match, and suddenly there we were, leaping back to the most charismatic man the game had ever known, Bill Tilden.

"I took lessons from Bill and just loved him. During the war, we would travel around to Navy bases and Marine camps and hospitals here in southern California giving exhibitions. He had his little entourage, and we'd pile into his car with maybe another car following and play for the U.S.O. or the Red Cross. And Bill didn't have much money then, and he got paid $15 for doing this. Yet when it came time for lunch, nobody picked up the tab but Tilden."

"Let me ask you something. If everyone loved Bill Tilden so much, why didn't they help him out when he was alone at the end of his life and without funds?"

"Well some did . . . that is, if you can call going to his funeral helping out. I know that Joseph Cotton and Arthur Anderson, Bill's protégé, and his mother helped out. I think Joe Cotton took care of most of the expenses. Bill left all his trophies to Arthur Anderson. Marge Hall, who used to be married to Frank Hunter, also helped out. Ellsworth Vines was at the funeral. I was in New York. It was 1953, and I was having my nose done in Buffalo . . ."

"What was wrong with your nose? It looks fine now. I don't remember you with an odd nose."

"It was more aquiline then. I had it done for cosmetic reasons. There wasn't really anything *wrong* with it . . .

"So my mother met me at the airport when I returned. I had gone to Buffalo with my future husband, Eddie Hand, and he had arranged for the operation. Anyway, my mother was crying when she saw me. 'Your nose, your nose,' she would say and weep, and then the next day I went to the funeral with the pro at the Beverly Wilshire Hotel. The funeral was very sad. They'd bought new clothes for him because he liked to dress so well . . . you know, when he was arrested for contributing to the delinquency of a juvenile—I believe the boy's mother worked at the Los Angeles Country Club—a good number of people felt it was entrapment. Bill was really, as far as I am concerned, asexual. I always thought of him as impotent. Certainly toward the end, he was chaste. He just liked being near people. He would lay a hand on

202

you. But he did this with us and with men too. He liked to *touch* people. I never saw him act overtly homosexual in all our time together."

Again we paused. The Tilden mythology had taken a new turn. The picture I got was that Bill Tilden liked to be near youth—male and female. Gussie said, "He would lay a hand on you, but he did that with me as well as with a guy." I knew that George Lott would scoff at her thoughts, but now in 1984 things had changed so much it was really social history we were talking about, not tennis. What Gussie was referring to was the way things were thirty years ago. She thought of the great Tilden as impotent, asexual, and chaste. He loved other human beings of both sexes, and I felt more than a twinge of respect for the man. We let the subject drop.

"What was your greatest singles match?"

"My greatest singles match was one that I lost. I lost to Pauline Betz at Forest Hills in the quarterfinals. But that was the only set *she* lost all year. That was in 1946. I played well, and I was pleased."

"How about doubles?"

"Well, winning never turned me on all that much," she said, avoiding the question, even though in 1949 she won the indoor singles, beating Nancy Chaffee, took the doubles with Marjorie Buck, and the mixed doubles with Pancho Gonzales. The year before, she won the U. S. Hard Court Singles Championship. Suddenly breaking a silence, she mentioned Adrian Quist. There was a wistful fondness in her voice, but she didn't elaborate. "Other than Adrian Quist," she said, and then she paused again, and the mention of Quist brought me back to Fred Perry, who had given me "good old Quistie's" address in Australia.

While Gussie was searching through her memory, I was thinking of how very fond I had grown of all the players I had met. They didn't know me at all, not one, yet I felt close to all of them. Some little phrase or gesture would recall Gardnar Mulloy at the California Country Club in North Miami, talking of his new job at Boca Grove, or perhaps Billy Talbert looking regal in front of the River Club, or Shirley Fry, so indomitable yet positively sweet in front of her son's old basketball hoop extending from her garage. I looked at Gussie, whom I was falling for as I had for the other women players. She was getting over the flu, was on antibiotics, and couldn't play tennis for a few more days. But she would be glad to play later, she said, and there was "good old Lennie" standing by (again I thought of Fred Perry), and for the hundredth time, I felt at home in this world and wondered why I had waited until I was fifty-four to go out and find athletes and write about them.

In 1948 Gussie was ranked fourth in the United States, with only Margaret Osborne duPont, Louise Brough, and Doris Hart above her on the ladder. In 1948 I was going to New Rochelle High School in New York's Westchester County, as a postgraduate so that I could get into a good college, and wondering why anybody would consider voting for Henry Wallace for president of the United States. That was the year I met Bud Freeman at the old Stuyvesant Casino in New York—he a great Chicago jazzman, a fellow now seventy-nine, whom I met again in Chicago between interviews with Frank Parker and George Lott. Time seemed to be collapsing around me as Gussie pondered my questions and thought to herself about Adrian Quist.

"Adrian taught me a lot. If I had gone to Australia and been under his tutelage, I would have had a different attitude. The Australians in those days had a great attitude about how to train. They lived normally and drank their beer, but they worked hard at it and they had fun working at tennis. But getting back to Adrian! I started playing with him in Alexandria [Egypt]. We beat Patricia Canning Todd and her partner, Philippe Washer, for the title. Yes, that was a good victory."

"Can you go back to women's doubles?"

"Pat Todd and I played well together. We got to the finals at Wimbledon. But she really did better with Doris Hart. Pat needed a stronger partner. Then there was Marjorie Buck, who later married John Van Ryn [of Allison and Van Ryn]. We won the ladies' indoors, and she was just great. When we played the indoors at the 7th Regiment Armory in New York, she would open up her apartment—that's when she was still Marjorie Buck—on East Sixty-third Street, and we'd all go over for an early lunch after the morning play."

It occurred to me that tennis for Gussie was a very good time, almost lighthearted. She denied this. She said, "It was very serious."* I said something to the effect that she wouldn't storm off a court scowling, and she said that yes, she could. She did not take it lightly at all, and indeed in India when she was on tour and was playing with Adrian Quist, there was a marked improvement in her game. For a brief period in the sun of the subcontinent, she thought of the major trophies.

I then asked her about the great women players she had competed against. She said Pauline Betz was a very honest player. "You knew she would go all out in a straightforward way to beat you. With Louise Brough, you found a deviousness. She looked like anything *but* a tennis player. You never knew what she was thinking. She had a fantastic serve, but she looked like someone who should be gardening, not playing tennis. But I would place Pauline at the top."

"What about Althea Gibson?"

"You should ask Pauline that question."

"I did."

* Later in a phone conversation, she said: "*Amateur* tennis was serious. I had a lot of fun as a professional. But that was different."

204

"Then you know the answer."

Yes, I knew the answer to that question—at least from Pauline Betz's point of view,* but I didn't know the answers to the large questions that seeped forth from the personality of Gussie Moran. Why was she alone? Why didn't she sell that house for a bundle of money and move to Palm Springs? Why didn't she ever settle down and have children, as Shirley Fry had, and still play tennis? She could have played in the seniors. Dodo Cheney had been cleaning up in the seniors' divisions for years. With Gussie it seemed to be all or nothing. Wimbledon or you can forget it. But I could be wrong. She matured during the chaos of World War II. As with Don McNeill and others, the war was always behind the curtain—lurking, shaping, and establishing attitudes. It was a very romantic time, and Gussie traveled from tennis to radio to manufacturing to television, through many romances, and now to the likes of me and Lennie Baker and my tape recorder. At the end of our talk, she said that she would like to have a job to keep busy. But none was forthcoming. She was wearing tan elastic Indian Punjabi pants and a red sweatshirt, and her black hair helped to give her an exotic look that recalled the days in India with Adrian Quist. She looked at me and talked about going back to work. "When I apply, nothing happens. I applied to J. C. Penney and never heard from them. I didn't care about what I did for them. I'd work in the stockroom or on the floor. But I never even got a reply."

I couldn't understand it. What, pray tell, was wrong with J. C. Penney? Maybe people had "Gorgeous Gussie" all wrong. They wanted her to stay gorgeous forever when, in her own words, it had been "an embarrassment." All she ever wanted was to be herself. That much I knew. Like her Punjabi pants, she had a label. Sometimes that happens to pretty and talented women. In fact, it happens very often. I left, knowing I would return in May for a game and for dinner, perhaps.

I had fallen for an enigma. I couldn't keep her still in my mind. She had traveled too fast and to too many places, crossing many roads of differing construction.

Gussie Moran is sixty years old and has the grandest-looking house on Ocean Avenue in Santa Monica, California. That is what is known as a "given." I thought of the song from Gussie's time, "Laura," with the opening line, "Laura is a face in a misty light." I'd gotten many glimpses of Gussie Moran, but I couldn't get the picture straight.

Lennie and I rose to leave, and Gussie Moran walked out with us to her

---

* Pauline had been diplomatic, but she said that she lost *one time* to Althea. She was pregnant with her fourth child and played Althea in Cleveland. Later on, and not pregnant, Pauline beat Althea with ease.

small aromatic lawn where greenery kissed the air. She posed for a few pictures and then stood next to her own star, Lennie Baker of Sha Na Na, and I snapped the two of them. I was thinking as I got into Lennie's Mercedes, "I'll never get a handle on all of this—this crazy book of mine. But it sure beats anything else I can think of." Lennie laughed as though he had read my mind, and we drove away.

13

Alice Marble:

Queen Bee

"Gussie Moran! Why did you see Gussie-eee [she hissed the name like a viper] . . . Moran?"

That rather acid comment or question was made after a series of events I will endeavor to describe with as much accuracy as memory and notes will permit. I left Los Angeles the evening after visiting Gussie and flew to Palm Springs in the dark, thinking about the past as I had in Hartford back with Shirley Fry. I was remembering Tom Wolfe's book *The Right Stuff*. It was not so much the champions whom I had seen but the area I was going to. How far was Palm Springs from Edwards Air Force base, the home of test pilots Scott Crossfield and Chuck Yeager? Maybe it was over there, out my window. I fantasized about it for some time. When all that right stuff was transpiring, I too was in the Air Force, but I was as far from the lines of courage as a man could get. I was working on a computer system, still classified, that was designed to drop the hydrogen bomb. I was a mechanic, or what they euphemistically called a "systems analyst." Colonels deferred to me because they thought I knew what I was doing. Out there in the dark at the old Edwards testing center, it would have been unlikely that anyone would have deferred to me, yet I might have risen to the challenge and done well. "Who the hell knows?" I thought. And I suppose subconsciously I was thinking of the champions because they were all taking me seriously and I was taking them seriously as well, but was I doing my job right? People who don't write books will never know the self-doubts about such matters. Just suppose I was writing what my father would call "tripe"? It nagged at me, and by the time I checked into the Hilton in downtown Palm Springs, I was becoming cautious. I ate quietly by myself and went to bed early. I wanted to be in top shape for my next appointment, which would be with the queen of American tennis, Alice Marble.

The *Columbia Encyclopedia* has her being born in 1913 in Plumas County, California. In fact, to be precise, she was born on September 28, 1913, in a tiny town on the California-Nevada border called Beckwith. As Don Budge had told me, she was such a good athlete as a kid that later when she was somewhat grown up, she worked out with the San Francisco Seals and practiced alongside Joe DiMaggio. I was not surprised when she reminded me of that. She could throw a ball as far as the best outfielders—a natural athlete, almost superhuman when you consider she was a girl, and not a large-boned masculine girl but wiry and of average height.

I awoke feeling very well and called her from my room. A charming voice answered and invited me to come right over to her house in the outlying town of Palm Desert. We would talk for a while and then go hit a tennis ball and have lunch at her club. At breakfast I said to myself that this would be my moment. I had Don Budge on tape and would go to see Ellsworth Vines, but Alice Marble would *actually play*, as well as be interviewed. The battle raged for years as to who was the best woman player ever to hold a racquet. The consensus was that Suzanne Lenglen of France and Helen Willis (Moody, then Roark) shared the top, but no one, absolutely no one, dared to doubt that Alice Marble, on the attack, was the most fearsome and dynamic player in the history of the game. She had been beaten, it is true, by Helen Jacobs, in fact, in the semifinals at Wimbledon in 1938, 6–4, 6–4. But it must be remembered that in 1939, she did what no other woman player has ever done. She won the singles, the doubles, and the mixed doubles at Wimbledon and then repeated that feat by winning all three corresponding championships in the United States.

Alice Marble changed the game of women's tennis. She took the net and used her overhead and could volley and did not play baseline tennis with long endurance-testing rallies. I remembered that Althea Gibson had seen her play in Harlem, and I told her about that and what an influence she had been on the young black girl who grew to copy her game and ascend to the throne. She smiled and said, "Yes, that's right. I'd forgotten. Bobby Riggs and I were doing an exhibition up there." But then she added, "But I wasn't as much help to Althea as she thinks I was. I didn't get her into Forest Hills. All I did

31. Alice: the woman who changed the game of ladies' tennis

was write one letter." One letter from the queen, I thought to myself, would be enough.

Naturally I had studied her record. She won the U.S. singles title four times, the Women's Doubles title four times. She won the U.S. mixed doubles four times, playing with Gene Mako, Don Budge (twice), and Bobby Riggs. She took the singles at Wimbledon once in 1939 and the women's doubles twice, playing with the delightful Sarah Palfrey. She won Wimbledon three times in the mixed doubles with Budge and Riggs. It was also true that she had had tuberculosis and was being treated for it, and her career is that much more outstanding when you think that she could play and suffer and win. No doubt her record at home was so great and lopsided because she felt more comfortable here than abroad. (In 1933, practicing in France for the Wightman Cup, she collapsed on the court. That was when she learned that she had tuberculosis.) You didn't find her name in the records of the French and Australian championships.

Alice Marble's house in Palm Desert is modest in size. She has a small living room, and in the back is a miniature swimming pool—not really large enough to exercise in but roomy enough for cooling off.

Between the house and the pool is a Ping-Pong table, and she told me that every afternoon a friend comes over, and they play. Her tennis days are almost over, as I was to find out, but Ping-Pong and swimming were what she could do, and she appeared to enjoy both activities. I asked about Ping-Pong. Her contemporary, Fred Perry, had sternly corrected me and called it "table tennis"—he having once been the table tennis champion of the world. "Ping-Pong!" she almost shouted. Like the cactus that grew nearby, she could spike you with her tongue. As American as Yucca Flats, she didn't give a hoot for fancy names. It was "Ping-Pong" and that would be that. I did not try to correct her or even ask her if by chance there was a difference that would account for Fred's being stern on one hand and she equally stern on the other. She had intimidated me almost from the start.

She is still wiry, and hard as a knot in a redwood tree. Her hair is cut so short she looks like a woman who is supposed to wear a wig, but that is not the case. It is broiling hot in Palm Desert, and her short hair makes sense.

After showing me around, we sat across from each other in her living room. I went to my tape recorder and made an awful discovery. In my excitement, I had forgotten to buy more cassettes. Lennie Baker had promised me back in Los Angeles that he would not let me forget. "You can buy them almost anywhere," he had said. But I did forget.

"No problem," said Alice. "I'll just get one of my own, and we can record over it." She drew out an old Boston Pops cassette that she had recorded some time back, and I inserted it in my contraption—a word I used often because I was forever pushing the wrong buttons. And then, I couldn't believe this—the thing didn't work. I had packed it in my suitcase on the flight from Los Angeles, and apparently it was broken by the way that baggage men throw baggage about, regardless of what is inside. So there I was, without a tape recorder and without my own cassette, and still it would be no problem. We would use hers. I needn't go on. Hers didn't work either.

She looked at me and suggested that I take notes. I agreed—what else could I do? And then she said, "You know, I can't write a tennis book," even though she had her autobiography published in 1946, *The Road to Wimbledon.* "I can't write more than I did for a little Wheaties pamphlet I did over twenty years ago," she added. It was clear that she was hoping for me to do a good job. She was as straightforward as a good fairway shot (she had taken up golf and thought that Ken Venturi was wonderful) and was sick of foolishness in the writing of books. She wanted the record straight. She wanted the truth to be known, the anecdotes to be honest, the facts of her life to be lined out as they actually had happened, not as people would have wished that they had happened.

I was with a scrupulously honest woman, but I did not know shorthand and had never attempted an interview for my book without a tape recorder. Some years back when I wrote for *The Vineyard Gazette,* I was able to work from notes, but lately I had grown to depend on the cassettes. I was in fine fettle physically and mentally, but I knew I was doomed. There was no chance that I could get the Alice Marble story on notes. As with most stars, she would presume too much. She would throw out a name, and I would have to ask her whom she was talking about, and she could tell that I didn't know my ass from my elbow, and I am sure she would not mind my saying that. A trooper, she could curse, but the point is this—I was up a tree.

So we just talked. She had received an award from the Bay City (San Francisco) Hall of Fame, which raised $75,000 for youth groups in the area. She was proud of that, but how it all worked out I do not know.

She said that for the first match after the war, she went to Wimbledon because she had been invited by Queen Mary. "I tried to teach the younger girls about etiquette, and I remember Pauline Betz saying, 'I am not going to curtsy before the queen.'" Pauline, who won, did indeed curtsy, probably because Alice Marble, Pauline's heroine, was there to tell her she damn well better—or else. So Alice Marble sat across from me, this energetic and at that time gracious, elderly woman, who talked rat-a-tat at me, recalling things from her past, not bothering to watch her language, as open as a brilliant Palm Desert star-filled night when it seemed everything was wonderful and everything was possible and you would not hold yourself in check. I listened to her extol Bobby Riggs. Her tennis coach, Eleanor Tennant, known as "Teach," used to instruct both Bobby and Alice on Carole Lombard's court, she said, and then she followed that remark with "Bobby was the most lovable player I knew."

This was not the first time someone had mentioned that Bobby Riggs was lovable or kind or helpful or generous. Indeed it was apparent to me that Riggs had always had a bad press. For reasons unknown, he was the bad guy. Surely taking on Margaret Court and winning was not his best move, although it made him infamous with women who did not know about tennis and brought him to the attention of many thousands of men reeling under the pressures of the Women's Movement. But Riggs' press had been bad even in my father's time.

Alice Marble went on. Once she and some other players were standing outside in the rain at Forest Hills. She was in high heels and was looking forward to a night in New York City, but no one could find a taxi or any way to get back to the city. The matches were over, and in the downpour, it looked hopeless. Dressed to kill, as she was, she felt like a fool. No one had thought to arrange for transportation. Alice stood downcast with the other players and when everything looked dreadful, along came Bobby Riggs, who had commandeered a limousine, and he scooped them up for the ride to Manhattan. She mentioned that only to show that the man cared very much for others, and though he could hustle and be callous (Carole Lombard once gave him a present on Thanksgiving Day, and he sold it on the way home), he had more than a touch of chivalry. Pauline Betz had said as much back in Bethesda, Maryland.

And at the mention of Carole Lombard's court, I thought again of the movie connection and how Don Budge said that the movie people looked up to the tennis champions as much as they did to the movie crowd, and there was this quid pro quo in which they intermingled and became good friends. Good grief! A million or more people would have paid a small fortune to play tennis on Carole Lombard's court back in the 1930s. Carole Lombard was married to Clark Gable and was the best-looking comedienne in the world. And here was Alice, now seventy, and Chaplin and Flynn and Lombard and Gable and Gary Cooper and Robert Taylor—the crowd that had clustered to the tennis players—were all dead. William Powell, Don Budge's "hero," died at 91 years old as I was in Palm Desert. It made me think that the movie legends who had played so much a part in the lives of the tennis champions were older and probably in their own narcissistic way needed the youth of the younger athletes. And what a way to stay young and handsome or pretty—go out on Carole Lombard's court and slug away with world champion Alice Marble, who in turn would be flattered by the experience. Younger people or, let us say, the post-Actor's Studio movie audience, may never understand the spell that movie stars cast on the English-speaking world. I remember crossing the Atlantic, going first class, and Charlton Heston was aboard on his way to film *El Cid*. All I wanted to do was to shake his hand, just so that I could say, "I shook Charlton Heston's hand."

No amount of nuclear age cynicism can take that away from me. She will never remember it, but once I kissed Ginger Rogers at a bar, and when I told my father, who adored Ginger Rogers, his eyes popped. Ava Gardner and I got in such an embrace that I asked her to be my date for a football game at college (Wesleyan University in Connecticut), and she accepted. Unfortunately, I never got her address and never confirmed it, but I can't forget that either. Movie stars and tennis stars went together as, I suppose, golfers and show business people do today. How many golf matches that one sees on television in the dour days of winter are sprinkled with the likes of Andy Williams and Clint Eastwood. Business leaders used to fight their way into the Bing Crosby tournament at Pebble Beach just to rub elbows. All of this came rushing back to me as Alice Marble kept talking.

She said that she was on the Tilden-Budge tour in 1940, and her female counterpart was Mary Hardwick. Of course, Budge was supreme by then, yet every time Tilden would say to her, "Today I am going to give him a lesson." And then he would lose. Tilden, she said, played five sets of tennis on Charlie Chaplin's court the day before he died. And all along, I had thought that Tilden lived out his last days alone and lonely in a small apartment, a disgraced man. Not so. Big Bill played tennis right to the very end of his life—just as Don Budge had told me Tilden said he would. Tilden had told Budge, "When I can't play tennis anymore, I'll die." And so he played five sets, his last, and passed away.

And I had never known that Alice Marble had been married. She married an Air Corps captain named Joseph Crowly, who died in the last two weeks of the war. By the end of the war, she had recovered from her long battle with tuberculosis that put her in a sanitarium. It is such a story in itself that she spent twelve years on the lecture tour, talking of her recovery and of good health. She also had her name on thousands of tennis racquets, which produced a good income, and with all her trophies behind her and her pro tour over with, she was a true heroine—as much a heroine as were the great glamour queens of Hollywood.

Alice Marble made quite a bit of money, although when you look at her small home, its walls made of poured concrete, and the minuscule front yard on a road laid down in a housing grid, you might not believe it. But as she said, "I live alone and have my job [she is the tennis advisor at the Palm Desert Resort Hotel and Country Club, which is just fifteen minutes from her house], and what do I need a big house for?"

But once she almost did have a big house. Somewhere back in time, a millionnaire, William "Will" duPont, fell in love with Alice Marble. She was making "about $75,000 a year" then as a tennis professional and lecturing on

32. At seventy, Alice still rushes the net

the side. In any case, Will duPont invested her money for her and established a trust fund. She admits he saved her neck because she would have spent her healthy income.

"Will wanted to marry me. In 1964 I got my Tennis Hall of Fame award, and Will sent a car with a chauffeur up to Newport, Rhode Island, and brought me back to his estate in Wilmington. I stayed for the weekend, and it ended up that I would look after his house in La Quinta—a suburb of Palm Springs—and oversee it for him. I did this for ten years. I'd get a check for this.

"Then Mary K. Browne [the same Mary K. whom other women comment on as the greatest woman athlete of her day, who could combine golf with tennis interchangeably] and I built this 3,600-square-foot house on Will's estate. He paid for it, and it was for us to live in and be near his own place. Brownie and I moved in with all of our things—I mean everything. It was a hell of a move, and then two days later he died. His heirs wouldn't let us keep the house, and rather than battle over it, I moved over here to where I am now."

I thought of Will duPont. Previously he had married Margaret Osborne, but they had divorced. I wondered about Mary K. Browne and figured that she must have passed away or else she would be there now—Brownie and Alice together. I thought of many things, but I guess admiration was my principal emotion. What times? What a life? Seventy-five thousand dollars a year and

Will duPont and Palm Springs—and now this small home with walls of poured concrete and a trust fund and a job that she was able to retain even through five cancer operations.

In the car driving over to the club where she is tennis advisor, she talked about her cancer. She had cancer of the colon, and for a while she had to wear one of those bags that collect the excrement, which otherwise would exit through the colon. Fortunately the bag was only temporary, but it was a nuisance. "When I played tennis, for instance," she was saying, "I had no backhand. I was forever keeping my backhand tight to my hip to protect that damn sack from being struck by a ball." She laughed loudly at her remark, the timbre of her laughter like a cowgirl's. But those days were fortunately over.

At the club, we got a court at once and went to work rallying, and the queen of tennis was stroking the ball with a definite alacrity. Her legs were wrinkled, however, and the tone of youth had definitely faded. Though but two years Frank Parker's senior and a little less than a year older than Gardnar Mulloy, she was showing her age. She had been tubercular and had had so many cancer operations. They could take a toll and did. But she pounced along the baseline like a jackrabbit, and once she rushed the net as she had done in the old days. I saw her coming and stung one right at her as she reached the net. It whizzed by before she could respond, and for a second I saw a flash of surprise and a "so-that's-the-way-it's-going-to-be" look in her eyes.

She suggested a set of singles and that I do all the serving. Since her shoulder was lame, I agreed at once. But this posed a problem for me. I knew that I could not sting her with fast shots—the one I had hit toward the net was a reflex and not on purpose. Yet I didn't want to play pat-a-cake either. So I just played my normal, rather ponderous, game and after four games when it was clear she could not run well, we stopped. Her generosity was amazing, I thought. She had played me only for the purposes of my book. She had even played me before spectators—several people were watching—so I could say that I had once played the great Alice Marble, because she knew I was a fan and was living a fantasy. She had accommodated me with uncommon kindness. Also it was clear that she didn't give a damn what the onlookers might have thought. Her games now were Ping-Pong and golf, and her tennis record was so spectacular that benighted comments (if there were any, and I am sure there were none) could not faze her. She looked grand at the game—her spunk was a marvel. I loved her spirit, and I was thanking her with a full heart when we stopped.

We walked around the clubhouse in our tennis clothes, and she introduced me to everyone. She pointed out a showcase where there were wonderful pictures of her under glass. At lunch she asked if I minded if she had a drink, and I said that I wished that she would and that I would join her. We dined in good cheer, talking on about the good old days and her life in general and who I was and about my book. Often we were interrupted by well-wishers who wanted to pay their respects to the champion. It was all good-natured, and I was no longer taking notes. "The hell with it!" I thought. "The experience is enough." And then after we finished, she introduced me to the club manager, who had his own Sony tape recorder with a fresh tape. "What good fortune," I thought. I could go back with her now and tape a real interview. The only hitch was that she had previously—again through her innate generosity—introduced me to a very good woman player from Vancouver, British Columbia, named Rhonda Dorman. Rhonda could hit like Jimmy Connors, I was told, and I had agreed to play her after lunch. But that was no problem. Alice would drive home and then come back and pick me up when I was through. Then we would do the interview properly and get it all on tape. Out there in the desert, time did not appear to be a problem. I had all day and all night, for that matter. Alice had the day free. No problem at all, I thought. But boy, oh boy, oh boy, was I wrong!

The lunch went very well. She talked about the most graceful women players she had seen. First was Maria Bueno, and later on came along Evonne Goolagong, both beautiful women to watch.

She mentioned Bobby Riggs again. She said, "He beat Margaret Court because he trained . . . I mean really trained. So he won. Then he goes to all those talk shows and stops training. Well, by the time he played Billie Jean, he was out of condition. Had he stayed in condition, he would have beaten Billie Jean. I won $100 betting on him against Margaret Court, but I wouldn't bet the second time. I knew his condition. I knew what the round of talk shows and all that celebrity would bring."

And so the lunch went on. We dined and drank just a bit, enough for me to get feeling very loose and eager for my game with Rhonda Dorman. I remember looking at the clock in the lounge as we went by. It was 2:30. I said good-bye to Alice and walked down to the composition asphalt court and found Rhonda already playing against the assistant pro, Rich Collins. She waved me on the court, and Rich went back to his office. We rallied for a long time, and her ground strokes were very strong. Her one trouble, I noticed, was that she did not use topspin. Whereas Alice, at seventy, could bring her ground strokes right down a few inches inside the baseline, this younger woman would often hit them out by about a foot. But she could hit hard and I, feeling light on my feet and exhilarated, gave her everything I had.

We rallied a while, just slamming ground strokes at each other, and then her husband, George, who is a bit older than I, showed up. With him came the professional, Rich Collins, a very engaging young black man, an ex-Marine whom I grew to like immensely. We played a set, with Rich and George playing Rhonda and me, and they prevailed. I do not remember the score. George Dorman had a mysterious, unorthodox game, but he was very effective. He reminded me of Gussie Moran's crack about Louise Brough—he looked like anything *but* a tennis player—he had a sizable pot belly and did not stroke the ball. He just hit at it, and it went in. I had played a little paddle tennis or what some people call "platform tennis," and that was how he struck the ball—slap!

For the next set, we switched partners, and George and I played Rhonda and Rich. I don't know what came over me, but playing with George, who I believe is fifty-seven years old and I am fifty-four—playing against Rich and Rhonda, who are both young—my game took on heights it had never had. George Dorman and I beat the assistant professional, who had played tennis for City College of Los Angeles, and Rhonda, who was a contender in British Columbia, 6–2. I can tell you that George and I were up there in the clouds after that. We went on playing, switching around, and finally at the end, I went back to hitting ground strokes against Rhonda, and Rich Collins pretended to sulk back in his office, but whenever he popped his head out to watch us, I could catch a grin on his face.

The time had come and gone. It was 5:30, and George and I were having a celebrative drink at the bar when I realized I had better call Alice Marble. We had played almost three hours straight out—in the broiling desert sun where it was eighty-five in the shade, but there was no shade, not even by the court. There were no nice chairs with parasols stemming from round tables as there had been back at Gardnar Mulloy's old California Club. It was hot and I was hot and could feel it as I sipped my drink and then walked over to the phone.

"No," she said. She would not drive over to pick me up. I would have to get a ride to her place "to collect my junk." I had left my street clothes cluttering her small bathroom, and the shower rod had fallen from the walls, and the curtain was lying there like a dropped mainsail on a sailing boat. My broken tape recorder and notes and other pieces of "junk" lay around her living room. Yet I was not apprehensive. All I knew was that I needed a ride to Alice Marble's house, and finally I was able to get George and Rhonda to drive me. The indefatigable Rhonda was still on the court, practicing with Rich Collins. By the time we were able to drag her from the court, get into George's car, and get going, it was about 6:00. Still I did not know I was in trouble. This had been one of the best days in my life, I thought. I had never played better tennis. I was unaware that I had, in effect, forgotten about Alice Marble.

As I walked in, all smiles, I realized that Alice Marble had not forgotten about me. She greeted me with, "I want you to know that I wouldn't wait two hours for Gary Cooper, much less for the likes of you. It just so happens that I had nothing planned this afternoon, so I just sat here. Otherwise I would have been gone and thrown your crap out on the front lawn."

I sat down and felt the old panic return. It was a panic I had known before when my mother in her cups waited up for me at night and snapped burning words at me for staying out too late—even when I was a veteran of the U.S. Air Force at the time of the Korean War and had been through college and was supposedly on my own. I remember my mother saying, "Won't you ever learn?"

And so I sat and listened to the tirade from Alice Marble. She said, "You know your friend Pauline Betz. Well, Bob Addie, her husband who before he died was a damn fine sportswriter, well, he told me that sportswriters were the most egocentric, conceited people on earth. They are parasites. They cling to athletes who play the games that they cannot play. Egocentric, conceited bastards like you." I immediately thought of the late Red Smith. What a wonderful, unassuming man! A great writer he was, hardly a parasite, but I dared not argue.

I tried to defend myself. I said that I was *not* a sportswriter. I was a writer who was a sports fan. There is a difference, I told her. It did no good. She lashed at me and lashed at me, and I looked up at her from my bowed head and saw her sitting there like my mother, a drink in her hand.

I admitted that I had made an error. Indeed, I had. I should have gone directly home with her after lunch and done my work before I went off to play. I always knew that you should get your work done first—then goof off if you want to. It was a rule I had violated. Yet—and this was my excuse—it was she who got me into the game. I didn't even think of playing with anyone else until she suggested it. My mind swirled around, and in my fear I grasped at straws. Was she jealous of Rhonda Dorman? Did she think she owned me? I had made a mistake, but it was an honest mistake, and I thought that when I reached her house, she would say, "Hi, Stan, I hope you had a good time. Now come on in and pour yourself a drink and let's do that interview." Instead, I had walked into a viper's nest. I was being bawled out as I had not been bawled out in almost twenty years. And somewhere along the way, she hissed, "Gussie-eee," casting her venom toward a writer who would include Gussie Moran and Alice Marble, almost side by side, in the same book.

So there I was. I called a taxi to come and get me, and finally I rose to collect my things. I went into the bathroom, and she had fixed the shower curtain. I was momentarily pleased, because one thing out of many I am no good at is trying to get a shower curtain rod back in its proper position. There are those suction cups that attach to the walls, and you have to adjust them and be patient, and hell, I could never do it without taking a lot of time. I had no time now. I wanted to escape. Patience was the last thing I could proffer from a soul now wretched with turmoil.

I dressed in a hurry, putting clean clothes over my sweating body, and grabbed my tape recorder and my camera and stuffed my tennis shorts and shirt into a little bag I had and started for the door. I wanted to cry because I was wounded and because she had triggered in me this undercurrent of emotion that went back to my mother.

With the taxi waiting, she gave me one parting shot. "I want you to know something. A long time ago, I was having some trouble with a man, and I went to a psychiatrist. You know what he said? He said, 'Look, Alice, you are a champion, and you don't need to take any crap from anybody.' " With that remark she pointed her finger at me and said, "And that means you."

I jumped into the cab and, shell-shocked, tried to assess what I had done. I had been thoughtless to a point, it was true. But damn it, I said to myself, it was all her idea that I play tennis after lunch. But I recalled that when I said that in my defense, when I said that to her, she answered, "*You* can always walk off a court."

For some reason, she had expected me to be at her house by 3:30 or so. There was hardly time for me to get in much tennis and arrive on that half hour because, as I have said, we hadn't even finished lunch until 2:30. But the trouble was, she was basically right. I had gotten carried away with fun and discarded all notions of work. I had offended her sense of being Alice Marble; her well-earned regal disposition had not been deferred to. I had taken her as a pal, a regular woman, a good egg. I had taken her as she appeared to be prior to the end of our lunch. Now, I had blown it with the most dynamic woman tennis player the world had ever known. She had changed from being a scrappy, good-natured woman to a person of immense stature who could chew me out like a drill sergeant. But I remembered the drink in her hand, and I recalled my mother.

That night I felt ill and blamed it on Alice Marble's upsetting me. I went out on the town and ran into a man who had once played for the Los Angeles Rams. He told me that Jackie Robinson was the greatest athlete of all time and said that he had been a class behind Jackie at UCLA. He was a giant black man, and he leaned over the table where we were sitting and said, "Jackie Robinson held four track records at UCLA. He was lightning fast and powerful in football. Hell, man," he said, "Jackie Robinson's worst sport was baseball!"

That is all I remember of that night. I was sick and exhausted, but the stranger—the ex-Ram—had changed the subject. Alice Marble for the moment had gone from my mind. When I awoke in the morning, I went down the street to a place called Thrifty's and bought a new tape recorder and six cassettes. I felt pretty good when I reached my room, and then I dialed Alice's number. When she answered, I said, "Hi, it's Stan. I have a new tape recorder that works and some cassettes."

"Well, let me think about it. Maybe we can get together. I don't know my schedule yet, but why don't you call me back later." She sounded wonder-

33. Alice Marble and the author: Balm before the Bomb

ful, just as she had prior to her departure from the Palm Desert Resort Hotel and Country Club after lunch. A change of attitude again. No drinking yet, I thought. Then I worried about my own drinking the night before. I had stayed up too late. I was feeling sick again, and I did not call her back. I let it hang. I was not doing a profile of Alice Marble for *The New Yorker*. All I had wanted to do was meet her and play her in tennis. As a matter of fact, I rationalized, I had a better story now—the ways things had gone made for good drama. But the real reason I did not call again was because I was afraid to. She might have turned around once more, and who knows? I just couldn't take a chance on another tongue-lashing. I would not see Alice Marble that day and so be it. And anyway, I was sick. I did not know it, but I had suffered something quite serious playing out there in the desert in the hot sun. The cardiologist in San Diego diagnosed it congestive heart failure. But that would be several days down the road. In the meantime, I was losing oxygen, and my lungs were slowly filling with fluid. I didn't feel well, and I blamed it on drinking and on the pressure of my work, or I blamed it on something I had eaten. I had no idea that I was in trouble—physical trouble that would take a doctor and an intensive care unit to get me out of. I just plunged on. I had to see Ellsworth Vines.

CHAPTER

$\backsim 14$

Ellsworth Vines:

"There was one time in his life when he was the best tennis player in the world. There was another time in his life when he was the world's greatest golfer."

Fred Perry
October 1983

But I waited another day before I went to see Ellsworth Vines. Because of Jack Kramer's flu, I had arrived in Palm Springs a few days ahead of schedule, and Vines wasn't expecting me. I took a day off to drive about in my rented car and see the sights. I wanted to go back to the Smoke Tree Ranch, but didn't. Instead I returned to the Palm Desert Resort Hotel and Country Club to see the assistant pro Rich Collins and to play some more tennis. I knew that I was feeling ill, but I assumed that a good tennis game and some friendship with the Dormans, who were expecting me in an "if-you-can-make-it" kind of way, would pull me out of whatever I had picked up.

We did play, but my game was off. Although it was fun, it was not like the first time when George Dorman and I had taken his hard-hitting wife and Rich and sent them home with second thoughts. We went to the bar afterward, however, and soon I was there at a table talking with a retired Marine general, who called himself "Smiling Jim." His real name I have forgotten, but he had commanded the Second Marine Division in either World War II or in Korea. At any rate, the guy was a pocket of power in the bar, and he bellowed orders everywhere, always with a smile. He wore a beard and was small in stature, and I teased him about another small, powerful man, the famous "Chesty" Puller of the First Marine Division. Whenever I mentioned Puller, a great hero of World War II, he would grunt and let the name ride

222

past his mind. Sitting with the bombastic Smiling Jim who, when teased, would growl, "Don't push me too far," had a loosening effect. Later I went back to his house to meet his wife. Some time during the night, I returned to the Hilton and never did visit the Smoke Tree Ranch. I know I dodged it because of the memories it held. I was sure that I could have talked my way past the guard at the gate, having once been a guest there. And I knew I would visit the office and then the dining room, where my name had been burned on a clothespin hanging from the ceiling along with hundreds of other similar pins, each with the name of a guest. But those had been my salad days when I would run free with money in my pocket and a woman at my side and a car to propel down the long desert roads near Palm Springs.

I also remembered that while I was at Smoke Tree, I would detect a slight tic of confusion in my father's face. He had come West to ride horses and lawn bowl and make friends (a Hotchkiss graduate and a Yale man, he fitted well with the Republican business leaders he met), and had indeed done all that but found it all kiboshed by a wife who was deteriorating from a combination of multiple sclerosis and alcoholism. I recalled them sitting out on the back patio of their cottage and my father rising to pour my mother another drink, and then he would stare out at the desert and the mountains. At night you could hear coyotes howling as my mother lashed out at my father for some minor infraction. He might have stayed too long at lawn bowling, or perhaps he had met a woman rider along the trail into the desert and remarked about it.

Those were dreadful memories, and I thanked the good general of the Second Marine Division for getting me away from the pain of recall and from the pain I felt when I thought of Alice Marble. A woman lashing out at a man (or at another woman, for that matter) was and still is one of the deadliest forms of punishment. At least for me.

The La Quinta Hotel is about twenty miles from Palm Springs, and as I drove down the road to the main entrance, I realized I was a long way from George Lott's Midtown Tennis Club or Frank Parker's McClurg Court Sports Center. The road was lined on each side with a row of perfectly groomed cedars, and everywhere I looked, I saw greenery springing from the desert. It was plush and lush at the same time, yet the hotel looked old and understated and Mexican and had a flavor to it that suggested Hollywood and salaries that were almost unimaginable. Out here people lived on residuals, and they talked of percentages. It reminded me of New York's Twenty-One or the old El Morocco. The hotel had been built for people who were somebody whom other people would know about. It had class that evolved from fame and fortune, not from old families of colonial heritage. This was the rich West.

The La Quinta Tennis Club, I would learn, was where at least ten ranked tennis players worked out when in Palm Springs, and the Golf Club, the domain of Ellsworth Vines, was the home of Marlene Bauer Hagge, Althea Gibson's old roommate, as well as other touring professionals. Cheryl Tiegs and Johnny Carson stayed at La Quinta, I was told, and so it was that kind of hotel-resort. It had glamour and, in its way, was the very opposite of Billy Talbert's elegant River Club. Yet if you drew a circle, La Quinta would be at the extreme left, coming around until it touched the extreme right—the River Club. It admitted people who were of a different type, but who, in their way, were very much alike. They were rich. La Quinta was the West, and the River Club was the East, and I, always touched by glamour and natural beauty, found it a fairyland. The River Club was Eastern establishment and hardly surprising. This place was a glorious Hollywood hacienda, and it held me in thrall.

Ellie Vines has a normal-size office, and he sits back at his desk and is often interrupted by his secretary. There are thirty-six holes out there, and he is the vice-president in charge of golf operations. He looks his age, which is seventy-two (exactly, to the day, two years older than Alice Marble). He is six-two-and-a-half, of senior citizenship, and there is no Hollywood aura to

34. Ellsworth Vines

him. He looks quite simply like a working man at a white-collar job. He wears rimless glasses with a metal bridge across his nose, and were it not for "La Quinta" on his polo shirt, he could be transplanted to a country store in New Hampshire and fit right in. He could run a small insurance agency in Portland, Maine. You would not suspect that he was once the greatest one-on-one competitor the world has ever known. Indeed, by beating Henry "Bunny" Austin of England at Wimbledon and Henri Cochet of France at Forest Hills, he reached the summit in all of tennis. Then later by taking on the great golfer Ben Hogan, at the height of Hogan's supremacy, head to head, and winning, Vines accomplished something that no one else can lay a claim to. There is no parallel to what he did in the history of American sport.

I told him that I was not just another sportswriter trying to do still another interview with him. I said, "I am a sports fan who just wants to meet with you and talk to you." I said, somewhat lamely, "I suppose you have had many sports articles written about you."

"You can say that again," he answered, rocking back in his chair, his hands clasped behind his neck, a grin on his face, with more than a trace of forbearance. Earlier I had told him that I had the pleasure of being with Alice Marble for perhaps three hours or more, and he looked at me aghast. "Well, you won't get that from me," he said, not unkindly. Rather it was his way of telling me that he was in midseason, and there was no time.

I did not wait to plunge into the question I had been dying to ask. I looked at the wonderous Vines and said, "How did you become the world's greatest tennis player, go back and practice golf, and then go on to Chicago and beat Hogan at the Tam O'Shanter? As far as I can see, no one can rival that feat. Can you see anyone who could claim to equal what you did?"

"No," he answered, "I can't." Then he went on to explain. "I quit tennis completely in January of 1940. The last match I played was for the British Relief in New York. I had had it as far as tennis is concerned. I had been playing tournament tennis since 1926. Budge was coming on very strong, and I couldn't see any place but being second, and golf intrigued me. I knew a lot of the old-timers, so I decided I would just try to get as good as I could. I worked very hard at it."

"George Lott said you practiced golf from sunup to sundown."

"I did that for two years. I played all the competition I could, both amateur and professional, and I would go to the golf course each day at 8:00 in the morning. I had four or five lessons a week. I would practice till 11:00, come back and rest a bit and have lunch, and then go out and play and then practice some more. I did this practically for five days a week for two years."

"With this athletic gift of yours, could you have, say, played baseball?"

"Oh, I played baseball, too. When I was fifteen, I played first base for a semiprofessional team down at San Pedro."

I mentioned basketball and said that obviously he wasn't tall enough—he was sitting down, and it was a stupid remark, anyway. Think of Bob Cousy.

"I am not tall enough now, but in those days I was tall enough. I played basketball. I was all-Pacific Coast center at Pasadena High School. I played center on the freshman team at USC and was *starting* center for the varsity in my sophomore year. But I had to quit the team to go play Davis Cup tennis. My coach thought that I had my best chance at tennis."

"After you beat Hogan, didn't people come around and ask you about it? Wasn't it considered kind of a miracle?"

"Yes, they did. They asked the same question you are asking. I told them that it was the product of hard work and competitive drive. I always had fast hands, so to speak, and had always been a good athlete at anything I tried, and so it was hard work, that would be my answer."

"Did you drink or smoke as a kid?"

"No."

"How about later?"

"I didn't smoke, but by thirty-five or so, I picked up drinking. I have drunk my share of scotch since then."

I asked him about making money as a golfer.

"I did all right. One year I was the leading money earner on the tour. I made $14,000."

"I suppose that would translate to about $140,000 now."

"Easily," he said. "Easily."

"How did you do on the professional tennis tour?"

"Very well. Very well. I started off against Bill Tilden, who was nineteen years older than I was, and I ran him out of gas. He could still play, but his legs were just gone." (*The Los Angeles Times* reported that Vines made $52,000 on the 1934 Vines-Tilden tour.)

Then came the famous Fred Perry-Ellsworth Vines tour, and he did well on that, too. He took Perry in a rather close series. Overall he beat Perry 86–71. From 1934 through 1939, Ellsworth Vines won 257 matches and lost 130 as a professional.

Trying to get at him for a moment, I told him that many of the other great players shared the same opinion of him. On his best day, he was the best the world had seen. But when he was off, almost anyone could beat him. "Even me," I offered, laughing as I said it.

"Well, many did," he said, smiling, and I remembered Frank Parker talking about the low trajectory of his ball—how it had to be hit exactly right or it would go into the net. Then I felt the pressure of time and went right to my standard question: "Who were the top five players in the world, thus far?"

"I would say Tilden and Budge and Kramer. Then Laver and . . . up to now I guess McEnroe. No, not McEnroe, Borg."

226

35. Ellie Vines in the old days. Later he turned to golf. Alas.

A secretary interrupted him, and I had time to think of Vines' own record as an amateur. One thing I knew was that it was brief. He started out in 1926 with the juniors, which John Doeg won, and it ended in 1933. But when he was at the top, it was quite something. Take 1932. That year he won both the Wimbledon and the U.S. singles. He also played Davis Cup tennis and in 1932 lost to Jean Borotra but beat Cochet as America failed to wrest the cup from France. His complete overall Davis Cup record was 13–3.

By 1933 he was losing ground and ready to turn professional. Fred Perry of Great Britain beat him in an interzone finals, which went 1–6, 6–0, 4–6, 7–5, 7–6, the last game won by Perry as (I was guessing) an exhausted Vines retired from the courts. He was ranked first in the United States for two years in a row, 1931 and 1932. In 1930 he was ranked below George Lott, with Johnny Doeg and Frank Shields at the top two positions.

His brief tenure testified to what others had said: his game had to be perfectly honed. Yet when it was, he conquered anyone in sight. With Bill Tilden waiting for him, along with the big money of a professional tour, Vines dropped from amateur competition after a relatively dismal 1933 season, in which he was runner-up to Fred Perry at Wimbledon and his only major victory was in taking the title at Longwood in the mixed doubles, playing with Elizabeth Ryan. But by then he had become a legend. His sweeping serve was the world's fastest. The cliché that "at his best he was unbeatable" was just that, a cliché, because it was grounded in the obvious truth of the statement and was repeated everywhere that tennis players convened.

Finally Vines' secretary left the room, and I looked over at his forehead, which I noted was somewhat mottled with little brown sun spots that look like freckles. I have one over my right cheek, and I had always supposed it came from being exposed to the sun. Ellie Vines must have logged many thousands of hours in the beating sunshine.

Incidentally, the secretary who had interrupted me was concerned about some checks that Ellie Vines had deposited and then drawn on. Apparently the checks had not cleared prior to his drawing on the money they represented. He said, "I know they are just piddling amounts, but I don't want to pay the bank the damn overcharge."

Immediately I thought of George Lott, who had made the crack that Ellie Vines would walk up and down the street before going to the movies, just to see which movie cost less, regardless of what was playing. And here he was, worrying about an overcharge. "They're all drawn on local banks and should clear in one day. I am going down to the bank and find out when they were presented," he stated firmly. I snickered to myself because I love such personality quirks. Obviously when it came to money, Ellsworth Vines had not changed very much. It was just as George Lott had said, only Lott was talking about the 1930s—fifty years ago.

We went back to tennis. I repeated the often stated opinion about Vines and his "given day."

"Well, I had one of those days against Budge. I beat him 6–0, 6–2."

"How much older are you than Budge?"

"I'm seventy-two." (Budge is sixty-eight.)

I asked him who his favorite doubles partner was.

"I won the national doubles with Keith Gledhill. But I would say, though we only played one tournament, I would pick Lester Stoefen. You know, he was so big and rangy and six five, and he had a devastating serve."

On that comment, I mentioned that George Lott said that he and Stoefen were ahead of Tilden and Vines 11–9 in the pro tour before Stoefen "got a dose."

Vines took immediate exception. "Tilden and I won the first part of the tour . . . we beat them so badly that they wouldn't play us for money anymore. I would say that out of twenty matches Tilden and I beat Lott and Stoefen."

"What would be the best doubles team you ever saw or played on?"

"I would say that would be Stoefen and Lott. They were far better than Allison and Van Ryn. They were tops."

"How about mixed doubles?"

"My favorite partner was Elizabeth Ryan. We won the nationals at Longwood. Then I would say Helen Jacobs. I won it one time with her." (On this matter, I checked and could find no major tournament that Helen Jacobs and Ellsworth Vines won as a team. He gave me the impression that it was at Longwood, but once again, it appears that memory plays tricks. Of course, this problem had been constant throughout my book. Facts may get distorted by time, but I would not have argued with him, even though I recalled only one mixed doubles win at Longwood. A hacker doesn't correct a professional, a star. And, as with the others, I did not want intentionally to alienate anyone's affection, though I may have done so by my habit of conversing rather than just interviewing. My style was to slip into a bull session, which must have seemed odd to some of the champions who were used to rather formal interviews. This distinction between a sportswriter and a sports fan had to be maintained. Yet I did not want to sit stiffly in awe or in *total* respect. I wanted to have fun with my idols, and one of my aims was to humanize them but not be directly contradictory. I almost got in trouble with Don Budge in this way, so I said nothing more about mixed doubles.)

I asked Vines what he would say to a graduating class from high school. I repeated my often used question: "What words of wisdom would you impart?"

"First, I would tell them they had to be honest. Then I would say that they should diligently apply themselves to whatever work they have chosen, even to the exclusion of other activities. And try to be the best in your business, whether it be sport or anything else. You see, I have a different philosophy on sport than others. They are still thinking of amateur sports, which was great years ago, but sports today is a hell of a big business. Whether you are a player or a promoter, there is so much money in it that if you are an exceptional athlete and you get a football contract or are like one of these pro tennis players who are in the first sixteen or something, you have to work in a business for years to make what they are making in a year—sports is such a big business that even the amateur athletes are getting paid—those in track and the skiers are getting paid . . ."

"But suppose that we can assume that only about 10 percent of the graduating class has athletic aspirations. What would you tell the others? Would you say something like 'Love thy neighbor,' or some such . . ."

"No, not really. I am not one who loves thy neighbor too much. I mean, I get along with people. I have hundreds of friends."

"Here is a question. Do you believe in God?"

"Sure."

"Do you go to church?"

"Yes. I go about eight to ten times a year to what they call the Palm Desert Church of Scientology. Their belief is in God, but they believe that heaven and hell are right here on earth. I believe in the hereafter, but basically I was brought up as a Baptist. I've got to believe that there is some supreme power out there, somewhere."

"Going back to tennis, what was the greatest match you ever played?"

"I think the best I ever played was against Henri Cochet at Forest Hills when I beat him 6–4, 6–4, 6–4 [for the title in 1932]. My quickest match was when I played Bunny Austin at Wimbledon and beat him 6–4, 6–2, 6–0." [Again for the title, but Bunny Austin of England had his revenge in Davis Cup play in 1933. He beat Vines 6–1, 6–1, 6–4.]

"Why doesn't anybody place John McEnroe in the top five players of all time?"

"I feel that overall, the competition is better. The top sixty or one hundred players are better than in my day. But, at the top, I don't think the basic competition in the top four players is any better than it was in my day. It's the same with golf. You can take Byron Nelson, Sam Snead, Ben Hogan, and Jimmy Demaret, and they'd hold their own with Nicklaus and Watson and the others."

We went on talking about the old days and comparing the game of tennis as it was to the way it is played now. Vines agreed with the other players I had met. There is this incredible depth where even a player no one had heard of could make money. But at the top, there was little change. He agreed with Don Budge, who said that in his time if a player had a fault or weakness, he would go home and practice for about six months to rid himself of it. Today players just keep on playing. "It's because there is so much money," I said.

"Sure," said Vines. "I agree with the others."

"If you had your life to live over again, would you make any changes? Be born richer or poorer or taller?"

"No, I don't think so. I have a marvelous family—my mother and father, wife and kids. No, I don't think so."

"Were you very close to your father?"

"No."

"Your mother?"

"Yes. My folks were divorced when, I guess, I was eleven. I kept in touch with my father, and when I got older and realized some of the problems between my mother and father, I grew a lot closer to my Dad."

"I guess my point is that you always had a supportive parent. You weren't just on the loose?"

"No. My mother was a great support."

"You have children, you said."

"Two adopted."

"And you have been married to the same woman?"

"Fifty-two years."

"How did the Ellsworth Vines-Fred Perry Beverly Hills Tennis Club work out?"

"It worked out fine—if only we had held on to it. We had two managers, but Perry and I were traveling all over the world, and we didn't have time to watch it. So we were being ripped off and ripped off, and then we had an opportunity to sell it at a good profit, so we did."

"I suppose that many Hollywood movie stars would join the club, hoping to play with you or Perry. It must have been disappointing to them when you were away."

"Oh, we played with them. Gilbert Roland and Errol Flynn were both good players."

I asked him if he had written his memoirs or was writing them.

"No, I never bothered."

"Why wouldn't you sit down with a tape recorder, the way we are doing, and tell your life story?"

"It's too much work. I'm having too much fun playing some golf and writing a few letters."

"Suppose you had a heart attack on the golf course. Your life story would go unwritten."

"I'd leave that to my wife or son. You know, it might be interesting to some people, but I don't think it's really worth it."

"When you were on the tour, say playing with Perry, was it a lot of fun and kind of flashy?"

"It was a damn grind. Perry and I would play sixteen nights running—these younger guys kill me [with long layovers between tournaments, as opposed to the exertions of the old-fashioned, almost whistle-stopping tour]—and we would travel all day in between our matches. We went by car or train or whatever way we could, and not only that, we were playing singles and doubles the same night. For instance, we had a match in Milwaukee and we were traveling by car and the next night we had to play in Pittsburgh. We didn't get through the match in Milwaukee until midnight. We took turns driving and got to Pittsburgh about ten or eleven in the morning to play in the arena down there. We slept four or five hours and then had to get up and go play."

"At your peak, how much did you make as a touring pro in a year?"

"Oh, $75,000 or $76,000."

I told him about Don Budge making $148,000 in one year.

"I wouldn't doubt it. That was the year that he and I played. He had a very good guarantee . . ."

"When you were an amateur going around the world playing tennis, were you paid under the table?"

"No."

"How did you support yourself?"

"Well, in the first place, we had the Southern California Tennis Association. They paid the expenses to get East to the tournaments, and in those days, once you got there, you stayed at a private home, and if you didn't, like at the Westchester, you'd stay at a hotel, and the tournament would pick up your bill."

I mentioned that some of the players I talked with said that they *had* been paid. I said that in those days if you were on the Davis Cup team, there was money around.

"There is no question about that. But," he went on, "I had had it with Spalding racquets. I think it was something minor like I couldn't get a free stringing job or something, so I picked up a Bancroft racquet and won Wimbledon with it. Now, Allison and Van Ryn, Keith Gledhill and I were invited to play in Australia, and we were put on a daily stipend of, let's say, ten pounds a day. On top of this, the Southern California Tennis Association would pay our hotel bills. This was 1932. So Bancroft had a man on the coast named Wally Bates, and Bates came down to the boat in October just before we were to leave and presented me with a check for $1,000 from old man Bancroft because I was playing with Bancroft racquets. And I told Wally Bates that I couldn't take it because somebody might find out and turn me in as a professional.

"As far as telling a club back East that I wouldn't play there unless they slipped me something—that just would never happen. And getting back to Australia, after our two-month tour down there, I was able, on returning to the States, to buy a $900 car. I lived frugally and saved my expense money."

The time that Ellie Vines had allotted me was beginning to run out, and I could sense it. There were more letters to write, and there was that bank business in the back of his mind. However, he was smiling and still leaning back in his chair, obviously enjoying the nostalgia that was wafting in the warm air of the room at La Quinta. I had no more questions to ask then, so I told him about my strange and ultimately upsetting encounter with Alice Marble. I told him how her attitude had done a flip-flop and that when I returned to her house, she was irate and had a drink in her hand. Apparently I couldn't let this problem lay at rest.

He waved me aside. "Look," he said, "Alice and I share the same birthday. I see her all the time. When she gets to popping those drinks, she gets that way. Don't think anything of it."

"I felt that she had been home, stewing for two hours."

"She'd probably been drinking for two hours. She has a marvelous memory about tennis, and she is a great gal, but when she gets going on that booze, her personality changes."

"It was amazing," I said, "to return to her house and meet a totally different person."

"That's Alice," he replied, and he laughed as I showed my puzzlement over the striking events of my day with her, trying to shake them off. I had no business being puzzled, however. I knew what had happened and why, but I told Vines so I could get it off my chest.

"She was a great player," he said, kindly shifting the theme to a positive note.

"At her best, how would she do against Martina Navratilova?"

"I don't know if she could beat her, but she would get her fair share. Alice had a marvelous high-kicking serve, and she was a very good net player. She wasn't afraid to serve and come in. I am sure, in my own mind, that she could have beaten Helen Wills and Helen Jacobs and those girls without any problems. But Martina? Martina has marvelous strokes and a devastating serve, and she is dedicated—but, of course, all champions are dedicated. Chris Evert is a good backcourt player, but good offensive players, if they are on their game, can beat a good backcourt player any day of the week. Helen Wills was really a backcourt player, too. But Marble wasn't. She was a net rusher and a hard hitter and had a lot of speed. To me, Martina and Alice would be very close."

Remembering my discussion with the ex-Ram about Jackie Robinson, I asked Ellie who was, in his opinion, the best pure athlete the nation had known.

He paused for a while and said, "Let me think." Then he answered, on cue, "I think Jackie Robinson."

Dumbly, but instinctively, I reacted with my guess and said, "Muhammed Ali." I could not help attempting an argument—a sports argument, although I had already been convinced about Robinson. It was an example of a bad habit of mine—always the devil's advocate, trying to provoke. I said, "I think that with Ali's obvious sense of coordination and timing and rhythm and courage and size, he could have played anything."

Vines replied, "I think he could have, too," and so the "argument" was defused before it began. We settled on Robinson.

"Who were the heroes of your youth?"

"Dempsey for number one," he said. "And, of course, not knowing what went on, Tilden was one of my heroes. They were all pretty much sports figures. When I think of political people, the one who I really looked up to and thought was the absolute greatest was Churchill."

"How about when you and Perry had your tennis club, were there some Hollywood people whom you liked a good deal, became friendly with?"

"Yes, I liked the Marx brothers an awful lot. I played golf and tennis with Zeppo. I also played tennis with Groucho, although he wasn't very good."

"But it must have been fun, though."

"Oh, yeah. I had a lot of laughs. When I was getting in shape for the winter tour with those guys, we used to play at the Beverly Hills Tennis Club, and they could hit the ball anyplace within the enclosure as long as they didn't hit the fence *on the fly*, but they had to win the last game legitimately, within the lines. Well, of course, every time I got the service and they hit it back, they would hit it right to the fence. They would go to 5–love right away, but they could never get that last game when they had to stay within the lines."

"Back in those days, did you and your wife socialize with that crowd, people like Gary Cooper?"

"Oh yeah, Randy Scott . . ."

"It must have been a glamorous time for you."

"It was great. Those were fun days."

"Looking back, who, out of that whole crowd, would you say was a really good egg, the best person of them all?"

"I would say, when he wasn't on the tennis court, it would be Gilbert Roland. He was really a nice guy."

"What happened when he *was* on the tennis court?"

"He was pretty intense—let's put it that way. He was married to Constance Bennett at the time, and she would sit at the back of the court, and when he made a mistake, you wouldn't hear a truck driver who could swear the way she did."

I had one last question. I wanted to know some details of his great golf victory at the Tam O'Shanter. I knew that in the playoffs, it was not just Vines and Hogan; there was also a very good golfer named Sammy Byrd.* But, naturally, it would be Hogan whom Vines would fear. However, Ellie was on the phone again. I held my query in reserve as I said good-bye and left.

I drove out of La Quinta with a feeling of great elation. With Vines on tape, I had met the big three of men's tennis: Don Budge, Fred Perry, and now Ellsworth Vines. I also had seen and played Alice Marble, but I still needed a few more of the truly great women players. I had to find Helen Wills, and Alice had told me that Helen Jacobs was in Connecticut. Then there was the formidable team of Louise Brough and Margaret Osborne duPont, whose major victories were sky-high when compared to the men. They had stayed amateurs, piling trophies on trophies. Somehow I thought I would get to them all. I even hoped for Helen Wills as I drove out Eisenhower Drive and past Bob Hope Drive, and leaving Rancho Mirage, where Nancy Chaffee Kiner played and taught tennis, I kept on into Palm Springs and the Hilton.

Late that afternoon, feeling restless, I put on my tennis clothes and strode down to the court that belonged to the hotel. There was a married couple playing singles, and I asked if I could join them. The man was a local Palm Springs doctor, and they both agreed, so we played Canadian doubles for almost an hour. We were about the same level, which surprised me. My breath was short, and I did not feel like running. My game had dropped many notches since the doubles victory out at Palm Desert. Rich, the pro, would have been surprised at the difference. I just shrugged it off and went back to my room to shower.

I awoke and felt fresh enough to call Nancy Chaffee Kiner. Like Gussie Moran, her forte had been the indoor championships, where she had done splendidly. But she was no Wimbledon winner, nor had she won at Forest Hills. She did not really belong with the others, as Alice Marble had indicated when she hissed, "Gussie-eee." For that matter, Don Budge (on my one phone call to him) had shown surprise mixed with distaste when I mentioned Sidney Wood's name, even though Wood did win at Wimbledon (by default) and was ranked in the United States for years and had played a number of Davis Cup matches (often with disastrous results). There was a pecking order among the great players—I had found that out. They, themselves, knew who belonged in the pantheon.

At any rate, I did call Nancy Kiner and got a friend of hers named Bootsie, who giggled on the phone. Nancy was giving a lesson and would be

---

* Incidentally, Sammy Byrd was another "crossover" athlete. He spelled Babe Ruth for the New York Yankees and played in a World Series. Babe Ruth referred to him as his "caddie."

out for a while. I could call back in the afternoon. So having looked at the phone book, I realized that right below the name of the tennis star was the name and number of her ex-husband, baseball Hall of Fame member, Ralph Kiner.

On impulse I called him and asked him to lunch. Ralph asked, "What for?"

I said, "Although I am writing a tennis book, I am a baseball fan. And my book is about heroes and being a fan, so I thought, 'What the hell, ask Ralph Kiner to lunch.' "

He agreed, and we ate at a favorite place of his called Mort's Delicatessen. We were back at Palm Desert again—an outgrowth of the sprawling Palm Springs nexus.

I liked him very much, but I will not go into our interview. This lunch was much like the long lunch I had with the great seventy-nine-year-old jazz saxophone player Bud Freeman in Chicago. I had strayed from my book but found the temptation to be near someone whom I admired to be irresistible. There was one bit of confusion, however. I had called Nancy again to let her know where I was, and Bootsie said she would leave my message. I had hopes that if I hung on at Mort's after Ralph's departure, Nancy Kiner could join me or get in touch with me there, so I could make a date to see her. Just after Ralph Kiner left, I received a message from the waitress that Mrs. Kiner was on her way. So I sat for over an hour sipping coffee and waiting. She did not arrive. Finally I went to the phone and called her, and she was at home. "Why were you with Ralph?" she asked, and I sensed that she thought I was some kind of snoop probing into their marriage, now ended. When I told her why I had seen Ralph, the timbre of irritation left her voice. She said that she had never called the delicatessen to say that she would be coming over. We could meet later on, she said, and I said I would call at a later time.

I was to deduce that there were emotions at play here under the clear desert sky. Perhaps she had said to herself, "Well, why don't I join this guy to see what he is doing?" (I had explained to Bootsie what I was up to.) But perhaps, then, she thought, "Oh, oh. Mort's is where Ralph goes," and maybe she smelled something fishy. At any rate, she had denied ever calling Mort's to say she was "on her way," and I never called her back. I looked up the records and figured that Nancy Kiner was just about my own age. To be honest, she was not a heroine of mine, nor was I a fan of hers. What had interested me was "the sports marriage of all time," her marriage to Ralph when he was in his prime and she was becoming a tennis star. Indeed, she was right if it is true that she had smelled something fishy. As I considered matters, I knew that I wasn't interested in her thoughts about tennis as much as I was in the human aspects of a celebrity marriage. When she went to England to play, she wore earrings, each one being the number 4, Ralph's number with the Pirates. I recalled the marriage of the champion swimmer Zoe Ann Olsen and baseball star Jackie Jensen. Too much talk about movie stars and glittering romance had gotten my mind off track.

Celebrity was entering my head more than was tennis, overtaking the purpose of my book. I was very pleased to have met Ralph Kiner, who is now a television broadcaster, working the New York Mets games. I have ninety minutes of baseball talk on tape. And I suppose meeting Kiner would be like meeting Pat Summerall or Frank Gifford or any other sports figure now in the public eye via television. I was straying from my book, and I realized it.

I had to call Ellie Vines about his golf because in his office I had surmised that he was not the kind of man who wanted to reminisce too long. He might want to do so with someone like Fred Perry or Don Budge or John Van Ryn (who I heard was still living in Philadelphia) but not with someone who was not his peer. So I telephoned him, and we talked.

"What was the name of the course where you played the Tam O'Shanter?"

"It was the Tam O'Shanter Country Club, right in Chicago," he answered. "In those days, it was the biggest tournament dollar-wise on the tour."

"And in the sudden death you played against Sammy Byrd and Ben Hogan . . . I suppose you were concentrating most on your game [obviously], but the guy who worried you was Hogan?"

"There was no sudden death," he replied.

"Well, then in the tournament that you won by beating Hogan . . ."

"I didn't win the tournament," he answered. "Herman Barron won the tournament. He beat me by one stroke. I remember it well. I had finished ahead of him and was watching by the 18th green. Herman Barron parred the last hole and won by a stroke. I beat Hogan by a stroke and came in second."

I couldn't believe him, and for a minute or two I argued with him, knowing that it was not so much that I *could not* believe him, I did not *want* to believe him. His memory has gone, I thought. I had been told about this match by an eyewitness. It was part of the record, I thought. Even Fred Perry agreed with me.

"Well, you still *did* beat Hogan?" I finally stammered.

"Yes," he answered. "I won by a stroke over Hogan for second place."

"When was it?" I asked.

"I think it was 1947, in the summer."

Still reeling, I let my first question lie. There was another thing that I had to ask. "In 1933, in the interzone match against Britain for the Davis Cup, you lost to Fred Perry 1–6, 6–0, 4–6, 7–5, and 7–6 and then it says in the record book that you 'retired.' "

(I had already figured that it could be from exhaustion, but I wanted his exact explanation. In any event, the record book indicated that it was a meaningless singles match—the English players had already locked up the match because they were leading at that time, 3–1.)

"I fainted," he said. "We were playing in Paris under the hot French sun and on the Roland Garros courts [clay], and I just fainted."

"Well, it was meaningless anyway. Had you won, the Americans still could not have beaten the British."

"No, no!" he almost shouted. "It was a crucial match. I had taken Bunny Austin in singles, and I know Allison and Van Ryn won because they always won. So it was important. It was crucial and I fainted."

I thought to myself, "What in hell is going on here?"

The *Tennis Yearbook* clearly showed that Vines had been beaten by Austin at the start of the match and that it was Van Ryn and *Lott* who played doubles and that indeed our doubles team did win. But Perry whipped Wilmer Allison in singles, as did Austin beat Allison, and it was all over by the time Perry took on Vines.

"Yes, I fainted all right," he repeated. "Is there anything else?"

I asked him what his exact title was at La Quinta.

He said, "I am vice-president of the La Quinta Golf Club."

I thanked him and, very much confused, I placed the phone back on its stand.

Then I called my informant in New York.

"He's mistaken," said Mac Muir, who had covered the Tam O'Shanter as a newsman. "It was 1946, not 1947, and it was what was known then as a playoff. They had tied—Byrd, Hogan, and Vines—and so the next day they went out and played it off. That is when Vines won, beating both of them. Why, hell, man, Vines played hundreds of tournaments. He probably beat Hogan several times. He was the biggest money earner one year, the best in the world, and so had probably got it confused in his mind. In 1947 I was at Sea Girt watching Frankie Parker play tennis. I know the Tam O'Shanter was in 1946, and I remember the playoff perfectly."

Malcolm Muir said he would go over to *The New York Times* to check it all out. He had a bad back the day I called him, but he would look it up as soon as he could. Muir, sixty-eight years old, was almost a contemporary of Vines, and I trusted his memory.* He was a great squash player and had played in national senior tournaments. He always knows what he is talking about, I thought, but Vines certainly should know about his own record. Yet Vines was wrong in his remembrances of that Davis Cup interzone played in

---

* In the summer of 1945, Malcolm Muir died of a massive heart attack while jogging on Martha's Vineyard. He never did get to *The New York Times* for verification.

1933. I am sure he was correct when he said he fainted. You don't forget something like that, and what made it doubly bad, he said, was that he fainted with his serve coming up, a serve he would probably have won, which would have tied matters at 7–7 in the fifth set. I recalled George Lott saying that Fred Perry was half stone wall and half rabbit. I could almost feel the red hot sun bearing down on that red *en tout cas* clay surface at Roland Garros.

Vines—who didn't care about his memoirs, who probably never kept a journal or diary, who married very young and kept on the move—had simply forgotten the details of his Davis Cup play. But he had been absolutely adamant in straightening me out about the Tam O'Shanter—to his own disadvantage.

It was the same old thing again. Uncertain memories. Matters went askew as time passed. I had to gamble, and I guessed that Vines was right about the golf and that Muir was wrong. And one thing was sure. He did beat Hogan in Chicago. He had triumphed over the best golfer in the world, as had Herman Barron. But I laughed. I really didn't care much about Herman Barron. The man I liked and respected more than ever was Ellsworth Vines, a man who could say flat out, "I fainted," and who could set the record straight and disabuse me of wishful thinking and more than a touch of hero worship.

The next day, I flew back to Los Angeles to see the king of tennis, Jack Kramer. By now his flu would have abated. I had dawdled long enough in the beautiful desert country, transformed into a lush paradise for rich sportsmen. I loved Palm Springs, but I had business to attend to. I thought that if Don Budge is the elder statesman of American tennis, then Jack is its supreme leader. All roads had been pointing toward Kramer who, I was told, knew everything that there was to know about the game. Tennis was his life, and he was still deeply involved with many aspects of the sport. Of this I had been assured. There was no excuse to play more tennis, to socialize in town, to drive out into the other communities and meet celebrities and be an endless and simple fan. I let Nancy Kiner hang fire. Maybe I would return to meet her, even though she was too young. I liked older people.

"Let's face it," I said to myself. "You do not lionize someone you could have had as a classmate in school. You lionize those far above, older grownups, people who can take the place of your parents. That is what hero worship is; it's parental surrogates." Or maybe, I reasoned, thinking of Shirley Fry and Pauline Betz and Gussie Moran, surrogate older sisters. And McNeill, a brother. In any case, they would be people you threw your emotions at, afraid or shy as a kid to throw them within your own family. I thought I had a clue to all of this. A fan transfers his emotions of admiration, loyalty, and even love to a star. To stretch a point, it is like an analysand in psychoanalysis. It is a subtle transference. It is usually subconsciously done. But when open feelings are quashed in a home, those feelings find a home in another person who

239

plays or performs for the public. Fred Exley, who wrote his excellent book about himself and Frank Gifford, *A Fan's Notes,* was not writing about a fan. He was writing about envy. Yet envy is part of it, too. Or so I was thinking as I flew from Palm Springs.

Also I was thinking that in a sports world full of baloney as well as truth, I had met someone special when I met Ellsworth Vines. He could have left me with my illusion over his greatness at golf. He did not have to say he'd fainted in a crucial match against Perry. I did not even like the thought of it. Ellsworth Vines would never faint in his life. I hung to the myth as the plane droned on toward Hollywood.

CHAPTER

15

Dorothy Bundy Cheney:

She Outlasted Them All, Becoming the Enduring Senior Champion of the United States

If there is a senior citizen of competitive tennis—a champion of all champions, one who has outlasted the best of them and surely could have the last laugh, if she chose—it would be Dorothy Bundy Cheney. If there were a contest of hanging in there to the final rounds and then knocking them off, one at a time, in some kind of crazy tennis brawl, no doubt the winner would be the smiling, graceful, engaging Dodo, who at sixty-seven looks healthier than anyone I had ever seen at her age. She wears her hair quite short, but it looks as though she fluffs it up with a blow dryer, and she has a Yankee look, an old New England way about her that made me think of Connecticut, of gutsy women who outlive their husbands by twenty years. Her face is slightly wrinkled, but only slightly, and her eyes are often narrowed by too many hours of looking into the sun. She has a strong nose and a face that belongs in town meetings. Not a large woman—in fact fairly small of stature—she glides and scampers like a kid, with no extra weight, no apparent arthritis, and seemingly no body problems at all. A phenomenon, Dodo Cheney has been almost unbeatable for decades as she racked up her many victories. I can only list some of them below—after a comment or two on her younger days.

Dodo started getting ranked in the top ten in 1936. She was third in 1937, following Helen Jacobs, who in turn followed Alice Marble. In 1938 she was also third behind Sarah Palfrey, and again, Alice Marble was at first

241

36. Dodo: Just a girl. In later years she became the all-time senior champion on all
surfaces

place. For ten years, she was ranked in the top ten and did, in fact, win two major tournaments before age began to creep up on her and turn her into a born-again dynamo.

Dodo won the U.S. Clay Court singles title in 1944. She also won the indoor doubles in 1941, playing with Pauline Betz. And on March 4, 1984, I would play her in singles at the Riviera Tennis Club in Pacific Palisades, a section of the Los Angeles sprawl.

Here is Dorothy Bundy Cheney's record in Senior Tennis:

U.S. Indoor: Women's 50 and over

           Singles—1976, 1977, 1978
           Doubles—1978, 1979, 1980, 1982

U.S. Indoor: Women's 55 and over

           Singles—1977, 1978, 1979

U.S. Indoor: Women's 60 and over

           Singles—1977, 1979, 1980, 1981, 1982
           Doubles—1980, 1981

U.S. Indoor: Senior Mixed Doubles

           1971, 1977, 1978

U.S. Clay Court: Women's 50 and over

           Doubles—1978

U.S. Clay Court: Women's 55 and over

           Singles—1977, 1978, 1979
           Doubles—1978, 1979, 1980, 1981 (in 1981 she was 65 years old)

U.S. Clay Court: Women's 60 and over

           Singles—1977, 1978, 1979, 1980, 1981, 1982
           Doubles—1979, 1980, 1981, 1982

U.S. Clay Court: Women's 65 and over

           Singles—1981, 1982

U.S. Hard Court: Women's 40 and over

           (Probably a record of some kind) Dodo won the singles title

thirteen years in a row from 1957 through 1969. In the doubles, she won it ten times from 1957 through 1977.

U.S. Hard Court: Women's 50 and over
        Singles—1971, 1975
        Doubles—1976, 1977

U.S. Hard Court: Women's 55 and over

        Dodo won all five years from 1976 through 1980 in singles
        (ages 60–64)
        Doubles—1979, 1982

U.S. Hard Court: Women's 60 and over

        Singles—1979, 1980, (1981 not held), 1982
        Doubles—1982

U.S. Hard Court: Women's 65 and over

        Singles—1981, 1982
        Doubles—1981, 1982

U.S. Grass Court: Women's 40 and over

        Singles—1964, 1967
        Doubles—1969, 1976, 1977 (at 60 years old)

U.S. Grass Court: Women's 50 and over

        Doubles—1977, 1980

U.S. Grass Court: Women's 55 and over

        Singles—1978
        Doubles—1978, 1979, 1980

U.S. Grass Court: Women's 60 and over

        Singles—1979, 1980, 1981, 1982
        Doubles—1979, 1980, 1981

U.S. Grass Court: Women's 65 and over

        Singles—1981, 1982
        Doubles—1982

The *1983 Official USTA Yearbook*, which I use as my source, does not include 1983 results. But 1983 would show the name Cheney once again.

By last count, Dodo Cheney has won 133 national titles, starting in 1941, when she won the indoor doubles with Pauline Betz as her partner.

Dodo's mother, May Sutton (Bundy), won the Wimbledon singles championship in 1905 and 1907 and the U.S. title in 1904, and was ranked off and on nationally for many years, all the way up to the 1928 listings. Dodo, who had also been a member of the Wightman Cup team for three years (losing once with the venerable Helen Wills as a partner, and also with John Van Ryn's wife, Marjorie Van Ryn, and winning in the doubles with Mary Arnold), had tennis in her blood. And I knew all this when I asked her to play on a hard court where she does not lose. Ever.

All of this came about because I was still a day early for my meeting Jack Kramer, who was still recovering. Once again I was staying with Lennie Baker at his apartment on Hollywood Boulevard. I called Kramer to make a date for March 5, leaving myself open for Dodo, who knew nothing about me. But she agreed to play at once. So I packed up my suitcase and carrying bags, called a taxi, and went off to the Riviera Tennis Club. I knew I was feeling "funny," but I was still not really concerned. It probably was the heat—either heat sickness or some kind of sunstroke. I did not pause to buy a hat. I was pleased that I had another game forthcoming with a woman who intrigued me—a late bloomer. After that I would move to the Bel Air Sands Hotel to be near Kramer.

We met on a cement veranda, where you can look out over the tennis courts and watch the play. I left my bags on the veranda and found the men's locker room to change into my tennis clothes. Dodo was waiting for me, dressed to play. She smiled a good deal—a kindly, grandmotherly smile, and I respected both of her names: Bundy and Cheney. They had a strong Yale-Hartford ring to them. Indeed, she is some relation to both the Bundy family of note (William and McGeorge—Yale men) and, through her husband, to the Cheneys of Hartford (the Cheney Mills—once a major industry in the Connecticut Valley). Oddly, Gardnar Mulloy's wife's maiden name is also Cheney, and she is from New London. Curious, I thought, but inconsequential. The fact was, I had to play the old gal. I'd try to hit it to her and be gentle as I had hoped to be against Alice Marble.

But no dice. She covered the baseline, corner to corner, and moved in easily on my shots to midcourt. Thump! and she'd put away anything I hit to midcourt. My serve was good, but it always came back at a sharp angle. And with a succession of excellent placements, crosscourt thumps on the sweet spot of her racquet, she had me perplexed. She did not err. Ever.

I suppose I could have given her a better game. No doubt I was losing stamina and was slow to move. I appeared stunned. I recall being tentative and never forceful. Yet, had I been my peppy self, it would still have been thump!

on the sweet spot. Her ability to return shots and her tendency to scamper like a child were my undoing. At her age of sixty-seven, she wasn't supposed to play like that. I like to think that under different circumstances—in better health—I might have won a few games. But I was playing a woman who *did not lose* on a hard court. I knew her record. She would have beaten me at my best. As it was, she triumphed 6–0. And though I kept thinking that a hard court was her surface, I also shuddered at the thought of grass. Maybe, just maybe, I might have given her a match on clay. I wondered about that as we left the court, Dodo aglow and I smiling and shaking my head in disbelief.

We had lunch in the club restaurant, and I turned on my tape recorder. She was wearing a pretty white warmup jacket embroidered with little tennis racquets. After I gave my recorder a quick testing, she went right into our interview. She was born in Santa Monica (a "native Californian"), which I knew from past experiences on the Coast was something you did not hesitate to point out if, indeed, you were a native. It was the California equivalent of a Boston Brahmin, but proper Bostonians *never* talked about it; they *assume* you know. In California it meant you were from a family that predated the migrations of the Depression, that predated Hoover, and nowadays I suppose you could say the migrations from Mexico. It meant "old family" and was a way at getting even with stuffy Easterners. I kind of liked it. One heard that "native Californian" business a lot around San Francisco. Now I was getting it here in Pacific Palisades.

Her father was also a champion. He played with the "California Comet," Maurice McLoughlin, and they won the National doubles at Longwood three years in a row (1912, 1913, 1914). In 1910 he was runner-up in singles at Forest Hills. All of this Dodo was happy to impart. She was proud of her background and said she had started playing tennis at eight years old. It was interesting, I thought, that she had done so well following in her mother's and father's footsteps. Often this is impossible—real achievers often place too much pressure on their offspring. Examples of this are commonplace. But as I looked at Dodo, I saw the pride she had in her parents and the pride she had in herself. She was happy talking with me. I got the idea that she was delighted in being "discovered," that just maybe she had been overlooked. Winning everything in sight in the seniors' might have neither sex appeal nor charisma. What a lot of nonsense, I thought as I listened to her. A stunning example of power, she outshone, in my eyes, a dozen Tracy Austins.

"I went to both prep school and high school in Santa Monica and then on to Rollins College. Jack Kramer went there too. I went the whole four years, and I think Jack went for perhaps one year . . . he had better things to do."

"Gardnar Mulloy says he got Jack Kramer to go to Miami for a while."

"Oh, no! He did go to Rollins, though," she said rather firmly, proud of her alma mater.

"If you had to rank the top five women's players of your time, how would you rank them?"

"I would say Maureen Connolly, Helen Wills, Alice Marble. Pauline Betz. Sarah Palfrey was my favorite, but I don't believe she was as strong as the other players I would put on the list, but she did have a superb volley, and . . ." she paused.

I mentioned Suzanne Lenglen.

"I never saw her play, but I have heard from various persons that in their estimations, she was the best woman player who ever lived."

"How would you rank Doris Hart, as an example?"

"Well, she was a beautiful player, but she had that handicap with her leg. I think she had polio as a child. Didn't she? I think she did, but even with that handicap, she was a beautiful player."

"What would be your greatest match? What match stands out in your mind as the best that you played?"

"Oh, my biggest thrill would be in 1937 when I beat Alice Marble in the semifinals at Forest Hills." (In 1937 the rankings were the following: Alice Marble, Helen Jacobs, and in third place, Dorothy Bundy. At Forest Hills, Anita Lizana beat Jadwiga Jedrzejowska 6-4, 6-2 for the title. Alice Marble returned for the next three years to win Forest Hills three times in succession. Whatever happened to Lizana and Jedrzejowska is a mystery. Were they East Europeans who were subsumed by Hitler and the Nazis?)

"Alice didn't mention that loss to me," I said.

"Oh, no, she's forgotten about that match, I'm sure, but I've never forgotten it."

"In women's doubles, who was the best player you played with?"

"Sarah [Palfrey]. She was one of the best doubles players who ever played because she volleyed so well."

"How about mixed doubles?"

"I played with Bobby Riggs a couple of times, and he was great fun to play with. I played with Jack Kramer, and we were runners-up one time at the National Doubles at Longwood."

"Don Budge was telling me that there are players you never heard of, club players who are very good in their later years—men who could give anyone a game."

"Oh, I doubt that. Frank Parker, if he competed, could beat anybody his age. Gardnar Mulloy is the best right now, but Parker would beat anyone were he to compete. Don't you think so?"

I agreed. "In fact, Parker did beat Mulloy a few years ago in straight sets.

But Parker is a bit younger than Gardnar, and maybe at that age this makes a big difference.''

"Going back to your club players. Those men [Parker, Mulloy, and Riggs] could beat any of them."

"But, I wonder," I said. "Look at someone like Chauncey Steele, Jr., Alex Swetka, and Bob Sherman—names you would not think of from the old amateur tournaments. Yet they win as seniors."

"Well, I think you hit the nail on the head. We who missed the big victories have stayed in shape and have kept on trying. The champions, like some of those you have met, don't have anything left to prove. They achieved the highest levels of success, and there is nothing left for them."

But I was thinking: so-called club players play in regional tournaments and win. It's just that you never heard of them in the big national tournaments. They didn't play the circuit. We got back to Frank Parker and his record of winning the boys, the juniors, and the national singles—the only man alive to do so.

"He may be the only man to do so—*period*," she said.

"Could be."

"How about Gonzales?"

"No, no," I answered. "I can't believe that Pancho Gonzales could have done that. Not the boys. I have a hunch he was still working his way up in the sport as a boy. He wouldn't have been a winner at that age." (He wasn't.)

"Well, he's out in Las Vegas," she said. "I hear he's trying to lose weight and give up smoking."

"Well, so am I," I said gleefully. "Maybe we can do it together."

"Oh, you're not fat," said Dodo Cheney. "You're tall and you need weight."

At that I beamed. Here is the kind of woman whom I need, I thought. But later I would hear myself on tape, and I was breathing hard and wheezing. And I am not tall. I am barely six feet, and I know I am about twenty pounds overweight. But back then, it sounded just fine. She asked me if I wanted anything else with lunch, and thinking of Gonzales, I wanted a cigarette. Before I could do anything, Dodo was up and trying to find me a pack. Apparently they were not for sale, and I had to borrow a Marlboro from a man at the next table. I said, "You shouldn't be doing this for me. I should be doing this for you [jumping about]," but she waved me off, still trying to get me a pack of cigarettes.

I went back to my questioning with the familiar, "If you had your life to live over again, would there be anything you would change?"

"Probably. Probably . . . but I have no complaints. I had a wonderful husband. I have wonderful children, lots of travel."

"Now, your husband was who?"

"His name was Arthur Cheney, and he was a pilot for Western Airlines. He passed away two years ago."

"When were you married?"

"In 1946."

"So you went through the same name change as did Sarah Palfrey. First it is Dodo Bundy in the record books, and then suddenly it is Cheney—in a way you lose something by this, a mix-up in image—this problem that besets women."

She acted as though she didn't hear my remark. She said, "I have three wonderful children and seven great, beautiful grandchildren . . ."

I interrupted, "To get back to my question, I can see that you really wouldn't want to change anything. Not be richer or poorer or more glamorous . . ." At this point she interrupted *me*.

"More glamorous! Definitely more glamorous," and she laughed loudly at the thought.

"But basically, though . . ."

"Oh, I just think you should be content with what you *do* have."

"If you could make up a scenario in which you had control of the whole world, what would you do?"

"I would have no more wars. But then I guess you have to have a little conflict in order to evaluate, to appreciate things. To balance it out. I would allow a few feuds and so forth, but not all the killing. And crime! I think crime these days is . . . oh, I don't know, it's so scary."

"If you look back over your life, who are the people you admire the most—across the board, not just in sports?"

"Evonne Goolagong."

"I mean across the board, not only sports figures." I knew what she meant about Goolagong. An Australian aborigine, she had worked her way to victory at Wimbledon.

"Right now I admire Ronald Reagan. I think he has been a wonderful president. He has a lot of class, an awful lot of know-how, and if he had some important support, I think he would steer our country the right away."

"How about some others?"

"You always have to admire someone who contributed to mankind."

I let the subject dangle, because she did not want to go on. Apparently the glow of Ronald Reagan was enough. But lest any liberal take offense, this feeling for Reagan and for the political right was fairly common. Only Pauline Betz and Althea Gibson would argue from a liberal bias, I thought, as Dodo paused to think. Maybe Gardnar, the agnostic, would find Reagan hard to swallow because Gardnar insisted on honesty, but clearly out here in the West, in Reagan territory, I was feeling vibrations from the right. I sensed that you would not go around in the tennis crowd championing welfare or social programs to the champions. I don't mean this as an unkind remark. It just seemed to be in the cards. Superb athletes are often conditioned to make it on their own; Horatio Alger is *real* to them. It seemed to be an old-fashioned definition of "character" that had seeped into their souls. Weakness is not lauded.

"Oh, I'll tell you something. Going back to my favorite mixed doubles partner, I would have to say Hugh Stewart. He now plays in the Masters, and we played some together. And then going way back, I played with Geoff Brown at Wimbledon. I liked him. He was a Canadian, and in 1946 we reached the finals at Wimbledon. [They were beaten in the finals by Tom Brown, Jr., and Louise Brough.] Basically, he should be my favorite partner because, oh gosh, he was good. He played two-handed like Bromwich."

"You dominate the seniors so totally—I wonder, to what do you attribute your good health and longevity?"

"To my mother. She was a very good player and strong and healthy, and she had three sisters who were the same, and I think I inherited the Sutton genes."

"And you have good health habits, I would guess?"

"Yes. I have good health habits. I don't smoke, but I will take a drink in the evening."

"You play every day?"

"No. I like to be fresh before each tournament. I don't work out between them. I play social tennis and fun tennis in between tournaments, but I like to be raring to go when it is time for a tournament. I want to be able to bear down when it is time."

"When you play one of these senior tournaments, are you paid for that?"

"No. Now, some of them have cash awards, so I might win one of those—possibly, occasionally."

Possibly, occasionally. She wins on clay, indoors, on a hard court, and on grass. What else is left, other than the Public Courts Championships, which she doesn't enter?

I told her that I thought she was one of the nicest persons I had met—certainly as far as meeting the great players. It was one of those things I just blurted out because she seemed so pleasant and so very unpretentious. I told her that I had felt the same way when I had met Sarah Palfrey.

At the name of Sarah Palfrey, she jumped right in. She said, "Sarah is just a few years older than I, and as I was growing up, she was my idol. I thought she was lovely."

As she ended her tribute to Sarah, I could not resist asking her what I called my off-the-wall question because I always felt that it took people by surprise. "Do you believe in God?"

"Of course," she answered immediately and almost by reflex, as though she were waiting for the question and was right on cue.

"How would you describe God?"

"The Creator, a spiritual being . . . I am continually thanking the dear Lord for all my blessings."

"Do you go to church?"

"No. I try to live by God's ways. I believe in the Golden Rule absolutely. All you have to do is to look at nature, and you know that there is a supreme power. There has got to be a designer of all things."

I asked her, "If someone came along and gave you a lot of money to use, how would you use it?"

"Oh, I would give it to my children to help them with their mortgages," she said, but she was laughing. She knew I was trying to get at some form of charity.

I mentioned that Alice Marble and Bobby Riggs had once played an exhibition match in Harlem, and that it changed the course of Althea Gibson's life.

"Well, for twenty years, I had a tennis program in Santa Monica, where we tried to encourage kids to play tennis. I arranged competitions for them."

"But with an outright gift, you'd go to your own children first."

"Oh, yes, and I would build myself my own tennis court." She was laughing again. This was all fantasy, and she didn't want to pretend that she would go to the needy or into the jungles to "do good." I told her that if I had been asked the same question—what I would do with a windfall of money—I would say, "I would not know how to answer the question."

"Knowing you," she said, "I think you would give most of it away—to where it would do the most good."

I was somewhat stunned by her remark. No one had ever thought of me in such eleemosynary terms. I wasn't given to charity as much as I was given to charitable thoughts. My deeds hardly matched my words, but I was nevertheless flattered. I'd been called a libertine, a sybarite, and worse. But no one had ever called me charitable.

Dodo drove me on to the Bel Air Sands Hotel. On the way over we chatted about Pauline Betz, a fellow alumna of Rollins. Dodo was pleased that I had seen her. She was very fond of the younger tennis star and called her an intellectual. I agreed—knowing that Pauline had pursued economics at Columbia University, was now studying tax law, and was a bridge lifemaster, but Dodo's use of "intellectual" had to be taken in the context of athletes. Pauline would not have thought of herself as an intellectual when set against the academic community or the hot minds of New York and other cities, where (for some people) the very process of thinking, in itself, is the prime en-

37. Dodo Cheney

joyment of life. As far as I was concerned, I had met a group of outstanding people, but on my tour, had yet to meet an intellectual. Wheezing as I was, it seemed a haunting choice of words. Suddenly I had been thrust back to the East Coast and *The New York Review of Books, The New Republic,* and *Commentary*—all blessedly absent from my life since I had started on my project. Sitting in Dodo's car, I was reminded of dim cafés where coughing, cigarette-smoking, skinny men talked of Ezra Pound.

Dodo asked, "How do you think I would do against Pauline in singles?"

I answered, "You would beat her. I think you would have no trouble," but I was thinking of all the women I had played and concluded that only Shirley Fry would have given Dodo a game and won. She was eleven years younger, but Dodo had been playing tournaments—it would be close. "I would like to see you and Pauline play, however," I added. "Her backhand is still a thing of beauty, and she has a nice, hard, flat forehand. But I don't see how she could win because you are so steady."

"Well, I'll be darned," said Dodo. "You really think that I can beat Pauline?"

"Absolutely," I answered.

"After all these years?" she said.

And it was true. After all these years, Dodo Cheney was supreme for her age and supremely above women everywhere to at least five years her junior. Her record seemed to be conclusive proof of that. I fantasized, "Wouldn't it be fun to get Shirley Fry and Dodo and Pauline and Althea and make a weekend of it. Singles and doubles. I'd love to witness such a tennis weekend."

I thanked her for the ride and the set of tennis and checked into the Bel Air Sands. Jack Kramer lived nearby, up there in the movie-star hills, and Dodo Cheney, a grandmother with a New England town-meeting face, drove away.

16

Jack Kramer:

Period

I would soon learn that if Ted Williams had turned hitting a baseball into a science and then had mastered the delicate art of fly casting, Jack Kramer was also a master and had correspondingly taken tennis to heart and mind and let it consume him. So consumed, Kramer had become the expert on the sport, an expert from every conceivable angle. His playing days were over, but he was as much involved—probably more involved—with tennis than he had been when he was unquestionably the premier player in the world and a man who is ranked in everyone's top five since the dawn of the game.

Scientific, professorial, and always enthusiastic, Jack Kramer reminds me of no one I have met. He adores the game that made him wealthy and commanding and a leader. A very fortunate person, he took a glamorous sport and rode with it into an era where it became big business. He could work at something he loved and keep himself in the big time while doing it. No professional shaking hands around the tennis court at some club; no teacher of tennis at a college; not one to switch careers—he simply kept riding the waves that rolled him to world reknown.

I would quickly learn that Jack Kramer was indeed the man to see if you ever wanted to get inside the game of tennis. He saw all the angles and the subtleties of the game, and he knew his business the way a great tailor knew his material. It seemed that he could take the game and actually "handle it." He was an inspector, a connoisseur. He could talk of tennis the way Ted Williams might talk about fly casting or baseball. Many of the great players had said in effect, "Find something you like and go with it." Jack Kramer had done that to perfection. He is not a futile jack-of-all-trades. (I recalled Budge's warning.) He is a sportsman and the "Jack of Tennis."

I called him from the Bel Air Sands, and he said he would meet me in the morning. We would, in fact, spend much of the day together. He, a whizbang of energy, just having had the flu, full of newly released power, and feeling his energy.

Kramer arrived at the Sands in his bright red Cadillac Seville coupe, and we went to his house to talk. He lives in the hills in Westwood, near the actor John Forsythe, who forsook a Broadway career for Hollywood gold and who is now the star of a series called "Dynasty." Kramer was quick to point out his friend's house as we wound our way up into the hills, so verdant with shrubs and flowers and exciting architecture. The Cadillac had red leather seats, and though cigarette smoking had dulled my senses, I could still smell the leather as I gazed at the affluence around me and thought of the dour East. I thought of the term "hearty New Englanders." What, I wondered, was so hearty about being chilled all the time by the raw wind off the sea? I lived only a matter of yards back from the winter beach and the Atlantic Ocean. "Hearty," I said to myself, sarcastically. I could get good and hearty living this kind of life, I thought. If nothing else, I could spend all day just gardening. The place reminded me of Melbourne, Australia, or Perth—flowering shrubs, a blue sky, a climate conducive to exercise. Some people say that the Los Angeles climate is impossible, and I had heard all those jokes about Californians and light bulbs—but in these hills, I was turning as green as the shrubbery with envy.

We settled in his kitchen, and I placed my tape recorder on the table and let it catch Jack Kramer in action. He was fired up, probably overly enthusiastic because of his late incapacitation. Since his wife was at the Gene Autry Hotel in Palm Springs, he was without familial pressures. Though he could not play tennis—still too weak—he was at liberty to give me all the time I wanted. What could be better for a writer, and would I take advantage of it? Not thinking too much about that, I let things start, playing it by ear, winging it with the man I had come so far to see.

By the time we were sitting at Jack Kramer's kitchen table, we were talking loosely to each other. By that I mean it seemed that we were old friends, and the first thing Jack recited was a short anecdote about George Burns.

"We were out at the Hillcrest Country Club, and George Burns joins us for lunch. I was with a nephew of a friend of mine from my Coast Guard days

255

and he organized this lunch at this marvelous country club. George Burns comes over and sits down just to have a bowl of soup before he runs back to his bridge game. Now, George Burns is ninety, and the very first thing he says as he sits down is, 'Do any of you guys still———?' "*

At that Jack clapped his hands and roared and continued, rapid fire. "Norman Krasna [columnists used to refer to Krasna as a movie mogul] is with us and he has just shot his age, which is seventy-four. So I tell him that another man, Ellie Vines, shoots his age—I play with Ellie a few times a year down at La Quinta, and then who should walk by but Ellie himself. He was at a meeting right there at the club for the Senior Golf Association."

A gregarious, loquacious man, Jack Kramer was pacing his kitchen shaking his head over George Burns. He looked about six one and he was wearing an Hawaiian shirt, open at the neck, and patterned to suggest tropical seashells. His face is lined, and his eyes are narrowed the way Dodo Cheney's were. His face has that leathery look that goes with the eyes. He made me think of the Everglades and the men who spent their lifetime out in the broiling heat, running outboards into the deep glades, looking for snook and redfish and hidden oyster beds. It would be hard for him not to be expressive. He moves his large hands a good deal, and his deep jaw thrusts outward. I noticed that he has long ears and, of course, his hair is no longer the brush cut that he wore in his youth when he played "the big game" just before and after the war. It is thick and slicked back, straight and full over the ears that from top to bottom cover half of his head. No pretenses. Jack Kramer expressed himself excitedly as though no one had listened to him for a long time. I knew that was not true—his nature is such that he makes every meeting an adventure in locution.

"Ah, ah," he stammered, groping for the right way to put it and then regretfully breaking the news, he said, "I am not going to play any tennis. I'll tell you why. I played about eight or nine sets last month with my lawyer and my doctor. My doctor, Omar Fareeb, is the Davis Cup doctor, and he has been with me since 1948, and for some reason or other, I got very, very sore—so sore I couldn't even play golf. And now I am trying to get over this damn flu. 'Look,' my doctor says, 'if you want to go out and play once in a while with Frank (my attorney—this is after my operation on my back) and not go back for lobs and not go to the net after your serve and be happy to stay back and get your ass whipped, then go ahead.' Well, I did go out and play, and I got awfully sore, and I don't want to let you down, but after I shave, I've got to run down to the Olympic Committee—I'm the competition director for the

---

* George Burns used a word that is graphic and indeed funny when you envision him saying it. But it appears inappropriate when set in print.

Olympic Games—I've got to go by the office to pick up some mail, and I'll take you any place you want to go."

I looked across at him, still walking about his kitchen and took a breath and said, "Fine with me. All I want is ninety minutes with you, but . . . yeah, it's fine with me. Maybe we can have lunch together."

"Absolutely. We'll have a nice day, and anything I can do to further your request for information about these people [the champions I was interested in] I will do because they are my favorite people, too.

"But you're not going to talk to Segura?" he said suddenly.

I said I had to make a limit. "Otherwise, my book will go over 500 pages." Segura, one of the most popular stars of the past, had won two big singles tournaments—the U.S. Clay Court Championship in 1944, and the National Indoors in 1946. Occasionally the record book shows him winning a seniors' tournament and the National Intercollegiate singles three years in a row during the war, but top competition was scarce at that time. I knew of his professional career when he toured with Kramer, and I knew that he was an excellent instructor of tennis, and what tennis player did not know his name? But his 1944 victory was during the war, and that left the indoor title, but it was not enough for me to rank him. After college he was swallowed up by returning tennis stars. And he did not monopolize as a senior as did Dodo Cheney, and furthermore and more important, I was never a fan of his. To me, Francisco Segura was a star journeyman—a top player among the great men players but not a winner as an amateur who had captured my imagination. I tried to explain that to Jack, but he was running free. I tried to make it clear that my book would be about amateur tennis, for the most part, and would avoid professional tennis when possible. Segura was a great professional, but "pro tennis" before 1968 when "open tennis" came in is a story in itself.

"I thought Segura would be good for the interest of your book. I have written three damn books, and there is a guy who is a wonderful guy, brilliant, smart—Sy Ramo—who put together that big company, TRW. That character wrote one book on friendly tennis on the weekends and outsold all my three. He rubs it into me, and he gave all the receipts to the University of Southern California Medical Center—that's the kind of guy he is."

"Well, I would like to talk with Segura, but . . ." I said.

"Look, Stan. You can talk with anybody you want. I think the idea is rather infectious and I think everyone will want to cooperate, and I just talked to Louise [Brough], because I have most of the people you are talking about, and I got them to join the Olympic Games in what we call a Jury of Appeals—I've got Gonzales and Trabert—Tony's out here, incidentally . . ."

"Tony Trabert is just a little on the young side."

"But Segura—Segura is *out and away* the most popular tennis player who ever walked on a court among the guys you are writing about. We have more memorable stories about Riggs and Segura than anybody. Alice Marble was just a bit ahead of me, and I don't know too much about her. Ellsworth Vines was my coach, so I know him, and Budge is one of my closest friends, and I always say that day-in and day-out, he is the best player I have ever played against or seen. And Gardnar [Mulloy], we go back a long way together. I was sort of an altar boy at his wedding, and it was Gardnar's father-in-law [a doctor] who figured out that if I put something on my racquet instead of my hand I'd be able to play, which allowed me to win the national championship in 1946. I put a Dr. Scholl's moleskin on the butt piece of my racquet, and Ted Schroeder and I won the doubles down at Newport, and then I won the singles at Forest Hills.

"Where is Segura, again?" I asked, knowing I had better give in and get this Segura matter over with.

"Oh, he is down at La Costa, about twenty miles north of Schroeder. There is an angle to Segura. He is what you could call 'the players' choice.' You see, Segura learned to play watching Riggs and me, and Gonzales and me, and playing against us. Then he had a chance to play, and he beat Gonzales at Forest Hills and beat me in Cleveland in five sets for the Professional Championship, and he owned guys like Rosewall till he was thirty-nine."

I promised that I would see Segura and said timidly that I was getting so much material that I could get my subjects mixed up. Details would get jumbled.

"Are you getting pressure from your editor?" he asked sternly. "They [the editors] loused up my last book [The Game: My Forty Years in Tennis]. They put some pressure on Frank Deford and me at the very end, and we left some things out and we okayed a lot of things that I wouldn't have wanted in. Ned Chase, Chevy Chase's father, was in charge of the project—a marvelous man—and he moved on to another publishing company, New York Times Books. Deford did the writing, and I went along mainly because of Ned, and when he moved on, they put someone else in charge and we lost it. So," he concluded, "don't let them push you around."

I said that I wouldn't let them do that and that I had my own deadline, that no one was bothering me. Once again I mentioned the scope of the book and how I had to omit some people. I mentioned Beverly Baker Fleitz. I made the mistake of calling her "second tier."

"You can't put her in the second tier," he said. "Beverly was there for a short time. She was cute as hell, and she had those two forehands! So, you give her a short chapter," he cautioned me.

With that remark, I thought, "Here we are, going at it. The competition never ends with these guys." On the verge of bickering, we were going over the contents of my book. "Good grief!" I said. "I have written more than three hundred pages already and have hardly left the East Coast."

"Did you see Parker?" he asked.

"Yes. I played Frank Parker in Chicago, and also George Lott. I beat Lott, but he is seventy-seven years old."

"That son of a gun," Kramer said with affection. "Now you're bringing back some thoughts. I know we are going to talk about what it was like being a player. Hell, I quit being a player really seriously in 1953. I had it in my mind to make pro tennis work like pro golf so that my friends and I would have a chance to make a living without playing in bad places at the wrong time of the year. You know," he said, "all of us remember it like it was yesterday."

"Who do you think was the greatest player of all time?"

"On his record, you gotta say Bill Tilden—Big Bill. Of those I saw and played against, it was Budge. And my allegiance, as far as affections, leans toward Ellsworth Vines on one of his hot days, and in my mind, watching him hit the goddamn ball, and knowing what he could do with it and knowing he played with a somewhat dinkie shoulder when he played Budge on the tour— you know (shoulder and all), on that tour Budge only beat him 22–17. When he was helping me back in the period of 1937, he used to have to go to a certain place, and we'd go through a gate where there was some heavy piping, and he would hang and twist around so he would stretch something back there so he could go out and hit. So if Ellsworth had been in shape and ready on that tour, I don't know if Donald was better."

"Budge and others said that on a given day, no one could touch Ellsworth Vines."

"Well, there were three guys like that. Vines, number one. Laver, number two, and Hoad, number three. But you have to think of timing. Laver came up just at the right time. Hoad and Rosewall were older, and Gonzales, who was still a hell of a threat, was gone [to the pros], and the younger kids hadn't really come along, so timing as far as that record book goes is very important."

I then told Jack how Don Budge had ranked the top five and how he had left Tilden out because Bill Tilden had no net game.

Jack interrupted me. "He didn't need one," he said, laughing, and I remembered that his remark was almost the same as George Lott's.

"I saw Bill enough," Jack said. "I would skip school to play Bill Tilden"—the net game apparently irrelevant.

"Who was your favorite doubles partner?"

"Well, Schroeder and I did quite well. We sort of grew together in 1940 and 1941. Then the war broke us up, and we came back and played the 1946 and 1947 Davis Cup and lost a match in Boston [to McNeill and Guernsey], or we would have won four [U.S. Doubles Championships—they won in 1940, 1941, and 1947, but couldn't match the record of Talbert and Mulloy who *did* win four titles]. But the funny thing is, even when Budge was over the hill, he and I could beat Segura and Gonzales. Segura is my age, and Gonzales is seven years younger, and then Segura and I were a hell of a team. I won Wimbledon playing with two guys I hardly ever played with. I only played one tournament in my life with Tom Brown, and we won Wimbledon, and Bob Falkenburg and I only played together in four or five tournaments. I'd say when you consider consistency and so forth, I would say Schroeder, but we had developed an awful good feeling for each other, which has lasted through the years, and when you play in a tournament and it comes to a real good fight, under pressure you have to play with a guy you like. You have to be able to let the guy blow his serve and say, 'That's okay. We'll get them next time.' If you don't like your partner, you don't want to say that."

"How about mixed doubles?"

"The mixed doubles game was fairly big when I was a kid. In 1940 Dodo Cheney and I were runners-up to Riggs and Marble. And in 1941 Sarah Palfrey and I won it [at Longwood for the U.S. title], but I have a sense that—after the war I played a little mixed doubles with Helen Wills—I would suspect that *she* would have been my best mixed doubles partner. Helen always ended up doing what a good lady's mixed doubles partner should do—she got the ball over the other gal's head and then turned the court over to me. So we were able to beat Pauline Betz and her partners, and Louise Brough and people like that, even though Helen Wills wasn't even playing singles. She was a marvel."

Jack Kramer was rolling now, and he continued with his thoughts on mixed doubles. It was sad but true, he told me, that nowadays when the big money highlights the singles at night, you don't want to play in the mixed doubles that might be scheduled in the afternoon before your match, or even in the men's doubles for that same reason. A modern player who has a chance at the singles title will want to save his strength. Kramer recalled the old days when you had to enter all three events in order to stay in the tournament and get your room and board. But with professional tennis and night tennis the way it is now—"Doubles is becoming obsolete. Of course," he added, "by playing night tennis at Flushing Meadows, you will get ten sellouts in a fourteen-day tournament, and a lot of money goes back into tennis. But with that kind of pressure, the afternoon matches, particularly the mixed doubles, can get sidelined in importance. Of course," he said, "at Wimbledon and Paris, you still only play daytime tennis, but who wants to play mixed doubles well into the late afternoon and into the early evening and then have to rise early the next day for singles when maybe your opponent will be fresh?"

Most people had thrown off my next question to Jack Kramer, taking it

260

lightly, but Kramer was serious when he answered my standard query: "If you had your life to live over, would you change anything?"

"I think there were a couple years there, Stan, where I didn't apply myself as hard as I should have. I had a reputation as an awfully hard trier. I was a nut on equipment and trained hard and, generally speaking, I made a total sacrifice to be a better player. But from the time I first played the Davis Cup in 1939, I was as good a player who was around. Yet, at eighteen I was damn good, but I had other interests. Not necessarily dames, but I loved to play cards and poker and stay up at night, and I didn't practice so hard for a while, and quite honestly, the war shook me up so much that I realized that I was a hell of a tennis player who excelled at doubles and might have won the singles in 1942 if I hadn't gotten screwed up and missed that year—I had an appendix taken out—and I was in California and Schroeder won. I don't like to take away his winning, but at the time it appears that I had a hell of a shot of winning that. So that might have changed my life a little bit because had I won that 1942 championship, I might have been used differently in the war effort. Instead of being at sea for twenty-two months on a LST, I could have been stationed in the States, where I could screw off the war being a tennis player, playing exhibitions . . . The point is that I couldn't play, and when the war was over and I got back, I knew (because I had screwed up my education) that my future had to be on the tennis court. I knew I had to follow Budge and Vines and become a professional. All the dedication and practice I put into tennis *after* the war—had I done that *before* the war, I would have been a better player. So, I was a little stupid as a kid."

"Forgetting sports for a minute—if you could change the world to make it better, what would you say?"

"You mean the *general* world?" He seemed shocked by my question.

"Yes."

"I come from rather nice parents. I come from Las Vegas, Nevada, and because of my Dad, not from me—my Dad couldn't participate in sports, he had to go to work at eleven years old and never went back to school, I got wonderful treatment from him and a good set of values—I never had any 'antis.' I had friends who were blacks. I played football against them, and baseball in the old days in school—I remember sharing a bunk with a kid named Popeye Powell, and we would run up to another place in Nevada and play basketball. I never had any problems with Jewish situations either, even though in the early days there *was* a real problem. Blacks weren't allowed to play, and they circumvented Jews in the very club where I played most of my tennis by denying them membership. Yet I was raised without any of that stuff and counted blacks and Jews and anybody among my friends, and that came from the traveling and experience and from the training I received from my Mom and Dad.

"I think I am generous in a way. I have done awfully well in business and have no problems financially. In some ways, I think I would be a happier and more fulfilled guy if I had not spent as much time making tennis a better sport —spent that time trying to get into the political world. Had I done that, I might have done something important. Sports are nice and they are fun for those of us who do it for fun and end up making it our livelihood and set up our families. It is really terrific, but it is so small compared to . . . I'll tell you if you want to do something big, you have to do it in the political area, that is all there is to it."

"If you did go into politics, what would you be? What party would you choose?"

"I am a very conservative Republican. In tennis, for example, I use my conservative philosophy. You take a youngster, and if you give him help, the nature of which he doesn't understand, eventually it will ruin him. I have seen talent indulged by parents and associations that make it too easy, and by the time someone gets to be seventeen, he can't play at all."

"You came from a lower-middle-class background where your father worked his way up?"

"He started work calling crews—that is, waking people up to get to work on the engines, and he ended up being a fireman, then an engineer, and finally road foreman for engines. I remember my father coming home one time when they, the Brotherhood of Railroad Employees, took a 30 percent cut in pay to help out the Union Pacific. This meant he went from $240 a month down to $180 a month. It was in the early 1930s, the Depression, and it put a damper on everything we were trying to do, so we never had any money."

"When you were a kid, did you have any heroes?"

"Baseball was my favorite sport, and of all things, the Philadelphia Athletics were my heroes. It probably was my Dad's influence. He couldn't play games, yet he was a sports enthusiast, so I played them. I started playing catch as soon as I could stand, and we started playing Ping-Pong almost by accident on our table, which led us into tennis. I had a basketball backboard in my backyard. I was a pole vaulter as a kid, but baseball was my sport, and when the World Series came on, my Dad would let me skip school to listen to the games that were coming out of the East—there were no teams on the Coast in those days. As I recall it, the big series in those days was the one with the Cardinals against the Athletics, a team that had Jimmy Foxx, Lefty Grove, Al Simmons, and Eddie Collins. It all came in on radio, and I played a lot of baseball in those days. I could hit the hell out of the ball and played first base. In those days, when I lived in Las Vegas and went to junior high school, you had a lot of time for sports.

"Sports were a seasonal deal, and with my Dad's urging, I went from sport to sport. When the Olympic Games came to Los Angeles, my Dad, who had saved up his money, put my Mom up at Long Beach with an aunt of mine, and my father and I would drive up every day for nine days to see the Olympic Games back in 1932.

"But I really started playing tennis in San Bernadino. My Dad had to go there two, maybe three, years for the Union Pacific for retraining, and I went with him. The second time I was there, it was 1935, and I was introduced to a man named Robin Hippenstiel, who was the local tennis champion in San Bernadino. Now the best thing he ever did for me was to take one of his younger brothers and me over to Pomona. There was a racetrack there where they held the fair, and Vines and George Lott and Stoefen and Bill Tilden had laid down a court and played an afternoon exhibition. Ellie Vines played against Les Stoefen. That was the first time I had seen anybody really good, and that was when I saw Vines. The impression that he made drove the idea—look, I have a rib and a nose broken from playing kid football in Las Vegas—that impression I got of Vines drove the idea or any image I had of Jimmy Foxx and baseball right out of my mind. I wanted to play tennis from then on."

Jack Kramer moved back to Las Vegas and won a local junior tournament, and his father, seeing what his son could do, and having seniority with the railroad, arranged a transfer. The Kramer family moved to the Los Angeles area, to the town of Montebello, where Jack went to high school and where he could find good tennis competition and training. "I went to school until 12:15. Then I caught a bus to catch a streetcar to catch another bus so I could play tennis at the L.A. Tennis Club." In 1936, playing in the boys' fifteen, Jack Kramer's name entered the record book. He was the U.S. champion. And three years after seeing Ellsworth Vines and throwing down his first baseman's mitt, he became the interscholastic champion of the United States. In a rush to fame, Jack Kramer took two National Championships, one almost immediately upon turning his full attention to tennis. To paraphrase Gardnar Mulloy, Jack was already too good for college tennis at Miami and stayed only a year at Rollins, according to Dodo Cheney.

By 1939 he was on the grass circuit. The Southern California Tennis Association paid his way East, and his father, the railroad man, had a pass so that Jack could entrain East to the tournaments and ride free. "It didn't cost a hell of a lot of money that way," he said.

"Did you ever get paid under the table?"

"Sure," he answered.

"Well, Don Budge [or Billy Talbert, I thought later] said he never made a dime from amateur tennis."

"He's wrong," said Jack.

"That's what Frankie Parker said," I replied.

"The next time you see Budge, ask him about Prague. It was the year he won Wimbledon in 1938. I think Helen Wills came back that year to win the women's as well.* Anyway, he couldn't go to the ball on Saturday night because he had to go to Prague to play a kid named Jaroslav Drobny [later a Wimbledon singles winner]. He didn't go all the way to Prague and miss the ball just for fun!

"Look," he continued. "There was no way to avoid it. If you traveled as you did and came from moderate means, you needed help."

I mentioned that Gardnar Mulloy had told me that he could play off conflicting tournaments in Los Angeles and Dallas and then go with the one that paid the most money. I said he went to Los Angeles over Dallas one time or vice versa. I said, "I think they paid him $500 to go to the tournament in Los Angeles."

"Well, Jughead [Jack's name for Gardnar] never came out here too much. But I can tell you the going rate. It was $1,200. Riggs set the pace, so Perry Jones, who was the president of the Southern California Tennis Association and a close friend, told me, and when Parker came along after the war, *he* was getting $1,200.

"So when it came time for me to win in the Pacific Southwest Championships in 1946, Jones called me into his office and said, 'I paid Frank Parker $1,200 because he needed the money, even though you are the champion. I want you to have $1,200, too.' I said, 'Mr. Jones, you have helped me through the years, and why don't you consider my share a donation? As long as I'm an amateur, you won't have to pay anybody because I am the champion. I will want to play just for the fun of playing for you.' He thought that was great, and the next year, Frankie and I played our long five-set match which I was lucky to escape, as a matter of fact, and we went through the scene again, and Perry was kind of embarrassed. But I said, 'Perry, you won't have to pay Parker because I am the champion.' He said, 'Oh, well, Frankie was having some problems,' and so forth, so that was the first time I ever took any money from my own association.

"But the first time I took any dough was—when you travel as a junior, your parents and the association sort of help you, and [as he had said] I had an edge because I had a railroad pass—but in 1939 after we played Davis Cup at the Merion Cricket Club outside Philadelphia and Australia beat us 3–2 [John Bromwich easily beat Frank Parker in straight sets, and this lopsided loss had much to do with later events], we went on to New York, where I lost a tough five-setter to Joe Hunt, and I was a good friend of Johnny Bromwich, the top Australian player, and one of the vice-presidents of Celanese Corporation of America happened to be Australian. His name was Fred Small, and he talked Harry Hopman, the Australian Davis Cup team captain, into taking

* True indeed. She beat Helen Jacobs in the finals 6–4, 6–0.

John Bromwich to a place called Cumberland, Maryland, for a match. So Hopman and Bromwich and Joe Hunt and I went down to Cumberland, Maryland, on our way west to Los Angeles and the Pacific Southwest Tournament. Bromwich and I drove Gene Mako's car [Mako achieved stardom as Don Budge's doubles partner but was an excellent singles player as well] and after the match, Mr. Small came to me and said, 'We all enjoyed you down here, Jack, and I know we paid your expenses, but I want you to have a present,' and he gave me $100. That was the first time I got paid as an amateur.

"Later on in New York, I had played an exhibition with Harry Hopman, and a man came up—I didn't know his name—and he said that as a token of his appreciation, he would give me $50. We stayed at the Vanderbilt Hotel, and our expenses more than covered our needs, and the thought occurred to me immediately (you know, it's a terrible thing about life when you start getting paid for things), and I thought, 'Doggone it, Mr. Small is a lot better than this guy,' because Small had given me $100. And that was the second payoff I had ever gotten."

"Were you ever afraid that if this sort of thing came out in the press you would lose your amateur standing?"

"Well, the thing came up a little later. I imagine it was 1941.* Don McNeill and I had become very good friends, and Don had made a deal with the San Francisco tournament, which in those days was called the Pacific Coast, and it was a very big tournament, older than the L.A. tournament that started in 1927 . . ."

Suddenly the phone rang, and this was the second time he had to rise to answer it. This time it was from his son, who is executive secretary of the Southern California Tennis Association, a group that Jack has deep and kind feelings for. Apparently there was a problem regarding the composition of a committee, and I heard the name "Charlie" as in "Pasarell" being mentioned—'Give him seven years or so, and he'll be a good asset,'—and the name "Don," as in "Budge." Finally, Jack, trying to break off the conversation, said he was being interviewed. He said over and over again to call the judge, and the judge could in turn call him, the judge being Judge Robert J. Kelleher, president of the Association and the successor to Jack's mentor, Perry Jones. The name "Arthur Anderson" filtered through the house as Jack was talking very loudly and I recalled the name from interviewing Gussie Moran. Anderson had been Bill Tilden's protégé. I mention the telephone in terruption only to emphasize that tennis in southern California is very big and

* The year before, in 1940, the Berkeley Tennis Club had set Kramer up at a hotel with signing privileges and given him $125.00 as well. The Pacific Coast Tournament wanted Kramer and he says "for some reason they gave me $125.00 on top of all expenses."

very complex. If anything, it appeared to be overorganized. Committees, sub-committees, names, dates buzzed through Jack Kramer's house.

Then he was back talking to me, and not surprisingly, the Don McNeill story about being up in San Francisco and perhaps getting in trouble for taking money was lost. Previously he had told me why Don McNeill had not fared well at Wimbledon after winning the French title in 1939. He had been forced to play on wet grass with his regular tennis shoes. The other players had black "pole-vaulting shoes" and Don had gotten himself a set of spiked shoes that were not authorized. Thus, he slipped and slid in his sneakers on his way to defeat in the opening round because of wrong footwear. Later at Forest Hills, McNeill won the U.S. Championship. I could tell that Kramer was fairly protective of a man who he had thought was a great guy. In fact, at a major anniversary of the French Championships—at which all the former champions had been invited back, all the way to Cochet, Lacoste, and Borotra—it was Kramer who helped a disabled Don McNeill onto the court to take his bows. "He was in awful shape," Jack had said.

So the last story got lost because of the phone call, and we were suddenly back in 1946 talking about the factious Davis Cup squad that convened after the war. It was composed of former Lieutenant Commander Gardnar Mulloy, Billy Talbert, Frank Parker, Jack Kramer, and the slightly denigrated (by the Easterners) Ted Schroeder. The last member was Tom Brown, Jr.

By now the story is familiar and almost tedious in its retelling, but I was eager to hear what Jack had to say about Ted Schroeder getting the nod over Frank Parker. I was also interested in how they got along "down under." It had occurred to me many times that what we had sent to Australia was a group of men with very secure egos, each of them with a host of trophies. Only the young Tom Brown, Jr. was yet to be a national champion, but he was ranked fourth in the United States and was runner-up to Jack Kramer at Forest Hills. Above Brown were Kramer, Schroeder, and Parker in descending order. Behind Brown came Mulloy and Talbert. This was a hot group to be sent off as a team. It was a group of chiefs with no Indians. And although Talbert and Mulloy may have grumbled about Ted Schroeder, his name stands out in the record book prior to Davis Cup play in 1946. Ted Schroeder won the singles at Forest Hills in 1942, and playing with Kramer, he won the doubles twice, in 1940 and 1941. To dislike Ted Schroeder only four years after his taking the title at Forest Hills seemed odd to me. And those four years were war years. The Detroit Tigers did not exactly ignore Hank Greenberg when he came marching back to civilian life. It appeared to me that in 1946, there was an East-West confrontation, with Parker and Mulloy and Talbert versus Kramer and Schroeder and young Tom Brown. This is great stuff to the incipient novelist. There were loyalties on the line, egos at large, and a lieutenant commander (Mulloy) getting increasingly upset with team captain

266

Walter Pate's authority. And so I sat back and let "Mr. Tennis" inform me as to what had transpired.

First off, he said, both versions of Talbert being off his game or being sick with diabetes "are bullshit. Just bullshit." The inference I drew was clear. Billy Talbert just wasn't good enough at that time, in that place.

Now as for Mulloy teaming up with Parker after Billy Talbert more or less withdrew, I said, "Parker and Mulloy say they beat you and Schroeder in doubles every time."

"Bullshit," said Kramer. "Just bullshit."

"The story you got back East is false," he continued. "Now Perry Jones was a very strong man in amateur tennis. For at least ten or twelve years, southern California produced all the junior champions in both boys and girls—believe me, it was a very enviable record. And when you look back over the record, you will find that southern California produced more champions than did Australia or the rest of America. Now Perry was not a big-time politician. He was a big man in a small area—southern California. He *did* go to Australia for the Davis Cup in 1959 with Alex Olmedo [who won both his singles, and combined with Ham Richardson to win the doubles for an American 3–2 victory]—and I had a hand in that. [Alex Olmedo was not an American citizen, and this was a very touchy business—the idea of getting a foreign college student to play for the United States.]

"Now as far as Schroeder goes, he had beaten Frank Parker in 1942 at Forest Hills. War came, and by 1946 we are all back. One of the cute things that Perry Jones did—this shows his brains and so forth—there was a Davis Cup team *and* a Wimbledon squad. America and Great Britain had a deal where England would pay our two top players to go to Wimbledon, and we would pay their two top players to come to Forest Hills. Well, Perry got Tom Brown, and I elected to go on to England, where I got my blister and didn't enter the tournament, and Tom Brown (I think) lost in the semifinals. [He didn't bother to say that he and Brown *did* win the doubles, beating Dinny Pails and Geoff Brown.] Now at the same time we are over there, Talbert, Mulloy, Parker, and Schroeder were playing Davis Cup against the Philippines. Schroeder had a job with the Kelvinator Company, and he could not play the total circuit. He did come East to play the Newport event, which I recall that he won, and we won the doubles. Now after Newport, you go on to the national doubles at Longwood in Brookline, Massachusetts. We should have won that, but we got the stuffing kicked out of us by Don McNeill and Frank Guernsey in the semis. Billy Talbert and Gardnar Mulloy won the tournament on a disputed call that most people think was out—Talbert's shot that both Guernsey and McNeill were shaking their hands over, having assumed victory. But we all go on to Forest Hills except Schroeder. He has to go back to his job. At Forest Hills, I played McNeill in the semifinals, and I was scared to death of him because he had beaten me many times. But I won against him, yet it was supposedly Tom Brown's tournament, because he had beaten Parker and, I guess, Mulloy, and Falkenburg had upset somebody, and I beat him, and then in the finals I beat Tom Brown."

He stopped talking for a moment, his rush of words bringing back the great postwar games when no one really knew who was number one or two or three. Upsets dotted the landscape, and finally Kramer had come out of the turmoil of seedings to take the U.S. title.

"But Walter Pate was a problem. My best friend in the East was Alrick Man, who succeeded Pate as Davis Cup team captain. But Pate had made a deal—you see, the Australians didn't look too good. Bromwich did not come to Forest Hills. Dinny Pails played, and he looked pretty good, but I had played him before and wasn't worried. But the deal was made by Pate because he wanted revenge against Australia, which beat him in 1939 after Budge had turned professional. [On that squad, a young Jack Kramer and his partner, Joe Hunt, were beaten in straight sets by Adrian Quist and John Bromwich.] So Pate was made captain. His team of Talbert and Mulloy and Schroeder and Parker had gotten us through the Philippines. Now we had to play the Swedes, and Mulloy and Talbert and Parker and I shut them out. With that victory, we are in the finals against Australia. Schroeder and I were a team. I wanted him to play, and this is where Perry Jones entered the picture and exerted some leverage. He got Schroeder on the team. [Schroeder played one match in the Philippines and won it. In the follow-up match, prior to the match against Sweden, he was absent in America's sweep of the Mexicans, apparently back at his job with Kelvinator.] So the squad consisted of six players. Now both Schroeder and I are married, but Walter Pate had allowed Frank to bring his wife, Audrey, along. But not ours. I believe that he did make it clear to Frankie Parker that he would play the singles. But it was clear that I would play, and if he told Parker that, which I think he did, he kept it a secret from us so we would all be fighting for our spots in practice. Later at a meeting that was unusual for its frankness, Walter said that unless there was something wrong with Jack, he was going to play both singles and doubles—understood?"

I said, "Yes."

He went on. "So Schroeder is added to the team because I want him on the team, and Perry Jones lended his support. We go down there, and there is a pretty good fight in the practice all the time, and we play for the Victorian Championships in Melbourne, the scene for the upcoming Davis Cup match. Schroeder gets to the finals. Mulloy loses a good five-set match to Bromwich, who wins it all by beating Schroeder. Colin Long and Bromwich beat Schroeder and me in the doubles finals. I didn't play the singles because I went down there fighting a tennis elbow. Now all of a sudden, there is a problem. It is

Frank Parker. He didn't play the tournament in Melbourne at all. He wanted to practice himself into shape. So with six guys, there was plenty of room for Walter Pate to juggle us around and get a good deal of singles and doubles play. I believe that there was no doubt that Walter wanted Parker and me to play the whole thing. Parker was his man, and they held a meeting. This was a day before we had to name our squad. That is when the captain enters his four people and they draw the names from the envelope. So we had this meeting. So there it was—who is going to play? It was obvious that because Schroeder had gone to the finals, he had eclipsed both Brown and Talbert for sure. Mulloy had extended Bromwich in five sets, but no one knew anything about Parker. We knew he had won Forest Hills in 1944 and 1945. [These were service years when Mulloy and Kramer and Schroeder were unavailable, although Army Sergeant Frank Parker had been able to get to the tournament.] But he had not played in Melbourne. Yet there was this secret deal, and Walter said we are going to practice, and there was this juggling around, and Walter said we will nominate the four—Schroeder, Parker, Mulloy, and Kramer. As a matter of fact, Talbert and I might have been the best doubles team, but he was staying up nights, and he wasn't married yet, and he had a couple of romances going."

I laughed at this because I suspected all along that Talbert was sowing his oats. No doubt his diabetes did kick up and no doubt he was, indeed, off his game. I could sense this flair, and Talbert confirmed it when I had met him that he had more than just an inkling for the high life. But none of this explained Mulloy and Parker continually beating Kramer and Schroeder. Or did they? "Bullshit" had been Kramer's terse reply.

"Billy was better at it than the rest of us in that league," he continued. "He was one and Mulloy was two, but Billy had a damn fine time with the dames, and so did Gardnar, but I rather think that Billy was better at it because he was more entertaining. Gardnar always was a difficult sort of guy with dames all of his life.

"And, anyway, we have the four, and Walter Pate called the meeting. He did not want to select the team to play. Tom Brown and Billy Talbert were there as well—along with the four of us. Now, Walter always had a way of saying, 'Boys.' He said, 'Boys, now it is time for the big decision. So, boys,' he said, 'who are we going to play?' In my mind, I thought it had already been established. I was in good condition—these kids today have to take three and a half hours to play a three-set match when we would play a five-set match in less time—three hours. Those delaying tactics are all nonsense. Anyway, Pate said that he was instructed by the ATA [the American Tennis Association in which Perry Jones had leverage] to play me in both singles and doubles. Well, I spoke up and said that I was in good shape and that I had worked my ass off and I was ready for it, and I thought Schroeder should play the second singles match. [Because Pate was asking the question, the apparent arrangement with Parker was now uncertain at best, and Kramer plunged in with his nomination.] I said that Schroeder won at Forest Hills, that he was capable of the upset, that he always had been capable of an upset, that he was a fantastic fighter and had guts for the game. And besides all of that, he is going to play doubles with me.

"Walter said, 'Well, we haven't decided that yet, but yes, you are right, he's going to play doubles with you.' And then I looked at Frank Parker, and I said, 'Frank, I know the records as well as anybody, and there was never a time that you went further than your seeding.' So I said to Frankie, I said, 'The last time you played Bromwich he beat you *one, love,* and *three* in 1939. And along with this feeling I have that if Schroeder plays the doubles, he ought to play the singles, please forgive me . . . but you had a lot of shots at it, and you never upset anybody at Forest Hills.' I said, 'Frank, we need someone to upset Bromwich. He is the favorite over you and Schroeder and even me, if you read the papers. (The next year, you know, Parker did upset Bromwich at Forest Hills, but we are back in 1946 when he had not upset anyone) . . . so I want Schroeder in there for two reasons: he is capable of the upset, and he will improve his doubles by playing the singles.' Then Frank talks and says that he has done well against me through the years and that he was promised the singles. So Cap'n Pate begins to hem and haw.

" 'Now wait a minute, Frankie. I know we talked about it, but I didn't absolutely promise you.'

"And Frank says, 'I wouldn't have come down here if I wasn't going to play. I have been doing my own practice, and I haven't had a chance to prove that I can beat Bromwich and Pails because I haven't played them.'

"Well, what killed him was the other guys. Gardnar Mulloy stepped up and said, 'I agree with Jack. I don't like Schroeder at all, but if he is going to play the doubles, he should play the singles, too. He will have a better chance of upsetting Bromwich. And as far as I am concerned, Tom and Jack and Bill and Frank and I and Ted will all beat Pails.'

"So we all agreed, and the guy they almost didn't pick wins the Davis Cup. The draw came out Schroeder-Bromwich and then Kramer-Pails. So while I am sitting on my ass listening to the radio, Schroeder is out there and wins a five-set match, and it is all over. I played Pails and won, and we had a couple of close sets, but it was really all over with Ted's upset in the opening match. Then the dummies selected Quist to play with Bromwich in the doubles. All Quist hit were lollipops, and we wrapped it up in three sets. The only other thing worth mentioning was that there was a rain delay, and neither Bromwich nor I wanted to play. Bromwich was considered to be the loser of the whole thing and was pissed off because he lost, and I was afraid he might win against me. I had not played him since the time we took Gene Mako's car to Cumberland, Maryland, and then drove on to L.A., where I lost to him. And with the cup already won, I wasn't sure I would be up for the match.

"So there was the rain delay and then a Sunday when they don't play down there, and finally we agreed to play, and Ted Schroeder said, 'Jack, there is no way this guy can hurt you.' "

And he didn't. Jack Kramer took Bromwich in three close sets. Gardnar Mulloy went on to beat Dinny Pails, giving up fewer games than Kramer and presumably won his bet. Jack said that on further reflection, he just couldn't remember if they bet or not. The score was 5–0, and America had the cup in spades after a disappointing start in the preliminary tournament for the Victorian Championships. It had all come down to a vote, and Mulloy had spoken up for the one man he did not like. The lieutenant commander had let his intellect do the talking and Frank Parker did not play. In Jack Kramer's mind, this was a crucial decision, and he cannot recall anything like it in tennis— that is, a vote taken by the players themselves. Surely it is fixed in his mind that the opening match was the big one and that the right man (Schroeder) had risen to the task. Schroeder started the landslide that the great American all-star squad pursued with vigor. I would see Ted Schroeder soon, but in the meantime, I was still with Kramer and had a chance to observe him.

At sixty-two he is no longer the slender athlete. Now he is a man of some

38. Jack Kramer

bulk, tall and broad-shouldered and full-chested. His graying brown hair that wisps over his ears gives him a careless look. The grain of his skin combined with his Hawaiian shirt and a barker's checked sports coat makes him look like a roustabout. At home and unkempt, he sashays about his house, loose-jointed—his back problems notwithstanding. He is very sure of himself, and if you say that he is a man who has seen a few things in his life, it would be the plain truth. If Billy Talbert is sartorially attired and appears somewhat fastidi-ous, this man, Kramer, gives himself *room*. He is not the kind of man whom you would catch looking at himself in a mirror. He roams his kitchen and, when interrupted by the telephone, he tells his son, "If you can believe this, I am talking with Stan Hart about something that happened forty years ago. You will have to try me later." He can go back in time with the delight of a man who once outclassed everybody and will give a fellow the time of day to tell what it was like. He is open as a freeway that leads out of town, heading into the wild desert, and when I looked at him, I thought—*full throttle!* While Don Budge has the cast of a country squire, and Ellie Vines appeared just a touch patronizing, surely Mulloy could still be—even at seventy—in com-mand of an LST. And Parker, whom I liked immensely—he smiled like a Cheshire cat. Talbert was urbane. Lott, who is an earthy presence, could have been a baseball star—and acted like one. But Kramer? Kramer is all tennis. His rambling western ways evoke leadership because he lets it be known that he is right. You give a man like Jack a wide berth. You know he is the champ. Not to believe in Jack Kramer would be not believing in mountaintops. That is what I thought as I watched him and heard the lore of the game.

He wanted to talk about doubles. It should be remembered that he started out in Davis Cup play as a doubles player, and he and others consider him to be one of the best, if not the best at that specialty. But to me, hearing Kramer talk of doubles was like hearing Babe Ruth talk of pitching. With Kra-mer I had images of his big game in singles, just as I had of Ruth hitting a home run, although Babe Ruth had been a great pitcher in his brief tenure at that position. There were so many good doubles teams back through time—Lott and Stoefen considered the best, though Lott says he played his finest with John Van Ryn, who in turn almost always played with Wilmer Allison. But Kramer? He shifted partners. He therefore was not a doubles figure. Yet look at his record and listen to him talk.

"Starting in 1940, I win two years in a row playing with Ted Schroeder—[the National Championships at Longwood]—then in 1943, I win with Frank Parker. Then in 1946, I play one tournament in my whole life with Tom Brown, and we win Wimbledon. I play four tournaments with Bob Falken-burg, and we win them all, including Wimbledon in 1947. So by that time, in five out of the last six doubles championships at Forest Hills or Wimbledon, I am a winner." (Not quite. He is the winner in five out of the last *seven*. During the war in 1944 and 1945, he was on his LST. There was no Wimbledon during the war years, and for some time, he was absent from Longwood, otherwise detained in the Pacific.)

As far as the war went, he did manage some tennis action. He said he played three tournaments with Parker (including their win at Longwood in 1943) and won them all. Parenthetically he said that they were a pretty good team. Much later on, on the pro tour, they beat Gonzales and Segura. Segura by now had risen to high prominence, and Pancho Gonzales, the new champion of the world who rushed his professional entrance, doubtless felt as others had before him that there was money to be made, so why go on repeating yourself with additional amateur victories? Kramer, elated with his remembrances of himself and Parker, almost muted my tendency to deflate his enthusiasm with the name of George Lott, who had won doubles everywhere with Lester Stoefen, John Van Ryn, Johnny Doeg, and John Hennessey. I recalled that it was George Lott, himself, who had extolled Kramer's doubles ability. He told me Kramer was the best because of his second serve. When I told Jack what Lott said, he was very pleased and said, "Well, I'll be darned." Yet it all seemed strange to be talking this way, quite simply because Jack Kramer was a nonpareil singles star. Like the home run, the singles in tennis was where the fans had given their hearts. Listening to Jack, I could not even recall the current U.S. doubles champions. Were they McEnroe and Fleming? In 1982 Steve Denton and Kevin Curren won the U.S. doubles—not exactly household names, which just reinforced the obvious. Money went with singles. Money went with home runs. And fame came to those who stood alone: the broken-field runner, the boxer, the batter at home plate, the tennis player who wins it all . . . by himself. But Jack wasn't reading my thoughts.

"My point," he continued, "is that I could play with anybody. I could play with Mulloy or Talbert or Parker, as well as with Schroeder, and we would have won. I played the backhand court, and Mulloy and Parker could go either way, but Talbert and Schroeder were forehand court players."

Then he went back to the great Mulloy-Talbert victory over Guernsey and McNeill. "I was holding my breath because I wanted Guernsey and McNeill to win. Otherwise Billy and Gardnar would retire the cups with all those great names inscribed on them. Well, they didn't have kinescope then, and you couldn't freeze the shot on a regular motion-picture film as you can now with the kinescope. Hell, I had to default Billie Jean when she walked off a court—I was the official referee—and she thought the call was bad. On kinescope it showed that the ball was in and that she was wrong. But they didn't have that back then. And just remember that when Gardnar and Billy won two of their three championships, Schroeder and I weren't around."

Going on about Billy Talbert, Jack said, "In 1943 Parker and I beat Billy and a guy named David Freeman in the finals. Now I bet you don't even know

273

who David Freeman is. But I'll tell you. He was a miraculous badminton player, who also beat me in the national junior tennis championships." I had wondered about that tournament because Jack had won the National Scholastics (high school age) but had not won the juniors even though he had won the boys at fifteen.

So it was Freeman, the badminton player, who beat Kramer, I was thinking as Jack was highlighting this man I had never heard of, a man who got all the way to the finals with Billy Talbert in a game that was not his specialty. This was interesting because Jack was paying a compliment to Talbert. "Freeman was a fantastic athlete," said Kramer. "He was the quickest man, reflexwise, we have ever had in tennis, but tennis wasn't his best sport. So in 1943, while Schroeder was out on his damn destroyer, I lost to Joe Hunt in the finals, and Parker and I beat Freeman and Talbert. But you ought to ask Billy about this: Good as he was, and he was a damn good doubles player, I can't recall a time when he or Gardnar ever beat me in a legitimate doubles."

Jack then went into some trivia questions. He wanted me to give him the names of partners that Mulloy had, other than Talbert, and then the same for Billy. They did not always play as a team, so I was stymied and could not come up with the names of Henry J. Prussoff, Wayne Sabin, and Budge Patty for Gardnar Mulloy. That last team won Wimbledon in 1957 when Gardnar was forty-three years old. For Talbert, other names came forth from Jack Kramer: Pancho Segura, Billy Sidwell, and the aforementioned David Freeman and naturally Tony Trabert. Kramer was having fun showing off his keen memory.

So I asked him what I thought was a stumper. "Who is the only player alive who won the boys title, the juniors, and then the national singles?"

Kramer appeared stuck and finally said, "Joe Hunt."* But Hunt is deceased, and this was not the answer. "But he did do it—I know that," said Jack, and he was correct. Yet he was stopped by the phrase "still alive." Kramer went down his list eliminating Schroeder, Patty, Riggs, McNeill, and Falkenburg, and then stood silent.

I said, "Your old friend, the guy we have been talking about so much."

"You mean Parker?"

"Yes."

I said that Parker won the juniors at sixteen and then won it the next two years.

"You're wrong on *that!*" said Jack. "Look it up!" he commanded.

---

* Joe Hunt was an Annapolis graduate and a Navy pilot. He had served in both the Pacific and Atlantic theaters and died for his country, thus becoming the only tennis star who did not make it back at war's end. In 1943, Joe Hunt was ranked first in the nation, ahead of Jack Kramer, who was in second place.

I argued that I was right but, of course, I was terribly in error. The best of them all, Don Budge, won the juniors after Parker, and he, in turn, was followed by Gene Mako. How had I gotten the crazy idea that Parker took three national junior championships in a row was beyond me, but I was distracted. Internally I kept harping on the statement made by Mulloy and confirmed by Parker that Kramer and Schroeder had lost to them, and Jack's refutation "Bullshit, just bullshit," was not a clear enough rebuttal. I was thinking of the days when I had seen Shirley Fry and how she reminisced over the matches she *lost* and how lucky she was to win the big ones. For reasons understood by theorists on aggression, this matter of winning and losing was what competitors carried with them. Kramer, speaking of the unsatisfactory publication of his book *The Game: My Forty Years in Tennis,* instinctively said, "We lost it"—as he would refer to a match. The first time I mentioned that Gardnar Mulloy had placed a bet with him over beating Dinny Pails, Jack said with considerable humor and astonishment in his voice, "Mulloy has grown senile!" He never gave ground on a tennis court, and he didn't like to give ground when it came to memory or to image. He was no Shirley Fry.

But we kept at it. I asked Jack, "Who won a national tournament at age fifty-one?" There was no response, but I did not wait for very long. I said that Gardnar Mulloy had won the National Public Parks Championship in 1961, which would have made him fifty-one, but I was wrong again. Jack and I did some arithmetic. Mulloy had been forty-six. But still, at forty-six!

"Old Jughead," said Kramer and smiled.

Then suddenly he said, as though we had never stopped after my error with Parker, "Parker won in 1932, beating Gene Mako, but he almost lost because Mercer Beasley had him tied up to a new racquet.

"Mako then loses in 1933 to Don Budge and comes back and wins in 1934 over Gilbert Hunt. In 1935 Joe Hunt loses to Riggs. Julius Heldman beats Joe Hunt in 1936, and Joe Hunt finally wins in 1937." As he spoke, I was leafing through the record book, and when I finally found the correct page, Kramer's memory was right on the money. Fifty years ago when he was a kid, events stuck in his mind and stayed there in the same way I could recall Joe Cronin's grand slam for the Red Sox in the summer of 1941, listening to the old Philco in our summer cottage. Fearfully they'd walked Ted Williams to get at Cronin, one of the game's greatest clutch hitters. Bango . . . out of the park.

Eventually we left Kramer's kitchen and had lunch at a fancy hamburger joint, and Jack picked up the bill. I thought of Tilden when he did that; he wouldn't hear of me paying. I also thought of the Australian champion, Jack Crawford, who lost the Wimbledon finals to Fred Perry because he was drinking brandy as an antidote to his asthma. I was doing the same thing: I thought that a drink with my hamburger would lift me up and rid me of the sinking, depressed feeling I had. Still, it did not occur to me that I was sick, that I'd been ill since the three hours of tennis in Palm Desert on the day I met Alice Marble. I supposed that only Jack Kramer—who had grown up in small town Las Vegas, always in awe of his own prowess, of his father's abiding faith in him, of his own good luck amidst tight living conditions—only he would have put up with me. I was dropping into no-man's-land. Almost witless and breathing hard, I had a hero at hand, whose confidence I was sure to lose if I appeared weak. When he drove me back to the Sands I realized that I was sinking but we agreed to meet for dinner. I don't know what Jack thought of me, but I felt like a failure. I felt like a man who'd taken home the belle of the ball and concluded the evening with an appalling display of impotence. I did not have the power to keep things going.

But Jack Kramer did. He was remembering when he won the boys fifteen-and-under and how it was a big jump into the juniors. "When you passed fifteen, there was this big discrepancy. It was big guys playing little guys. In fact, Perry Jones kept me out and sent me up to the Northwest to get practice on a little clay and a little grass, and he didn't let me go back till I was ready."

"How did you get to know Perry Jones?"

"He was the secretary of the Southern California Tennis Association then, and he laid out the schedule. The sunshine, the concrete, and the playing sched-ule developed the record for southern California. We didn't have any magic for-mula. Tennis was made available to kids, and these things seemed to work.

"In 1935 I was sent down from San Bernadino to play in a thing called the Dudley Cup in Santa Monica. In that tournament happened to be Bobby Riggs, Joe Hunt, and a fellow named Ted Schroeder, among a couple of hun-dred girls and boys. Well, I lost in the first round, but some guy came up to my father and said, 'You've got a good kid there, but he needs to get on the playing schedule.' My Dad didn't know anything about that—all he knew was that we had gotten something in the mail when I was in junior high that in-vited me down to play. It was spring vacation, and I was local city champion for my age, and I came down wearing a camel's hair sweater and carrying one racquet, and all the other kids had the Tilden-V sweater [for decades *the* ten-nis sweater], and they were carrying several racquets each—the Vines racquet and the Eleanor Tennant racquet—she was Alice Marble's coach, known as 'Teach.' So my father realized that we were sort of second-class citizens around there and went out and found that the magic name was Perry Jones. So my father finds out that Perry Jones has an office at the L.A. Tennis Club, and as we are driving back to San Bernadino, about a seventy-mile ride, he takes a chance and goes to the club and knocks on the secretary's door. We are met by a woman who is Perry's assistant, and she says that he is out playing tennis at the club. They have seventeen courts, and we find him, and when he is through, my father talks to him, and Perry Jones takes us back to his office and gives my father a booklet that lists all of the tournaments. Perry said the only way a boy will improve is to play the tournaments.

"But it was Easter vacation and a little late to start playing tournaments, so we stayed in San Bernadino during that school year of 1935, and then my Dad moves down to Los Angeles, and I started playing over at a place called Southgate in Huntington Park. I had this booklet in my hand, and I entered the City Championships and played with Andy McLaglen, the actor Victor McLaglen's son, and we upset a good team and won the Metropolitan Boys' Championship. I had not yet turned fourteen at the time. And that is where I ran into this fellow named Dick Skeen, and Skeen improved me out of sight. So in 1936, after a default in my first tournament at Bel Air, where I had sprained an ankle, I entered the same Dudley Cup and won it. I had come from nothing to a winner."

"Now, you were just a poor kid showing up in old tennis clothes and . . ."

"Yes, but I'll show you how fast things work. After I won the Dudley Cup, Perry Jones had the Association buy me a membership in the Los Angeles Tennis Club. In those days, a junior membership cost $25 a year, and it cost my Dad $2.50 a month for me to play there every day."

Jack then began to repeat the story of how he would make his way from school each day to the club for tennis. I interrupted him and asked him about the history of the Jack Kramer-Wilson racquet, which was and still is so very popular.

"My first was a Tilden Top Flite by Spalding. The original manufacturer of the Vines racquet was the Magnum Company, but a man named L. B. Eiseley purchased Vines' contract for the Wilson Meat Company and talked them into starting a sporting goods company. Eiseley had been with Wright and Dixon, which was controlled (really) by Spaulding. Now I had played with Spaulding equipment up to, I think, 1941 when they were a little slow over something and Elwood Cooke (Sarah Palfrey's husband) was with Wilson. Well, he talked me into using the Wilson-Budge racquet (superceding the Vines), which I played with from that time on until the Kramer came out in 1948. [The year he turned professional.]

"The Budge was called the . . ."

"The Ghost," said Kramer. "It was white, and then it became the Budge Autograph racquet."

"Was there much difference between the Kramer and the Budge?"

"It is very simple. The first racquet they gave me (with my name on it) was also all white, like the Budge. Anyway, I turned pro and beat Riggs with the Budge and went to South America and came back, and on our way to Australia, we stopped in Hawaii. Riggs and I and Segura were to play a few matches there with a local professional. Well, anyway, they sent me a dozen of my new Kramer racquets—pure white—and I still had my Budges. But when I

39. Kramer electrifying tennis court

started to play with the Kramer, it was too damn stiff for me, and I wrote from Australia that, dammit, I couldn't play with it. It was more like the Beasley that Parker played with—very stiff. So I wrote to them and suggested that they just put my decal on the Budge racquet. Let the Budge racquet become a Kramer—the same wood, ash, or whatever laminations—same thing only with a new decal. [Then he could play with a Budge that was called a Kramer.]

"Well, they didn't want to admit that they had two racquets that were the same but with different autographs. At that time, Wilson had the Vines, which was phasing out, the Marble, the Betz, the Riggs, the Budge, and the Kramer. So what they did was to take some of the stiffness out of my racquet by changing the number of laminations. So I played with it and said, this is more like the Budge, and I used it."

"In 1950," I said, "I was in Fargo, North Dakota, and I bought a Jack Kramer racquet that was red."

"That was a Kramer signature, and it had my picture on it. You know, at one time, I had sixteen different racquets with my name on them.

"Now, when I was able to win my pro tour over Riggs, and Gonzales came along having won at Forest Hills, and I put Riggs in the position of promoter and was able to handle Gonzales, the Wilson people thought they had a staying champion, and they started to put all their development into selling the Jack Kramer racquet. They eased Riggs out of the picture, and they were starting to promote me. In those days, we all had almost the same contract: a five-thousand-per-year guarantee, and with Budge they gave him a 3 percent royalty, but with me a 2½ percent because they thought Budge was a smart guy but didn't think I knew my ass from third base. But because of some of the guys in promotion (one was Charlie Hare who played Davis Cup for Great Britain), they began putting my racquet into the hands of some college players who they thought would become very good. So about 80 percent of the racquets were mine—they were showing up in Kalamazoo in the juniors and in Philadelphia, but it took till 1954 for my royalties to exceed my guarantee for the second time. They were selling them for cheap in those days. They were selling for something like $3.75. Well, one year, as things got better and better, my 2½ percent royalty added up to $238,000. All still at a 2½ percent royalty. Now, here we come to the climax of the story. A computer goes to work. No racquet had won so many major tournaments. McEnroe and others were using a Wilson. So the computer goes to work for Pepsico, which bought out Wilson. The computer was figuring out how many types of Kramer Pro Staff, Autographs, and so forth, the company is going to have to grind out. By 1985 or 1986 they come up with 600,000 of one kind, 400,000 of the other, and as they start to project those figures in terms of increasing inflation, they say, 'we're going to have to pay Jack $800,000 a year.' [Obviously the tennis boom and the royalty arrangement, though seemingly very low, was a pleasant combination, not only for Jack but presumably for Billie Jean King, Chrissie Evert, and other stars whose timing jibed with the emergence of countless indoor courts and exhortations for exercise, particularly running.]

"So they call me in. The nicest guy, who is president of the company, says, 'Jack, we've got a problem here. Inflation is going to force us into cutting down. We can't afford to give you this kind of money. We're going to have to work something out where you are happy and we're not getting killed because you know that you are making more money than I am right now.' So what we worked out was that they gave me a damn good guarantee but no royalty for my name for my racquets and clothing—there was a time when they wanted to use my name on a line of tennis shoes—and this goes for fourteen years. I get, quite frankly, a guarantee in excess of $200,000 a year, and it goes up slightly every year. I'm in what I think is my fourth year. After seven years, they cut it in half and start over again.''

At this remark, I sat amazed at his candor. I had vague notions of how sports could pay off for those who had reached the top. I knew what people made as players. But I did not think players could have made such an amount afterward by just lending their names to what used to be a minor sport. We weren't talking baseball or football, but the old sissy game. But then I realized that it was the Kramer name and the Kramer expertise that brought attention to the stiffness of a racquet he was not going to use—he'd use the Budge with his decal on it—and his image as a champion had pulled so many youths and hackers into the Wilson fold. And, too, it was his style that had helped to mold the game. Among the pros whom I had seen, the Kramer racquet was everywhere. My friend Dick Craven had just bought two more to add to the one he had used for years. It would be fair to suggest that had Kramer not gone with Wilson, Wilson would have been noncompetitive in the surge of tennis that overtook the country back in the 1960s and 1970s. So he had earned it. But I was marveling at the size of the stipend he would get until he was seventy-two years old. This on top of what he had invested from his touring days when he was the best and took in the big purses as he barnstormed across the nation, playing Riggs and Gonzales and later being a promoter with his own entourage.

And there he was still talking to me, telling me more and more about himself, and I at last gave up the idea of asking him the few questions I had asked the others. Perhaps unjustly, it did not seem to matter what Kramer would say about God. I had a good idea of what a man his father had been. The Almighty could wait, as could other standard queries.

But then he said, ''Everything had to be big and apparently black or aluminum or something other than wood. So under the old deal at my peak, I was selling better than now. I am now getting way overpaid. From my peak I am down to 35 percent. They have my wooden racquets in warehouses, and I think they have given up on Chrissie because of the new development. So I am getting what amounts to retirement pay. But there is one thing I don't understand. To be a good tennis player, you need control, and the real good players will choose wood for control. Plus, there is a little element of sound. When you play with a graphite, you get a thud. It's not the same. But it's all a marketing thing. They're selling things for $150 to $300 that if you made them conventionally would go for $60 to $70. Well, if you're a manufacturer like Howard Head and the others who were involved with skiing and found that tennis-racquet manufacturing was a crossover product from skis—they decided, why not sell everybody Rolls-Royces? Who wants Chevrolets? So I think the public has been hustled,'' he added.

At the word ''hustle,'' I thought of Bobby Riggs and felt tempted to open up the whole subject of professional tennis before 1968 when Wimbledon opened its gates to the professionals and the division of talent was finally ended. Yet I was hesitant because I knew that Kramer, one of the innovators of tennis professionalism, would go on and on and that, though fascinating, it was not a part of my book. I had always been interested in the amateur game because that was where the glory lay, the excitement that came from reading the newspapers—*The Hartford Courant* and later *The Washington Post*—as a kid. But I mentioned Riggs anyway, and Kramer told me how Riggs and Budge had asked him to join the tour right after he had won at Forest Hills in 1946 and was ranked number one in the country.

"It is a matter of timing. Bobby had beaten Budge, and they had a backer, and they wanted me, and I said, 'Well, I haven't even won the Davis Cup back. I haven't even won Wimbledon.'

"Well, you might get a bad shoulder, I was told. (This would be like telling a college basketball star to turn pro as a sophomore and make his money quick, lest he hurt himself before he can cash in.)

"Well, if I hadn't lost to Joe Hunt in the finals at Forest Hills in 1943 (nobody knew it but I had clam poisoning—hell, I had beaten Joe about thirty-four sets in a row)—if I had won then as I was supposed to have, then I would have been more of a political tennis player during the war (and been able to keep playing), and the timing would have been okay by 1946 or so. But I had to wait."

Wait he did, and he took back the Davis Cup in 1946, retained it in 1947, winning all four singles matches; won Wimbledon in 1947, took Forest Hills twice in a row, and was ready to run for the money. Yet he is still bothered by the loss to Joe Hunt. It cost him the time of his youthful life, in which he could have dominated in the United States and undoubtedly racked up many titles, including the big ones at Forest Hills and Longwood; and the war took him to dangerous areas in the Pacific, where he made seven landings on his LST, emerging at the end as an ensign. Of course, it was evident that Gonzales had rushed his professional entry, as Don Budge had told me earlier, and this led Kramer into his talk about waiting until he felt he was ready. Gonzales, however, made a great comeback in 1954 after being crushed by Kramer in 1949. All of this was running through my brain as we started to leave for lunch. In the book* I had in my home, it was written: "On the tours from 1948 to 1953, Kramer demonstrated his invincibility winning against each opponent. In 1954, Kramer, apparently feeling he had no more worlds to con-

* *The Encyclopedia of Sports* by Frank G. Menke. 6th Revised Edition. A. S. Barnes and Company, South Brunswick and New York.

quer in competition, turned all his talents to promoting world professional tennis tours."

It was a simple statement of fact. I liked the line "having no more worlds to conquer."

By the time we went for lunch, Jack Kramer had talked for almost three hours. I could not converse intelligently with him because he is not a generalist as were some of the others. As I mentioned earlier, he reminded me of what I had heard about Ted Williams. He spoke his mind and used specifics. He *asked* to be challenged, and when I timidly did so, I was flustered and found myself losing names and dates and foolishly turning the pages of my *Yearbook*, looking for facts. He probably assumed, to my benefit, I thought, that if I weren't up to his level in knowledge of the game, I wouldn't be in his kitchen. But the fact I bore with me was that no one had yet given me so much time.

I thought of his own assessment of his play, pretending there had always been open tennis with professionals included. It was in his own book* and I had an excerpt in *The Tennis Book*. According to Kramer, he would have won Forest Hills five out of six times from 1947 through 1952. He would have taken Wimbledon from 1948 through 1953—again five out of six times. He had Budge winning Forest Hills six times in a row and seven out of eight. He had Gonzales winning Forest Hills in 1951 and then again in 1953, 1954, 1955, 1957, 1959, 1960, and 1962. As he had implied, Kramer was never too high on the Australians and told me he did not think Australia should be among the "big four" tournaments. It should not be a grand slam event. Although I had heard rumors of Kramer-Gonzales misunderstandings, it did not appear either in conversation or in his own writing. What he barely whispered was, "The war shook me up." Imagine a tournament tough Kramer in 1943, 1944, 1945! But he did not slight Rosewall, the Australian. He wrote, "Little Rosewall would have won four Wimbledons to go with five at Forest Hills." Yet in our talk he had said, "Segura owned Rosewall." Kramer's chauvinistic attitude concerned me. The Russians were to come to Los Angeles for the Olympic Games, and Kramer, a major sports figure, would have a role. Since conciliation was important, if not absolutely necessary, I was alarmed by thoughts of the bright, unruffled, strong-willed Kramer railing against the Russians. I recalled him saying Mulloy and Talbert had won their doubles while he and Schroeder weren't around. He might be behind the scenes, per-

* *The Game: My Forty Years in Tennis.* Copyright © 1979 by Jack Kramer and Frank Deford. Published by G. P. Putnam's Sons.

haps, but his voice would be heard. All we needed was another boycott, this time by the Soviet Union. Kramer spoke his mind, but he also emitted an attitude of the very self-reliant American who would scorn socialism in all its forms. It was an attitude that brooked no nonsense, and that attitude might confound normal diplomacy. Strangely, I worried about that as I got ready to have dinner with him. I had a hunch that Jack Kramer's attitude was a typical one in southern California. He was so "American" and such a believer in free enterprise, I found his enthusiasm would reflect the general approach to the Olympics, and I could not imagine Russia fitting in.*

Earlier, after we had our light lunch of a hamburger and a drink, Jack drove me over to the headquarters for the 1984 Olympics, where he had to pick up a letter, read it, okay it, and then let it be posted. I took some pictures of him standing before the brick edifice, now full of offices running at a high pitch. He looked as unaffected as he had in his kitchen. He had not yet shaved, as he had told his son on the phone he would. He stood patiently as I photographed him a few times, and then he drove me back to my hotel.

That evening he again swung by the Sands to pick me up for dinner. I mentioned something to the effect that it would be nice if Gussie Moran came along, and he quickly said that I could go down to Santa Monica and dine with her—it would be okay with him. I don't think he knew I was suggesting that we include her, that somehow we would get her up to the hills of Bel Air. Because I didn't want to lose him, which is to say, give up the chance of having dinner with him, I let the Gussie idea go, even though I had called her in the afternoon and suggested that we meet. Fortunately it turned out that she had other obligations so that when I did not confirm my invitation, as I had told her I would, there were no hard feelings. She had other irons in the fire.

We dined with a friend of Jack's, a large man who was also a sports fan.** The restaurant had a miniature railroad running around the wall on a ledge—an imitation of the Atchison, Topeka, and the Santa Fe. We ate in a darkened room, and I listened to the two older men discuss the intricacies of running or advising tennis organizations. They talked of esoteric tennis matters and of tennis, which was to be a demonstration sport—on trial, as it

---

* My hunch may have been well founded. Not long after I saw Kramer, the Russians announced their boycott. Of course, Kramer, personally, had nothing to do with this. But I sensed in him a buoyant belief in the business community, which I think was symbolic of the overall Olympic Committee Organization.

** Bob Briner was a partner of Dave Dixon, a man who talked Lamar Hunt into forming World Championship Tennis in 1967. Briner works with Don Dell at Pro-Serv, an agency for tennis stars.

were—at the Olympics. They talked as old friends, and I occasionally joined in, but the interview was long over. Finally, I asked the two of them to name their all-time, all-star baseball team. This question fit their mood, and they grabbed at it with delight. After a moment of pondering, they both came up with the same team. They had Ruth, Williams, and Cobb in the outfield, although Jack's friend was edging toward Tris Speaker, but no one knew whom to drop out to make room for him. Finally I said, "What about Mays?" We paused over drinks and food and in the gloom of the room with a toy railroad train whizzing by (Kramer's memory of his father?), we again could not delete any one of the three, although Williams came under suspicion as the one who might have to go.

The rest of the team was unanimously approved, except for my choice of Nettles at third base over Hall-of-Famer Pie Traynor. Both men nodded and said I could be right. And that was how the evening went. Jack did say that the most important development in all of tennis was in professionalizing and opening of the game, and in my scribbled notes written in the dark, I wrote the name "Joe Hunt." Clam poisoning had robbed Jack of a title. It was not something he would forget, even at dinner.

And there was another thing Jack would not forget. It was his first encounter with Bill Tilden. He had been asked to play Tilden in an exhibition match when he was only seventeen. This would have been in 1939. By then, the young Kramer was a phenomenon in the Los Angeles area, and to get "the greatest player the game had ever seen" to play with a boy who could possibly be his successor—such a match would be a dream even though Tilden, by 1939, was forty-six years old. But it was not to be, though it was a memorable event for Jack Kramer. Early in the match, Tilden sprained his ankle, and Jack had to rush to the other side of the court and carry him off. The kid and the champ, the new and the old, the flowering and the wilted, the young male of the pack and the old and deposed leader of the pack—it was a day of high drama for Jack Kramer, and it came flooding back to him as he recalled the event with awe and excitement in his voice. And so we dined in quiet merriment mixed with nostalgia—the great Kramer, an old friend, and a tagalong who was just a callow sports fan whom the champion had befriended.

I slept well that evening but awoke forcing myself to breathe. It didn't matter, I thought. Once I was in La Jolla with Ted Schroeder, the lore of the game, more reminiscences from still another person's perspective would enliven my stay in the West. Kramer had been the most stimulating athlete I had ever met. At dinner he once more took care of the bill, just as "Big Bill" Tilden would have done. I spent almost a whole day with a whirlwind who seemed involved with tennis in a number of ways—an organizer, a committee man, a meddler, a strong man, an advisor, an advocate, a leader. I looked for the right descriptive phrase. But there was something I could *not* employ. I could not say he was still a tennis player.* As a player, he had not played the game with me. That thought was the only sad intrusion in a day of unbounded ebullience.

* In a telephone call I made to him from my home, I discovered he had just returned from Monte Carlo, where he'd had "too much tennis." He said that he would play, but not for publication. Unlike Billy Talbert and Alice Marble (who both had to endure serious illnesses for much of their lives), Jack was keeping the quality of his game to himself and to his close friends. But the ebullience already mentioned was hardly diminished by his admission. It would be nice to play tennis just for fun and not for the purpose of a book. But I couldn't have it both ways with Jack Kramer.

Ted Schroeder:

"Who shot Charlie?"

I had arranged an appointment with Ted Schroeder at his home in La Jolla in the late morning, so I was up at dawn's light to leave Bel Air. As with Kramer, he could no longer play tennis. He had injured himself and the game that made him famous was out. But the night before had been pure fun and I was happy as a winner in center court. Out on the town with an idol, the phrase had a nice ring to it, and I did not mind rising with the birds one bit. Nor did it bother me that the man Jack called "Schroeds" would not don his whites. In fact, it seemed that I had not yet gone to bed. My energy was running wild, almost like a kid at an all-night party. Who needed sleep? Who needed more tennis?

It was off to Los Angeles International Airport and then to San Diego and then a cab ride to La Jolla and to Ted Schroeder, ranked first in the country in 1942 and a junior champion in 1939. (In 1939 Kramer took the junior doubles playing with Ted Olewine.) Schroeder was also the intercollegiate champion playing for Stanford University in 1942, which must have pleased the people at Palo Alto very much. You don't often have someone ranked first in the country playing singles for you. And as an aside, I knew that he had won the U.S. hard court title three times in singles and twice in doubles. Of course, none of this comes close to his victories at Forest Hills, where he won the doubles with Kramer three times and the singles in 1942. The Wimbledon singles title was his in 1949, and the same year he was runner-up in the doubles with Gardnar Mulloy, purportedly not one you would call his best friend. It bears repeating that Mulloy had been runner-up the previous year, playing with Tom Brown, and had won the doubles in 1957 at forty-three years old. But Ted Schroeder was one of the truly great players and was in the Tennis Hall of Fame, where a helpful soul had given me his address.

He met me at the door to his house, which was modest in size and typically Californian in that it had a small green lawn, green shrubs, a verdant appearance, and was not made of wood. He is a round man now. He wears glasses and looks like a dairy farmer. But he was smiling and polite, and he spoke with a quiet voice that reminded me of a movie actor of years back named Guy Kibbee. He said that he had started playing tennis in 1928 in Beverly Hills at a place called Roxbury Park.

"How old were you when you started playing?"

"I was eight years old."

I calculated that he would be sixty-three now, and looking at him, I saw his clear eyes through light, framed glasses and thought as I had so often that the people I was meeting in southern California bore no resemblance to the southern Californians I saw on television. They were straight-shooters and homey, and thinking back to Dodo Cheney's understated Riviera Tennis Club, they were not showy. Schroeder wore clothes that might have come from the same J. C. Penney's that had ignored Gussie Moran's request for work. He was, in a word, unpretentious. The Riviera Tennis Club was also unpretentious, but I had an idea it would be tough to join.

40. Ted Schroeder today

Ted, more than anyone, looked less like a champion. There was not even a hint of dash or glamour. He talked like Guy Kibbee or Cecil Kellaway in the original movie version of *The Postman Always Rings Twice*. The dash of tennis stardom had left his stride and was now deep down in his soul. What he had done, he had done. Now he could look like a dairy farmer or an herbalist, if he chose. All that was to the good, as far as I was concerned.

And then there was La Jolla itself. Thirty-four years ago, I had camped on the beach when I was twenty, at the Torrey Pines State Park, which is nearby. Looking back, 1950 was still a continuation of the time of innocence when sleeping on a beach meant nothing more than a night under the stars without fear of rowdies, perverts, or police. And La Jolla still struck me that way as my cab driver drove me up to Schroeder's house. Gentle, well-heeled, noncommercial La Jolla appeared to be a town to retire to when it came time to give all your button-down shirts, your three-piece suits, and your tassel loafers to a thrift shop. I would lay a bet that the people of La Jolla knew right from wrong even if they were wrong about what they considered to be right. The feeling I had was that I was among people who were happily unmuddled by the confusion that whirls about in the minds and drives the emotions of the rest of us. Oh, not to have to worry, I felt as I was driven to Ted's house. What a blessing it would be to be comfortable with my opinions.

But I was worried as I listened to him talk. It had been an arduous journey.

"I played on cement courts until 1938, when I got my first touch of something else."

"When you were a kid, who were your heroes?"

"I had no heroes. But as I grew older, in the 1930s, Tilden and Vines became heroes to me. Later it would be Fred Perry and Johnny Van Ryn and Wilmer Allison—people who were preeminent in the game."

"Looking back over your life, whom would you say you respect the most?"

"Well . . . I didn't think of that sort of thing in the old days, but in retrospect, I would say anybody who did things the best. Babe Ruth. Franklin Roosevelt, even though I wasn't of his political persuasion. Churchill. The doers."

"Are you a Republican?"

"Let's say that I am on the conservative side because of my upbringing, and I haven't changed with the times, probably because I have not been able to adapt as well as some others.

"I was born of moderate circumstances and went only to public schools until I went to Stanford University, where I graduated in 1942, where I paid my own way."

"Where were you born, and where did you grow up?"

"I was born in Newark, New Jersey, but grew up out here in the Los Angeles area. I moved to Los Angeles in 1927 and then moved on to this very house where I have lived since 1957."

"Have you been married all this time?"

"Forty years last February."

"Were your parents influential in your becoming a champion?"

"Indirectly. I came from a split family, and I wanted to prove I could do something on my own. I was motivated but was very small for my age. And I have been on my own ever since I went to Stanford in 1938. Being on my own was the background for my motivation. It was a means to an end."

"Your favorite doubles partner was Jack Kramer?"

"Of course. You must remember that my association with Jack dates back to March 1935. We talk to each other maybe five times a week. It is an association of almost fifty years. He is the only fellow in my life whom I have known who really hasn't changed. He is the same person he was fifty years ago."

"How about mixed doubles?"

"Oddly enough, I played a mixed doubles tournament in 1940 with Helen Wills, who was in the twilight of a very distinguished career. The game was very different in those days, and bear in mind, I am not comparing her with Martina and others, but for her time, she knew more about the game than any woman or anyone else. We won that tournament—the Southern California Championship. She never came to the net, but she was a dominant player at all times."*

"If there was an overhead?"

" 'Yours, partner!' "

I shifted the subject, as I knew I would sooner or later. I went back to 1946. I told Ted that there was still a differing of opinion concerning the Davis Cup team that whitewashed Australia.

"Well, I don't know about that, but I can tell you what happened. Essentially, the choice of who would play the second singles was left to the players by the captain. Billy Talbert was in no condition to play. Tom Brown was in no condition to play. Parker wanted desperately to play. Mulloy thought he should play. So it came down to a vote. Tom Brown, Kramer, Talbert, and I voted for me to play the second singles. Parker voted for Parker, and Mulloy voted for Mulloy. We thought that it was all over and done with. Then a couple of days later, Captain Pate called us all together and said we had to make a

* In 1940, Ted Schroeder won the Southwest Pacific singles title and the doubles with Jack Kramer. Add his victory with Helen Wills to those feats, and you have the best player in California. Oddly, in 1940, Ted Schroeder was ranked tenth in the nation behind lesser-known Henry J. Prusoff and Elwood T. Cooke.

decision as to who would play the doubles. We went through the singles again, and it remained four-one-one, the way it had been. Parker then says that if he isn't going to play singles, then he isn't going to play doubles."

I interrupted. "Parker and Mulloy say that as a doubles team, they beat you and Kramer every day." [Even though with Parker defecting because of the singles exclusion, it was to become academic.]

"Well, that might be technically correct. Let's say that the point is arguable."

"That they maybe had had an edge?"

"Let us just say that the point is arguable. But the point became unarguable the moment Parker tells the captain that he won't play doubles because he can't play the singles. So I am not getting into any argument about who shot Charlie; so what is the point? Even if Mulloy and Parker did beat us all the time, without Parker, Mulloy is alone."

I ventured to say that I supposed that the real issue was that some of the players resented Perry Jones' foisting Ted Schroeder on the squad when they didn't really know much about him.

At that, Ted ran down his record as it stood in 1946. It was the same list of victories that I stated earlier in this chapter, with two additions: he had been national intercollegiate *doubles* champion with David Freeman [the badminton player] and the national mixed doubles champion with Louise Brough.

Then he said, "They can dislike Perry Jones, but I'll tell you something that Perry Jones did for Frank Parker. After Frank married the ex-Mrs. Beasley in 1937, Perry Jones made it possible for him to survive and go on with his tennis career until he turned professional in early 1948."

"But I know that Frank Parker worked for MGM and at other jobs to support himself and his wife during that time."

"Of course he did. But I mean that Perry Jones helped him in a *tennis* way. He had a wife to support, and he was an *amateur* tennis player."

"Enough," I thought. "In a tennis way" intimated more than it said, and I could guess what Ted meant. It meant expenses.

"How would you rank the top five players in your time?"

"In my time? Well, I am going to cut it off for you. I am going to cut it off in 1951 because that is when I quit. And I won't arrange them in any order because I am not qualified to. You had Budge, Riggs, Gonzales, Sedgman, and you had Kramer."

"How about Budge versus Tilden? How would you place them?"

"You're comparing apples and oranges. It would be like comparing Helen Wills and Martina Navratilova. In my opinion, Martina would beat Helen Wills the way she beats Chrissie Evert Lloyd. But when you go back in time, Helen was better than Martina is today."

He was speaking relatively—in terms of mastering one's opponents. Weeks later, Peter Schwed, editor and tennis author, would tell me that Helen Wills went a whole year and lost only one set, that being to Mary K. Browne.

I let the point about apples and oranges sink in for a moment and then mentioned Rosewall, whom I have used as my yardstick to show that you *can* compare players from different eras—he being an Australian champion over a twenty-year span.

"I would say that from, say, 1953 to 1978 (twenty-five years), Ken Rosewall was the most consistent and outstanding player there was."

Warming up a bit, Ted took the initiative with his own question. "I have another category. Who were the best underrated players of all time?"

I was mute.

"Bobby Riggs and Kenny Rosewall. Riggs was a clown; Riggs was a hustler—he was a this and a that, but boy, could he play tennis!"

I threw my "given-day" theory at him. "Who was the best player on his best day?"

"On their best day, there were two players. I will go back to 1928. The two best players on their best days I ever saw were Lew Hoad and Frank Kovacs."

Again there was silence in the house as the name Kovacs wound its way slowly through my mind. Kovacs. No one had mentioned him thus far. Frankie Kovacs was one of those colorful men who appeared—at least in the press—to be his own worst enemy. He showed off, they said, and was a "I-could-have" player. He could have done this and could have done that. But there was scant mention of him in the record book. In the juniors, there was one three-time winner—the immortal and now deceased Vincent Richards. Several players had won it twice, including George Lott, Frank Shields, and Budge Patty. But there was no mention of Kovacs as a lad. In 1941 he did win the U.S. Indoor Singles, and that year he was runner-up to Bobby Riggs at Forest Hills. As a professional, the right-handed Kovacs won the title, beating Segura with a left-handed shot. They called him the "Clown Prince," and Ted Schroeder was a Kovacs loyalist. I was amazed.

"What about Vines?" I asked. "Most people argue that Vines on his best day . . ."

Schroeder continued, "When Hoad was on . . . when *they* were on, they did as much with a ball as Vines did, as Tilden did, and more. Tilden had an understanding of the game that was second to none. All Vines could do was to hit the ball, and as you say, when he *did* hit the ball, he hit it very well."

"Don Budge said that for 365 days a year, the best player would be Kramer."

"For one reason. Jack could apply pressure to such a level that in the end, he would kill you."

He seemed to be finished and let the melodramatic ending of a tennis death from Jack Kramer's big game settle in the air. And Ted Schroeder was getting tough. I could sense that he was becoming impatient with me. There was a testiness to his voice, and I knew it was unrelated to my questions. It was instead related directly to me. For the first time since we had met, I recognized that I was failing. I was getting weak, and later when I played the tape of our talk, I could hear a low rasp to my voice and a diminished ability to express myself. The exhilaration of the night before and the fine feelings of the morning had gone. And so had Guy Kibbee or Cecil Kellaway. I was now with a tough hombre who most probably felt he was being interviewed by a lunatic.

So I did what I suppose my instincts directed me to do. I jumped right back into the 1946 Davis Cup, and I told Ted that the problem that winter in Melbourne appeared to be with him. I said that Mulloy and Talbert and Parker still felt uncomfortable about those days and that one reason was Ted Schroeder. I was using the others to buttress up my own sinking condition. It was as though I was calling in the troops to help me while I was in the enemy's camp. I was trying to get Ted's goat and go back to the offense. Mike Wallace had told me months before—in the summer when I had him on a radio show I was doing for a local station on the Vineyard—he had said, "Never lose control of the interview."

I said, "There are still bad feelings about those days, and the bad feelings revolve around you. Apparently they did not know much about you or where you came from or how you got there—to Melbourne."

"It's very simple," he said, almost as though he had anticipated the question. "All the time these guys were playing tennis, I was either going to school or working for a living. While they were on the circuit, taking handouts under the table, I was doing what I thought I should be doing—going to college, getting a degree, going into the service . . . I didn't play any tournaments. [He meant in the East, on the circuit.]

"I graduated from Stanford, went into the service, and then went to work for an engineering organization in Los Angeles. I think what you have here and what they resent is that for my entire career, I was a part-time tennis player. For their entire careers, they were full-time tennis players."

I stared at him and said as though I had discovered Shakespeare, "That's a damn good line." I liked the way he had put it, and I liked what it implied. People who futz around with life usually have an underlying respect for those who take life seriously. I liked the hard-working Ted Schroeder. He could come and go in the tennis world. He took the rest of his life seriously.

I asked him, "Do you believe in God?"

"Sure."

"Do you go to church?"

"Yes."

"Where?"

"I go to the Catholic Church. And I am *not* a Catholic."

292

"Do you go every week?"

"Almost."

Grasping at the spiritual angle, I asked him the same question I had asked Billy Talbert about what makes a champion.

"Suppose you and I go to the same school and we are equal, yet you go on to become great, while I slip back, go into, say insurance, and drop out of the game. Wherein lies the difference?"

"Very simple. Motivation. Jack Kramer, for example, came from modest circumstances, but there was never anything as long as I knew him but that he was going to be a professional tennis player. That was the way out from being a railroad engineer or a freight-train conductor or something like that. What made Gonzales? What made all the great Australians? It was a way out of their environment."

At that point, I told Schroeder that I was through interviewing him because I was in no shape to interview anybody. I could feel that I was losing not only the interview but my whole self. There was something really wrong with me. I had a hunch that a good day's sleep and a following night of lying low was what I needed. I had met the man, and we had talked. He had ruled out playing tennis because he couldn't play anymore. There was reason to abbreviate our meeting.

But he went on. "Before we conclude, I want to place this whole 1946 thing in perspective." Again I had the feeling that he had somehow anticipated my bringing the 1946 Davis Cup situation to his attention. He and Kramer talked five times a week. I was betting that Jack had called "Schroeds" on the phone and told him that I was still rehashing the old days—almost forty years ago in Melbourne.

"There is no doubt," he was saying, "that Perry Jones exerted an influence. Jack Kramer undoubtedly exerted an influence. But I will stack my record against any of the other people who think they were done evilly—with regard to the selection itself. Look, did Mulloy or Talbert ever win Wimbledon? Did either one win a national championship? [He was talking of singles.] I did not play in a national championship from 1942 to 1949, and yet I was almost good enough to win Forest Hills a *second* time seven years after winning it in 1942." (He lost to Pancho Gonzales 16–18, 2–6, 6–1, 6–2, 6–4 in the finals. His victory in 1942 was over Frank Parker: 8–6, 7–5, 3–6, 4–6, 6–2. In 1949 he *won* Wimbledon, beating Jaroslav Drobny, also in five sets.)

"What did you do in the war?" I asked.

"I was either at sea or back in the States learning to fly."

"Did you become a pilot—fly off a carrier?"

"Yes. I was in destroyers and then on the aircraft carrier, the *Enterprise*. But sticking with the 1946 thing. I didn't have anything to do with Parker's arrangement, with Parker saying that if he couldn't play singles, he wouldn't

41. Ted Schroeder: the upset man showing his power

play doubles. Talbert didn't have to vote for me. Brown didn't have to vote for me. But we haven't answered the question: 'Who shot Charlie?' That begs the issue of who was the better doubles team. Mulloy and Parker were a good team."

But Kramer had been picked for both singles and doubles, and Ted Schroeder was his man. It now looked irrelevant as to whether or not Parker and Mulloy were better. They just weren't in the running once Kramer was in the doubles, which appeared obvious from the start. Parker had replaced Talbert and then removed himself from the doubles, leaving Mulloy alone. Had he stayed, it would not have changed anything. It was Kramer and partner . . . that was the call all along.

"So what have they to complain about?" persisted Schroeder, feigning a look of astonishment. "If Parker had played the singles and Kramer and I were arbitrarily picked for the doubles, then there would have been room for a complaint." (Especially if Parker and Mulloy had beaten the other two with a regularity that a candid Schroeder does not really contest.)

I moved back to Perry Jones. "At any rate, Perry Jones did seem to have an inordinate influence over things."

"Perry Jones had a tremendous influence. He was the dominant figure in the game from an official standpoint because California produced all of the good players. Parker really wasn't a good player until he came to California. Players outside of California in those days were a rarity."

I remember a good Californian, Pauline Betz Addie, telling me almost the same thing when I began my book. I was somewhat shocked. Locked in the East with all of its traditions, I had assumed that the best grass players came from the East. But no. The great champions, almost without exception, were (as Schroeder reminded me) from California. They had gone from concrete to grass and won wherever they went. Vines, Budge, Kramer, Betz, Marble, Budge Patty, Schroeder, Riggs, Falkenburg, Tom Brown—how long was the list? Louise Brough, later Maureen Connolly. Ted Schroeder, of course, was correct about California, and it appeared immensely logical, if not a relief, to recognize that Perry Jones should have been at the helm of amateur tennis. Indeed, with the talent he had as an official, he could have been a tennis czar. It now appeared foolish for people in the East to quibble over the power of Perry Jones. I, for one, was convinced that he deserved it and could pull all the strings he wanted to pull. The only question of ethics in this whole business about 1946 lay in Captain Walter Pate's deal with Parker. All had agreed that he had reneged once Kramer's abilities were obvious. Kramer's abilities foreclosed all options. He would have a lock on the singles and the doubles, and *his* commitment was to Ted. Jack ruled the roost.

We broke off after that. Ted Schroeder had been a good host and had made his point about California, Perry Jones, his selection to the Davis Cup squad, and being elected to play against the Australians. And as far as his life went and his home went, he appeared very content. I had seen pictures of him when he was lean and rough-looking, and now he was a smiling milkman, although I felt he could get testy when he wanted to. I had also noted that his Stanford education and subsequent exposure to the bigger world outside of tennis had made him decently articulate. He spoke with an educated, nonjock manner that was at once soft but very penetrating. He could take command but did not wear his ego on his sleeve.

But all that speculating and assuming and deducing came later when I was recuperating in a hospital, a few hours out of the intensive care unit. All that kind of rumination went into a notebook while it was fresh in my mind, but my mind, as it was in Schroeder's home, had begun to go just as we concluded our brief talk. I remember chiding him about his supposed poor table manners down in Australia, and I think he looked at me and said that he was just a kid in those days—a brash innocent. I believe he said something about not being polished. Also, I suspected as I lay in my bed in a San Diego hospital that being an aircraft carrier pilot had touched him somewhat. It was hairy work, and if he had been uncouth, perhaps it had to do with his recent return from a scary world of survival where manners had slipped by the board. Who knows? I just recall his saying something to the effect that he hadn't known any better when he irritated Gardnar Mulloy and Tom Brown at the dinner table.

But what I do recall is that I was suddenly very much out of breath and had asked for a beer to revive me and had found that the beer did not work. I was dying in Schroeder's living room, and I think he knew it. He called a cab for me, and when it came, I got him to pose for a few photographs outside his house. Strangely, the pictures came out and are not too bad. The driver took me immediately to a hospital in San Diego, where I was hooked up intravenously and had an oxygen mask clamped on my face. Later the nurse said that when I arrived, I had about ten minutes to live. My lungs were filled with fluid, and I was down to less than 20 percent of my breathing capacity and the percentage was falling. They injected me with something to reduce the fluid and gave me a melange of pills to knock me out.

After San Diego, I flew home. The West had been a wild place for me, and I had gone somewhat haywire out there. It had been almost twenty-five years since I had been West for anything other than a short stop. I had overdone things and back in Palm Desert, the sun had burned down for three hours on a head nearly devoid of hair and a body unused to heat and had contracted congestive heart failure. Not many days after that great day on the courts, Ted Schroeder telephoned for a taxi, and that ended my first trip to see the Californians who once streaked to victory on tennis courts around the world. I would come back for more.

⌇18
E. Victor Seixas:
Total Tennis

It was May 4, and the rain was falling gently but steadily, and the wind was picking up. The Atlantic Ocean was a gray blanket, ruffled by the wind but hazy in the overcast. As I sat at my window contemplating my next trip West, I wondered if maybe enough wasn't enough. I had written over 350 pages and had seen most of the players on my original list of tennis champions. Surely, it seemed to me, I had enjoyed a rich and varied fan's experience, and now, recorded as it was, I could quit.

I write this because I want the reader to know how my mind was working two days before leaving again for another trek in search of athletic greatness.

I was again afflicted with a bronchial condition. I had had this condition when I flew to Chicago to play Parker and Lott, and I suffered for it. Also, and more important, my right knee had given out one week earlier. I was tuning up for my first match, against Vic Seixas, and was running hard and playing well, and I had lost weight. I was still smarting over the thumping I had taken from Dodo Cheney and was getting in trim and hitting the ball with smooth strokes and covering the court better than I had in a long while. But snap! went the knee or a tendon behind it or the cartilage around it. It hurt and began to swell, and after a day, I was walking on one leg. I finally went to an orthopedic surgeon, who drained off the fluid. By May 4 the knee looked normal, and most of the pain had gone. I knew that in three days I would be on the court, but I would not run very well, and I'd be light-years away from the condition I had been in on the day that it snapped. All hopes of showing off to Vic Seixas were dashed on that day.

My schedule was formed to the extent that I had a date with Vic on Monday, May 8, near New Orleans. I would see Louise Brough in Pasadena for a game on May 11 and had a match arranged with Tom Brown, Jr., in San Francisco on May 13. On my way home, I would see Margaret Osborne duPont, who might or might not play—she had recently undergone a gallbladder operation. She had not said that she wouldn't play tennis; she did say that she would be happy to see me on my way home from California. She lives in El Paso, Texas. Others I wanted to meet and play with were Frankie Kovacs (near San Francisco), Gene Mako (in the Los Angeles area), Bobby Riggs (near San Diego), and, if I could hang on until he came back from Europe, Pancho Segura, a pro at the same club where Riggs played. Gonzales ruled out playing tennis with me, but nevertheless, I planned to visit Caesar's Palace in Las Vegas just to see the place and to see Gonzales and perhaps to watch him stroke a few with someone else. As for an interview, he was neither impressed nor available.

It was a tough schedule, and there were still others. There was the mysterious Bob Falkenburg, who had beaten Bromwich in the finals at Wimbledon in 1948. But where was he? I had an address for him, but he had not answered my letter, and his phone number, like those of so many others, was unlisted. Beverly Baker Fleitz should be seen, as should Nancy Chaffee Kiner in Palm Springs. But neither Fleitz nor Kiner was really necessary to my book. Falkenburg was. A Wimbledon singles winner, he was a challenge to play, and I had a hunch he would be fascinating to interview. And then—and this was the big one for me—what about Helen Wills (Moody, Roark)? She lives in Carmel, near San Francisco, and by all reports lives a totally reclusive life. No answers from her to my letter. I would be able to see her only if I stood near her mailbox and waited for her to come by to pick up her mail, and even that was dubious because she could very well have someone else do that errand for her. But I wanted to get a glimpse of the woman thought by many to be the greatest woman who ever played the game. Even considering the overpowering Martina Navratilova, there were the Wills loyalists, and those who were more sensible about such matters would say, "I'd like to see the match." In any case, an authentic legend, Wills lived away from the public eye, and if I could break that barrier of isolation, I would be proud of myself, get a scoop, and play private detective. It would be an adventure, tracking her down.

So I had these thoughts as I wondered about leaving. My knee might obviate all tennis. In fact, if it went to pieces, it would ruin my ability to travel. I could not carry suitcases and other paraphernalia in and out of airports with only one good leg. Having already suffered congestive heart failure with the attendant and dangerous effect of my lungs filling with fluid, I was worried about my bronchial condition. Suppose it got worse, and my lungs began to fill up again?

So, as I have written, I could have called it quits. I could have let what I had already written come out as Book One and then start all over again with the remaining Americans, then go on to Australia for Crawford and Quist and Bromwich and Dinny Pails and others, and then to Switzerland for Budge Patty, and finally to England to visit Wimbledon and to locate the last of the great English champions. Would Dorothy Round still be living? And what of the great Frenchmen Borotra, Brugnon, Cochet, and Lacoste? I would fly to Paris for Book Two. And so Book Two was looming larger and larger—it would take me around the world. Therefore, the remaining Americans had to be dealt with *now*. I said to my dog, Lexi, "People don't stop just because of a bad knee and a rotten cough." People who did would never become champions. By now I was identifying with the great players and was one of them. "The game will be played," I said, and my dog looked at me with gloomy, soulful eyes.

I flew out of the Vineyard airport on one of those lovely May afternoons that occur only a half dozen times in the month. It was warm enough for swimming and lying by a dune, and I knew that New Orleans would never match what I was leaving. To my surprise, I learned that I could leave this small island on the North Atlantic coast at 2:20 P.M. and be in my hotel room in the New Orleans French Quarter by 7:00. I could be having dinner by 8:30 (as I did) at Brennan's, which was just up the street from the hotel. The night went smoothly. I dined on raw oysters and frog's legs, and then walked the streets for a while until I found the Monte Leone Hotel, now noticeably refurbished since my last visit in 1951. Indeed, everything was different from 1951, except for the Old Absinthe House—and that was enlarged. Somewhere on the wall among a thousand old and tarnished cards was a card with my name on it, and I remembered how at twenty-one, I had written my name on the back of a stranger's business card and saw it mounted on the old, dusty wall where calling cards were a part of the decor. I went to the Court of the Two Sisters but forgot about Jean Lafitte's Blacksmith Shop, which was a bar I used to haunt as a kid. It was late by then, and the streets were full of foolish people milling around anticipating the forthcoming World's Fair, but nowhere did I hear any authentic New Orleans jazz. It was Sunday night, and the one great jazz band left, the Preservation Hall Jazz Band, was not playing, its members having gone home to bed. I finally went to bed at the Hotel Richelieu, tired from walking and irritated by the sound of rock and roll that flooded out of Bourbon Street. I was pleased that I was there, though I was remembering the glittering sunlight of Martha's Vineyard, which could take the small scraggly lawn of an airport and make it look like a putting green.

I awoke early and strolled by the bar just off the lobby. I looked in to see what was going on. Two men who had not been in bed yet were talking. One

42. E. Victor Seixas

asked, "How about another?" The other replied, "Well, it's a little early in the day. I think I had better do my laundry," and then he walked away. This was New Orleans. The toper exited with a face creased like that of John Huston, and I thought, "There goes a man who at least thinks he has his priorities in order. It was 9:00 in the morning and time for a break. He might like a clean shirt for the next round."

There was a period many years back in time—back in the years that bracketed World War II—when Will duPont collected tennis players the way a book dealer collects rare editions. DuPont dealt in world-class competitors, and one man who was known to visit his estate was a young and handsome Vic Seixas, who drove down to Wilmington, Delaware, with his wife from his home outside of Philadelphia.* They played on elegant grass courts that Will

* Source: Margaret Osborne duPont

duPont had built so that the great stars could sharpen their games and commingle within his purview. There were women there who turned their heads toward the handsome athlete who they knew was trying to sink Frank Sedgman and other Australians like a U-boat, hoping to retrieve for America the Davis Cup and become the number one player in all the world.

This is pertinent because now at sixty-one, Vic Seixas is still darkly tanned, lean at 175 pounds, and carries his six-one height on a pair of bowed legs that are endearing—the one blemish to make a female heart flutter. His high forehead presumes an intellectual mind, his manners are courteous, and his gentle good humor suggests an accomplished gentleman jesting at the center of genteel living. He is an Easterner, and there is no rawness to him. He is as smooth as an opal in the window of a store in Melbourne or Sydney or wherever they play the Davis Cup and where for one time, his star ascended, and he brought back the trophy. Concerning his intellect, he wrote a typically self-effacing book, full of anecdotes and humor, *Prime Time Tennis*. "I wrote 75 percent of it myself, in longhand," and that remark, if not his speech, testifies to his keen mind that flashes from his green-gray eyes alive with life. His handshake is warm, and his smile makes you think you have been pals all the way back to the time when Will duPont opened up his array of grass courts and told the best players in America to give them a try.

And Seixas is proud. Not so much for his tournament tennis anymore, although he is quick to point out that he must play in the forty-fives in order to get a game—but he is proud of his four-and-a-half-year-old daughter, Victoria, his first and only child. He is also proud of his home, set in the heart of an Eden called the Beau Chêne Golf and Racquet Community. Beau Chêne is a serendipity in "good-old-boy" country, just the other side of the longest bridge in the world, a causeway that crosses Lake Pontchartrain from Metairie to Mandeville, Louisiana. If you leave his home, you can be in the French Quarter in forty-five minutes, but as Vic said, "I have only been there about four or five times in my life." The tawdry squalor of the Quarter is too far a cry from the tranquil, almost meticulous beauty of Beau Chêne, surely one of the best designed, loveliest resort communities I have ever seen. Mandeville, itself, is a typical Southern roadside town, and you would never know that about a mile in from the bridge—a bridge so long you lose sight of land—that a mile from the toll booth is a dead-end road with just one sign overgrown with vines to lead you on to Beau Chêne.

But all is not bliss in Eden. Elias Victor Seixas, Wimbledon singles winner, U.S. singles titlest, Davis Cup star, a man who has been ranked in America over a longer span of time than any other player (starting in 1942 and ending in 1966), and the man who could beat Sedgman and Hoad—Elias Victor Seixas is out of work. He represents the classic case of a man who traded opportunity for geography, and now he must stroll his lush Shangri-la, waiting for a job that will take him back to work but also allow him to keep his home in an area no man in his right mind would want to leave. He has found a vast playground for his beloved daughter, a good school for her to attend, a job for his wife, Toni (she is the tennis pro at the club), and even an attached marina for the yacht that has yet to come. He strolls the grounds and thanks the good fortune that brought him to Mandeville and Beau Chêne. But what is there to do? He clearly loves his neighborhood—if you could call it that—but he hates being idle. Over in New Orleans, the name Seixas does not ring too many bells. If name recognition on a local level is essential, he may be tilting at windmills. He is a long way from Philadelphia and Wilmington, where Vic Seixas could sell sand to an Arab. "I would never go back to Philadelphia," he says. "But no one knows what I am doing here." Like the other people in this book, he peaked too early for television fame and the tennis boom. It is his fate to remain anonymous in God's country.

We met at 1:15, he in a pair of khaki Burma shorts—the kind Hollywood thought were worn by Wingate's Raiders, and I noted that his full, brown hair had a touch of gray. He greeted me warmly, even though it had taken me an inordinate amount of time to get to Beau Chêne. I had waited for an hour to get my car (reserved) because it was "blocked," or so they said, and then, of course, I got lost driving to the hidden dead end that marks the entrance to his club. So it was after 1:00, and instead of playing, we thought it best to have lunch and then to play. Vic drove back down the country road, onto an access road, and to a small cafe he fancied, called Mande's. We ate hamburgers that "were dressed," which in Louisiana means were served with salad ingredients and french fries. We drank Dixie Beer, the local brew. Vic had never tried it, he said, but I was doing things the local way and could not resist.

By 2:30 we were on the court, but in the meantime, we talked and the tape recorder picked up a rather unusual story.

Vic's father was Portuguese and his mother Protestant Irish, and he grew up in a middle-class inner Philadelphia community, which he says is now gone. He played tennis as a boy—he played all the sports and says he is an athlete who plays tennis rather than being a pure tennis player. But we didn't start talking about his heritage or his youth. My first question had to do with his amazing span of years of being ranked in the United States. I had thought that it was for eighteen years. "No," he said. "You can look it up. I was ranked in 1966—I bet you overlooked that [which I had], and I was forty-three years old then. I had played in two or three tournaments and beat Stan Smith in the Nationals that year and had a good enough record to be technically ranked, although I wasn't playing for a ranking. I was working full-time in a brokerage business in Philadelphia [Goldman, Sachs] and could only get in a few tournaments."

He wasn't ranked for the years 1960 through 1965 because, as he said, "I only played a few tournaments: two for fun, down in Puerto Rico and Jamaica, and then the one at the Merion Cricket Club [his local club] and the Nationals. But in 1965, playing the same casual routine, he was suddenly ranked again. "Number 33 or 34." He wrote to the ranking committee of the USTA to complain. "Look, I am not playing for any ranking, and I would appreciate either being dropped or having 'insufficient data' beside my name. So they dropped me. Then the next year, I played the same tournaments and maybe won a couple (Smith, and I think Krishnan),* and I was ranked in the top ten. That just shows you how ridiculous things are."

I didn't argue with him because in 1966 when he beat Stan Smith, Smith was only a sophomore in college and was very much unranked, and that fact seemed to buttress his assertion that caprice has its way in the rankings. Of course, in no time Smith would be a power in the game, and perhaps the ranking committee could see Stan Smith coming and were impressed that a forty-three-year-old man could take a youth with such potential. But that is the kind of thing you can ponder on forever. The point is that Vic Seixas holds the record: twenty-five years, inclusive.

I asked him what his best period was as a player.

"I'd have to say 1953 and 1954. In 1953 I won the singles at Wimbledon, and in 1954 I won the U.S. singles title, and we won the Davis Cup. That would be my best." (In 1954 he had also won the U.S. doubles and the French doubles, playing with Tony Trabert, his partner with whom he beat Rosewall and Hoad for the Davis Cup.)

"Was there pressure in 1954 for you to turn pro?"

"Well, Kramer was running everything then, and what they were looking for was one dominant amateur who could play Gonzales, who was beating everyone. In 1954 I was probably the best, but I didn't win Wimbledon that year, and I didn't win the French, and there really wasn't any dominating amateur. Later, of course, he took Trabert and Sedgman and Hoad and Rosewall, but in 1954, that ingredient of domination wasn't there. So from Kramer's point of view, there really wasn't a very good marketing attraction. Of course, I never played tennis with the idea of turning pro anyway. In 1958 I went to work for Goldman, Sachs."

"What did you do between 1948 when I saw you and 1958 when you went to work?" (I had seen him beat Henri Salaun, a great squash player, who played number one for the tennis team at Wesleyan, where I went to college, and I could remember the ballyhoo: *Vic Seixas is coming.* Seixas, who was ranked ahead of Gardnar Mulloy and Herbie Flam that season, played for

* In 1959 Ramanthan Krishnan won the U.S. Hard Court Singles Championship.

303

North Carolina. The match with Salaun seemed to offer the chance for an upset. The college body thought Salaun was unbeatable in the cold New England spring.)

"From 1948 to 1958, I played total tennis," he answered.

"How did you live—on *what* did you live during those years?"

"You lived on expenses. If you were good enough. And I was married, so they paid for my wife, too. You never made any money out of it. At the end of the year, you might break even."

"What about Kramer who said Perry Jones paid Frankie Parker $1,200 to play in the Pacific Southwest Tournament?"

"Under the rules, they paid your expenses, and if you were married, your wife's expenses as well, and that would include first-class airfare, hotel rooms, and anything else you needed. Now if you translate that into dollars, sure it may have cost Perry Jones that much to get Frank Parker (and wife) to come out to California to play. Now if Parker should take the $1,200 and go live in a flea bag, well . . ."

"His wife took the money, he told me, so he never really saw it. Just thought I'd add that," I said.

"Anyway, there was a limit that you could receive legally. Now if there were the under-the-table payments that everybody says there were, I didn't participate in that because my wife was with me all of the time, and if I was getting double expenses right off the top, I was getting more than most people were. Furthermore, I don't know where the money would come from."

"Well, Gardnar Mulloy was saying that he could play one tournament off against the other and . . ."

"Sure, you might be able to get a little here and there, but anybody who says he made money at the end of the year from amateur tennis is either lying or putting you on. For instance, I played twenty-nine times at Forest Hills, and they never gave me a nickel. Not even your expenses. We lived ten days in New York and paid our own way, so if I made anything else along the way, it would go right out the window at that one tournament. Now at Wimbledon, they give you a little graft, maybe £50 or £100. But you had to pay your way over there. So if someone was making money, I sure as hell wasn't."

"So if you sat down at the end of the year and did your income taxes, you would show zero income."

"That's right. But we lived awfully well if I was playing, and I was playing most of the time."

"In the back of your mind, did you think of becoming a club pro once the tournaments were over?"

"Either that or go into something else, which is what I did. I didn't want to be a teaching pro, and bear in mind, there was no thought of open tennis yet. So after I went to work, I still played when I could and played in the Nationals until 1970, and I couldn't play in 1971 because I was the referee. In all the twenty-nine years that I played, I lost only once in the first round."

Vic was named after his father, Elias Victor Seixas, and his mother's full name was Hannah Victoria Moon. "We named our daughter after her, and we call her Tori. Not after my father nor me, Victor, but Victoria for my mother."

To be precise, he was born in Overbrook in west Philadelphia and went to grammar school there and junior high school and then for four years to Penn Charter, a prep school that is also in Philadelphia.

"Did you go on a scholarship to Penn Charter?"

"Believe it or not, I went on a tennis scholarship. It was a pretty good tennis school."

"So you started playing tennis pretty young. About ten?"

"Oh, before that. I was playing by four or five at a little community club my father belonged to. There were four clay courts."

His father was in the plumbing supply business and brought to his home a standard middle-class urban life. Victor senior worked hard and played a little tennis and had a tagalong boy, who picked up on the game in ways his father could hardly have visualized. At Penn Charter, for instance, Vic won the Interscholastic singles in 1941, one year ahead of Bob Falkenburg, who was playing at the other side of the continent, for Fairfax High School in Los Angeles. In 1940 he and a teammate named Bill Vogt won the doubles.

At North Carolina, he received what he calls a "half scholarship—a kind of grant in aid," and he joined a fraternity and waited on tables to pay for his meals. In October 1942, he enlisted in the Army Air Corps and was called up in February of 1943 in the middle of the basketball season during which Seixas, the athlete who also played tennis, was on the basketball team. I mentioned to Vic that Ellie Vines had been a starting center on the USC basketball team as a sophomore, and Vic said that he was already playing as a sophomore but was not yet first string. On that and other matters, Vic refused to attempt to outshine the great tennis stars we both admired. In the Air Corps, for example, he served in the South Pacific, but he quickly pointed out that he did not see combat. Rather, he was in "testing."

"We had a rear area depot in New Guinea, and by now they [the Allies] had started back up the road toward the Philippines. My job was to check out the new airplanes that would be shipped in by boat. It was like a miniature right field where we assembled the planes. I would fly anything they brought in, and then we would ferry them up to the outfits—everything the Army had over there. And then all the planes they had would come back through the depot for overhaul."

But no combat—just ferry service and testing. He wound up in Japan for about eight months after VJ-Day, and then it was home to college at North Carolina on the GI Bill. Like so many of the champions, he had lost time in the service and, like the rest of them, it was just something you did. Only Kramer, perhaps, would regret that he might have worked a better deal had he won Forest Hills in 1942, which should have been Jack Kramer's year. Instead, Victor Seixas said that he had an interesting time of it. I doubt that in hindsight he would have changed a week of his tour in the Pacific for a week at the Merion Cricket Club, though surely he must have griped and moaned and wished he were home a thousand times during his tour of duty. I would suspect from hearing him talk that when you go through something like ferrying "everything the Army had" north to where the action was and survive, you'd get a glow of pride that is unequaled by winning one more trophy on one more playing surface. And because we had talked quite a bit before our lunch, I had the notion that Seixas was a man born to duty, one who took things as they came and could sleep well at night because of it. But by so doing, the big bonanza would elude him.

Back at North Carolina, he played basketball in the winter and squash whenever he could. In the spring, he played tennis for the university and spent the summer on the circuit. By 1948 he was ranked again, this time number seven behind the great Pancho Gonzales, who was then number one in the world, and other illustrious players such as Ted Schroeder, Frank Parker, Billy Talbert, and Bob Falkenburg. He graduated in 1949 and married his first wife, who was in the same class—then a coed who was five years younger than he.

By now he was debating whether he should withdraw from the circuit. He was twenty-six and had yet to go to Wimbledon. But he hung on to the game, and in 1950, the United States Lawn Tennis Association (now the USTA) sent Vic, Doris Hart, Shirley Fry, and Art Larsen to South Africa—all expenses paid—to begin a tour that took them through Europe and finally to Wimbledon, where Budge Patty beat Frank Sedgman, and Louise Brough conquered Margaret Osborne duPont for their respective championships. Seixas, however, got to the semifinals, where he lost to the eventual winner, Budge Patty. In France he thinks he also reached the semis, losing to Jaroslav Drobny. In the mixed doubles, it would have been natural for him to have won with Doris Hart (they did win in South Africa), but Doris was still Frank Sedgman's partner, and Vic and Doris didn't team up together until 1953, when they started their almost historic mastery of the mixed doubles. They took Wimbledon three years in a row (and he won a fourth straight with Shirley Fry in 1956), as well as taking Longwood by storm, also for three years running. In this matter of mixed doubles, only Margaret Osborne (not yet duPont) and Billy Talbert outdid the team of Seixas and Hart by winning the U.S. title four years in a row. But no other mixed doubles team in the history of Wimbledon has won the title three times in succession. As a footnote, it should be noted that when Frank Sedgman turned pro in 1952 and Doris Hart

306

joined Vic Seixas, they played for three years and lost only one match in all the tournaments that constituted "total tennis."

Of Doris Hart, Vic says, "You know, she was the best mixed doubles player of her time. And she couldn't run. She had had an automobile accident that almost cost her the use of her legs. That's how she started playing tennis. Her brother Bud Hart (about my age) was a pretty good player, and he got her interested in tennis. The crux of it is that she could do everything except run. She had great racquet control, volleying, half-volleying and . . . well, she could do everything. First of all, she played doubles with Shirley Fry, who is a great runner, and she played mixed doubles with Sedgman and me, who I think are, were, the two best runners in the men's game. So she had just what she needed. I don't think she hardly ever lost a mixed doubles match. She lost one with me, but I don't think she lost once with Frank Sedgman. Frank was perfect for her, and I was perfect for her, and she was perfect for us. When she lost to Maureen Connolly in the singles finals at Wimbledon (8–6, 7–5), that was the greatest women's match I have ever seen. She was so personable and outgoing and had a fine sense of humor."

"Then why won't she let me see her?" I asked.

"I don't know. It seems funny to me," he answered. "But you know, I sent her a copy of my book and never heard a word."

"Well, I guess she has turned secretive," I said lamely, and I let the subject of Doris Hart drop. Truly one of the great women stars, and handicapped at that, what a story she would have made. But no dice. I went back to Seixas.

And going back to Seixas, we got back to Ted Schroeder. Once again the man the Easterners love to pick at rose from the West out of a setting sun to cast his shadow on a trio of Easterners: Seixas from Philadelphia, Savitt from New Jersey, and Trabert from Ohio. It was 1951, and Dick Savitt had won Wimbledon. It would be Seixas' first year playing for the Davis Cup. Tony Trabert, a superior left-court doubles player, would be on the team, and Seixas had eyes on being his partner. The year before, Australia had trounced the United States 4–1, the only victory being Tom Brown's triumph over Ken McGregor 9–11, 8–10, 11–9, 6–1, 6–4 in an ordeal of victory that should be noted. And it should also be noted that Ted Schroeder lost three matches. But in 1951, with Savitt on the squad and a man named Seixas reaching his prime (he lost in the finals to Sedgman at Forest Hills) and the young Trabert, who was superb on the odd or left court, there seemed a chance to wrest the cup from Australia. Frank Shields was the captain, and Jack Kramer, at the urging of Perry Jones, was signed as coach. And along with Jack came Ted Schroeder. Now, as most players on the circuit were aware, Ted, who worked hard for a living, had the annoying tendency to pick his tournaments. If there was one single thing that irritated those who were grinding out the year, going from club to club, match to match, "knocking ourselves out," said Vic, it was

43. Vic Seixas: A pure athlete and a great champion

this man from the West Coast who would suddenly enter the picture, looking toward the finals without (in a sense) doing the dirty groundwork, which was constant and grueling competition.

So suddenly there they were in Australia, and Savitt seemed to have a lock on the number one singles. Seixas, looking at Schroeder, was worried. How did he get there? Why was he there? What about me? Ted, once again, had been among the missing, and to repeat, he'd lost all three matches the year before, beaten by both McGregor and Sedgman, and playing with Gardnar Mulloy, he lost to Sedgman and Bromwich. So as Seixas said, "I had to work myself onto the team." And this he did by playing match after match and making a record for himself that was better than anyone else's. Shields would have to play him. And Schroeder? He, too, played well, and in any case, where Kramer was the coach, Ted Schroeder would play. And remember Ted Schroeder was the man who was capable of pulling the upset. And as in 1946 when they all feared Bromwich, in 1951 they feared Sedgman, who had won the U.S. title in both singles and doubles and had won the Wimbledon doubles with his partner, Ken McGregor. So clearly, Ted Schroeder would get the nod over the man everyone assumed would play number one singles, the Wimbledon winner, Dick Savitt. And that is what happened. Savitt was left out and went home, vowing never to talk to Frank Shields again (which he didn't). Schroeder and Seixas each beat Mervyn Rose for two wins, but the doubles team of Schroeder and Trabert were crushed by McGregor and Sedgman in straight sets. Sedgman beat both Vic and Ted, and the cup was retained by Australia.

Could Savitt have beaten Sedgman? No one will ever know. He had taken Wimbledon but never got his shot at the Davis Cup. Again Schroeder appears, plays, and departs for his job, and a rather angry (to say the least) Dick Savitt goes back to the East with fury in his heart, adding more fuel to the Ted Schroeder legend. And Vic Seixas wonders what might have happened had he been Trabert's partner in the doubles. And all the time we talked about this, I was thinking that in those days, the Davis Cup was everything. As Frank Parker had said, "If you don't play Davis Cup, you don't count."

One last note. In 1951 Schroeder was ranked seventh in the nation. Seixas was first, Savitt was second, and Trabert was third. By 1952 Ted Schroeder dropped from the rankings, never to return. I recall him telling me, "I quit playing tennis after 1951." Thirty-three years later, we were still talking about a man who I think looks today (in 1984) like a dairy farmer. Yet his legend will not be diluted. Other people on my trip will raise his name. Was Ted Schroeder one of the great men of the game? Surely Jack Kramer would think so, and so would the loyalists from the West. Back East, as the Californians are wont to say, no one is sure. There is more puzzlement over this enigmatic figure than animosity, but the verdict is not in. Quite probably with Ted Schroeder, you will get a hung jury. So at Mande's Cafe just across Lake Pontchartrain, I let Ted go the way of Doris Hart. I was interested in Victor Seixas, but the thought lingered. I wondered if Ted Schroeder quit tennis after 1951 because of what had transpired in Australia, when playing with the impeccable Tony Trabert, they lost the doubles.

Vic was an only child from solid parents. Because of his father's membership in a tennis club and his mother's strong personality, Vic went into sports early. I asked him if there was a time then when he thought he might go all the way and be a world champion.

"No. This is because I was very good, very young. I was winning all the fifteen-and-under tournaments in the area when I was twelve and thirteen. I don't think there was a kid in the country who was any better at my age. I think back then, the feeling was that I had the potential, but being an Easterner and not playing all the time, I was not in the same boat as the other guys."

"So that was a handicap?"

"Well, in a way, but hell! I was free to do something about it. I could have gone to college in California. I could have moved there, but I didn't. I elected not to play tennis in the winter. I played squash. Actually I took up squash again after I stopped all my tennis and played in the seniors, which in squash is 'over forty.' I won that three years in a row."

I mentioned that many tennis stars could play anything. I thought of Ellsworth Vines and Don Budge and Althea Gibson.

"Some could and some couldn't. There is a fine distinction between athletes who play tennis and just tennis players. Althea Gibson is a good example of the former. I think I am a good athlete who plays tennis. Gonzales is a good athlete. So is Gardnar Mulloy. Lew Hoad is another one. Some of the Australians are *really* good athletes. They could be good at almost any sport."

"How did you get ranked in 1942?" I asked, switching the subject.

"Nineteen forty-two was a semi year. There was the war, and a lot of the guys were in the service. I was still too young. It was not exactly a banner year for good tennis players."

"Who were your heroes when you were a kid growing up?"

"Well, I liked baseball, and I still follow baseball avidly. But do you mean sports heroes?"

"Anyone. Some people might say Churchill."

"I'd say Franklin Roosevelt, because I can't remember anyone else as I was growing up. Four terms, and I can remember being on an island in the South Pacific when he died, and I sat down with a lot of other guys, and I remember sitting there and crying. It may seem strange to say now, but there were a lot of us who wondered if we would ever get back to the United States, and then you take away that father image, if you want to call it that, and . . .

after all, he was president for over half of my life. And this is not a political thing. It's just the father image, I guess.

"But getting back to baseball, I was always a Detroit Tigers fan, and you can imagine the kind of year I am having now!"*

"You mean growing up in Philadelphia you rooted for the Tigers?"

"Well, I was an American League fan, and in 1940 the Tigers won the championship, and I have been with them ever since."

I then asked him to name the 1940 team and he flunked. He flunked on Birdie Tebbetts at catcher, Pinky Higgins at third, and Barney McCosky in right field. So I had him, and we laughed over our coffee as the time drew on, and the tennis game continued to wait. But he did say that, yes, his heroes as a kid were Hank Greenberg, Stan Musial, and Ted Williams. "I loved sports," he said. "Call for a game of tag, and I'd play."

"Now that you are almost a senior citizen [he laughs] and you reflect on your life, who are the people you respect?"

"Golfers," he answered, which was a stunning response. "I'll tell you why. I like the way they behave toward their sport, the way they treat their sport—the Watsons and the Crenshaws, the name players—they all seem to have a deep-seated reverence for their sport."

"What about tennis players? Don't they have that reverence?"

"No. I think *some* do, but nowhere near the number nor not as much. I mean, this came to light when Ben Crenshaw won the Masters. Everybody was so happy that he won. Here is a guy who has read everything there is to read about the game, loves it, has a respect for the game, and it seems to me that if you are going to be great at a sport, that is the way you have to be."

"Well, Kramer has that."

"Yes, I believe he does."

"What about McEnroe in terms of reverence for his sport?"

"Better than most. I think he has more of a feeling about wanting to do something other than to just make a lot of money. I think deep down he would give a lot of that money back just to see his name in certain places on certain things—in the record books. And that is the way the golfers feel."

"What about his manners on the court? How do they show reverence?"

"McEnroe is an enigma in a sense. He can be an s.o.b. on the court, but he is the only guy who plays doubles all the time, who plays Davis Cup, and I think he has a certain love of the game that goes beyond making money out of it. Some of the other guys couldn't care less about the record books; it is purely the money."

"How would you rank the five best players of all time?"

---

* It is 1984 and the Tigers are 13 games ahead in the American League East.

"I can only go back to Budge's time. I didn't play Tilden. So from Budge on, I would have Budge one, Kramer two, Gonzales three, Laver four, and Sedgman five."

"On your best day, how would you do against McEnroe?"

"I don't think I'd beat him. I could stay with him because of my serve, but he is the one kind of player who plays the way we did. What I am getting at is that his game is built around the serve and volley. He is the only one that plays that way. Of course, *we* did because we played on grass so much of the time."

"In other words, he could beat you at your own game. So what about Budge? How would he do against John McEnroe?"

"I'd have to go with Budge. I don't think McEnroe could give anyone I have on my top five a hard time."

"On the 'given-day' theory, most people say Vines."

"I've heard that, too."

"And Hoad?"

"Well, that's for sure. I have played Hoad, and he is the only guy who scared Gonzales. He hit the ball so hard he scared everybody. If he is playing well, he can blow you right off the court."

"Didn't Gonzales beat Hoad on the pro tour?"

"Yes, but it was close. But oddly enough, I play best against that kind of player. I played well against Hoad. I beat him more than he beat me."

"You know, Billy Talbert told me that he 'outdistanced Gonzales'—the only man to have a better overall record."

"Not quite. There is one other."

"Who?"

"Sam Match. Do you know who he is?"

"Sure, because he was your partner in the Interscholastics when you won the doubles. I suppose they played once."

"No. They played a few times, and Sam just was able to win.* He just had a funny way of beating him. It's like Laver and me. I never lost to Laver, but that was a question of timing. When I played Laver, he was just coming up, and I was at my peak. Now, when he reached his peak, I don't consider myself a better player than Laver."

"In your book, *Prime Time Tennis,* you rank the top ten. Do you include yourself?"

"No, to be realistic about it, I played most of them, and I beat them, but I lost more than I won."

"To what do you attribute your youthful appearance, now in your sixties?

---

* Sam Match, a relatively unknown player, is still winning. He won the fifty-five singles at the Pacific Southwest Championships in 1982.

I mean, you and Mulloy and Parker are going to be in your eighties and still look, maybe, fifty."

"Exercise and good sense—moderation in things, and luck. I was lucky I never got hurt."

"Moderation. Did you ever smoke?"

"Sure, in the Army. I never knew a pilot who didn't smoke. But then I gave it up. And I never drank much when I was playing. I mean, after a long tournament is over, you might go out and whip it up to relax, but I trained pretty hard when I was playing because I didn't have that good a game. I depended on really feeling good. Kramer could go out hurt and play. He played better hurt than anyone who ever lived. But I'll tell you one thing. I am the oldest first-time winner to win the national singles [at 31 years old]. That's a record that will never be broken. They're getting younger, not older."

"What was your toughest match?"

"Oh, jeez. I guess the year I won Wimbledon I had my two toughest matches. In the quarters, I beat Lew Hoad 8–6 in the fifth set. In the semis, I beat Mervyn Rose 6–4 in the fifth set. Against Hoad—now this sticks out. It was six–all in the fifth set, and I was serving love–forty, and somehow I pulled it out. So Lew Hoad is now serving, and I have him love–forty. Well, he hits a ball that is called in but looked out, but hell, I didn't care. I figured I had him—let him take the point for 15–40. But then he serves two clean aces, and it's deuce. Then I got an ad when he hit a ball off the wood of his racquet, and then he double-faulted on match point. So you might say that match stands out."

"On women's tennis, who do you think is the best?"

"Prior to Martina, I would say Maureen Connolly, but right up there would be Alice Marble. Alice came to the net and changed the game around."

"If you had not gotten involved in tennis, what do you think your life would have been like?"

"I would have tried like mad to be a baseball player."

"You would have been an athlete in some way or another?"

"I think so."

"If you had your life to live over again, would you change anything?"

"Knowing what I know now, I think I would rather have put all that effort into something else, other than tennis. Tennis hasn't paid off, for me, anyway."

"But look where you live!"

"Yeah, but I don't have any money at all."

"Neither do I, but at least you're better looking."

"Well, when you think of all the other sports, tennis is about the worst one to play in terms of money, up until recently. People always ask, 'Wouldn't you like to be playing now, at thirty years younger?' Let's face it, I had a pretty long run, and if I had been playing now, I would be a multimillionaire. Yeah. I'd like to be thirty years younger with the run I had. I'd also be a millionaire in my losses. I had more losses than anyone else, but they were good ones—you know, in the finals. So going back, knowing what I know now, I would rather have been a golf pro. You can go on playing golf until you're seventy years old (profitably). The way I am playing tennis now, I could go on playing golf until I was ninety."

"Forgetting sports?"

"I guess I would have gone into law, because it leads to everything else."

"Do you believe in God?"

"Yeah, I believe that there is somebody who knows what is going on, but I am not really religious in that I go to church every Sunday. I used to go to church when I was a kid. I was a Presbyterian."

"Who was the major influence in your life?"

"When I was a kid, I used to chase balls for my father at that little club across the street. That's how I got into tennis. But my mother used to chase me around and scream at me all the time. I think I was closer to her, but I had a rather basic childhood. I don't think I was spoiled as a kid."

The interview over, we got back to his Lincoln and drove to the club. Vic was tired, and his knees hurt from the long tournament he had played the previous weekend, which had ended only the day before. He had played in the men's, the mixed doubles, and the men's doubles. It was clear to me that he was doing me a great favor to run again. He did not want to. He hurt and it is his custom to take aspirin before playing to dull the pain. His knees ached and his left hand is gnarled with arthritis. Were it his right hand he'd be finished as a player. But as we drove, we talked, and he got back to Frank Shields who had been his Davis Cup captain.

"Shields," he said, "was one man who should never have taken a drink. He was charming and delightful and then with a drink in him, he went wild. I was at the Meadow Club in Southampton one time with a bunch of us hanging about after a tournament, and Shields began throwing all the furniture out of the room. The thing that strikes me about that was that not one of us dared get up to stop him. He was really a big guy and he was out of control. We watched him. That was all we could do. And then there is the story—I don't know if it is true, but I am told that it is—about the time Frank Shields held Bitsy Grant out of a hotel window, way up. Held him by one hand.

"And you say Schroeder injured himself and can't play anymore. I have a hunch he quit because he got fat."*

---

* It should be borne in mind that this represents friendly banter. Seixas and Schroeder teamed to win the U.S. Hard Court Doubles in 1948. When one player talks of another, there is a warm admixture of friendship and competition.

The last thing I recall Vic saying as we got out of the car was (subconsciously, perhaps, but referring to Schroeder's girth), "Now that I have eaten lunch, I'll skip dinner. I usually never eat lunch. Only two meals a day."

And then we began to play. At once I laid down the ground rules. I said, "Vic, because of my knee, in order to make a match you have to hit each shot within my reach—that is, don't make me run too far. If you do, I get the point."

He chuckled at this and said, "Look, I have spent an entire career hitting *away* from people. How do you suppose I am going to hit it to you?"

"Try," I said with a grin, and we began rallying.

It was an exalting experience because I was doing pretty well. As we played our set, I had him going from corner to corner and actually hit many past his grasp. He, in turn, was edging ever so slightly away from our bargain and was stretching me. I was unable to make the corners on defense, and so he had me, but I did keep the ball going, and we played fairly closely. I was thinking as we hit, "Thank the good Lord he doesn't drop-shot me," because I would never have been able to hobble to the net. And he never did drop-shot me. He just kept me going a few strides, from side to side, and I made him run from side to side, and at one time we were at 2–3 with my serve. But then he got serious, and though his knees were hurting and he was exhausted from the previous weekend, he pulled ahead and ran it out.

I suppose that I could go on with a more detailed analysis of our game, but tennis, the way we played it, would be too tiresome to recount. Just let this impression stand: I ran the legs off the man by ground-stroking to his forehand, and when I suggested a second set, he declined. And he (playing by my rules) kept hitting it just within my reach so that I could, indeed, run him. Only once did he violate Hart's Law, and that was when he hit a hard backhand deep to my left corner that no man alive could have retrieved, even assuming a good knee, great speed, and quick anticipation. As I picked up the ball, I yelled across at him, "My point!" He laughed loudly at that, laughing the way he does so easily, and the game went on. At the end, at set point, he shouted across at me. He was serving, and he said, "Now I will show you my *real* serve." He sent a bullet that missed the line by a couple of inches. Then like Babe Ruth, he called his shot and struck his second serve that hit right on the center line and spun away. This pleased him immensely because he had shown me what he could do if he had wanted to: he could ace me at will.

We drove around Beau Chêne. He showed me the marina and parts of the 27-hole golf course. In case of rain or in the short, cold season of a Louisiana winter, there are indoor tennis courts. He pointed out his house and houses of local business leaders. He showed me the condominiums, and as we passed the club house, I said, "Gee, I would wait on tables in there, just to live in a place like this."

Vic answered, "If the pay was right, so would I."

It was clear to me that he was in no hurry to say good-bye. I felt that he was deeply pleased that someone had come down from the Northeast to see him, but as we drove, I kept thinking of his rejoinder about waiting on tables. I was remembering 1954 when Trabert and Seixas had brought home the Davis Cup. In all, he had played for his country a total of 23 matches over seven consecutive years. In 1954 he and Trabert beat Hoad and Rosewall in four sets. In the singles, he beat Rosewall 8–6, 6–8, 6–4, 6–3. He had been a hero.

Later he worked as a tennis pro at the famed Greenbrier, along with Sam Snead, who was the resident golf professional. From there he went to New Jersey to be tennis director for a Caesar's Palace-style hotel and resort in Atlantic City. For reasons that elude me, that project failed or was delayed, and Vic, after buying a house in that state and settling in, was out of work. He then took a job at the Hilton Hotel in New Orleans where, as he said, things were so petty that he had to "punch in and punch out" like a bank teller, and so he quit. His second wife, Toni, had been his assistant at the Greenbrier, and now after all the traveling, she is the one who has the job and E. Victor Seixas—a hero, a legend, a man who may at his age be the best tennis player in the world—was driving me around showing me the sights and did not appear to want to say good-bye.

Once I was across the long causeway and at the Landmark Hotel in Metairie, I called him on the phone. I wanted some more information about Shields. His first response to my call was to say, "So you made it okay." He thought I would get lost again. The guy cared about me, and that was a nice feeling for a sports fan to have, especially since I was a long way from home and alone in a hotel room.

Vic Seixas. I had first seen him on a clay court in Middletown, Connecticut, playing for the University of North Carolina in 1948. Reverse the last two digits, I thought, and there we were again. "I'll bet he is sitting in that house of his having a drink," I thought, "and I'll bet he is remembering what it was like through all those years."

⤳*19*

Pancho Gonzales and Louise Brough:

The Gentleman Said No, The Lady Said Yes

The Las Vegas sky was white with the heat, and the human beings who strolled in the glare were wearing sunglasses, not for affectation but in order to see. The pool was not crowded, and the tennis courts were empty. Only the air-conditioned casino at Caesar's Palace had any action and, at best, was just sporadically busy. The town was hot and tired in the heat of May, and a strike by hotel workers had stripped some of the fun from this city of pleasure.

I had used the pool and had sunned myself, and finally I felt I had enough nerve to approach the lion's lair, over the door of which is inscribed: "Pancho Gonzales Tennis Shop." The letters are large enough so that you can read the words from the pool.

I thought that trying to see Pancho Gonzales would be useless because I had written from my home—a rather lengthy and comprehensive letter—and he had answered me as follows:

Dear Sir:

I do not allow myself to become involved in these types of ventures. However, I do wish you the best of luck with your new book.

Sincerely,
Pancho Gonzales

The young woman who stood by the counter was courteous, albeit idle and somewhat imprecise. She had no idea where the great Pancho was, nor did she know when to expect him. "He sometimes comes in around 2:00, after lunch," she said. I probed a bit and finally found that he might play an "exhibition" that very afternoon, beginning at 4:00 at a downtown hotel called the Union Plaza. Because it was already almost 2:00, I held no hope of catching him prior to game time in his office, a small cubicle within the structure of his shop. The thing to do, I felt, was to go for another swim and then head down to the Union Plaza and watch him play. Perhaps after seeing me, he would change his mind, and we could rally on another day, and I could get him to talk to me. After all, I'd come a long way to see the champion who had won Forest Hills two years running and had taken the doubles at Wimbledon with Frankie Parker.

The woman was right. There was a game scheduled at the Union Plaza, and it was for money. And it was a doubles game that teamed Pancho Gonzales with Bob Howe, a transplanted Australian who had once won the French mixed doubles playing with Maria Bueno and Wimbledon with Lorraine Coghlam, and was now a high-ranking senior singles player. Their opponents were the venerable Hugh Stewart and a man I had never heard of, Jason Morton. Stewart had a national record of some note. He had taken the juniors eighteen-and-under, playing doubles with a player named Alex Hetzeck in 1946. That year he won the juniors eighteens as the Hard Court champion. In 1955 he and his partner, Earl Baumgardner, won the U.S. Hard Court doubles. Playing for USC, he had won the National Intercollegiates, and as a men's senior, he had earned a lot of tournament trophies, some national. Stewart shows up in the record book as a Californian who occasionally made it to the national level and won. In southern California, he had taken doubles championships in the 1950s with Herbie Flam and Barry MacKay. He had name recognition, but he was not comparable to the great Gonzales. Morton, on the other hand, had no recognition, yet there he was with Stewart, ready to do battle against Gonzales and Howe. Beside the court, a television camera was picking up the action, and two spectators sat on the hard seats to watch the game. A small knot of Rossignol officials were also on hand because Rossignol—a ski manufacturer—was sponsoring the match and, I was told, a series of matches for world-class men fifty-five and over.

And all of these odd goings-on were held on the seventh floor of a hotel in the burning heat of a late afternoon. So I watched Gonzales. He was sliding back and forth in the sunlight, his body stooped and his eyes intent on the flow of the ball. By playing on an elevated deck of a rather impressive old hotel, it seemed that he was even closer to the source of the heat than he would have been at a lower level. It was roasting up there—on a plain, hard surface, which was painted green, made of concrete, but carried its own special formula, and which, most likely, was constructed the same as any other western court where they are all hard and knee-jarring and terrible on the spinal disks.

As the game continued, you could see great beads of sweat pouring down Gonzales' face. The regal Mexican looked tired, and every so often he came to the near sideline for a glass of Gatorade. Once in his high voice, he asked, "Is this all we have . . . Gatorade?" A Rossignol official scurried over to inquire as to his preference, but he just shook his head and went back to the burning surface.

At fifty-six, he has a paunch, but his broad shoulders would normally negate its appearance—if he were wearing street clothes and not running and bending and reaching for high lobs. His legs are slender and so well-formed that he could make Cyd Charisse take notice. And, of course, he is handsome. There may never have been a world-class player—not even the striking Lester Stoefen nor the dark and classy Frank Shields—who could cut such a figure in shorts. No wonder, I thought, that the tennis world turned upside down when this rangy Latin arrived with his racquets and beat the best of the best.

Moody and silent, Gonzales stalked the ball and seldom showed any emotion. Only once did his personality shine. He had served to Hugh Stewart, and the ball flew long over the service line. He then stroked the same serve into the corner for an ace. Looking across at the waiting Jason Morton, he repeated the performance—his second serve, coming like a blurred pellet for another ace. *Both on second serves.* He grinned and stood there and yelled across at Morton, "Seems like old times, Jason!" and then he strode manfully around the net to receive service, having at last established himself. Later on, I regret to add, he missed four consecutive overheads and simply shrugged. But he stroked well and automatically, but too often his shots would hit the net. (He had a backhand wrist-volley that erred far too often.) He was rusty, and the extra weight was wearing him down. Meanwhile, Bob Howe, his partner, was missing easy shots and grimacing. Hugh Stewart, on the other side of the court, was playing with an immense knee brace and was using finesse to angle soft shots away from the tired Gonzales and the erring Howe.

But it was Jason Morton who held the day. He ran like a youngster and made one spectacular put-away, hitting the ball behind his back as he dashed backward after a deep crosscourt. Watching Morton, I again recalled Don Budge, who had told me that there were many club players who could come out and take on an ex-champion and win. Morton was such a man. I vowed I would try to look up his record, and I did manage to gather a bit of information. In 1979, Jason Morton won the U.S. Hard Court men's fifty singles. He also took the title on grass that year, again in the men's fifty singles.

In 1982 he was ranked tenth in the nation in the men's forties. His hometown is listed as Houston, Texas. In the men's fifties, doubles, he was ranked *number one,* with Russell Seymour as his partner. In the men's forty-fives, he was nineteenth with none other than Gonzales as his teammate in doubles. In any case, whatever his record, the amazing Jason Morton had superb reflexes and carried Hugh Stewart along to victory in straight sets: four and three.

When it was over, Pancho Gonzales came to the side of the court to drink more Gatorade, his shoulders slumped and his graying hair tousled. He sat on a chair and drank a drink he did not enjoy, and a few people came by to pay their respects. The winners, Morton and Stewart, remained on the other side of the court, ignored and resting. Gonzales had a tiny audience, and Bob Howe had slipped away. I went to him, then, and introduced myself. He looked at me with eyes that were narrowed from fatigue and also, I felt, narrowed with irritation. I said, "Hello, my name is Stan Hart. I wrote you about a book I was doing?"

For a moment there was no answer. Then in his high voice, he said, "Didn't I write you a letter?"

I said, "Yes."

"Well, then you know my answer."

I said, "But maybe if I just came by your pro shop tomorrow . . ."

44. Richard "Pancho" Gonzales: no interview. Oodles of charm

"Look," he said, "all that is wishful thinking. And besides, I am playing in tournaments now. I don't know where I will be tomorrow. And look," he repeated, "you're just wishful thinking. You have my letter."

I said, "Thank you," and smiled down at him sitting there and then walked back to the exit door. The sportswriter Dick Schaap had called him the "Lone Wolf of Tennis." I would think of him as some fallen Montezuma—a regal man who may have lost a fight at this point in his life, but not the war, and was too busy for me, for you, for anyone, as he contemplated defeat in the bright glaze of sunshine on cement, aloft on the upper deck in a silver-and-golden city called Las Vegas.

Caesar's Palace was generous about letting me check out yet remain at the pool, "picking up the rays," as they used to say in Las Vegas. Wearing my "shades" and striding about, I imagined myself as a millionaire from Milwaukee or Moline, Ohio. The night before I had looked for something to do and found the town almost deserted of talent—that is, talent that appealed to me. For instance, Caesar's Palace had the irreverent Joan Rivers, but in order to see her, you had to sit through the mediocre wit of the Smothers Brothers. And down the yellow brick road, as it were, was a man named Andy Gibbs. Who was he? A teen phenomenon, a Bee Gee! Well, that wasn't my cup of tea, so I asked around and found out that El Rancho had a country and western singer named Kathy O'Shea. I liked the sound of her name and yearned for the heartbreak of country and western music. I was alone and had lost Gonzales, so the chance to cry in my beer was overwhelming.

As it happened, El Rancho was hardly booming. I was one of five customers to watch the show, and when I returned to enjoy it again at midnight, I was alone. There was one other man, sleeping with his head on the table. He had cried himself to sleep, I thought, and as the endearing Kathy O'Shea belted out Hank Williams' songs, I was the only recipient of her perfectly pitched plaint of woe. Eventually she joined me, and I taped her for an hour and a half. Why? I was angry at Gonzales and used her to replace him. In my mind, fairly askew at the time, I thought I had discovered a great talent and that I would write an article about her. I may still do that. Five-foot-three, with auburn hair, she is a delight and sings the way they did when I was a boy and heard Patsy Kline at Dyson's, a roadhouse in the forgotten southern Maryland town called Charlotte Hall.

So the next day, I ambled about the pool and then flew away. Simple as that, I flew to Los Angeles and then went by cab to Pasadena, where I stayed at the Pasadena Hilton so that I could be near the apartment of Louise Brough. We were to play at 2:00 the next afternoon. Yet, on the way, my mind strayed back to Vic Seixas. He had played Gonzales "maybe three times." He had never won. "Gonzales had the kind of game that gave me fits," Vic had said. But, of course, Gonzales had turned pro at twenty-one, and when Vic, much his senior, was hitting his peak, Gonzales was already a prodigy playing on another circuit. But mentioning Gonzales brought Vic back to Frank Sedgman. Vic said that the most underrated, great player was Frank Sedgman. "Frank could run—he was the fastest man I have ever played against." And Sedgman won most of their duels. By the time Seixas won Wimbledon, Sedgman was a professional and did not stay in Vic's path. As for Hoad, Vic could handle the great Australian except when he was really hot. And Louise Brough. At one time or another, this agreeable woman (as I would soon discover) beat everybody. Except for Maureen Connolly, many years her junior, Louise at the top of her game was as good as they came. This was what I thought as I flew into Los Angeles once more. Once more I would play on cement courts and challenge a world champion—it was still heady stuff, and remembering the ebullience of Kathy O'Shea and the proud bearing of the great Gonzales, I did not regret my trip to Las Vegas. Hell, you can't always have everything your own way. Even the roulette wheel had made that bromide obvious to me. I had gambled unsuccessfully but not dangerously, and Kathy O'Shea had told me her life story. You win a few and you lose a few.

In Pasadena, the word was out that the Russians had boycotted the Olympic Games. This news was distressing to everyone, and there were two responses: one—screw the Russians; two—the Olympics won't count because the Americans will just roll on to gold medals, with the Eastern Bloc countries out of the picture.

And this is pertinent to my book because I remember writing my chapter on Jack Kramer. I said then that if his kind of attitude pervaded the Olympics, the Russians couldn't possibly take part. His was a firm belief in free enterprise, and even if their athletes won, the USSR would lose. By winning and making the Los Angeles Olympics a competitive success, it would prove once more that our system (Kramer's system) works. For us to be successful at wooing the Russians, you had to be tricky and use finesse. Jack was an open advocate for the private sector. I knew then that the Olympics would fail. Kramer was no Hugh Stewart who angled his shots. He still played the big game and so did his friends and so did the Los Angeles organizers. How could the Russians go to a city where perhaps 20 percent of their athletes would defect, where the Olympics would be run to perfection, and America—regardless of its strength in gold and silver and bronze medals—would triumph? In short, America could win even if it came in second or third. I knew there was trouble afoot when I saw and listened to the untroubled true believer, Jack Kramer. Kramer would not compromise over the way you cooked bacon, much less the finer points of international diplomacy. He would never forget his open game that belted weaker people off the court. His friends were millionaires. The whole town was full of millionaires who had made it on their own. This would be hard for the Russians to swallow. Their very system would be jeopardized. It would be Russian Marxism versus McDonald's.

I called Louise Brough at 2:00 and, as she had promised, she came right over to pick me up, and off we drove for our game in the sun. On that bright, beautiful, apparently smogless day, all thoughts of a messed-up Olympics were erased by the prospects at hand. I was with Louise Brough, a woman who had been a presence in my book from the very start. The familiar question—whatever happened to?—was what had started me off, and Louise Brough and Margaret Osborne duPont were the first names to come to mind. As a doubles team, they had won the national title at Longwood twelve times, nine of them in succession from 1942 through 1950. In 1942 she won the mixed doubles playing with Ted Schroeder and was runner-up in the singles to Pauline Betz. In 1947 Louise won the mixed doubles with John Bromwich, the doubles with Margaret Osborne (not yet duPont), and the singles, beating Margaret Osborne 8–6, 4–6, 6–1—all three titles in a blaze of supremacy. She won the singles at Wimbledon three times in a row, starting in 1948, and in 1947, the year she made the triple play in America, she won Wimbledon with Bromwich in the mixed doubles. Indeed, her name should be especially enshrined, for she also took *every* championship in 1948 at Wimbledon. I doubt if anyone has played in America and won all three titles one year and then repeated this feat the next year in England.

Admittedly, with John Bromwich and Margaret Osborne, Louise had the finest of partners, but on her own as a singles star, she had four Wimbledon titles (she came back in 1955 to beat Beverly Baker Fleitz in the finals) and one United States victory (1947). Her competition was fierce: Margaret Osborne, Pauline Betz, Maureen Connolly, and Doris Hart. And as has been noted, there was one stunning year when Sarah Palfrey returned from out of the blue to win, 1945. And you can add to that list Shirley Fry and Althea Gibson—a golden era for American women tennis players. In fact, in 1957 Louise Brough lost to Althea Gibson in the finals at Forest Hills—a time span of fifteen years after she had reached the finals against Pauline in 1942.

But on the day I played Louise, we were a long way from the impeccable green lawn of Wimbledon or the old and lovely grass at the West Side Tennis Club in Forest Hills. Instead of such august playing surfaces, we played on plain, white cement; the kind of court that the outstanding California tennis players grew up on. We played on a court adjacent to the McKinley Junior High School in downtown Pasadena, and near where she parked her car, there was litter, dying grass, and sand and pebbles meshed into a landscape that reeked of public access and of wild kids running like miniature express trains about the courts with old racquets and old balls and high spirits. Who could help thinking of a youthful Kramer or a blond whirl named Pauline Betz playing their hearts out with whoops of victory on just such a court many decades ago?

Naturally, I told her about my knee, and she looked briefly at my elastic wrapping, which I hoped would hold the tendons together—or the cartilage. My knee hurt, but it seemed to have improved with the short respite it received in Las Vegas. Louise also had an injury, and she somewhat gleefully pointed to her ankle, which was encased in an Ace bandage. "I guess I sprained it," she offered, but her merry disposition indicated that there was nothing to be alarmed about. Of course, we would play, and we would play on a court where she sometimes gave instructions to students she was working with. I didn't mind a little old court made of cement, and I said that anything she wanted was all right with me.

We rallied for a short time and then started a set. I felt that with Louise, not quite up to par with that bad ankle, I had a good chance to win. I noticed that she hated my forehand, a forehand I was driving at her. I also figured she would not have much of a serve. At sixty-one I doubted that there would be power in her game, and she did not appear to have the placements that Dodo Cheney had shown me. If I could keep forcing her from right to left, I could slip in and put it away from midcourt—even though I could not run and, of course, could not take the net. But I could slip in on her, I thought.

She briskly moved ahead to a 4–1 lead. However, her first serve of the match to my forehand, I belted back on an angle for a put-away, and she seemed stunned. I did not look that good to her as we warmed up, but boy, did I have a forehand that afternoon! So she worked my backhand and even aced me four times to take a commanding lead.

Then I gave her a backhand drop shot that amazingly she returned. She said, "Had that been on clay, the ball would have died," and I was pleased. But more than pleased, I was enthusiastic and went on to take three games in a row. Finally, she had me at 6–5 and forty–love. I knew that if I just looked at the ball and hit it deep, I could take her, so I did just that and came back to even the score. At 6–6 she opted for a tie-breaker. Alas, she won it quickly since I had used up my powers of concentration by that time and was just swinging away as though we had two more sets to play. We did not. She declined another set because her ankle was hurting, and I did not press her. My knee felt pretty steady, but why overdo it? Anway, she had the right to stop. I always had to remember that people were doing me favors.

Louise Brough is of medium height and is lithe and quick. Her hair is brown and her face is slightly lined and hard from the sun, the way Dodo Cheney's face is. She has an elfin twinkle that I loved (again like Dodo Cheney), and *she was amenable.* It was 3:30, and there we were in sweaty tennis clothes and nowhere to go, so I suggested the Hilton. In my mind, I rather

45. Louise Brough

thought we would end up in my room ordering room service because it would look odd going into a city cocktail lounge in wet tennis attire. But Louise just smiled and said that she doubted they would mind because I was staying there and paying for a room. So we went into the lounge. It was called the Madagascar Café and was appropriately touched with exotica. We drank beer and she began to reminisce. She was a Pasadena resident with another home down the way in Vista—not too far from San Diego—and, well, you could tell that if the Hilton was fine with me, it was fine with her, and I felt secure and supreme over any functionary who might stare at us. Louise Brough had met the Queen of England. Her record as an amateur athlete was unassailable. Unlike others who had turned professional, she had kept on winning and winning. Winners do not worry too much about the state of their tennis sneakers in a cocktail lounge. I had learned that much over the course of my trail. And if she didn't worry, neither would I.

Louise was wearing whites, and her shorts stopped at her upper thighs, showing nice slim legs. Her hairstyle could best be described as "short straw-cut," the kind a farm boy might have, and for a moment I thought of Louise Brough riding a tractor. There may have been gray in her hair, but I did not notice. It was short and brown and curly in the back and straight in the front. She looked young and in excellent condition. Sitting at the table in the

Hilton wearing a white tennis jacket, she was a picture of health. Others around us were either hanging on from a long lunch or taking high tea—a little midafternoon pick-me-up. California and tennis seemed to be a salubrious combination—the other people in the room were missing out.

We started talking about Pauline Betz, whom Louise played against over forty years ago. In 1942 and 1943, Pauline beat Louise in the finals at Forest Hills. In the first match at Wimbledon after World War II, Pauline triumphed again, beating Louise 6–2, 6–4. After that Elwood C. Cooke (Sarah Palfrey's husband) signed Pauline to a professional contract that Pauline signed a bit prematurely, or so said Louise Brough. "She wanted to play Wimbledon again in 1947, and they found out about it, and Pauline fessed up that she had signed a contract with the Cookes. Elwood wanted the two girls (his wife, Sarah, and Pauline) to play against each other. I don't think she really had to tell them, but she told the truth."

Louise seemed shy, and I wanted to get her to talk about herself, so I asked her if anyone had ever won as many major tournaments as she had. "Oh, sure," she answered. "Margaret Smith [Court] and, I suppose, Billie Jean is next."

"But you are ranked second in the all-time list for being in the top ten. Sixteen years."

"Oh, someone sent me a little clipping on that," she said.

"Billie Jean Moffitt King leads with seventeen years."

"Who is third?"

"Nancy Richey."

"Well, that surprises me. Nancy could have played longer than she did."

Being number three, then, Nancy Richey could have surpassed Billie Jean, I gathered, and I told Louise that I hadn't even thought of Nancy Richey in such exalted terms.

"She could have gone on longer," Louise answered.

"Well, you were ranked number one in 1947."

"And I was in the finals four or five times, and there were two times when I had a match point and didn't win. I look back now and say, 'What a nut you are! What a waste!' "

We gossiped for a while about other women players, and when I told Louise that Doris Hart would not see me, she said, "She's a devil." She spoke in a kind of old-fashioned, schoolteacher way that was ambivalent. Was she scolding Doris Hart or giving her approval? As for Helen Hull Jacobs, Louise thought that she was ill. "She's not going to Wimbledon for the anniversary," she said. That event, forthcoming in the summer of 1984—only a matter of weeks away—would be the topic of much talk among the women athletes who had won in England. Indeed, Shirley Fry and Louise were going back, so was Alice Marble, and probably everyone who could. Their reunion would mark the hundredth year of women's tennis in the All-England Championships. I thought as I listened to Louise evince her concern for Helen Jacobs' health that I would love to tag along on that trip. Pauline and Althea, Maria Bueno and Billie Jean—boy, I'd like to be a fly on the wall.

Louise was born in Oklahoma City in 1923, she said.

"Did you go to the regular schools there—high school?"

"No, we moved here when I was four and a half. We moved to Beverly Hills. My parents were separated, and my mother moved to Beverly Hills, where her parents lived, and I went to Beverly Hills High School and then on to USC for a couple of years, and then I quit."

"Were you wealthy?"

"It was the Depression time, but my father had enough to buy us a home and we were all right, but I wouldn't say we were wealthy."

"I suppose by the time you left USC you were playing serious tennis."

"Oh, yes. I played in high school, and when I was seventeen, my mother took me East for the junior tournaments, which I won in 1940 and 1941. (The USLTA girls eighteen singles, after which she was followed by Doris Hart, who won it two years in a row, and then by Shirley Fry, who also won the national grass court championship two years running.)

"And I won the doubles in 1941 with Gussie," she added.

I quickly went to the *Tennis Yearbook,* and there it was—Louise Brough and Gertrude Moran. I had had no idea of that when I saw Gussie months earlier. I told her about seeing Gussie Moran, and Louise wanted to know how she was. I said that she was getting over the flu when I saw her, and Louise added that she was somewhat of a recluse—a word I had employed talking of Helen Wills.

"Going back to your college days, did you have a tennis scholarship at USC?"

"No. They didn't know what women's tennis was in those days."

"When did you hook up with Margaret Osborne?"

"When I was nineteen. Her husband, Will duPont, had seen me play the year before in the juniors, and he knew that Margaret's partner, Sarah Palfrey, was going to have a baby, so he suggested to Margaret that we play together."

"You then became a legendary team."

"Yes. We never lost. We played well together and got along together, and it was really a nice arrangement."

What a nice arrangement, indeed. For here was Will duPont, "who believed that tennis players didn't get an even break—they played as amateurs and didn't make anything"—and he would take them, Margaret and Alice Marble and Louise and perhaps others, all the way to Hawaii, as Louise pointed out. Finally Will duPont settled in Palm Springs for his bronchitis

327

and built himself a lovely house with a tennis court and a pool and another house for Alice Marble and Mary K. Browne and then died before he could sign the papers making Alice's house officially hers. But though this story was told to me before by Alice Marble, it sounded fresh coming from the quiet, almost tentative voice of Louise Brough. Again, I wondered about Will duPont. I thought that he must have been seeing Alice Marble at the same time he was married to Margaret Osborne.

"Yes, but they were always good friends. Alice was a good friend of Margaret's."

"Chummy," I thought, and I showed my confusion over the chronology of all of this. "Who came first, Alice or Margaret?"

"Alice," Louise answered. "Will started seeing Alice, I think, when he was still married to his first wife."

"Well, I can't get into this any further," I said. The whole matter of Will duPont, a great benefactor of amateur tennis, would make another story, another book. Like Frank Shields, Will duPont was emerging on the periphery, looming larger and more enticing all of the time. But I had to stick with Louise. I asked her about heroes and heroines.

"No. I didn't start playing tennis until I was twelve or thirteen, and I received tennis lessons from Dick Skeen on my thirteenth birthday as a present."

"Kramer mentions him," I interrupted, knowing that she'd misunderstood the question.

"Well, he taught a lot of the juniors—I think he even helped Pauline. And, anyway, my mother had a friend who had a daughter who was going to take lessons, and the two mothers thought it would be nice if I took them, too, so we could play together."

"You mean it was all luck! If your mother had not had a friend who was giving her own daughter lessons?"

Louise laughed happily. "Not really. I was already playing all the sports in school. I had a brother who played football, and I played with the boys."

"Were you always wiry and an athlete?"

"No, I was big and fat. Not fat, fat you know . . ."

"But husky. Well, you certainly have trimmed down," I said, recalling how slender she was on the old cement court we had recently left.

"Did you ever play Dodo Cheney in the seniors?"

"I played her in one tournament and, of course, she beat me, but I was never in serious training for the seniors."

I had to ponder that last remark. Dodo is older and "tournament tough." But suppose Louise *did* train. I knew that I hit a lob of hers, going full tilt backward toward the baseline. I had hit it over my head, and it landed two-thirds deep in her court. She was so astonished that she missed her return—with me

328

limping outside the playing surface. She would not have made such a mistake were she in training. But still . . . I thought about Dodo Cheney. I don't know why I thought of her except for the fact that Dodo Cheney had never gotten the rewards as a youngster and she's hungry now to atone. Louise had it all early in life. All things being equal, what would she have to prove?—which was almost precisely what they said about Gonzales back in Vegas in the lowering sun and high heat of the late afternoon.

Dodo Cheney, Louise Brough, and (as I suspected it would be) Margaret Osborne duPont were "sweethearts on parade." I know I may be biased to say this, but to quote Ned Rorem, I was "In Praise of Older Women." I admired spunk, and sitting with Louise, I realized that I was glad that she had beaten me—even though I would tell people it could have gone either way—a tie-breaker, et cetera, et cetera. And what of Sarah Palfrey, who had played in pain after a hip operation? And Alice Marble, the best of them all, who played after five cancer operations and with one lung—as I later learned? Where in hell were the men when you added them up?

Only the exquisite Billy Talbert had gone out to look bad. Kramer, Budge, and Schroeder had said in effect, "No way." Parker and Mulloy had nothing to hide because they were still superb. Although Talbert might be a bit of a stuffed shirt (I secretly thought), he was game. And so were the women. I adored them. Yet that was unfair, and I *was* being biased because I thought of George Lott who (as I write this) has recently called to challenge me to a game at Forest Hills for money when he comes East in the late summer. I had come to realize that I could not generalize on this. Some people were happy to be seen and talked to and visited with, and they welcomed the small attention my book might bring them. Others (Gonzales is a perfect example) needed me like a hole in the noggin, and I could sense it. Sidney Wood came to mind as Louise and I drank beer and were being just friendly—nothing to write about, just one of the best players in the world, and being herself. So my mind ran on. What *about* Sidney Wood? Should I end my book with one more futile phone call to the great Wood? Louise, I thought, tell me something exciting. Get me out of other people's lives. Take me to yourself.

"I am not in too good shape now," she was saying, although I could see no evidence of truth in that statement. But Louise being in shape didn't mean just looking well. It meant stamina. I asked her if there was any doubles team that she and Margaret feared.

"Doris Hart with anyone. Pauline played with her, Pat Todd, and Shirley Fry. I would get nervous before playing them. Doris was so steady.

"Now back to that hero question. You could say that I looked up to Alice Marble when I was a girl before I started playing myself. But I get a kick out of kids today who are always writing about someone and are so involved. When I was a kid in college, I didn't know beans about politics."

"Now that you are sixty-one years old and you look back on your life, whom do you respect the most?"

"Oh, I suppose that will take a long time to answer. I'll probably think of someone tomorrow."

"Off the top of your head."

"I guess Mrs. Wightman. [Hazel Hotchkiss Wightman of the Wightman Cup. Louise played Wightman Cup tennis for nine years and amassed the incredible record of 22 wins and no defeats.] Also Margaret [Osborne duPont]."

"No national leaders or spiritual leaders?"

"I was never philosophical until just the last couple of years." And then she shook her head and smiled, and though I gave her some names such as Eleanor Roosevelt, Winston Churchill, and Mahatma Gandhi, she stuck to her silence. She made me wonder if the constant grind of competition over a goodly number of years simply obviates any chance for a larger vision. She made me think of Senator Bill Bradley—the ex-Knick basketball star—and Congressman Jack Kemp from the Buffalo Bills. Did they have tunnel vision for years and then frantically have to catch up after their playing days were over? I could not imagine going through life placing Margaret Osborne duPont above Abraham Lincoln, and Louise Brough just smiled as though such a leader had never existed or was somehow irrelevant. Athletes refer to athletes, I thought.

"To what do you attribute your good health and youthful appearance?"

"Until three months ago, I was playing tennis with women who were thirty-five years old, so I would say exercise. But there were times in my life when I actually wished that I didn't have to play tennis. When I retired, I said, 'Ah, I won't have to play tennis anymore.' I thought I might be able to go into another profession."

"When did you retire?"

"When I got married in 1958 or 1957, I can't remember. I played through 1956. And actually I played the nationals one year after I was married. I didn't do too well. I played Maria Bueno and lost, and then I didn't play for two years, thinking I would find something that would turn me on, but I didn't find it. So I went back and started teaching tennis."

"What about smoking and drinking?"

"I never smoked. I drink some, but I am not really a drinker. Back during the Wightman Cup days, when we would win, we would celebrate with champagne, but, no, I am not a drinker."

"I suppose you don't worry very much about things."

"No. I *am* a worrier. I wish I were not, and I am trying now to be more of a positive thinker. I wish I had been a positive thinker when I was young."

"But you won almost everything you could win?"

46. Louise Brough and Mo Connolly

"Yes, but I would have won more. I used to think, 'What if?' all of the time. I would have done better in singles had I thought positively."

"What was it like when you and Margaret squared off in the finals?"

"Just competition. It didn't much matter whom you were playing."

"Was there anyone you were afraid of—someone you hoped would be bumped off before she reached you in a tournament?"

"There were quite a few like that. Playing Shirley or Doris would be like that, and actually playing Margaret was easier because when you like someone, you don't mind losing so much. There isn't as much pressure."

"How would you rank the top five women's players?"

"I think Maureen Connolly was the best."

"If Maureen played Martina, how would that turn out?"

"It would be the world's greatest match, but I think Maureen would win."

"What about you and Margaret?"

"At our peaks, I think I would be better."

"Where does Alice Marble fit into this?"

"She would have to be up there. But against Maureen, she might not win a game. And Pauline Betz would be up there. She didn't have a great serve and no volley to speak of and no forehand, but she could retrieve like crazy. She had a great backhand. I never felt particularly tired after playing her. My trouble was that I would make too many errors. I played Maureen after my peak, but I really felt it when we had done playing. We had close matches."

"What was your toughest match?"

"I don't know. But I guess, because it was later in my life, it would be the time I beat Beverly Baker Fleitz at Wimbledon in 1955 [7–5, 8–6 for the title]. I was thirty-two, and Beverly was at her best. She beat Doris Hart two and love in the semifinals. She was playing very good tennis."

"And the toughest player you ever played would be Maureen Connolly?"

"Yes. I think she would beat Martina because she had a great return of serve. And she had fine passing shots. So if Martina was forced to stay back, she couldn't compete with Maureen."

"Here's an off-the-wall question. Do you believe in God?"

"I don't want to say I don't."

"Well, why not?"

"Because then I would be an agnostic. I don't think that there is a being up there. I think that the best that is in us is God. I think it is in the mind and the heart of human beings. I think that here we are and we have one life to live and we do the best that we can and the best is that thing you can call God."

47. Louise Brough and her mighty forearm

"Do you go to church?"

"No. But I don't mind going to church. When I was a child, I was confirmed in the Episcopal Church. It was in my latter days that things changed. I read a good deal of Ayn Rand."

"Speaking of Ayn Rand, an opinionated conservative, most of the players I have seen are conservative."

"I think that's wonderful."

"I guess the reason is that they have the rewards of endeavor, from work?"

"Yes, taking responsibility."

"If you had your life to live over again, would you change anything?"

"Not in tennis. And, no, I can't think of myself as anything but an outdoors girl and an athlete and a nature-body. Back at my home in Vista, I can spend hours out-of-doors picking weeds."

"Are you a gardener?"

"Not in a real sense. I don't have a vegetable garden. We have flowers. My husband does the planting, and I do the maintaining."

"Any hobbies?"

"I read a lot. Right now I am reading novels, but I read books on nutrition and business."

"What novel are you reading right now?"

"A silly thing called *Solo* by Jack Higgins. I guess I read novels to avoid responsibilities, but that is what I am doing now."

"What do you mean by business books?"

"Books about investing, and there was that book about buying gold by Harry Browne."

"Do you follow through on these books and invest?"

"I do my share of investing."*

"Are you wealthy?"

"Comfortable."

"What about living expenses on your trips around the country and overseas to play tennis?"

"On my first trip to England, we received $12 a day to live on. That would have included the hotel and the three meals. It wasn't very much."

"Did you ever receive money under the table?"

"No. My mother helped me out, and you would sometimes get expenses and were put up in people's houses. I did hear, though, that some of the men would carry tennis racquets with them to sell. I heard a story that

---

* When Louise mailed me a picture of herself, she wrapped it in a magazine called *Dollar $ense*, published by the Georgia Federal Bank.

Don Budge, before the war, sold so many racquets, he was able to furnish his house."

"You mean, a player would fill up a steamer trunk full of racquets when he went abroad and sell them?"

"I heard that. Heard it about Mulloy, too. Wilson would give you shoes and clothes and everything under the sun. There was a time when you got anything you wanted. But then they cut it down to the top players, who might get four frames and a couple of restringings, something like that.

"Who or what were the major influences on your life? Your mother?"

"My mother, because she really pushed me to win. She made me serious about winning because I was almost afraid to come home if I lost. She would be so mad. But she took me everywhere and was a negative help in that I was afraid to make her mad by not winning. Otherwise, I might have just floated along and not done anything."

"Suppose you hadn't become a tennis player, what would have become of you?"

"I don't know. Maybe nothing. I really wasn't that bright. I could get good grades, but I didn't because I was always playing tennis. I wasn't serious about anything else."

"When you were a young girl, were you interested in guys or mainly sports?"

"I could take them or leave them. When I was in high school, I dated a lot, but it wasn't important. I didn't get married until I was thirty-three."

"What does your husband do?"

"He is a dentist here in town."

"Do you have any children?"

"Nope. I never felt that I could manage children."

"No maternal instincts?"

"I love other people's children. I just felt that I was so tired, I wouldn't be able to wake up at night to hear them cry. I'd probably (inadvertently) kill them in the first week."

"Looking back, wouldn't you like—say you were in your seventies—wouldn't you like grandchildren around the house?"

"No, I don't care about that. I haven't missed them at all. I have friends who have children and grandchildren, and my brother has two children, and one of my friends' children just had a little baby last week, and I love the little things, but I just would not want to take care of them. Someday maybe, but not yet."

"What about animals—dogs and cats?"

"No."

"In other words, if you wanted to stroke something, and you have no children, grandchildren, or pets, the only one around is your husband?"

"No. I am not a stroker. I don't like to touch people. The only reason I don't have a pet back at Vista is that I don't want to have to take care of it."

"You're quite a loner, then, aren't you?"

"I feel like I am now, and I feel right in tune with it. I feel that I don't need anybody."

It was quite an admission. We were very different. I hated loneliness and needed attention, the kind I hoped for the next day when I was seeing Gene Mako. Without other people, I'd destroy myself. For me, Sartre was wrong when he wrote, "Hell is other people." Hell is being *without* people. So it was that I was distressed to hear her say that. I hated to hear a woman of such grace and charm say that she was content to be alone. I'd flown from Phoenix with Paul Hornung, the ex-Green Bay Packer football star, which is to say that he was on the same plane. We collected our bags together, and I studied him. He was fat and pale and gray-haired and looked like a bartender from Meriden, Connecticut. But soon after getting our luggage, we both checked into Caesar's Palace, he at a VIP check-in and I standing in line. I looked over at the small cocktail lounge near the registration desk as I stood in a line of guests, holding my registration receipt, and there was Hornung already in gear, talking with someone—clearly a man *not* alone. But the contrast with Louise! Hornung was out of shape and looked dreadful in tasteless clothes and . . . clumsy. Louise was trim and smiling and laughing all through our talk, often at herself, and yet *she* was the loner. What did it all mean? I only knew that I was the Hornung type. Check in and start talking. Louise is so different, but then she is a champion nonpareil. Hornung was a great team player but just one among many great players. Surely a Hall of Fame member, but in truth, no Louise. As I wrote earlier, her back-to-back triple crown at Forest Hills and Wimbledon is amazing in a sport that depends on precision and concentration, as well as on guts and skill. Margaret duPont would tell me later that Louise would walk onto a court at Wimbledon in front of thousands of people and say, "Now I am alone."

"Sometimes," said Margaret, "she would be so tight or tense that she actually could not throw the ball in the air to serve. Her arm would become palsied."

I told Louise that I had five children and didn't know what would have become of me had I not been a father.

She said, "Well, once you have them, that's different. I only know that if I had children, I would never have done anything in sports. I would have been too worried about them."

"Would that be true for most athletes?"

"I think they are self-interested. I know that now I can take it or leave it, but I also know that tennis is good for me."

"If you wanted to leave some words of wisdom for the public, what would you tell the people out there?"

"Well, I don't have it organized. I just know that you can make life awfully difficult for yourself, and you can also make things a lot easier. You just have to have a positive way of looking at things. I have been listening to a tape called "Seeds of Greatness." In that tape, the message is, "I am *going* to do this. Never, I *can't* do this." It is forward and positive, and I have always been the type who says, 'I wonder if this will happen?' or 'I wonder if that will happen?' If I hadn't been that way, I think I would have been a lot happier and a lot better in a number of different ways. I remember when I was nineteen. I had left the juniors and was on the circuit, and I won every tournament. When I got to the finals in the nationals, I remember saying to a friend of mine, 'I don't deserve this. If I win it, I don't deserve it.' It was some years later that I realized that if I only had someone there to tell me, 'You *do* deserve it. You've worked hard, now go out there and win . . .' And so I lost it back when I was nineteen."

"You speak a good deal about winning. Do you have any sympathy for the losers in the world?"

"No. I am sorry, but I don't. I would have if I knew one personally, but not for the masses."

"But take World War II. You must have had sympathy for those who were being bombed out or for the Jews who were . . ."

"No. I wasn't there; I wasn't aware of the war at all. You know, when they bombed Pearl Harbor, I didn't know where Pearl Harbor was. What was wrong with me?"

"But I don't want you to sound insensitive. You are really a sensitive person."

"I am. I am very sensitive toward people I care about."

"Then it's all on a personal basis. If I were Jewish and came to you and was talking to you about my parents being gassed at Dachau, you wouldn't begin to cry because you didn't know them?"

"No. I wouldn't cry. I don't cry easily. But I am getting better. I finished reading *Sophie's Choice* and *The Little Drummer Girl*, and those things affect me now."

"I suppose that when you were an active athlete and on the road all the time, one would not have time to feel for others too much . . ."

"Pauline Betz did. I remember thinking about Rockefeller and other millionaires who would give to the poor, and I thought, 'Why, that's peculiar. Why would they feel guilty, having so much money?' and I wondered why they should feel guilty about it. But now I feel a little guilty—not that I have that much money, but I think of those without."

"Would you give a percentage of your money to the poor? I remember talking to Frankie Parker, and he said he would, providing it were done right."

"No, I wouldn't just give it away. If I wanted to give money, I would give it (straight out). I wouldn't give it to the politicians, to the bureaucrats, and let them drink it up with champagne."

"Did you ever make any money on your own?"

"Yes, as a tennis pro. I have had some lovely private courts and have coached kids from eleven years old, and now they are all in college or moved away or something, and the private courts went with them. That's why we played on the court at the McKinley Junior High School."

"But you couldn't get very affluent as a tennis teacher."

"No. My mother passed away, and I inherited some money."

"And your husband is a dentist . . ."

"But I don't depend on that," she said, laughing.

I mentioned Sarah Palfrey, who had been brought up with money, and now here was Louise, who had grown up in Beverly Hills and attended a private university (USC), admitting that she came into money, "enough to be comfortable—enough not to have to worry," and saying, "They used to say you couldn't be a good tennis player and be rich. That was dumb."

I threw her my final question—a question I had shied away from because of some male embarrassment. I asked her what happens when you menstruate, say, the day before the finals. "Don't you get cramps?" I asked.

"Not really. I don't think it makes any difference. Those women who complain about cramps—maybe if they'd been tennis players, they would not have gotten them."

"You mean, if Martina's time comes around right before a big match, it doesn't make any difference?"

"I think it's a disadvantage, but it's not a crippling one. I used to wonder about swimmers. But I am sure they just go through it. It's something you grow up with like anything else. The show must go on."

"Speaking of the show going on, is there one big day that stands out in your mind?"

"I remember playing five and a half hours of tennis at Wimbledon. You had to play all three finals on the same day. It was 1949."

"How did you do?"

"I won the singles and the women's doubles with Margaret, but John Bromwich and I lost. But the year before, in 1948, I won all three, but it wasn't so long. Not five and a half hours."

As she was speaking, I was leafing madly through my *Tennis Yearbook* and found Wimbledon. She had also won in all three categories in 1950. She won the mixed doubles with Eric Sturgess. That would mean, I thought, that in a four-year span, she had taken the triple crown three times. First in Forest Hills in 1947. Then in England in 1948, and then again in England in 1950.

I said, "I had a great time with you," still a bit awestruck by her records.

"Oh, so did I. I hope we can play again—when your knee and my ankle are all right."

"I might even win," I said, and Louise Brough smiled, but did not reply. Fat chance!

CHAPTER

$\mathscr{Q}20$

Gene Mako:

"You shut up and deal."

The thought of Gene Mako was a stroke of genius—my stroke of genius. I had forgotten about him even though months before I had heard from Don Budge's housekeeper that the Budges were in Los Angeles visiting Gene Mako. At that time, I had fired off a letter asking if I could fly out "even for two hours" to meet the two of them. But I had received no reply, and later when I did meet Budge and when a rather quirky order began to take place within the chronology of my book, Mako receded from my mind. He was a doubles player like George Lott. But not in George's league—or so I thought.

So the stroke of genius occurred when impulsively I telephoned Mako from my house on Martha's Vineyard and got his answering machine. I laid out the plan of my book and said that I would be in the area to see Louise Brough and Bob Falkenburg and asked if we could get together.

A day after my rather lengthy peroration to his answering machine, the phone rang. It was Gene Mako. "By all means," he said. "Just call when you are in town." Mako. I had found his number by calling the office of the Southern California Tennis Association. Mako, I thought. What a great name—the name of a shark. The man who played with Budge. I looked him up in my record book. George Lott, who had had a distinguished singles career, had been ranked in the United States, starting in 1924 and was still ranked in 1934, and as I scanned the top ten rankings, I finally hit 1937, and there was Gene Mako, number eight, one line above Don McNeill. But in 1938, he moved to number three, trailing only Budge and Riggs. After 1938 he disappeared—presumably turning professional, I guessed. But he was number three behind two of the great tennis stars of all time.

But let's look at the doubles. In 1935 Allison and Van Ryn beat Budge and Mako in the U.S. finals at Longwood. In 1936 Budge and Mako returned the favor and won the national title. In 1937 Budge and Mako lost in the finals to von Cramm and Henner Henkel. In 1938 (Budge's grand slam year) they took it again, beating the Australians, Quist and Bromwich. In both 1937 and 1938, they won Wimbledon. In 1937 they won the Davis Cup doubles, part of a lopsided four-to-one victory over Great Britain. In 1938 Mako and Budge were beaten by Quist and Bromwich, but the United States retained the cup because both Riggs and Budge played superbly in singles—Budge whipping both Quist and Bromwich, Riggs losing to Bromwich but beating Quist. The score was 3–2, America.

And like Lott, Mako was a junior champion. Lott won the junior singles title two years in a row (1923 and 1924), but Gene Mako won it in 1934, a year after Budge and a year before Riggs. But what is more important with regard to his later success as a great doubles player is the fact that Mako won the junior doubles three years in a row playing *with three different partners,* a feat equaled only by the now deceased (but often spoken of) Joe Hunt, and the man I would soon see, Bob Falkenburg.

So Mako, long obscured by his brilliant partner, Don Budge, was ready to see me, and the drama of it stays in my mind. I was thinking about it even as I waved good-bye to Louise Brough. Gene Mako had slipped so far out of the public eye that to bring him back would really be thrilling. If the candid and soft-spoken Louise Brough Clapp had been a treat, what, pray tell, lay in wait for me in the presence of Gene Mako? Mako, Stoefen, Lott, Allison, Van Ryn—all doubles players at the very top, and doubles was my game. There was strategy at work in doubles. It was like being a kid and playing war. I had really loved my time with Lott. What would it be like with Mako?

I was still feeling the jet lag, and after talking with Louise, I went to my room at the Hilton and took a nap. When I awoke, it was almost 10:00 at night, and I fled my room looking for a nearby restaurant that was still open. Fortunately, there was a superb Japanese restaurant across the street, and I dined there, the only customer in the place, eating shrimp and exotic dishes. The next night I planned to see the movie *The Natural,* which was about to open, but for tonight, I had only my memories of my game with Louise—a game that I would have loved to have gone on—for two more sets. I thought about many things that evening, but none of them have a bearing on this book. It just seems that when you travel alone, memories play their tunes. And yet if you clutter the mind with friends and activity, it will dilute the impact of the experience you have come so far to enjoy. The high point of my day had been Louise, and tomorrow it would be Gene. So I dined alone—a solitary Eastener in an Oriental setting. I recalled my early days and the mundane world I had lived in and the few high points that made it worthwhile; and, of course, I missed my children. I suppose that is the worst part of traveling. Amid all the excitement, there is the missing of people whom you love.

Mako. I met him in front of Daniel's Art Supplies in downtown Los Angeles. He was standing there, looking like a stronger version of Fred Perry. Big and robust and with a full military bearing and a large, strong face, he waved at me. He knew me at once. I knew him at once. No nonsense in our meeting. It was noon and time for lunch, only for Gene it was really breakfast. We went to the International House of Pancakes, and I listened to this worldly man talk.

I started out by referring to him as a remarkable doubles player. I erred.

"I won five national titles in a period of about two months. I mean in *singles* and doubles."

Mako won the national juniors and the national intercollegiates in 1934, playing both the singles and the doubles, and he also won the U.S. men's doubles on clay, playing with Budge. In southern California, he took the Pacific Southwest titles in both singles and doubles in 1933 while still a boy, at seventeen. Now at sixty-eight, he is commanding and a power to deal with. He went to USC as did so many great athletes, and looking at Mako, I had the feeling that I was with a man whom Seixas would call an athlete first and a tennis player second. With broad shoulders and a Mount Rushmore face and a poplin shirt with epaulets, he looked military. He didn't mince words, and when he said he had won national tournaments in singles at fifteen and sixteen, I didn't even bother to flick through my always handy *Tennis Yearbook* to find out where and when.

"I suppose the average tennis fan thinks of you primarily as a doubles player," I persisted.

"Well, that is not true. I was a better singles player for the first four or five years, up until I hurt myself. You see, I only played tennis till I was twenty-two years old, and then I stopped playing."

"How did you hurt yourself?"

"I hurt myself serving too hard on one occasion, and then it reoccurred when I was playing Brugnon in . . . I believe it was 1934 . . . at Forest Hills, when I served too hard, too quickly. Then I tore all the muscles in the arm that goes into the chest, at Queens one year, practicing with Bitsy Grant. After that happened, the doctors told me I could never play tennis again. That was in 1936. I was twenty years old at the time. So I played the last two-and-a-quarter years of my tennis career with no arm."

342

"How could you have done so well with Budge during that time?"

"You have to do things. I had maybe the best serve in the world and the best overhead in the world, and I had to compensate. You have to move better and concentrate better and play so you never miss a ball—you have to play an entirely different ball game."

"In other words, your serve was gone and your overhead was gone, and you still were one of the best doubles players—on record, at least?"

"Well, yeah. It's a God-given thing. I have good eye-hand coordination, but when all the injuries happened to me, I geared myself into the game mentally. I became a superior competitor, mentally."

"How did you get to the singles finals at Forest Hills to play Budge, the year of his grand slam, with no arm? Whom did you beat to get there?"

"John Bromwich, Frankie Kovacs. Then Gil Hunt beat Riggs, and I beat Hunt."

And he got a set from Budge that indicated how good he was. Budge was so overwhelming that year that it was only Mako who *did* get a set in the finals of the four tournaments that constituted the grand slam of tennis.

"But Don and I always played close. I think we played five or six matches, and I won two of them, but they were always close. [And staying with singles play] I have been reminded that when I was a youngster at thirteen, fourteen, all the way through eighteen, in those six years I played in the Southern Cal boys and/or juniors and never lost a set! The man who took Perry Jones' place told me that. I was unaware of it."

"I am still amazed that you could do so well later on with no serve."

"What you have to do is to run everything down and, by the way, it is much better to have never had a serve than to be without it after having a good one. The adjustment for me was great. So you serve, and you know that you are no better off than the guy receiving. Therefore, I had to be on the go, moving, and had to be able to pass very well, because everyone was coming in on me. You have to play a cat-and-mouse thing when they come in. You shouldn't even try to pass them on the first shot. You have to move them around and find an opening."

"Your conditioning must have been incredible . . . you didn't drink or smoke?"

"Never in my life. Not to this day. I often played two pro basketball games in the same day—one matinee and one in the evening."

"Basketball?"

"Yes, when I was at Norfolk in the Navy, we tried to pick up a few extra dollars, and we had a professional basketball team. That was in 1942 and 1943. There were six of us on the team, and nobody ever worried about getting tired. We played forty-minute games and got $90 per game, which was pretty good. Fifteen dollars a player."

"So by then, you had given up tennis and being a professional didn't matter?"

"I never intended on playing tennis anyway. I had stopped by 1938. Oh, I might play if someone invited me to play, but I didn't practice, and maybe for four or five years, up to eight years, I played here and there."

"But you were so good at it—even with that bad shoulder—how could you just stop?"

"I didn't have any trouble. I just didn't feel like playing, so I didn't."

"Going back to Budge, what was your record? I know that in his big year, 1938, you lost in France and Australia, and in Davis Cup play, you lost to . . ."

"Our first year [1936] when we were pretty young, we lost to Quist and Crawford in a five-setter after leading two sets to love, which was just a horrible loss to have. Then we lost to Quist and Bromwich when Don was very, very sick, which most people don't know because he's not going to tell anybody. We won the first set 6–0, and we were going along great guns, and then Don just couldn't move. He said, 'I got to play another singles match tomorrow, and I feel so lousy today.' I said, 'Don't worry about it. We'll just go through with it,' and I'm not trying to take anything away from Bromwich and Quist because they are a good team (but we beat them, two, one, and three in the nationals that year), but Don was just so sick—a food virus thing."*

"So on to mixed doubles. Did you ever win Wimbledon in the mixed doubles?"

"No, I never played mixed at Wimbledon. I won the nationals, playing with Alice Marble—it was her first big win. We beat Don and Sarah Palfrey. But I want to tell you something about playing sick or playing when you have something *really* wrong with you. I played with Don six weeks after I was told I could never play tennis again, and we won Newport. When I hear about someone with a sore back or a sore toe, I just want to laugh, because it is a joke."

I told him about my playing Alice Marble in singles, after her five cancer operations and one lung removed and with no hat in the heat of Palm Springs.

He said, "Ohm, ohm," in an approving way—the old guard lining up,

---

* When they weren't "pretty young" and when Budge was well, they took the Davis Cup doubles from the English in 1937, part of a 4–1 victory. Even when they lost in 1938 because of Budge's illness, the challenge round was a great one, with Budge beating both Bromwich and Quist in singles for a 3–2 U.S. win. Riggs played the other singles and took Quist.

48. Gene Mako

and then he said, "It's lucky I was an egomaniac because things didn't bother me, what other people said, because I always knew what I could or couldn't do. And the press was very cruel. Never in the two plus years that I played [after being injured] did the press say what a good team Don and I were. They said that I couldn't serve, I couldn't do this, or I couldn't do that—never the other side of the fence. And then Don would say something about it, and I would say, 'They don't know what the hell we are doing. What the hell do they know?' "

"What about your name? I can't help thinking of a shark."

"Hungarian. It's a pure Hungarian name, and there is a town in Hungary with the name, Mako. But you see, the Hungarians are supposed to have migrated from Asia Minor, and Mako is a common name in Japan. It is not a common name in Hungary. It's pronounced 'Mucko' in Hungary."

"Were you brought up here in southern California?"

"Yes, but I was born in Budapest, and when I was three years old, we moved to Buenos Aires, and when I was seven the family came up here."

"What did your father do?"

"My father was one of the greatest artists of the world."

"That's a strong statement."

"Easy to back up. Statements are no good unless you can back them up."

"In my wild mind, I am trying to remember an artist named Mako."

"Why would you?"

"I am semicivilized and I . . ."

"Look, I can name five thousand artists to you and, civilized as you are, you wouldn't know who they are."

"I can throw a few at you, you know."

"But I am in the business. I doubt you can throw too many at me."

"Did your father make a living at it?"

"One of the greatest artists of all time, and you ask that question?"

"Well, some people are discovered after they die."

"You're a New Yorker . . ."

"No, I am from New England."

"Well, that's worse."

"What's better about New York?"

"The action. Look, my Dad did murals for the 1939 World's Fair in New York. In 1939 or 1940, in San Francisco, more murals. St. Sophia's, a world-famous Greek church, my father did 90 percent—all the design, inside and out—he did the architectural engineering. He did the sculpture work for the church; he did the seating arrangements, the pulpit. He did everything but sell tickets for that church. He was in South America for about three years, and for the first year he was there, he painted the president of the country [Argentina]. When he came to this country, he did schools and churches because that was the way he made a living."

Like father, like son, Gene Mako is an art dealer, specializing in nineteenth-century art. He also designs and builds tennis courts, a job he is trying to rid himself of. It is the art world that intrigues him. We began talking about some of the great muralists, Rivera, Orosco, and Thomas Hart Benton. Of Benton, who used to live near me, Mako said, "Lousy painter, great artist. Hell, that is the reverse of the norm. There are thousands of great painters who are lousy artists," and so it went, the two of us talking about art.

Finally, I steered him back to sports, and I said, "Because I never wrote you, just called you on the phone and left a message, you don't really know what I am doing."

"And I don't care," he said. "I'm easy," he added and chuckled over his breakfast. "Whatever you do, whatever you say . . . I don't care."

I mentioned John Van Ryn, and Gene said that he lives in Florida with a lovely wife and is someone I should see because he goes back to the time when he played Tilden in tournaments. "I played Bill a lot but not in tournaments—oh, I guess we played a couple."

"How would you rank the top three doubles teams, going back to the beginning?"

"I'd rank George Lott and Lester Stoefen number one. George was a fine doubles player, who won five national titles with three different partners, but, by the way, I never lost to him."

"In singles?"

"In anything. I say that just in case you begin to compare. And let me tell you something. From some people, you'll get opinions. From me, you get the facts. Opinions are easy. Good opinions are tougher, but facts . . . that's what count."

"Well, would you put yourself and Budge up there?"

"I think I'd have to."

"Then who? McEnroe and Fleming or Allison and Van Ryn?"

"I'd lean toward McEnroe and Fleming. Fleming is a very good doubles player, a good partner for John. He is tough in the deuce court because he can do a lot of things others can't do—he can return the ball harder than most people, and every once in a while, he will put three or so of those shots together in a row, and so will McEnroe, and they'll be *doing something*. And they'll get their service break. Also Fleming has great mobility. And as for McEnroe—now you're getting an opinion from me—he is the only player I have seen, other than Don Budge, who is a super player. There are only seven or eight players that I have seen whom I can put in that category, but McEnroe is the only one I have seen, other than Don, who can play doubles as well as he can play singles. You can go back a long way, but you won't find anyone else other than those two who are superb at both doubles and singles."

"I would disagree on one man. Kramer. Kramer was a great doubles player."

"No."

"Well, that's what most people say."

"I am not interested in what most people say. He was a *fine* doubles player, but I have news for you. He was not a *great* doubles player."

"So we have our top three doubles teams, and number four?"

"Vines and Gledhill would be number four, but if we go out into the world, you have to put in Quist and Bromwich or Crawford and Quist."

"I am sticking to America or else it gets way too complex. Take France and the Four Musketeers."

"France didn't have good doubles teams."

"How about Britain?"

"I never lost in doubles to a British team in my life—from age fourteen on. And I am talking about a lot of partners, not just Don. I won four national titles with guys you never heard of: Jack Lynch, Ned Russell, Ben Dey, and Lawrence Nelson. These aren't household names."

"All at Longwood?"

"No! National boys and national juniors. Four years in a row with four different people. And Phil Castien? Ever heard of him? We won the National Intercollegiates."

"How about Tilden and Hunter? Wouldn't you include them?"

"Anything that Tilden had to do with had to be good. Tilden was one of the great players of all time, without any reservations or any question. If we go back to the 1920s, we find a super player in Tilden. He *had* to be one and he was one."

"Going back to the old days, it is interesting how memories differ. For instance, Lott thinks he and Stoefen had the edge on Vines and Tilden on the pro tour. Vines sees it the other way."

"That is what I call having a 'convenient memory.' People see things conveniently. I remember Lott and Wayne Sabin were training against Riggs and me for the Davis Cup. They bet us $200 that we couldn't get two sets from them in a three-out-of-five match. We bet them the $200, and won three straight. If I say something, I can back it up with facts. It's all there in the record books."

"But you had Riggs!"

"But Bobby wasn't a good doubles player. We go back to the time we were babies together. He was a good competitor, and we played a lot together and had a good rapport. But my secret in doubles is this: there is a very basic reason for how I could win with, say, eighty different guys. Everybody I played

348

with played better with me than they played with anybody else. The reason for this was because, psychologically, I made all my partners know deep inside that they were doing great. Now, you take Phil Castien. He was a basket case. He'd go along for an hour, playing well, and then make one error and think the world had caved in. So I would wrap him in cotton and make him think that *I* was doing poorly and that he was carrying the load. Castien was worse than Tidball in that, and Tidball* was bad enough. I had to make them think, regardless of how well I was playing, that they were carrying the load."

As he was talking, I was looking up Tidball and noticed that Gene Mako had won the Pacific Coast doubles championship in 1941 with Frank Parker. It would appear that he had not really retired at twenty-two years old in 1938. He said that he did play a few tournaments but gave up practicing. No serious tennis, in other words, yet he managed to win three more important major events—first, Tidball in 1939, and Parker in 1941, *and* 1939.

"How long has it been since you've played tennis—I mean, just horsing around tennis?"

"Oh, I play once every couple of months—that kind of tennis."

"If I got Louise Brough, would you find a woman partner, and play us in doubles?"

"I could, but I wouldn't. Hell, I can't play!"

"What about friendships in tennis?"

"Oh, the friendship between Don and me is unique. I think that in sports, you wind up with some marvelous friendships, and besides that, in my case, they go back for fifty to fifty-five years.

"Was there anyone along the course of your tennis career whom you didn't like?"

"No. I don't think so. I basically like people."

"And once again, what do you do now?"

"I have my tennis court business, which means I do anything you want. I design it, build it, anything. The same thing with art. I do my own appraising. I do my own looking. I do my own finding. I pay for everything myself, and I sell everything myself."

"So you have been very successful. You couldn't have used tennis as a springboard into art?"

"No. My success, whatever it may be, is basically from an attitude that

---

* Gene Mako and Jack Tidball won the Pacific Southwest in 1933. Also in 1933, they won the U.S. Clay Championships. They won the Pacific Coast men's doubles in 1939, the year after Gene officially retired. That year Gene also won his third U.S. clay court title, playing with Frankie Parker. Gene Mako's "official" retirement remains murky, but it is safe to say that after 1941, Mako left tennis for the war, for art, and for business.

rubbed off on me from my father. Whatever you have to do, you do it. You don't talk about it, you do it. You shut up and deal."

"What about heroes when you were a kid. Did you have any?"

"People who were the best at what they did. You might say Babe Ruth or Lester Stoefen, who was about five years older than I, and I looked up to him. Later, in college, I wrote one term paper on Lincoln and one on Edison, and they were heroes. My father was a total hero to me because he did everything better than anyone else—everything. Everything in his line. He was like Michelangelo in that he could do everything there was to be done for a church or a building, a portrait, a landscape, water color, charcoal, drawing, oils, acrylics, upside down, inside out, whatever."

"Is there any of his work around Los Angeles?"

"All over Los Angeles. In St. Sophia's* you go crazy. There is so much art in there, you go crazy."

"How about your mother?"

"Lovely, lovely. Let me tell you about my family, my mother and father."

"It was a happy family?"

"Unbelievable."

"Any brothers and sisters?"

"No. But let me tell you about my mother and father. If there is such a thing as the best educators in the whole world, you can't find me better ones than my mother and my dad. They never pushed anything, but encouraged everything!

"Father was a one-liner. I used to call him the 'one-liner of the art world.' You know Count Basie, well I grew up with people like that, guys like Tommy and Jimmy Dorsey. I was a jazz drummer. I knew Gene Krupa and Buddy Rich . . ."

"If you were in Chicago playing tennis, might you hook up with those people in the evening?"

"Might! I would. So one night we went to hear Basie, and my father was the kind of guy who told me that 99 percent of the artists screw up their work because they overwork it. So we are driving home, and I said, 'Dad, how did you like the Count tonight?' and he said, 'I love what he left out.' "

"What was his name?"

"Bartholomew Mako."

"So whom do you respect the most, looking back on life?"

---

* St. Sophia's was closed that day, so I was unable to see it. Mako told me to take Louise Brough along when I did go. "It will open her eyeballs," he said. "Tell her I said she needs some culture."

350

"The number one mind is Leonardo da Vinci. Painting was the least of his accomplishments, although he was a good artist. But the number one artist of all time was Michelangelo. But if you're talking about sports, the first name that comes to mind is Babe Ruth because to this day they can't make a pimple on his ass. And then in music, I'd say Basie and Jimmie Lunceford, Duke Ellington . . ."

"No political or spiritual leaders?"

"No. I pay almost no attention to that. Take Jimmy Carter who started all this Olympic boycott thing—as if the Russians going into Afghanistan has anything to do with the Olympics."

"Do you believe in God?"

"I was raised a Catholic, so that answers that question."

"You go to Mass?"

"No. I haven't gone to Mass in a long time."

"Are you married?"

"No. I have been alone for sixteen years. My wife is one of the most successful ladies. She does interior design and is about as successful as you can get. Laura Mako. We have no children."

"What was your toughest match?"

"Every match that I lost. But I can think of 1933 when Don Budge beat me in the finals of the juniors. I think the scores of the first two sets were 6–4, 6–2, and I won the third and fourth set, 6–1, 6–0, and I had him 3–5 and 15–30 in the fifth set, and he pulled the match out and won it 8–6."

"What about in the doubles? The year he won the grand slam, you lost the doubles twice?"

"Yes, and it was entirely my fault. I was playing around off the tennis court in Australia and in Paris instead of attending to my business."

"You weren't drinking . . ."

"I did worse than that. That was no way to train. Look, let me give you my top eight players. The ones I call my super players. I don't rank them. Just the top eight. Here they are: Tilden, Vines, Perry, Budge, Kramer, Hoad, Borg, and McEnroe."

"No Laver?"

"Of course not. I am talking about super players. And as far as athletes go, Vines could do anything. Swimmer, basketball star, you name it. But when it comes to athletic ability, I could do about anything, too. I was the California handball champion when I was eleven years old. I played on the national semipro softball championship team at Los Alamitos when I was in the service. I played AAU basketball; I played the post against a guy who was six-ten. I'm six feet. I was the best Ping-Pong player in America when I was fourteen and fifteen years old."

"Fred Perry was the world champion."

"Yes, in 1929, but he never beat me at Ping-Pong. How's that grab you? I got Fred later on when neither one of us was as good as before. In Glendale High School, I played baseball, which bored me stiff because I require action, like soccer, basketball, and tennis. But at Glendale High, there wasn't one guy batting over .300, and I was batting .630-something. Sports were so easy—I can't tell you how easy they were for me."

"Is there any way to compare the players of today to the ones of your day?"

"Sure, but you have to name the conditions and stipulations. When we played, we had a smaller ball, which was harder and had less fuzz. Now you can put overspin on the ball. And today you can foot fault. That's a typical monstrosity that associations will dream up. It's incorrigible. But if we are talking about super players, they can play anytime, anywhere, under any conditions. The rest of them will be where they are anyway. You have one McEnroe in the world now, and that's it. If Borg were around, you'd have the two of them killing each other in titanic matches."

As for a yardstick between then and now, Gene Mako chose Pancho Segura.

"Segura played for three decades: the 1940s, the 1950s, the 1960s. He played against Rosewall, Laver, Hoad, Sedgman, Kramer, and Gonzales. He was dead against Kramer because Kramer was too good for him. Gonzales beat him about three to two, and he either played even or beat the other guys."

"Kramer says Segura owned Rosewall."

"That's true, he owned Rosewall."

"If you had your life to live over, is there anything you would change?"

"Yes. I would never go into the construction business of any kind [tennis courts]. I would have started right off with the art world. The day I got out of the service in 1945, I should have gone into the art business instead of tennis court construction."

"What were you in the service?"

"I was in the Navy in the program Gene Tunney had—teaching the usual Navy drills and stuff."

"Did you ever get paid under the table during your tennis days?"

"Yes. Well, not really *under* the table. They paid our expenses, and you might get $300 for expenses, but you could save on that. It didn't matter if you slept in the Ambassador Hotel or a motel."

"So the amateur business is kind of cloudy."

"There is no such thing. That's how cloudy it is. There is no such thing as amateur sports."

"How about mixed doubles? Whom did you like to play with?"

"I didn't play much mixed doubles, but I loved Alice Marble and a girl named Helen Marlowe, and with them it was very enjoyable. And I played an

49. Mako today

exhibition with Helen Wills, and that was totally enjoyable because she was a flawless player."

"Didn't you have to play in all three categories in order to get your expenses at tournaments in Newport, for example?"

"No. You didn't even have to play the men's doubles."

"But other people have told me that you had to play in all three."

"They are wrong. If your home tennis association will pay your way to a tournament and then the local club or whatever picks up your tab while you're there, you could go all the way around the world free. I don't care if it's Newport or Rye, New York. All free. You can go around the world for nothing."

He drove me to the Ambassador Hotel in downtown Los Angeles in his Oldsmobile station wagon. He talked rapid-fire about his athletic prowess. After playing professional basketball in the Navy, he took on Jack Kramer, one-on-one. He beat Kramer, who had been a basketball all-scholastic at Montebello High School, 30 to nothing. He went back to Ping-Pong. He beat the reigning champion, a man named Coleman Clark, 21–10, 21–10 between the ages of fourteen and fifteen. He played soccer in Argentina at three years old. But baseball was his best sport, even though it was slow for him. "I could hit," he told me as we drove slowly through the streets of Los Angeles.

At the Ambassador I got him to pose for some pictures. I told him what I thought he looked like. I said, "You look like a German general."

"That's me," Mako said, and soon he was gone. He was off to buy more art supplies, driving his large station wagon around the city. I looked at the grand Ambassador Hotel and went inside. My parents had stayed there once, and my father had left my mother alone for a weekend while he flew off to Hawaii to see what Hawaii was like. My mother must have had a hell of a time without him because she was ill with multiple sclerosis and had to rely on room service. She probably chewed him out when he returned. As for my father, I would guess that he did a little of what Gene Mako implied he had done in Paris and Australia, which had cost Budge and him the grand slam of doubles. Good for Gene Mako and good for my father, I thought as I walked into the lobby of the old hotel. I sat in the Palm Bar and remembered my father because Gene Mako had brought his memory back to me. The next day I would go to San Francisco. That afternoon I just sat and wondered about life and made some notes and then threw them away.

❧ *21*

Tom Brown, Jr.:

He's Coming Back to Tennis

I suspected that both Tom Brown, Jr., and Bob Falkenburg would be sophisticated men, and they were next on my list after seeing Gene Mako. Also, I would play with them, both Wimbledon champions, and both are from the time period I am touched by—the period of World War II and its aftermath.

I had first heard of Tom Brown in 1946 when, seemingly out of the blue, this man who had never been ranked made it to the finals at Forest Hills and almost beat Jack Kramer in the first set. Kramer won 9–7, and then Brown's game collapsed as the great Kramer, at the top of his game, beat him 6–3, 6–0.

Falkenburg, on the other hand, had one of those names you just love to roll off your tongue, and as it happened, it had rolled off many tongues during the war. His sister, Jinx, was a pinup girl and one of the great beauties who adorned footlockers and barracks' walls and whose picture was pinned to the inside of my closet door at a military school that I went to from the fall of 1942 to the spring of 1947. I had pictures of Jinx and Ella Raines and Dusty Anderson all there to stare at. They wore bathing suits, and in my daydreams, I said to myself, "When I grow up, I am going to have a girl like one of those half-naked women. I am going to feast on a girl like that."

So, after seeing Gene Mako, I had to watch myself a bit. It would do no good to hit the town, to see Hollywood, and to stay up late and mess up the forthcoming games with two men I was especially interested in. I did not want thoughts of Jinx Falkenburg as she looked in the 1940s to lead me astray. So I went to see a movie, *The Natural*, taking a cab to a small theater on the edge of Hollywood, and if ever I was touched by a movie, it would be by *The Natural*, a film that held me in thrall. At the end, the entire audience applauded wildly as you would expect an audience to do in the legitimate theatre. I was clapping as well, and there were tears in my eyes. The movie was about a sports hero and the movie was set (at the end) in 1939, the year that Gene Mako and Frank Parker had won the national clay court doubles championship, and the year that Don McNeill had stormed France, unseeded, and won. I had met these men and liked them, and somehow the movie touched a nerve that triggered a sentimental longing for greatness.

By noon the next day, I was in a limousine on my way to the airport for a short flight to San Francisco to play with Tom Brown. I left most of my luggage in a storage locker at Pacific Southwest Airlines and was able to travel very light—the way I had imagined Gardnar Mulloy might travel—a pair of tennis shorts, some underwear, and a shirt and racquet. I checked into the Hotel Lombard on Geary Street, feeling like a man on a mission, and called Brown. We had a doubles game scheduled for noon the next day, he said, and he would pick me up at my hotel. He sounded pleased that I had actually made it to San Francisco and that I was real. I had telephoned him after getting his number from the California Tennis Club where he plays, having learned that from Jack Kramer. He really had no idea what I was doing—only a vague notion that I was writing a book and that he would be in it.

Of course, I had more than a vague notion. Brown would wrap up the story of the 1946 Davis Cup squad that intrigued me so much. He also would give me a good game. But what made him irresistible was the fact that he was another one of those players who had simply disappeared from public view. After winning at Wimbledon in 1946, in the men's doubles with Jack Kramer and with Louise Brough in the mixed doubles, his name and the media parted company. Checking closely, I did see that he won the Pacific Southwest singles title in 1950 and the Pacific Coast doubles as late as 1953, playing with Tony Trabert. But back on the East Coast, he was a forgotten man soon after his big year—the only one where he was ranked—the year he almost toppled Jack Kramer at Forest Hills, and that was almost forty years ago.

I walked down Geary Street, thinking of Tom Brown and wondering what he would be like, and stopped at the St. Francis Hotel for a drink at the bar. My parents used to stay there—it seemed that they had stayed everywhere for at least a night—in their search for a comfortable winter location. My father, who had retired early in life, and my mother, who was ill, were almost nomadic, moving about, hoping to establish themselves in a compatible setting. Finally they did when they found Smoke Tree Ranch in Palm Springs, but meanwhile they checked into a good number of hotels, one of which was the St. Francis. During the early days of the Korean War, I drove from Sacramento and stayed there myself, and I loved the sense of elegance it exuded.

Back in 1952, my older brother, who often visited San Francisco, introduced me to a small restaurant, the Blue Fox, and the night I arrived to meet Brown, I went there again, to dine alone and let my powers of retention roll back the fog of memory. The restaurant is now much larger, which was to be expected. I had pigeon, a tender and exquisite delicacy to someone used to chicken and fish and steak. The service was good, and I stayed clear of alcohol other than some California wine. It was a quiet, civilized evening, and I went to bed before 11:00.

The next morning I met him. Tom Brown is tall and very lean and has a long Randolph Scott face. He has more hair on his head than I do, and he acts like a man who can handle himself pretty well at most things. He is a lawyer, and I realized that if he dropped out of the national tennis picture after the war, it was because he was furthering his education. Of course, Mulloy had also been an attorney, but I got the impression from Gardnar that law came in a distant second to tennis. Tom Brown looked as though the law was a front-runner to any sport, even the game that took him to the top. But he appeared very trim indeed, and I shuddered at the thought of my pale, pudgy body with its wrecked knee out in the California sunlight with this man, playing before people at his own club and in a doubles game he had arranged and . . . perish

50. Tom Brown, Jr., today

the thought . . . I was under the terrifying impression that Tom Brown thought I was a good player. A really good player.

We changed quickly and went out onto the sparkling, typically hard courts you find in California, and there warming up were our opponents, the brothers Warren and Donald Low, the latter billing himself as a world-class tennis professional. After hitting for a while, Tom could tell that I had trouble running, although surprisingly my ground strokes were working well. He took the odd court, and I stayed in the forehand, or deuce, court and told him that he would have to cover the middle. He feigned fear and trembling at that, saying that he had his alley to watch, and on he went, but I knew that with his driving forehand, he would be in the middle anyway. This left me with about one-third of the court to handle. I would stay out of Brown's way and just use my forehand and keep the ball humming back at the Low brothers.

And that is how it worked. We built up a nice 4–1 lead, and my serve was giving them fits. I was getting my serve in, and Tom was putting their weak returns away. It should have gone on like that, but Tom made a few errors, and I began to lose confidence, and soon I was limping enough for the Lows to get a few ideas. One idea was to angle me to death, which they were able to do. Instead of hitting hard shots at my baseline, which I was jumping on, I began to get soft angle placements that I could not reach. And then, bang! A ball would come stinging at the far corner, and I couldn't reach that, having been drawn in by the softer spin shots and cuts that went crisscrossing my side of the court. Cursing myself, I watched our lead slip away, and they won 8–6. The next two sets the Lows also won, 6–4, 6–2. But we had played for over an hour and a half, and Tom had shown me some fine tennis. He looked much better than Pancho Gonzales—at least on the day we played compared to the day I saw Pancho and Bob Howe beaten. And he had that strong forehand, which he calls his "shovel shot," a shot he claims to have in common with Kramer. His serve was crisp and accurate, but if he had any tricks to display, he did not display them. He played straight, hard tennis with his share of errors. I played quite well, I thought, considering that I could hardly run. I did miss some key overheads that would have turned things around, and I could see Tom wince when I did that. I would curse and stomp the ground, and the Lows would grin.

It was good fun and a good workout, and I felt that for once I had been in a really competitive match with a male tennis star. Certainly my games with Louise Brough and Shirley Fry had been competitive, but here with Tom Brown, I had gotten a Wimbledon doubles winner to play doubles with me to the best of his ability, and I had given him a partner he could at least work with. I had nothing to be ashamed of, and the Lows shook my hand with firm grips and real appreciation in their eyes. They were damn lucky that they beat us. A couple of key overheads . . . if I had only been able to move, and maybe if only Tom had put that ball away . . . such were the standard thoughts you have when you lose. We all showered together, laughing, and as I dried myself off, the brothers gave me their cards. "If you are ever in town again and want a game, give me a call." I thought, "Californians are so very hospitable." In that locker room at the California Tennis Club, I actually wished I had stayed in the West after being discharged from the Air Force. I could be a member like the rest of these guys, I thought . . . maybe get into real estate back in 1955. I'd be a millionaire by now. Have all of San Francisco to play with. And to live in this climate. No more bronchitis. Good friends, good tennis, good food . . . such are the thoughts you have when you are second-guessing yourself to death. I grabbed on to Tom Brown and said, "Let's get some lunch."

Brown is a patient man. He let me tell the story of the 1946 American Davis Cup sojourn in Australia as though he had not been the sixth man on the squad. I was talking about Mulloy losing Talbert as his doubles partner and then apparently winning with Parker over Schroeder and Kramer. Except for Jack Kramer, who denied this, it appeared to be an accepted fact. But Tom Brown, an attorney, was not going to assert himself, and he said, "I seem to vaguely remember that in one or more practice sessions, they may well have beaten Kramer and Schroeder, but I am always of the opinion that if it is a team effort, regardless of what the sport may be—soccer or football—you play the players you think will win against the other team. You play the players who may *not* be the best practice players in the world, but the ones who on a given day will do the best against the people they are playing. It was a judgment call, but I think that Kramer and Schroeder were a longtime team and the best we had.

"Now, when you practice, you are tuning up for the match. You do not go all out to win the thing. If you turned practice sessions into trials, you would leave your best tennis on the practice court. For instance, when I go into the finals of a tournament, I will get up in the morning and maybe rally for a while, and then I will play one good practice set. Now, I don't concentrate on beating my opponent in that practice set. What I want to do is get my skills to the finest point—whatever they may be—for the match I am going to play.

"Now, as I understood it, and it seemed to make sense, the original Davis Cup team was only four players. It was Kramer because he won Forest Hills. It was me because I was a younger player and had been a finalist at Forest Hills. It was Parker because he had the most consistent record in singles. He would be a second singles possibility behind Kramer. Schroeder came out of the blue because he won the Pacific Southwest and had a top record before. He was, conceivably, a choice for the singles spot on the thing. So you had

359

one top singles player and three good possibilities for the second singles, and you had the doubles team of Kramer and Schroeder.''

"What were Talbert and Mulloy doing down there?"

"They brought them down because we needed practice and sparring mates. My understanding is that they chose the four of us initially and then sometime later on, they decided they needed two more players, which made perfect sense because it gave us variety. You don't want a sort of ingrown thing where you play against the same guy all the time. If we didn't have that variety, what our team should have done was to sign on a couple of Australians or some other foreign players because we were going to be down there a month or two before the Davis Cup, and we just can't go around begging for practice mates.

"Now, Talbert and Mulloy could have been considered as a second doubles team, but Kramer was the top player, and whomever he carried with him was going to make the top doubles combination. So Mulloy and Talbert were brought along for practice.''

"Did you have the impression about yourself, that you were being used for practice?''

"I had the impression that it was an open thing, that Kramer was the top player and a cinch, but then it would depend on how we looked down there for the second singles spot.''

"What about Parker who said he had a verbal contract for the singles slot?''

"I know that Parker had that impression. He would not have come on the trip if he were not going to play. I recall, however, that after Mulloy and Parker were playing good doubles as a team—I recall Mulloy's expression when Parker said right in front of him, 'I didn't come down here to play doubles.' Mulloy was flabbergasted.

"I'll bet that there was a misunderstanding between Walter Pate, the captain, and Parker, because I don't see how a captain could commit himself in advance of a trip like that.''

"Can you compare Schroeder and Parker? Is it true that Schroeder had a history of pulling off the big upset?''

"Both could rise to the occasion and both play top tennis, but Schroeder had an attacking game and Parker had a steady game, and Parker had a history of going against Bromwich. Parker had lost to Bromwich very badly in the last match in 1939. Straight sets, something like 3 and 1 and 0. [Bromwich won 6–0, 6–3, 6–1.] It would make no sense to send Parker against Bromwich, who had a steady game as did Parker, but had previously killed him. Bromwich was considered the best player in the world. And Schroeder had the attacking game so . . .''

"What about the vote as to who was going to play singles?"

"I can tell you exactly how the vote went. And I think Pate was a little nuts to put things to a vote, but the vote was to determine how the players would be seeded in a preliminary tournament—the New South Wales Championships. It came out with Schroeder last because Mulloy and Talbert disliked him, and I came in second ahead of Parker. I guess Mulloy followed Parker and then Talbert. Kramer, of course, was first."

"But I am not talking about *that* vote—I had never even heard of that one—I mean the one for the starting players to play the Davis Cup. You had six players, including yourself, voting to see who was going to play the second singles and conceivably, had Mulloy voted against Schroeder and for Parker, there would have been a standoff—a tie. So Kramer must be right when he said that Gardnar voted for Ted Schroeder even though he didn't like him, and that is when Parker walked off because if he can't play singles, he is not going to play doubles."

"I really can't remember," said Tom Brown, and then I realized that finally the whole story was over. Nobody really remembers, and what they do remember conflicts with other remembrances, and the precise human drama of it all is forever lost in the dust of old locker rooms. And as I had written earlier, it was always Jack Kramer's show.

I reminded Tom about the time that Schroeder stole his steak and ate it. Tom nodded and smiled and said, "Yes, he did that." And then he told a story concerning Billy Talbert.

"Talbert used to be kind of snooty and wear those long Bermuda shorts in the dining room of this fancy hotel, and all the people turned around to see Talbert in his shorts as we walked across the floor to our seats. Schroeder was needling Talbert about his shorts. Then during dinner, he arranged for someone to page Talbert to the overseas telephone, and so Talbert has to walk back and forth, and as he is coming back, Schroeder is doubled over with laughter because all the eyes are on Talbert in those shorts."

"Schroeder, by the way, flew off the deck of an aircraft carrier after serving on a destroyer."

"I was unaware of that."

"What did you do in the war?"

"I was a mortar gunner in the armored infantry, and we were sent to Europe in the closing days of the war."

"Do you have any regrets about losing time to the service, time during which you might have become a better tennis player?"

"No, that [the war] didn't keep me from being a better player. There wasn't enough in tennis to keep you going afterward. I did play for one year after I got out of the service and might have been a better player had I not gone back to law school. Had I stayed out of school for a couple more years, I might have been better."

"You went to college—where?"

"University of California, at Berkeley, and I went to law school there."

"What do you mean, there wasn't enough in tennis?"

"The U.S. Lawn Tennis Association was a very backward-looking group. I stayed on in Australia and played in the tournaments down there from the end of 1946 to the end of January 1947. This suited their purposes because it was part of the quid pro quo. We played down there, and then the Australians would have to send their players up to our tournaments. But when I wanted to play in a couple of tournaments on my way home, coming home around the world, they wouldn't let me. They said if I did, it would cost me my amateur standing. They said it is un-amateur—that I am playing too much tennis already and that I am supporting myself through my tennis. They would wire the tournaments and keep me from playing if I went against them."

"Did you get paid under the table?"

"I got transportation and expenses and so on, and sometimes you can save on your expenses and sometimes if you play in an exhibition, you get a little more, but as a practical matter you can't do very much. The United States Lawn Tennis Association was blocking everything. I might have played more if it had been easier."

As he was speaking, I was thinking of Gene Mako saying that you can go around the world free by collecting expenses for playing tennis. But apparently the USLTA put a crimp in Tom Brown's plans to do just that.

"So," he continued, "I thought it better to get a vocation and play tennis on the side. I was treated well by tennis, and I have no regrets; it is just that the people who were running things were back in the Middle Ages. The tennis association had an iron grip, and they saw that those clubs that had votes in the association got the players, and sure the top four or five would get money. After that, though, you had to be backed by your parents or work at your job to get to the tournaments. The association [USLTA] would make exceptions for themselves."

Tom Brown was born in Washington, D.C., and moved to California when he was two years old. As a small kid, he would follow his parents out to where they were playing tennis "at a class-B or class-C level" and "pick up a racquet and bat a ball around."

"I was a pretty strong-minded kid and didn't venerate anyone. I liked having my parents around, but I didn't like them trying to get me breaks by talking with officials or anything like that."

"But back at home?"

"My father was a newspaperman and later a public relations man for the

Western Pacific Railroad, and we lived a middle-class life. My mother was a school teacher and taught at San Francisco State."

"Did you love your parents?"

"Yes."

"Any brothers or sisters?"

"I had a half-brother because my father was married before, but he did not grow up with me in the same house."

"So essentially you were an only child."

"Yes. They were supportive and supported my tennis, but I didn't like them breathing down my neck, and I wanted it to be my own thing, and I was."

"Any heroes as a kid?"

"I didn't think of them as heroes. I thought of Don Budge and other high-ranking tennis players as great people."

"Not Lincoln or Roosevelt or somebody like that?"

"No. I didn't like Mr. Lincoln and I didn't like Mr. Roosevelt. I didn't like Roosevelt because he laid the basis for all the big deficits we've got going now and that kind of thinking. And somewhat facetiously, I don't like Lincoln because he made a big mistake trying to keep the South together with us. If he hadn't kept the country together, the South would be a union unto itself, and we wouldn't have any race problems."

"Wait a minute, let me get this straight, you say . . ."

"The South secedes, and we draw the line, and we don't allow any immigration. They would have had a far lower standard of living, and we would have had a better standard of living. And they would have had the race problem because all of the blacks would have been there, and it would have served them right because it was their ancestors, for greed, who brought all the slaves in from Africa to work the plantations."

"I think that is a pretty farfetched theory. I gather you are very conservative."

"I like to call myself pragmatic. I am not conservative the way they are in the South. The Southerners made a big impression on me when I first traveled down there. I went into a railroad station to get a drink of water, and they had two drinking fountains, one for whites and one for blacks, and I thought to myself that the kind of people I am going to meet at the clubs where I will play tennis are responsible for this. I said to myself, 'Who could possibly put up with this madness?'"

"So you are fiscally conservative but not racially conservative. If your daughter, say, married a black guy, it wouldn't throw you off."

"No. I want them to be happy. We didn't have race problems when I grew up. In school we had Orientals and some blacks, but they weren't the kind of blacks who emigrated from the South with chips on their shoulders because they had been screwed in the place they came from."

Tom Brown was the first Northern person I'd ever met who wanted the South to be a separate country and to stew in its own juices because of the greed of the plantation owners. He apparently disliked the white supremacy attitude of the South, as it had been, but at the same time, he wished that the blacks would all stay down there. Yet he didn't mind if a black should marry his daughter, and even said, "Hell, in sports it doesn't matter what the color of your skin is." What bothered him were blacks with "chips on their shoulders" and racial problems. Far better to keep racial problems off in another country—the South.

In any case, Tom Brown had said he was being facetious about Lincoln, and maybe he was pulling my leg as well as confusing me. So I left his racial problems to himself and went on to ask whom he admired the most, looking back over his life. He is now sixty-one years old, the same age as Vic Seixas, and as he puzzled over my question, I wondered how they would do against each other in a match.

"Well," he said, "there are certain qualities I like in people and when I find those qualities in people, I respect them very much. One of the qualities I respect is when someone is considerate. If they're not considerate, they go way down. Also, I might add, I deplore affectations, but when people are very considerate, they go way up. Another quality I respect is whether they are individuals—people who have their own thing and allow themselves to be themselves and allow you to be yourself.

"If you went from the above to the level of world leaders, I am a great admirer of Margaret Thatcher. I am a great admirer of Golda Meir. I would have traded either one of those women for Richard Nixon or Ronald Reagan, any day."

"How about Churchill?"

"He had faults, but he called them as he saw them and was willing to take the responsibility."

"I have a feeling he was an egomaniac and might not have been considerate . . ."

"Well, of course, he was an egomaniac, but if a guy thinks he is the best in the world at something and has a pretty good reason to think so, then I don't consider him an egomaniac. And take DeGaulle. He stood up for what he believed, and it's fashionable not to like him in this country because he was ornery, but . . ."

"Then what about MacArthur?"

"I thought MacArthur was a very fine man, a military genius. He apparently had some personal weaknesses."

"What about his decision to cross the Yalu and take on China?"

"That would have been a huge mistake. I felt about that as I did about the Vietnam War. I didn't march in the streets, but I felt it was a great mistake at the time. I tell my friends now, suppose we won the Vietnam War and the premier came to us and said, 'Okay, you win,'—I say, how would we occupy it? Pave the streets? Get it going again? It's the same thing with China. It would drain us dry. We would perish from winning."

"To change the subject, to what do you attribute your fine physical condition?"

"To tennis. I was away from it, but not so often I couldn't get back to it. I was sort of like a battleship in mothballs. I knew that in my twenties I could play twice a week and keep in shape. Now, in my sixties, I have to play at least four times a week. I have to run harder to stay in place."

"Have you ever had physical problems?"

"Yes. Like a car that runs several thousand miles a year, you're going to have problems. I had a shoulder problem for about three years. And now I have knee problems, but aspirin makes it playable. I had a tennis elbow that knocked me out for about a year, but I played right-handed with the strokes that didn't bother me, and for my backhand I played left-handed. I was playing with club players, and I found that I could keep my timing on with my regular strokes on my forehand, and it kept me in shape."

"So you played with two forehands—like Beverly Baker Fleitz?"

"No, not really like Beverly, but it gave me exercise, and it kept me going so that when I started to play again, I picked it up fast. And the last secret is, 'Don't take medical advice 100 percent.' "

"How about smoking and drinking?"

"I have never smoked. I do drink, but I don't get drunk. When I was playing in a big tournament, like Wimbledon, I wouldn't even have a beer (although I might have *one* beer, but I am scared of the effect). I am of the opinion that just a little alcohol will have an effect on your vision. For two or three days, it will have an imperceptible effect on your coordination. Now, of course, when I play a tournament, I have two or three drinks. But not back then. Who needs it? When you are in a tough match, why not have things going your way?"

"What was your toughest match?"

"In 1950, in the Davis Cup, I played a five-set match against Ken McGregor and barely pulled it out [9–11, 8–10, 11–9, 6–1, 6–4]."

Looking it up, I saw that it was Sedgman's tournament, beating Schroeder and Brown and winning in the doubles with Bromwich against those great antagonists, Schroeder and Mulloy, in five sets. For a second, I thought of the amazing John Bromwich. Here it was, 1950, and the man is still playing for his country and winning. And there it was, that tempest in the teapot—Mulloy and Schroeder as teammates. How much of all of this athletic competition

51. Tom Brown, Jr., playing in Czechoslovakia in 1947

and comparison was really hot air? I remember Kramer saying that in doubles, you want to play with someone you like. I would bet that underneath, Mulloy and Schroeder liked each other, but I shied away from the subject because Tom Brown was not the kind of man who would indulge in gossip. I just had this feeling that comes when you think of boxers who go one-on-one and end up lifelong friends and of men such as Babe Ruth and Ty Cobb who supposedly despised each other, yet showed up at an old-timers day and put their arms around each other. Soap opera is a long way from the truth. I daresay that among the great champions, there is a deep respect—so great that nasty little episodes have, with the course of time, turned into humor. And then there was Brown in 1950, still playing, even though he was working hard at being a lawyer,* and Mulloy, nine years his senior, still playing. I admired the concept of striving for one's flag, and so I did not mind asking people what they thought of their country. I was struck by Tom Brown placing Golda Meir

* In 1957 and 1958, he returned to the national scene by winning the U.S. Hard Court Singles title both years.

over Reagan. I was under the impression that he was a Reagan fanatic. Out West you cannot jump to conclusions. The word "eclectic" is operative. People choose values at will, sometimes in conflict with each other.

"What about the top five players?"

"I am glad you didn't ask for my number one player, because you can have a situation where player A can beat player B and B can beat C and C will beat A. So you give me five, and I would certainly put Budge in the five, and then you have Borg, McEnroe, and Kramer . . . now for number five, let's see. Gonzales was awfully good, and so was Laver."

"You wouldn't say Tilden?"

"I didn't see him play that much. I would be a ball boy and watch him well past his prime, and his serve looked awfully good, his forehand looked awfully good, but his backhand looked unsound. He hit his backhand with a dropped wrist."

(When he said that, I thought of Gonzales, who had a flip-volley backhand that erred so much—you could call that a dropped wrist.)

He continued. "I teach people sometimes, and I tell them to keep the wrist straight and the racquet head high on the backhand. And Tilden had a sloppy wrist."

"What about women players?"

"I never watched them enough. I am of the school that says that women don't hit the ball hard enough or deep enough. But I could give you Maureen Connolly and Helen Wills and Alice Marble. Martina would have to be there. Chrissie is very strong off-the-ground, but she doesn't seem to be an all-round player."

"Who was your favorite woman partner?"

"I'd have to say Louise [Brough]. I played with her only twice. Once we won the Wimbledon mixed, and the next time we won at Forest Hills. However, I have to recall Margaret Osborne. She was the first person I won a tournament with above the junior division. I used to brag that I was the national women's champion because I practiced with Margaret and Alice Marble.

"When you played with Jack Kramer, you won Wimbledon."

"I like to tell Jack, 'I am the only player you've ever been undefeated with.' We played just once."

"Can you compare the players of today to the old-timers?"

"Sure. I think my bracket spans it, and I don't think the players of today are any worse or any better than the group that I was playing with. And when you go back before my era, back before Budge, there were different conditions. It wasn't the same game. You have Billy Johnston hitting balls on grass that were over his head. Today you never hit a ball on grass that is over your head. It's a heavier ball. It's much more an all-court game from my time on. And I don't think the game as it is played today is any different than it was when I was playing the circuit. But there is a much greater depth today. In the old days, in the first couple of rounds, we would get wrapped, but now there are tough players, very close to beating a top player, and in tennis there is a very close margin. You give that away, and you will lose eight or nine times out of ten."

Then I mentioned Fred Perry's old fear of being knocked off by some unseeded player in the first round—some unheralded youngster who would go all out for the upset. Tom Brown said that Fred must have been "laying it on."

"Fred never got upset that I am aware of," he said, which, of course, did not negate the fear that it was possible—even in the old times when just a handful of men were to be considered as contenders.

"Do you believe in God?" I asked.

"No."

"But you mentioned the word 'Christian' back as we were dressing to play . . ." (I wondered at the time if I were going to be involved with a born-again person, and it interested me.)

"That was just humorous," he said.

"Are you an atheist?"

"No. I don't like the word because it places me on a par with those who say there *is* a God. I don't have any knowledge to say that there is or is not a God. So I am an agnostic."

"Do you have any children?" (I was thinking of the daughter who would have had his blessing to marry a black man.)

"Yes, four of them."

"Are you still married?"

"No, we were divorced back in 1966 or 1967. I was married late, at the age of 34, and then we were divorced about eight or nine years later."

"If you had your life to live over again, would you make any changes?"

"Oh, I would be a lot cagier. I am developing the philosophy that we don't know how much time we have left on this earth, so you had better make a lot of it count. I remember that when I was young, someone would invite me to go somewhere, and my parents said you shouldn't go with strangers. Well, now I wouldn't turn down such invitations."

"Would you say that this is the day that counts, the day you are in?"

"Well, I'd say that this is the day that counts, but you had better have a little in reserve in case you should last for a day or two. But you better live it while you can."

"If you should die today, what would you be remembered as . . . I am thinking now that I would hope my children would remember me for something."

"Well, I think they would know that they had a lot of good times with

368

the old man, and I had some good ideas that helped them along. 'He was a fine tennis player, a competent lawyer, and though he had his faults, he made a good deal of things.' That's what they'd say."

"How would you rank tennis among the other sports?"

"The more I look back on it, the more I like it. One reason it is a great sport is that it is a carryover sport. It doesn't end when you finish college or whatever; it is . . . you can do it all of your life. And another thing is that it gives you strenuous exercise, as much as you can handle. And one final thing. It will send you around the world."

"You, but not me."

"Let's say that you go around the world. You can find a local club wherever you go, and you can find some people to play with, and you will get a perspective of that place you would not have had otherwise."

"Were there any tennis players whom you did not like as you played the circuit?"

"There are always a few bastards, but you take a guy like Bobby Riggs. He will pull this and pull that, but he is funny as hell, and the most lovable rascal whom I have ever known, but a rascal nonetheless. But the camaraderie is fun. We were all down in Palm Springs, and Segura is there and so is Mulloy. So Segura looked over at Mulloy and says, 'Come on over here, coach, sit next to me,'—we were getting our picture taken—'I want to look you up.' Mulloy looks over at Segura [a three-time intercollegiate champion playing for Mulloy's University of Miami team]—so Mulloy looks over at Segura and says, 'If it weren't for me, you would still be climbing coconut trees.' "

"How would you do with the people in your age bracket?"

"There is only Vic Seixas. And he has knee problems. When you get to our age, it boils down to a knee, a shoulder, an elbow. It depends on condition. Vic and I would have a good match. It would depend on his problem with his knees. What he tells me is that if I could keep him out long enough, his knees would get tired."

We stopped then. It was getting late, and we had been sitting in a small San Francisco restaurant. The evening crowd was coming in, and I had a flight to catch. Tom wanted to drive me to the airport, but I declined. I opted for a cab because I felt I had already put him out and had been his guest, and he had been very interesting to be with. I knew one thing, though. Seixas would beat him in singles, and so would Frank Parker. I mentioned Parker to him, and he said that the age difference would favor him over Parker. I wondered about that on the ride to the airport. Tom Brown had played a hard doubles game as my partner and had to tell me not to play net because the brothers Low were lobbing over me, and I couldn't get back on my bad knee, and of course, he was charging in after his serve. He had surely played hard, but he was not really a tournament player the way Seixas was, and he was not

369

as steady as Frank Parker. As for Mulloy, well, he is a phenomenon who at seventy might have fallen prey to the younger Brown.* But there were two other players left, other than Seixas, to place against him: the incomparable Bobby Riggs and the alluring Bob Falkenburg. Brown had not mentioned Bob Falkenburg, but the great Falkenburg had said that he was playing again.

As Tom dropped me off on a San Francisco street corner where I could catch a cab, I said good-bye and thanked him. But my mind was on the senior match of all time: Sedgman, Seixas, Brown, Riggs, Parker, Mulloy, and maybe Bob Falkenburg. And then there were all those club players like Jason Morton. Get them to play a tournament and see how it works out. Let Tom Brown play Vic Seixas. Let Riggs play Parker. The best people in the world were over sixty, I thought as I waited for a cab. And one last remark. Tom Brown had said he was "phasing out of law—mainly estate and real estate law—and going back to serious tennis." If true, then E. Victor Seixas should beware.

---

* On September 9, 1984, Gardnar Mulloy beat Bobby Riggs 6–2, 3–6, 7–5 to win the U. S. singles on grass at Cedarhurst, Long Island. By playing at a lower level (by five years) and winning, Gardnar Mulloy became the greatest player at his age in the world. Brown and Seixas and Parker . . . their chances looked slim on that bright autumn day in New York when Mulloy mastered Riggs.

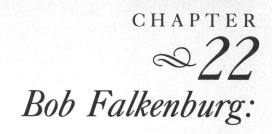

Bob Falkenburg:

Ice Cream Chic

Flying to Los Angeles, I had a chance to bone up on Bob Falkenburg's record. He won the national boys' fifteen singles in 1940 and 1941, following Budge Patty, and Jack Kramer, who was four years ahead of him. Again he followed Budge Patty and won the national juniors singles twice, in 1943 and 1944. In the doubles, he was victorious, playing with Budge Patty in 1942, and in 1943, he won the national title a second time with another youngster named James Brink. Still able to qualify for the eighteen-and-under, he won the doubles a third time in 1944 with John Shea. He was also the national interscholastic singles champion, playing for Fairfax High School in Los Angeles in 1942, a year after Vic Seixas. In 1942, playing with his brother, Tom, they won the national interscholastic doubles. But it was in 1944 that he hit the big time, because that year he and Don McNeill won the national doubles at Longwood, beating Billy Talbert and Pancho Segura. In other words, from young boy to young man, his streak of victories in national tournaments was prodigious. I might add that in the boys' fifteen doubles, he won twice, with James Brink and with Don Harris in 1940 and 1941, respectively. He went from a child champion to a national men's doubles champion without a hitch, or so it would seem, riding on a string of victories.

In 1946 the war was over, and he and his brother, Tom, were both at USC. That year he won the National Intercollegiates in singles and the national doubles with his brother. Two years later, Bob Falkenburg became the best amateur singles player in the world. He won Wimbledon, beating the much-feared John Bromwich 7–5, 0–6, 6–2, 3–6, 7–5.

Indeed, I was going to meet a man who I thought would be fifty-nine years old, assuming he was eighteen in 1943. I had written him from the Vineyard, and one day, just before I was to leave for the West Coast, he telephoned me. He said that I sounded serious in my letter and, yes, we would play. He would arrange a doubles game. He had just taken up tennis again after years of golf because he had a grandson who liked to play. He would be a far cry from his former self, and I said that I had a wrenched knee, so he had nothing to worry about as far as I was concerned. I had gotten his home address by calling the Southern California Tennis Association. As it turned out, he had two homes—a ranch at Santa Ynez near Santa Barbara and a beautifully appointed house near the Bel Air Sands, where I was to stay.

He came by at 10:30 in the morning for our game, and we drove off to a fairly famous tennis court. It is the same court where Jack Kramer plays and where I was supposed to play with Jack had he not had the flu and later changed his mind. I recalled that Kramer had arranged a doubles game for me on a court owned by his doctor, who had once been the Davis Cup physician. As it happened, this same man, Dr. Omar Fareeb, is a friend of Bob Falkenburg's, and Bob uses his court.

It was to be a regular Monday morning game, and Bob was a bit fearful that the other players might not show up. One was out of town, he thought. But that hardly mattered. I would play him in singles and get a good line on his prowess. If the others showed up, we would have a Tom Brown-type doubles match with a lot of action. Bob Falkenburg, in a way, *is* the Tom Brown-type. At six foot three, he is tall and thin and strong and has that wiry kind of body that serves a man well in all matters of life. Women noticed him, and in a conference room, men would take heed. For one thing, he looks smart and quick-witted. He wears stylized glasses that give him the appearance of an educator or a school teacher who can also work in high tech if he so chose—a genius entrepreneur. Like Brown, he smiled easily and was not afraid to speak his mind. He looks accomplished, which is the word I would use for Bob Falkenburg. Nobody in his right mind would take him lightly. Thinking of Brown and Falkenburg, I realized that I was seeing two men who are far more than tennis champions. And yet you just know that it was their bodies that took them to the top. Seixas, as great-looking as he is, has the build of a third baseman. Mako looks like a solid first baseman, and George Lott, as I have noted, could have been a bouncer. Kramer and some of the Westerners—other than my milkman, Ted Schroeder—simply look hard and lean and tough and long-lasting. It is that ectomorphic, loose-limbed frame that goes on until the heart stops at ninety-seven. Budge looked like a country squire, and maybe that is why he gave up serious tennis. It was the make of his body frame. Looking at Bob Falkenburg as we drove off to play tennis, I thought that this man would be hitting tennis balls as long as he lived.

And, indeed, that is his intent. His grandson had brought him back to the game and there quite suddenly I found myself playing him in singles. His "group" had not materialized.

I am not an analyst of great tennis strokes and such things as concentration, body movement, and placements. I am aware, however, of something called fluidity. Mulloy had that, as did Dodo Cheney. They glided across the court, and so did Bob Falkenburg. He just handled his strokes and his movements as though he were in a world of motion that did not allow any mistake. We played one set, and he won it 6–love. However, the games were long, the rallies were good, and the stroking—back and forth—was sweet as the supposed sweet spot on a racquet. The trouble was that I (obviously) could not run in singles—although my knee was repairing itself—but I think I played better than I did with Tom Brown. So Bob could shoot me a placement almost at will if he ever needed a point. In the meantime, I tried to keep him back on his baseline so that the fine flow of the game would keep on. I remember that one time I served a hard one right at his stomach, and he could not hit it. He barely backed away in time, and I yelled at him, "Was that an ace?"

"It was an ace," he answered, his body untouched by my bullet that caught him unaware. Other than that, it was a simple practice session for Falkenburg. He was just hitting them back at a nice pace—probably as he would to his grandson, only a little harder. What I recall the best was his effortless motion, his natural grace on a court. He just flowed, like Mulloy, and perhaps even smoother. I cannot recall an unforced error.

When we were through, we drove back to his house for lunch. He was very pleased with himself, and I was happy. He lived nearby, and when we drove up to his house, I realized that this was big-time living. It was Jack Kramer country and movie star country. I showered in his guest room shower stall and walked on the immaculate white carpets that lined the floor of much of his home, having dried off with puffy towels you buy at stores that specialize in towels, and when I saw his dining room set for our lunch and then glimpsed his lovely swimming pool, I said, "Okay." I said to myself, "Stan, this is the way you were meant to live," and my heart and my soul fled back to the 1930s when my parents had money, and we had a cook and a maid and a Packard and a Dodge that my mother drove very carefully until she couldn't drive anymore.

I thought of Martha's Vineyard, where we had a private harbor and where my grandfather and his brothers owned large, commodious summer

52. Bob Falkenburg

homes and wonderful driftwood-smelling camps on the Atlantic. I was thinking of old affluence and at the same time of California money. And, of course,
the foliage. It was everywhere. Had I used my brains and controlled my emotions, I would never have left this state where men and women lived in beauty
all year long. It was the same line of thinking that I had had at the California
Tennis Club, showering and kidding around with the Low brothers and Tom
Brown. I had come from a dead area of steadfast people. I was now in a place
alive with flowers and bright sunshine and sharp men who told the rest of the
world to screw off. The liberal East—the conservative West. At another time,
in another mood, I would try to make sense out of my emotional response to
this wonderland of riches, which I automatically compared to the old factory
towns of my youth and the staid country clubs and the lost souls whom John
O'Hara could write about with such accuracy. There was a time when I was a
rich kid. Now it was Bob Falkenburg's time to be a rich adult. My burning
question had to be answered: who was this guy?

Bob's wife was in the house, but he told me that she was shy and avoided
publicity. Therefore we dined alone, with a servant bringing us cold beer and
small dishes of deboned chicken along with an avocado salad. The dining
room was elegant, and I took a picture of him sitting at the head of his table,
wearing slightly shaded glasses and with a carafe and a glass pitcher next to
him. Later I met his wife, who is a beautiful woman from Brazil, but for our
lunch it was just the two of us—one man in charge and the other five years
younger trying to ask meaningful questions.

"I was telling you about my game," he said. "After we played, you suggested that we rally, and I said my ground strokes were no good, and they never were any good [pooh!], so all the players I used to play with used to kid me, and they said that if I didn't have ground strokes, I couldn't beat the women. That is, if I couldn't go to the net, I wouldn't beat the women. At that time, Pauline Betz was the best woman player, and she was around the club quite a bit [the Los Angeles Tennis Club—the land of Perry Jones], and so we had a challenge match, and if the challenge was accepted, there was always a wager on it. Well, I played Pauline, and I gave her thirty points per game and I said, 'I won't serve hard, and I won't take the net unless you hit the ball inside the service line.' So all the guys immediately jumped on it. They said, 'Oh my God! You have no chance,' because they were imagining that I would try to win all of my points from the backcourt, and Pauline was very fast and could run down everything. What they didn't know was that when I was a kid, my game was a dinking game. I could stay there all day and just dink the ball back. So that's what I did. I would just serve the ball, sort of like Harold Solomon or someone like that, and eventually she would hit one into the service court, and I could come to the net. Or else she would come to the net, and I would hit a high lob which, as you know, is difficult for women. It was just a different strategy that I employed—different from what they thought would happen, and I won the wager."

I said that Pauline still had a great backhand and could hit a flat, hard forehand as well. He said, "I'll be darned." Then I dumbly said that I doubted that she could still run as she used to, and he said, "Who can?"

I mentioned Seixas as a runner, and Falkenburg said, "Not really."

This led us into a debate over who was the best now, from sixty on up in age.

"I don't know," he said. "I have been away from tennis for twenty-five to thirty years. The only reason I took it up again is because my grandson, who lives in Brazil, comes up twice a year, and he is eleven, and I play with him. So I can't answer that question.

"But I can tell you that back seven years or so ago, when they started the Masters and played at Wimbledon, Frank Sedgman was far and away the best player. But he was younger. Then there was Torben Ulrich, who was always a useful player, but he stayed in great shape and got involved with yoga or something, and he came on strong after forty-five."

"Like Dodo Cheney," I said.

"I saw Dodo play after maybe twenty years, and I was amazed at her. She is fantastic. She looked just great—tan, smooth-skinned, lithe, active . . ."

"I think she looks like Louise Brough."

"But she is older, seven years."

"That's my point. The Torben Ulrich thing."

"Conditioning."

"I think *you* would even have trouble beating Dodo Cheney."

"You're right. Oh sure, I can't beat anybody who really plays. But, on second thought, I think I could beat any woman over sixty."

So we began talking about the older players, and I told Bob that he should be doing the talking, not I, but he said go ahead, and I told him how I would grade some of the men players over sixty, and I insisted that Frank Parker would be tough, but surely Seixas and Brown would have to be ranked somewhere in contending positions.

"But think of the players who are not name players," he said.

I did, and I thought of Jason Morton and Bob Sherman and others who fill the record books with senior titles. I mentioned Mulloy, and for a minute we talked of Mulloy and Schroeder.

"Ted is the kind of fellow who can say anything to anybody and then live with it or undo it as if it doesn't mean anything. In other words, he can let it go. Now, other people are different than that. I, for instance, rarely get upset with anybody, but if I do, it may well be for life."

"This is a good insight into you. I think I am more like Schroeder."

"Well, that's good. I think I wish I were more like that. Basically, I think what you should do is be yourself."

And about Mulloy, Bob said, "When I was a kid and over at Wimbledon in 1948, I looked at Gardnar and I said, 'What is that old man doing here?' He was all of twenty-seven or twenty-eight then."

As Falkenburg laughed at his own absurdity, I again searched through my mind and found what I wanted. Gardnar Mulloy had won the public court championships in 1961. And that was not senior tennis. It was a fact that had to do with our talk about age and conditioning and Bob Falkenburg's self-denigrating chuckle had affirmed what we both knew: tennis was a game where older people got younger.

The old times. That was what this book was all about. I loved the jocular give-and-take with Falkenburg. He was a most agreeable man, and we continued to dine while a young Latin woman smiled at us and gave me more avocados and another beer. The world was in bloom.

His mother was from Baltimore, his father came from California, and he was born in Flushing, New York, coincidentally the new home of the national tennis championships. Two weeks after he was born in 1926, the family moved to South America. His father was an engineer with Westinghouse, and their first home in South America was in Brazil. Then they moved to Chile, but things became a bit hectic in that country because it was torn by revolution. "Anyone who knew my mother knew that she made the decisions for the family—that she was the boss—so she looked at the map of the world to select a place to go. My mother, who had checked on the climate in other parts, selected southern California because it was very similar to Santiago,

Chile, where we lived. My father then got a job working on building the Boulder Dam. He had been offered a job in Russia, but my mother decided she didn't like the politics over there and vetoed it."

"So your mother was the major influence on your life."

"Yes, my mother. But my father was strong, but quiet. For instance, my brother, Tom, who is one and a half years older than I, is more rebellious—when he got in trouble, my father would step in."

We talked about Tom for a few minutes. I asked about the quality of Tom Falkenburg's tennis—he had won the intercollegiates with Bob—and Bob said that he was a better player than his results would indicate, but he "didn't have a good head for the game."

I asked Bob a touchy question. "Why did Tom get himself arrested?" [for armed robbery], and Bob said, "He was fed up with his marriage and trying to make things work, and he couldn't, so he wanted to do something drastic, to get caught—to sort of call attention to himself, almost like a child would do. And that is what he told me, and he is usually pretty straightforward."*

I then presented my theory that many people commit crimes hoping to get caught so that they will be jailed and at last someone will look out for them.

Bob got heated over this. "I am really a nonbeliever in these reasons. I get upset when I read of a criminal getting let off because of a technicality or because he is temporarily insane. I say, 'Who cares?' If a person commits a crime, he should be punished. Take the death penalty. I am for it. What good are these people? Eventually one gets released, and who is to say he won't repeat his crime? If the judge wants to take the responsibility for releasing a confessed killer, that is something else again. But judges don't."

He was referring to plea bargaining and getting reduced sentences, and we seemed to be off the track as far as tennis was concerned, but not off the track regarding the state of California, where the crime issue is a constant subject and where the athletes I have met take a hard line on human weakness or human venality.

Trying to get back to the great game and his life, I asked him when he had actually settled in California.

"When I was nine years old."

"When did you start playing tennis?"

"Right then. My mother always played the game, and she had been the champion of Chile. So she would take my brother and me to the tennis club whenever she went to play, and if there was an open court, we would grab a couple of racquets and start hitting."

---

* A fairly famous case of some years back, the details of which I did not pursue.

He played tennis from then on, especially after his family had moved from a section of Hollywood to a location closer to the Los Angeles Tennis Club. Almost to the day that he was graduated from Fairfax High School, he went into the Army Air Corps (his name shows up as a/c Robert Falkenburg when he won the national juniors—the "a/c" standing for "air cadet"), and he eventually wound up as a flight engineer with a pilot's rating on a B-29 Super Fortress.

"[That work] was interesting. I think it was worthwhile. They gave you crash courses on hydraulics, electricity, and just one thing after another."

"Did you end up bombing Japan?"

"No. Just two weeks before we were to be sent to Okinawa, they dropped the atom bomb, and we were almost immediately phased out."

"Would you say that the service messed up your tennis career?"

"Yes. More because of what it did to my physical condition. I don't really know why, but before I went into the service, I don't ever remember tiring. I could play five matches in a day and never tire. The first time I remember that I got tired was when I got a week off to go to the nationals, and I went along okay until I met Pancho Segura in the quarterfinals. I won the first set, and then I felt completely exhausted—about halfway through the second set—just completely exhausted, and this had never happened to me before. And from that time on, I had problems with conditioning."*

"Others say they were affected by the war and . . ."

"Oh, yes. Take Kramer and Bromwich. The war came just prior to the peak of their careers."

"When do you think is the peak time for a tennis player?"

"In the early twenties. That is when you have the youth, and you can combine that with some added strength. Of course now the professionals play all year long and they can keep in shape longer than we could. We played and then went back to school or our jobs. So we would have to work hard to get back into condition. Our peaks would be earlier than some of the players today."

"Yet Schroeder, who had to work all of the time, would breeze into a tennis tournament and win it. He would be an exception?"

"Well, Schroeder had a tenacity about him that most of the others didn't have. He also marched to a different beat. To give you an example, at Wimbledon after he won, he shows up at the ball wearing a tan suit and a yellow tie and red socks. Everyone else is in a tuxedo. And he's got his pipe, and that's Ted. He was just an individual."

---

* He may have had problems with conditioning but he won the Wimbledon doubles in 1947 with Kramer and the Wimbledon singles in 1948—three years after the war.

And that is how it went. We began to talk about players and games and some of the funny things that happened along the route. One thing that Bob Falkenburg is positive of is that Parker and Mulloy could not have beaten Schroeder and Kramer "every time" in Australia, *if at all*. And another thing—Bob was there right on the line when Billy Talbert hit the "out ball" that should have given Frank Guernsey and Don McNeill the match in the 1946 finals at Longwood. He said, "Talbert and Mulloy were going up to shake hands. The match was over, and then there was no call, and they thought, 'Wait a minute, no call.' They started to walk back, and then it was called 'In!' and Guernsey and McNeill had lost. Talbert and Mulloy were going in to shake hands as losers, not winners. But I am not going by a call. I am going by having played against many teams, and Talbert and Mulloy were

53. Falkenburg showing his stuff

a good team, but they were not a *great* team by any stretch of the imagination. They went to Australia to give Schroeder and Kramer practice. Of course, someone could get hurt or sick, and then they would be there. But they were not the top doubles team.

"And that was a year that changed my life because I thought I would be going to the Davis Cup that year, even though I wouldn't have played either the singles or doubles, but by the results of that year, I thought I would have gone because I had played both Talbert and Mulloy and hadn't lost to them. I also beat Don McNeill [who was ranked just ahead of him], and I have a lot of respect for Don because we played on a very bad grass court, and the serve was just bounding all over the place. After the match, he came over and said, 'Well this isn't tennis,' and I said, 'I agree with you, but what can I do? This is the court they gave us.' So anyone can make his case. But looking back now, I can see there was no reason to take me. I wouldn't be good practice for anybody, but Talbert and Mulloy would be good practice for Kramer and Schroeder."

"But they didn't know that they were there for practice."

"Well, *I* did, and where I say it changed my life, it is because I was not included that I went to South America in 1946 and met my future wife. And that is when I moved back to Brazil to start my business. It worked out well for me. And that's the point."

At that point, I felt compelled to say, "You and Jack Kramer have been awfully kind to me. I don't usually expect to be taken to lunch and . . . well, you both have been great."

"Oh, don't be ridiculous," he said. "I am not really very sociable," he added.

"Well, you sure have been with me—even with my cigarettes." (We'd opened the windows because neither Bob nor his wife smoke, and though he didn't appear to care, he didn't want his wife to smell the toxic fumes from my Merit Lights.)

"Well, I don't know about the second time around, but for now . . ."

Then he was interrupted by a phone call, and upon his return he began discussing horses and golf, and apparently he had been talking to Gussie Moran on the phone because he said, "My mother used to call Gussie another member of the family."

I then told him that he and Gussie held the record for the longest mixed doubles match in the world. He said, "Is that right?"

I said, "A world record!"

"I'll be darned," said Bob Falkenburg.

"Here it is," I said, "seventy-one games. Margaret Osborne duPont and Billy Talbert beat you and Gussie 27–25, 5–7, 6–1 in the semifinals at the West Side Tennis Club, Forest Hills, New York, in 1948."

"Well, I'll be darned," he repeated.

"You don't remember that?"

"No."

"How can you not remember that?"

"Well, you see, I always like to enter all the events for the competitiveness of it, but I never considered mixed doubles important. I likened it to a practice match, almost."

"But you don't remember an endurance test like that? Seventy-one games?"

"You'd think so, but I don't. Gussie and I were entered at Wimbledon that year, and there was a sort of unwritten agreement with the players that if anyone is doing well in the singles and if the mixed doubles interferes, you drop out. That was the famous year [1948] of her lace panties, and she was the number one attraction. All of a sudden I am in the semifinals, and we're backed up in men's doubles and mixed doubles, and I would have had to play the men's doubles after my singles and two mixed doubles, which would have finished around 10:00 at night, and then I would have another singles the next day.

"So I talked with Gussie and said, 'Do you mind if we withdraw?' and she said, 'No, not at all,' because that was what was understood. But then, of course, I became the hate symbol among the British press because they all wanted to see Gussie with her lace panties."

"Had you played the mixed doubles, how far do you think you and Gussie would have gone?"

"Oh, we were semifinalists, maybe. We wouldn't have gone further because any team that had Margaret Osborne or Louise Brough would beat us. They were too strong. You know, either Louise or Margaret might get into a rally at the net against a man and sometimes win."

"So to go back to your youth, you were a ball boy at the Los Angeles Tennis Club where Jack Kramer played . . ."

"Jack was the fair-haired boy, and Perry Jones was Hitler."

"How would you evaluate Perry Jones?"

"He was definitely needed for tennis. There were bound to be some injustices along the way, as there would be with any dictator, but tennis needed direction, and it was much better to have Perry Jones than to have chaos. Bascially I would say that Perry Jones was 90 percent correct and 10 percent wrong, and that 10 percent would affect some people, but he was basically a good person. He instilled etiquette, sportsmanship, dress code—things that stuck with you for the rest of your life. It was like going to a very strict private school. When Perry Jones taught you something, you didn't forget it."

"You went to USC, a private university, and you were from a middle-class background. Did you pay your way?"

"I wouldn't say always middle class—we had some tough times during the Depression. Yes, I went to USC on a tennis scholarship. As a boy, I was better by comparison than anyone else. And that was because of my physical condition." (Which he began to lose during the end of the war.)

Looking up his amazing record as a youth and noting his air cadet status when he won the junior singles, I said, "So you must have gone to college *after* the war. You probably went on the GI Bill and wouldn't need a tennis scholarship."

"You're probably right," he said. "I would have the GI Bill. That's probably what I went in with. I don't really remember."

"So you graduated from college and . . ."

"No, I didn't graduate. I went for two years and went to work for Fox Theaters."

"Was that through your sister, Jinx?"

"No. I got in on my own through my tennis. The guy in charge liked tennis, so I became the manager of a movie theater. I remember once a person was dying right there in the theater, and the people around him didn't even care. They're watching the movie!

"So I was doing that work for just less than a year, and one day Ted Schroeder called me and asked me if I wanted to have lunch. He was having lunch with a guy who owned a chain of ice cream stores in California, and without thinking much about it, I went to lunch, and this fellow says, 'How would you like to have the franchise for one of my ice cream stores?' And I said, 'Whereabouts?' and he said, 'Arizona or Hawaii,' and I said, 'How about Brazil?' and he said, 'Sure. You can have Brazil, if you want.'"

"How old were you then, when you took *that* flyer?"

"Twenty-three or twenty-four."

"Of course, you were brought up down there and . . ."

"It wasn't that. It was because I was married to a Brazilian girl. I met her when I was omitted from the Davis Cup squad in 1946, and I went on a tennis tour of South America instead. It was the first time I was paid any money. I had heard about money under the table and the famous Frankie Kovacs story of how he was offered and accepted $300 to play in a tournament, and then two days before the tournament, he calls up and says he has a tennis elbow, but for another $100, he is pretty sure the tennis elbow will go away.

"So I started out playing in Mexico and lost to Frank Parker 15–13 in the fifth set of the finals. And that was one of the most memorable of matches because we started out playing on a very dry court, and I couldn't get my footing to rush the net. So Parker has me running and slipping and sliding all over the place and wins the first two sets. Then we get a downpour, and after a wait, we go back, and I have my footing. So I win the next two sets. In the fifth set, Frank has me 4–5, love–40, and I served *five* straight aces. Well, the

Mexican crowd goes wild, and they throw everything they can find down on the court until it is completely cluttered. So the match goes on, and I have Frank at 9–8 with match point, but by now the courts have dried off again, and he hits a ball I would normally get as I rush the net, but my feet slip out from under me. And so he finally won the match.''

"What *was* the surface?"

"Slippery clay."

"And the drier it gets, the more slippery it gets?"

"Yes. I see on TV that they say the opposite, but not on that court. That wasn't the case at all.

"So after the match, this promoter from Brazil comes up and says, 'I'll give you $50 a day plus first-class accommodations to come and play through South America.' And I said, 'Wow, that's fantastic!' And then this Belgian player* and I took off, stopping in Panama and Lima, Peru, and other cities like Santiago, Chile, and we cross the Andes and play in Buenos Aires, where they had the big championship—the South American Championship—and they decided to only play on weekends, and it was fine with me. I met some very nice people, and it took four weekends to play the tournament. Of course, you're getting your $50 a day, plus expenses."

"How did this conflict with you being an amateur?"

"As I said, I had heard about others getting money, and this was the first time for me. And I thought, 'Well, I am way off in South America. Nobody is going to care anyway.' I couldn't have gone on my own, so that was the situation."**

"So that is how you met your wife?"

"Yes. The tour didn't end in Buenos Aires . . . We went on, and we played in Brazil—Santos, Sao Paulo, and then Rio de Janeiro, where I met my wife on the beach. We have been married since 1947."

"So, to bring things up to date, you were married because you went to lunch with Schroeder, and you really owe a lot to Schroeder because it was through him that you went back to Brazil."

"Well, nothing was meant to be, but that's right. Circumstances would show that Schroeder was the direct contact for sending me to Brazil and starting my business there. I stayed in Brazil for twenty-two years."

"So you played tennis down there?"

* Falkenburg could not recall his name at the time of our lunch.
** Of course, some official, somewhere, having read this could claim that Falkenburg's superb Wimbledon singles victory in 1948 is now voided, that the trophy belongs to John Bromwich because in 1946, Bob played for $50 a day. But all who know the game, *know* that there had always been some money in amateur tennis.

"A little, but I was working day and night at my business. Then in 1953, they asked me to play Davis Cup for Brazil, which I did in 1953 and 1954."

"How did you do?"

"Not great. We beat Switzerland, and then against England, I ended up playing a guy I had beaten easily in 1948. But now he looks so good, you know, and I get blisters, and, oh, it just shows what can happen when you don't play the game over a span of time, five years in this case. And I, indeed, lost to him. So we lost to England the first year, but in the second year, we started off playing Cuba, and we won. But the next match was against Australia, and we played it in Louisville, Kentucky, and they had Hoad and Rosewall."

"Oh, brother!"

"Yes, but by now I had played a little bit and was in better shape, and I won the first set against Hoad. I had a service break in the second set when I hit him with a serve in the lower extremities. He was out, and we were allowed maybe five minutes for this kind of thing, and after five minutes, he wasn't ready to play. So Harry Hopman, their captain, comes over and asks me what we're going to do. So we wait a half hour, and Hoad comes back and wins. But I didn't want to win on a technicality. Two days later, I played Rosewall, and he beat me quite handily."

As we lunched and he talked, I knew that this man could reminisce forever. He was starting to recall a good deal of his tennis history that he had forgotten. He mentioned that he had almost beaten Rosewall at Wimbledon in 1953, playing on grass. I knew that the trouble with my book would be that I had to stop people and their wonderful running monologues on tennis glory and get them into my old format. I asked him about heroes.

I said, "Were you a fan, like me, when you were a kid?"

"Yes. When I was a little kid, I was a ball boy. And I ball-boyed for all of the top players—Tilden, Vines, Budge, Stoefen, and Lott."

"How do you get to be a ball boy?"

"Well, if you are at the Los Angeles Tennis Club and are a tennis prospect, Perry Jones says, 'You are a ball boy,' and that is it."

"Now about Tilden, you were saying earlier, upstairs, that you were the youngest player to ever beat Tilden."

"Yes. I was about eleven or twelve, and he asks me to play over at Charlie Chaplin's court, and my brother and I jump at the chance and get in his car. My mother arrives at the club and says, 'Where are Tom and Bob?' And the guy says, 'They went off with Mr. Tilden.' Oh, my God, she went crazy and had the police and the whole thing. And, of course, Tom and I at that time didn't know what it was all about. [I was imagining the scene at Chaplin's court with police cruisers moving in and Tilden scared stiff.]

384

"Later, I played one of his protégés and I beat him easily (half-trying), and Tilden was watching and said that the match could have gone either way, except for a few points. Well, he was a genius, but to say something like that and then actually believe it! I was a notoriously bad practice player, but in tournaments, it was a different story."

"Something like Schroeder?"

"Yes. I always admired Schroeder for that."

"Was there anyone you feared in singles?"

"Only one. Jack Kramer. Everyone else I thought I could beat. When I went on the court, he was the only player against whom I figured I wouldn't win. I never put Gonzales or Schroeder or Parker in the class with Kramer."

"Who were the top five players?"

"Tilden was a virtuoso. He put on a show, and the show was more important than winning. He had so many shots. Like Laver. I saw Laver when he first came up. He was on center court at Wimbledon, and I said, 'Here is a player who is going to be great, absolutely great. His only flaw is that he has such a variety of shots, he won't know which one to hit.' That is a definite problem, because if you have a one-track mind on how you are going to play the game, it is a lot easier than when you have too many options. But he proved that, even with his variety, he could handle it, and that is the same case with Tilden."

We got back to heroes when Tilden again entered the picture, and we both agreed that heroism lies in the imagination. Bob began recalling the great boxing matches, and we talked of sportscasters like Bill Stern and Don Dunphy. We talked of how television dilutes this ingredient, and then we went into education and how some players missed out, and the phrase "A diploma doesn't mean a damn" came out of my mouth. Bob was quick to say that there is so much money in sports now that it is almost impossible to be a good student *and* a championship athlete at the same time.

"You have to choose one or the other. A man like Roger Staubach, who went into the Navy and still came back to become a star, is so unusual . . . You know, sometimes too much intelligence will hurt you in a sport."

"At eighteen, if you had the choice to become a bright, quick, educated man or a great athlete—what would you choose?"

"At eighteen you don't have the choice. Looking back, you would pick the education. But at eighteen, you wouldn't know. When I was thirteen or fourteen, I was working in the movies as an extra and making pretty good money for a kid."

"Now, *that* must have been because of your sister."

"No. As a matter of fact, she got into movies because of me! She was babysitting for me, and one day my mother couldn't go with me to the set, and Jinx, who is older than I, went instead, to look after me, and the director said, 'My God, who is this?' "

"How did you get into the movies to start with [and hence Jinx]?"

"I think it was through Frank Shields. He was in a movie, and they needed some kids, and he suggested my brother and me."

"Because you were ball boys."

"Yes, something like that, and that was how I first got in. Then they get your name and address, and I got into all of the Mickey Rooney movies, the Dead End Kids movies, and so forth. Then I came very close to getting the part of David Copperfield because I had been educated in the early days in South America and had an English accent, which is the way you spoke English down there, but just at the last moment, they got Freddie Bartholomew from England. I was in the movie but not the star. Then at thirteen or fourteen, I was in a tennis tournament and also in a movie, and I was more interested in tennis and wasn't available for the movie, and that was the end of my movie days."

It was fun to talk of motion pictures, but he had not yet answered my question as to the top five players in tennis history.

"The top five," he said, "would be Tilden, Budge, Vines, Kramer, and Laver, but I am not placing them in any order."

"What about Vines on his 'given day'?"

"When Vines was on, he would be the best of the group. His margin of error was so small, but when he was on his game, he would be the best."

Earlier we had been in his study where he had three television sets and a whole library of video tapes, reflecting a vast reservoir of sporting events that he could draw from. We discussed the fact that he can watch three networks at once, following three separate sporting events and tape each one. I wanted to know who, in his opinion, was the best all-around athlete in America.

"One indicator, and I don't mean it is an absolute, but after the football season ends, they have the "Superstars" on television, and I like to see that. They have the best athletes in every sport competing in ten different events. Now, it has turned out that almost invariably the very good athletes are pole vaulters. To be a champion pole vaulter, you have to be able to run very fast, to be strong, to be agile . . ."

"You say that a pole vaulter would be a better athlete than Muhammad Ali?"

"Not better, but *much* better. So much better!"

"What about Jackie Robinson? He could do anything."

"He could. He was a good track man, and that is where you start. The best athlete would be a good all-around track man."

386

"So a man like Bob Mathias [the great 1940s decathlon champion] would be a good bet."

"Yes. You would have to consider him."

"Another would be Vines. He could do anything, and switching to championship golf was a major feat."

"True enough," he said, "but look at Lynn Swann who won the 'Superstars'!"

I thought of Swann, who is as graceful as his name implies, and agreed. "Could Swann play tennis?"

"I saw him play Martina, and she was just jerking him around. Tennis players use different muscles and don't need to run the hundred-yard dash. They have to have the ability to sense a position. Swann looked fine on the court, but he didn't have that ability."

"Tennis players have to concentrate. You have to learn that," I said smugly, talking to a two-time Wimbledon winner.

"Oh, yes. I remember at Wimbledon after the war, the British were fairly hostile to the Americans and were always rooting for the Australians or the English, but I didn't hear anything. After the match, people asked how I could concentrate with the sort of oohing and aahing for my opponent and the rustling, but I didn't *hear* anything at all."

"Speaking of Wimbledon, I assume that beating Bromwich in 1948 and winning the singles must have been a tremendous thrill for you."

"Oh, yeah."

"I would assume winning Wimbledon is the amateur championship. Would you agree with that?"

"Definitely. No question about that! For sheer prestige . . . it's run on such a high level that even though I am very American and some Americans might prefer to win their own championship, there is just so much atmosphere—it's on a higher level."

My mind wandered again as he sat there in his shaded glasses, leaning back in his chair. He is six-three, and back in 1947, he won Wimbledon in doubles with Kramer. In 1948, with Kramer now a professional and the one man he feared gone from the ranks, he won the greatest title in the tennis world. Back in 1947, he won the doubles with Kramer for the indoor title. I remember Kramer lauding Falkenburg as a man he played with only a few times and they had never lost. And here he was, his mind again in England, and so neat and trim and well-dressed and living in a spotless home with a beautiful wife whom he met in 1946, rich from the ice cream business he had set up in Brazil because of a chance phone call from Ted Schroeder—and all of that from tennis.

Bob Falkenburg is a private man. He told me that he raises horses in Santa Ynez and that seeing me was really a one-shot thing. But he was running now with his memories, and I had to leave for my plane. The man had been superb, and we had dined in keeping with someone who wants to stay in perfect shape—on chicken and salad. His three television sets and the rows of video tapes haunted me. So did the shower and the bathroom and the fluffy towels—everything perfect. And then the swimming pool. It was all Hollywood with class, and he had started out in Hollywood as an extra.

I asked him about his sister Jinx, and he said, "You know, everyone always loved her. There was never a bad word about her, and on the U.S.O. tours during the war, the generals always wanted to entertain her. But she went where the enlisted men were."

And so did Bob Falkenburg, in his way. I was the enlisted man and he a man of high rank, and I knew that, much like Tom Brown, he was taking up tennis again, and I threw my curve ball at him with minutes to go before I left his house.

"Do you believe in God?"

"I believe—commonsense-like—that there must be something there, but I am not a churchgoer."

"If you had your life to live over again, would there be any changes?"

"No major ones. I remember some of the old movies where a businessman would get his son into the business and start him off, you know, sweeping floors and working his way up. I wish I had done that with my son. I had a pretty good-sized business in Brazil, and I wouldn't have sold it, had I been tougher on my son. I made it a little too easy for him, and he thought that is the way life is."

"How many children do you have?"

"Two. A boy and a girl, and three grandchildren."

"Look," I said. "I have walked all around this marvelous home, and you are telling me that all of this came from ice cream—from selling ice cream in Brazil?"

"Yes."

"No inheritance, no nothing?"

"No."

"Do you consider yourself retired now?"

"Yes, but I am in the horse business with the ranch, but I don't consider that much because for me, the results are the only thing that count, and I am just getting into the thoroughbred business. But I don't consider that by any means a profession."

"I am still astounded that you have done so well on ice cream."

"Well, I *did* have an inheritance of $8,000 from my father, and that is what I started with. I had $8,000 and sold my car and everything and ended up with $10,000 and went to Brazil and opened up one store."

"All because of Ted Schroeder?"

"Well, yes, basically. That would be pretty close to it."

"You must have had confidence in yourself. Most people would take the $8,000 but hardly sell everything and head to Brazil."

"Perry Jones used to tell my parents, 'Bob will go a long way.' I don't know why because I couldn't sense it in myself, but I do know that I have very strong feelings and disciplines about certain things."

"What about politics? What would you call yourself?"

"I am a little to the right of Ronald Reagan. And if you want my dislikes, they are Communists, unions, pickets, Jimmy Carter, and Tip O'Neill, and not necessarily in that order."

And that was it. Another conservative athlete from California. I had to say good-bye. I am not a Reagan fan. I believe in liberal causes, although I am suspicious that they do not work. Sometimes I feel that, were I like Falkenburg and others who went out and did things their way and had made it, well, who knows? I don't argue with champions, and as we parted smiling, I was as envious as any hacker in life who has been entertained by a man who had accomplished so much.

I had called a cab to take me to the airport, and as I shouted farewell and thanked him again, my head out of the window, he said one last thing. He said, "Last year, with a good knee, you would have beaten me. This year, even with a good knee, you would have lost."

And that pleased me very much. I wished mightily that I had seen him last year.

23

Margaret Osborne duPont:

At Home in El Paso

I had heard from Jack Kramer that Bobby Riggs was down at La Costa, the same place that employed Pancho Segura as its tennis professional. Riggs actually lives right near La Costa in a town called Leucadia, and I got his phone number by calling La Costa, where he is a member. Riggs was away— somewhere in Florida—and I had no exact idea when he would return. A young woman answered my call and said, helpfully, that he might be back in ten days or so. Well, I wanted Riggs in last place for my book, and ten days or so was just right. In ten days, I would have seen everyone in California except Riggs.

Previously I had written Bobby Riggs a letter, getting an address that is his brother's, and is, in a sense, a kind of clearinghouse for Bobby Riggs' correspondence from people such as me. Someone at the Hall of Fame told me that he lived in Coronado near San Diego. His brother lives in Coronado, and I learned all that much later. In the meantime (and to bring things up to date), I had a dilemma. By the time I had finished talking with Bob Falkenburg, I had gotten hold of Bobby Riggs' wife, Miriam, on the phone. She said that he would love to see me. "He'd like that kind of thing," she supposed, and I assumed she was correct. So my instinct was to fly immediately to San Diego and locate Bobby Riggs and try at least to get a look at Segura at the same time. Segura had said on the phone that he would not participate unless he got something out of it ("What would be in it for me?" he asked), and then he said he would have to consult his agent and his lawyer.

So there I was, flying to San Diego to try and find La Costa, which I had heard of and knew had a championship golf course because it was on the PGA tour. I had seen the course on television, drooling away in cold New England. But could Riggs be around and agreeable? Could I trust his wife? And the dilemma referred to earlier was this: if I saw Riggs now and visited with Margaret Osborne duPont on my way home, how could I get Riggs in at the end of the book? Margaret Osborne duPont lives in El Paso, Texas, and had welcomed me on the phone. But Riggs was fireworks, and I knew he had to end my long trek, and so for the first time, I would deliberately change chronology and see Riggs, if I could, and then place Margaret Osborne duPont *before* him in my book. In other words, Riggs would get the last chapter, no matter what. And then I was in San Diego.

But it is El Paso that I am writing about now and, in particular, a charming woman, slightly overweight, with a soft face and warm smile, who greeted me with enthusiasm and who led me into her home and showed me the sights on the Mexican border.

Margaret Osborne duPont was ranked in the top ten in the United States fifteen times, starting in 1938 and ending in 1958. Her Wightman Cup record against Great Britain was 18–0, playing singles and doubles in nine matches, starting in 1946 and playing her last set in 1962. This superior athlete won at Wimbledon in the mixed doubles with Neale Fraser in 1962. She started her ladies' doubles supremacy with Louise Brough in 1946. They won their doubles five times. She won the singles title in 1947, and this was all at Wimbledon. She won her country's singles championship for three straight years from 1948 through 1950 and the women's doubles thirteen times, always with Louise Brough, except for 1941, when she played with Sarah Palfrey. So with Margaret Osborne duPont, we have a woman who was a grand-slam event champion over a span of twenty-one years. It is doubtful that anyone can match that achievement.* She took the Nationals at Longwood in 1941 and was able to win at Wimbledon in 1962. Could the venerable Australian, Margaret Smith Court, equal that? I looked up her record for comparison. The answer is no. Court began winning in 1960. Her last win was in 1973 when she won both the ladies' doubles and the singles in Australia. Of course, she did win the grand slam of tennis in 1970, but for longevity, there is no one that I

* The USTA Yearbook is inaccurate in its list of all-time champions. It cut Margaret off in 1960 rather than in 1962, forgetting the Fraser-duPont mixed doubles win at Wimbledon. This list applies only to the four big "grand-slam events": the American, French, English, and Australian championships in all three categories. Margaret Osborne duPont is first in longevity, followed by Helen Wills (Moody, Roark) and Billie Jean King.

can think of who equals Margaret Osborne duPont. And this excludes senior participation in which Dodo Cheney, Gardnar Mulloy, and Bobby Riggs hold unbelievable endurance records.

And speaking of endurance, it should be recalled (which Bob Falkenburg did not) that Margaret, playing with Billy Talbert, beat Falkenburg and Gussie Moran in a 71-set match, the longest in mixed doubles history. In short, I was meeting a woman so extraordinary that El Paso, itself, was but an afterthought.

Years back, in 1954, I had been in El Paso. I had traveled there with a wonderful girl named Patty Price, who wanted to see Mexico. I was still in the service, and she worked at Lowry Field in Denver, and off we drove in my Chevy coupe over a long Labor Day weekend. We saw Juarez, Mexico, and then in El Paso, both of us were thrown in jail because I zoomed into a speed trap. I vowed that I would never return to that dismal city, but I had to.

I did what I had to do—I avoided it. I never went to Juarez, and I never went anywhere outside of my hotel, the El Paso Hilton. I only went to Margaret Osborne duPont's home and to her horse ranch and then in her car up on the ridge where we could see for miles of open, dry earth and the foothills of the Rockies. We crossed the Rio Grande at one point, and we drove into New Mexico, she steering her BMW, and I sitting there. She was taking me for a ride like a proud host. I sat there in her car and recalled our long talk.

She lives in West El Paso with another tennis player, Margaret Varner, which is a long way from the El Paso Hilton, and I had taken a $20 cab ride to find her home. They reside out near the El Paso Country Club in a sprawling white house that is as clean as one of Bob Falkenburg's towels and rests on several acres of land. Out back there is an old butternut tree, now dead—choked to death by vines. There are also two beagles and a Belgian sheep dog barking from their kennels. You can see a paddock and a field for horses to graze and nearby is an amazing track for a bicycle run that humps and curves over a large slab of brown, Texas earth. This is the province of Margaret Varner's son, who at thirteen may be looking for titles of his own.*

But she would talk, and talk with me openly and with appreciation—I believe that she was struck by the fact that someone would come to El Paso to find her. For me it was an honor, but I doubt that she would guess that. She

---

* I later learned that he had his share. We were in Margaret's garage, getting into her BMW. I saw a line-up of trophies—cheap plastic trophies on a back shelf. I asked: "Is this where you keep your great mementoes of victory?" She said kindly: "No, this is where the bike rider keeps *his*."

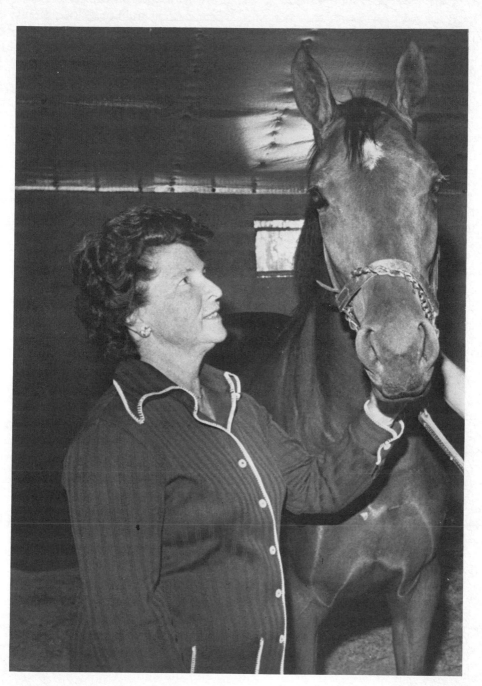

54. Margaret Osborne duPont

seemed very modest and yet very frank. It was evident that she lived with Margaret Varner (Bloss) and that they shared a long friendship. Margaret Varner's daughter had been named after Margaret duPont and had died in an accident riding a horse. Margaret said that the grief she felt would have been the same had it been her own son, Will duPont, Jr. It was clear that the child, Margaret Varner's thirteen-year-old boy, was a joy to Margaret duPont. I could see her grin as she showed me the obstacle course he had set up in what was once a penned-in area for her thoroughbreds. It was obvious and pleasing that there were two Margarets in the house and both had children and lived there . . . a thousand or more miles away from fame.

We started talking about her world's record match with Billy Talbert against Gussie Moran and Bob Falkenburg.

"Well, we had to end it on the first day at 22–all and then continued the next day. The wind was so strong that day at the grandstand court at Forest Hills that you couldn't possibly win a game on one side of the court and you couldn't possibly lose a game on the other. We just never could finish the set."

"It could have been 30–all or 40–all at that rate."

"Yes."

"I gather from people that Gussie Moran was really a pretty good player underneath it all [the publicity over her panties]."

"Yes, she really was. She was a nice player."

"And then you had that long 48-game match against Louise Brough at Forest Hills."

"That must have been the singles final (4–6, 6–4, 15–13) in 1948. It might have been the year that it rained off and on, and they had to keep postponing us, and the people in the stands were calling for the men to come on."

At that she laughed, as she did almost all the time, a soft chuckle that told me that she was not someone who was at all pompous. She could kid herself and her accomplishments.

"How would you rank the top five women players going back, say, to Helen Wills, whom I assume you saw play?"

"I never saw her play as a competitor. Coming from San Francisco as I did, I saw her at the California Club in practice games, but it was after she retired. To rank the top five would be very difficult."

"Well, then just lump them. You won't have to pin yourself down to an order."

"Alice Marble I saw in some competition, and to me she is one of the greatest players because she had that all-court game: good serve, good volley. I haven't seen Martina except on TV now, and she must be playing tremendous tennis. She also has that all-court game, and I think the great players have to have all the shots."

394

55. Margaret Osborne and Louise Brough at Wimbledon, 1948

56. Pauline Betz and Margaret Osborne: two stunning champions in 1944

"What about you?"

"Louise and I did well in doubles, but we came at a funny time. We were just good enough to be getting to the top when the war came in 1939, and during those years, we played a lot of patriotic tournaments, service exhibitions, and we weren't really in that tough competition. And then when we went abroad in 1946 on the Wightman Cup team—all six of us—it was the first year any one of us had gone abroad." (In the Wightman Cup matches of that year, Doris Hart joined Louise Brough, Margaret Osborne, and Pauline Betz for a team of four women, a team that most surely could never be seriously contested. They won 7–0. I do not know who the other two players were—perhaps Patricia Canning and Shirley Fry.)

"But you were ranked seventh in 1938."

"I was, but I took all of 1939 off and stayed in Berkeley, California, and took lessons from Tom Stow."

"So you are another Tom Stow student."

"He made me work."

"How many Tom Stow students were there who made it to the top?"

"Well, Sarah Palfrey and Elwood Cooke. Cooke and Riggs won the doubles in Wimbledon in 1939. And Don Budge, and I don't think Tom Stow ever got the publicity from Don Budge that he should have gotten. I am really a great admirer of Tom Stow. He did wonders with his pupils."

"What about Pauline Betz?"

"No. She was from southern California."

"Would you put her in that group of top players?"

"She was tough. She really was. She was good. She had that backhand that was so good, and she was a worker. She had a fine temperament on the court."

"Was there anyone you would not want to be with—on the same side of the draw? Someone you might have feared—as Pauline said she feared you?"

"Broughie and I never wanted to be on the same half of the draw. After Pauline turned pro, we were one and two (or two and one) for some years. We never threw a match to one another, as some people questioned us about, but on the other hand, we didn't want to be in the same half because both of us could get home."

"Were you actually born right in San Francisco?"

"No. I was born in Joseph, Oregon, up in the northeast corner, on a farm. My father was a farmer, but we had to leave the farm on account of his health, and we moved to San Francisco, where my mother's brother made it possible for him to work in a garage—to do the kind of work his health permitted."

"What was the state of his health?"

"He had ulcers and . . . I didn't know what else."

"So where did you start playing tennis, coming from a farm?"

"On the public courts at Golden Gate Park, right in San Francisco. My brother and I started there. He was two years older than I and just out of high school, and we played on every public court in San Francisco."

"Did you go through high school there?"

"Yes. I graduated in January 1936 from the High School of Commerce."

"How about college?"

"No. My parents didn't have the money, and there were no tennis scholarships then, and I had a choice of working my way through school or tennis, and I opted to play tennis."

"So, who helped you get going?"

"Howard Kinsey. He was the first one to help me get started—to make any kind of money, not much, but some. He was the pro at the California Tennis Club. He was very helpful in practicing with me and getting other people to practice with me, even though I wasn't a member. At the time, he was writing for *The American Lawn Tennis Magazine*, and he was paid so much per word, and he let me do that so that I could make a little bit of money. I also did his bookkeeping for him, and then I was secretary treasurer for the Northern California Tennis Association for years. It was not as big as it is now, and it just covered my expenses. They paid my way to the National juniors in 1936 when I was eighteen, and I won."

"You won both the singles and the doubles?"

"Yes."

"And you were on your way. But where I get confused is when you got married to Will duPont."

"That was in 1947, after the war. He was always interested in tennis and always had a lot of people at his home in Wilmington, Delaware. He had three grass courts, and he conducted some small tournaments during the war, some for men and some for ladies. We used to have a real grass court circuit in those days: Seabright, Southampton for the men and Easthampton for the women, and the men went to Newport, and we went to Manchester, Massachusetts, and then everyone came to Longwood for doubles, and we all went down to Forest Hills for the singles. They were super tournaments, actually."

"When you were on the Wightman Cup team, who would pay your way over there?"

"Every year I went abroad, I was sent as a representative of the United States Tennis Association."

"You would be put up in hotels and get a per diem."

"Yes. At that time, the tournaments themselves wouldn't send you any money, but the National Association did. You went as a team."

"As a kid growing up on that farm, did you have any heroes or heroines?"

"No. Joseph, Oregon, was a very small community, and we were too far away."

"So you were just out of touch?"

"Yes. Even the two years we spent in Spokane, Washington, before we got to San Francisco, I can't remember anyone."

"Not Helen Wills?"

"I can't remember anyone during those years. But once I was in San Francisco, I looked up to Alice Marble. I really liked the kind of game she played. And then, of course, once I started playing, I would read every magazine or book I could find about tennis."

"When did you start to play?"

"Ten years old. It was the second summer we were up in Spokane, and my mother bought my brother and me each a tennis racquet. And we took music lessons, and I would go by these shabby dirt courts on the way to my piano lessons, and I would stop and shag balls. Then when we got to San Francisco, I took up the game.''

"Can you give away your age?''

"When it is in the public record . . . I am sixty-six.''

"When you look back over your life, are you going to stick with tennis players, or were there other people you respected?''

"I was a baseball fan. Mother and I would go every week to the park to watch the San Francisco Seals.''

"But we are still with sports. I suppose you saw Joe and Vince DiMaggio . . .''

"Oh, yes.''

"But if you were asked to give a speech to a graduating class, what would you tell them?''

"I can't imagine being asked to give a speech.''

"But suppose you did.''

"Well, I do remember a speaker at the graduation for our junior high school, and this man really impressed me. He talked about athletics, and he said there is no such thing as a bad sport or a good sport. You are either a sport or not a sport. And from that day forward, sportsmanship was very high in my book. And it still is.''

"What would you do if you hit a perfectly good ball and someone called it out?''

"I'd be furious. And it happened at Wimbledon. Broughie and I were playing in the finals against Doris Hart and Pat Todd [Patricia Canning Todd], and Broughie hit a ball that was right on the baseline. We were down 30–40, and she was serving. Then all of a sudden, Toddy [Pat Todd] comes running to the net and says, 'The linesman called it out, he called it out.' But what can you do? But I really was furious.''

"There was nothing you *could* do?''

"No, not then. Nothing.''

"The other night, when I was playing near La Costa, Bobby Riggs called the last shot out when it was in. Both his wife and I were mad as hell.''

At that she went "Hah!'' and her voice, which reminded me of Molly's voice on the old radio show, "Fibber McGee and Molly,'' broke into a prolonged chuckle. She absolutely cackled.

"Sometimes,'' she said, getting serious again, "players make calls the way they really wanted them. It could go either way, but they call them the way they would want them to be. I never really worried about calls because I always thought that they evened up one way or the other. You never want to do anything to disturb the concentration.''

"What would be your toughest singles match?''

"I would think that long one that I won against Broughie in the third set, 15–13, at Forest Hills in 1948."

"How about ladies' doubles matches?"

"We really had straight set matches. I cannot think of a tough one. Not now."

"But the mixed doubles would be easy—the Talbert match?"

"Yes. That was the toughest I played in mixed doubles or any doubles."

"I suppose it is impossible for you to pick the best woman tennis player of all time?"

"Oh, that's tough, but you would have to put Alice Marble up there. And then there was Mo Connolly. I thought that she was a good tennis player but not a complete tennis player. I think the same of Chrissie Evert. I like her very much, but she doesn't have a complete game. She has a fantastic record, but it is mostly on clay."

"What would be wrong with Maureen Connelly's game? Where was she weak?"

"She didn't have a volley. She stayed mostly on the back court. But apparently so did Helen Wills. They say she could stand on the baseline and pound the ball forever."

Margaret mentioned that her son was born in 1952, and she took time off, and then we went back to her long career of winning, first in 1941, and then for the last time in 1962 with Neale Fraser—"which was the first time either one of us had won the mixed doubles at Wimbledon."

I asked her how she had kept fit for so long.

"I have never smoked, and I didn't drink until I got married in 1947. We didn't drink during the tournaments. We had a 'tennis season' then. It didn't go year-round."

"So you retired after your son was born?"

"Yes."

"Then that explains how Doris Hart and Shirley Fry slip into the picture. You win ten years in a row. Hart and Fry win four years in a row, and then you come out of retirement and win again with Louise for three more years, straight."

At that she cackled again, and I asked her about God.

She said that she believed in God in a general sense but was not a churchgoer, although she had been baptized in the Episcopal church. She said, "So many tournaments are played on Sunday, you know," and we both laughed because it was so true. The finals were always on the Sabbath. It would be easy to lose the habit of church, even assuming you had it, once becoming a contender.

"If you had your life to live over again, would you make any changes?"

"I don't think so. I am very happy with my life. I always looked forward to the next step, so to speak. When I was in junior high school, I always looked forward to high school, to the next year and the next year. I was always optimistic, always looking forward."

"If you had a characteristic about you that might have made you a champion, would you say optimism?"

"I would say concentration and hard work. I was an optimist in that when I went into a tournament, I never expected to lose, but when I did lose, I would learn something from it."

"How long have you lived out here?"

"Since 1966."

So four years after winning Wimbledon for the last time, she moved to El Paso with her friend, Margaret Varner, and settled in. She settled in an old section of El Paso near the Rio Grande, near enough to have a drainage canal cut through their property, where water sluices in from the famous river for irrigation. Years back this was cotton country, and "there are cotton patches dotting the area, but the area is being built up now, which is too bad."

"But what did you come to El Paso for [as nice as it appeared to be]?"

"A lot of people ask me that. But this was Margaret Varner's hometown. She had been working with my family. My husband wanted someone to be a guide to our son's education. He had been married before, and he knew he couldn't do it. His four children from that marriage had been sadly neglected in their education. So we both knew Margaret through tennis,* and she was taken on to work with our son.

"I didn't like the East after Will passed away, but I stayed back there two years after our divorce. I had stayed back there because he wanted to see our son, but after two years, I couldn't wait to get away. There was no reason to stay on with him gone. And I didn't want to go back to California because there are too many people out there. I just love it here. When I came here in 1966, the population was about 350,000. Now it's over 500,000."

"Then, to get this straight, you live here with Margaret, and your son, whom she tutored,** must be grown up by now. Where is he?"

"He lives in Lexington, Kentucky, and is married and has a boy almost four now, and is a commercial horse breeder. He is really into it—the thoroughbred horse industry. Margaret and I have just a small operation. We have

---

* Margaret won the junior doubles in 1944 and 1945 with Jean Doyle. Their team followed Doris Hart and Shirley Fry, champions in 1943. Margaret Osborne was both a singles and doubles winner in 1936.
** Margaret Varner has a master's degree. When I met her, I met a woman who could star in the old TV show "Bonanza." She wore tight Levis and looked as if she could twirl a lariat and run a bunkhouse full of cowhands.

a dozen brood mares, and we raise them four miles from here toward town in New Mexico."

"Was your mother the major influence on your life?"

"Probably. She would take me around to all those junior tournaments."

"Would you agree that when you have at least one strong parent, you get a sense of confidence from that person that spills over and maybe gives you a sense of confidence in yourself to become greater than you might be?"

It was a long question that was part of my need to understand how some people rise to a championship level; especially now when you can have two parents working or a single parent working, and children grow up without that enthusiastic push from above. I guess I was getting at the importance of parents and thinking of my own father, who never pushed me toward anything. Yet I revered him, but wished he'd been more directive.

"Yes," she said, answering my belabored remarks. "It is bound to spill over to you. My mother had confidence in me and I felt it." (Somewhat like Louise Brough, who was afraid to lose because of her mother, the young Margaret Osborne was aware that her mother had high hopes and that she wasn't being driven around to so many tournaments just to burn gasoline.)

"What about McEnroe? He has his father on the scene, watching in the stands."

"I admire his tennis, but I do not like his actions on the court."

"Are they detrimental to tennis?"

"Yes."

"Isn't there a sense of decorum that is important because if there is no referee, then tennis is a game that depends on honesty. You can't play against someone who will cheat, and making obscene gestures could give you the idea that this is the kind of guy who could break the rules, break the code."

"Yes, etiquette and decorum are important."

"What about wearing whites instead of these new crazy patterns or uniforms they wear?"

"I always liked pastels myself, and I always liked the whites. I thought they looked so nice . . ."

"Especially when you are tanned . . ."

"Yes." She laughed and appeared to be rolling back into another era, her laughter modulated by memory, her kind face full of care for people and places that she had known.

"What about television? Do you have any regrets that they didn't have television covering your matches?"

"I am glad they didn't, because had there been TV, I would have to give all those press interviews."

"But aren't you kind of sad that you don't have any recognition now? You came before television, and no one knows you. Are you known in El Paso?"

"Oh, yes."

"But I mean, if you called to make a reservation . . . well, if Chrissie Evert called, they would know who she is."

"Oh, that's right. They would know, all right."

"So fame is not a big thing with you. You just knew you were good."

"Yes. But I enjoyed the playing and the travel, limited though it was. I never went to the Italian championships or to Australia, and I never played on the Riviera. I did play the French championships five times."

"How did you do?"

"I won it twice, but don't ask me how. Pauline and I were the two girls and Tom Brown and Budge Patty were the two men who were sent over by the United States Tennis Association in 1946. I remember that Pauline had me at match point, but I won the match. She had beaten Broughie in the finals at Wimbledon."

"But I thought the French championships came *before* Wimbledon?"

"They do now, but not then."

For the record, Margaret, in 1946, won the women's singles and the women's doubles, playing with "Broughie," not Pauline. The mixed doubles were won by Pauline Betz and Budge Patty. Neither Patty nor Brown won a men's title, those events going to the Europeans, Marcel Bernard and Yvon Petra.

I changed the subject again. I asked her how long she had been married to Will duPont.

"We were married in 1947, and I divorced him in 1964."

"He must have been a great tennis enthusiast."

"Yes, he was. He was very charming, but he couldn't get along with his contemporaries in the business world. Alice Marble and Mary K. Browne were very good friends, and he just enjoyed the younger generation coming to his home, and he played with them, of course, as well as watching them play, and it was wonderful because we were able to get grass court practice before the grass court season."

"What about the weather? Didn't it rain a lot in Wilmington?"

"Very seldom."

"So you would get the practice in?"

"Yes."

Thinking of the duPont estate in Wilmington, I asked her if tennis has an image problem of being a country club sport.

"People always say that, but I wonder. I grew up on public courts and so did so many others, Alice Marble and Helen Hull Jacobs, as examples."

"Billy Talbert comes to mind. He started out playing, not in a country club, but found through tennis that he could get pretty far and one guesses he has been on the country club scene for many years."

"Billy worked for my husband once," she said. "Billy said, 'All he will do is let me lick stamps,' so that was the end of that." Once again she laughed and cackled and I could see her flash back to the days of Will duPont and Billy Talbert and the fun it must have been for a young woman—especially with the incredible and world-famous Alice Marble on the premises.

"What do you do with your leisure time?" I asked her. "You have books on bookshelves here in the living room. Do you read a lot?"

"Leisure time!" she said, and laughed again as if to say, "What leisure time?"

"Do you still play tennis?"

"I don't think I'll ever play anymore. I hurt my knee about five or six years ago and later when I tried to play, I couldn't get around the court the way I was used to, and I never had the willpower to take off the weight [that she put on while her knee was healing], and now I have so much interest in the horse business. Anyway, I still keep up with tennis and do administrative work, which I have done for years. As I said, I used to be the secretary treasurer of the Northern California Tennis Association, and then Will wouldn't allow me to do anything, even though I did write a few articles on tennis, and then when I moved out here, they asked me to be the vice-president of the Southwestern Tennis Association, which I did for about ten or twelve years."

"So when I say how do you keep busy, it is the horse business. You have this property here with horses and a bicycle track and acres to look after plus another ranch where you breed thoroughbreds. What about the Kentucky Derby?"

"Oh, we all hope for that."

"Can I see your horse farm?"

"Yes, I'll take you there, if you want . . ."

At which time, I was swept off. We went on an extensive tour of her property by the house and later to her ranch, or "horse farm," as she calls it. I asked her about her social life and she said she had never been a social person, but, yes, the university had grown (the University of Texas—El Paso), and it is more social now.

"But," I said, "you must have had a social life, married to Will duPont."

"Not really. Just the bare necessities that he had to go to, like the National Horse Show in New York. I went with him to a General Motors meeting *once* [duPont de Nemours, the family-owned duPont Company, was a major holder of General Motors stock, but it was broken up in a famous anti-trust case] and . . .''

"But the tennis social life. That must have been something."

"Those years that I was a champion, we went to Forest Hills, and we had to make an 8:30 train back to Wilmington that night. So we never had a party or a celebration—win, lose, or draw—ha! [She laughs delightfully, but her laughter is full of pathos]. Win, lose, or draw, we had to board that train and go back to Wilmington."

"To give him the benefit of the doubt, he sounds like a very eccentric human being."

"A friend of mine said that he was the most interesting character he had ever met. He could be perfectly good to people. He certainly was good to a lot of tennis players. He had three grass courts, one cement court, and two Har-tru courts, *and* two indoor Har-tru courts."

Indeed, as she spoke, I said to myself that this man, Will duPont, is taking on the whole West Coast. He has built himself a complex of tennis courts so that Eastern players have a chance to play in the winter—in the off-season. They would not be rusty when May came around, and the flashy Californians who had not missed a day of tennis would not have that overwhelming edge. But I wondered about Will duPont. Imagine taking your wife who has just won the singles championship of the nation and putting her on an 8:30 train to Wilmington, Delaware! What glory would there be in a Pullman car? The toasts would be made back at the West Side Tennis Club and Margaret *would not* be there. He *was* good to tennis players but indifferent to the best of all the women, his own wife. It was a hard irony to struggle with, to assimilate.

Walking around her "spread," as they call it down there, we talked about the duPonts and Margaret said that Will's closest cousin was a *third* cousin. Again, the mystery of Will duPont. What about siblings and *first* cousins? She did not pursue this obvious line of thought.

We dropped the subject of the duPonts and then went on to Margaret's plan to return to the hundredth anniversary of women's tennis at Wimbledon (she, a seven-time winner). It is a big year for the women. All who can are returning. And Margaret Osborne duPont will be there.

There is nothing much I can add to this. As I have written, she showed me her horse farm, and I saw a beautiful, spindly-legged foal and a mare that Margaret treated the way you would treat a rose petal that was about to fall. She is very gentle and very sweet and self-deprecating and in love with her life in El Paso. We had to send the cabdriver, who was on call to pick me up, away. She insisted that she drive me around the great ridges of the town and to her farm and to my hotel.

At the end, I left her grinning and smiling, and if the word "genuine" has any bearing on human beings, it rests with her. A special woman with a good life. I flew away in the morning, knowing that I had been touched by the genuine article. Margaret Osborne from Joseph, Oregon. From Spokane. From the public courts of San Francisco. Then Will duPont. And *all* those victories! She just drove me around and, I swear, she did not want me to leave. Her kindness made me like El Paso. Her house was right across from the El Paso Country Club, and I fancied myself playing tennis there. Her charm was such, I began to think the unthinkable: moving to Texas.

CHAPTER

24

Bobby Riggs:

"He's pretty slick and you really don't have a chance,
although we all thought we did."

Ellsworth Vines,
in a letter to the author

Bobby Riggs is the kind of guy you would want for your brother-in-law. He'd be ideal. You wouldn't want him living in the house, but you'd want him to be available. You could say to him, "Hey, Bobby. How about a game?" or, "Hey, Bobby! When you're in Florida, let me know. I want to get in on it,"—whatever "it" is. He is the kind of guy you love dearly but wouldn't want to live with—day after day, forever. But, then again, on reflection, maybe you would. He is a miracle. It would be tough to live with a miracle, but maybe it would be worth it . . . on balance.

I loved being with Bobby Riggs. I say this because he was a one-day "happy hour" of horseplay and good times and money. He was a compatriot in high jinks who knew exactly what I was doing and sympathized with it. But beyond all of that, I want to say at the start that he is truly a warm and friendly man. He would give you the shirt off his back and then hustle it back again. But he *would* give you the shirt off his back. Probably a genius, surely a rogue, he is undoubtedly a great champion, admired even by his supposed enemies, but I had yet to meet one. The great Bobby Riggs is in a class by himself.

I spent the night in a motel near La Costa, just outside of San Diego. In the morning, I called the La Costa Resort Hotel and Spa and asked for a room and got one. As for Riggs, he is an odd-looking man with no taste in clothes. He wears a "Caterpillar Tractor" hat, which looks like hell on a tennis court.

The cap does not say "Caterpillar," but says "Sugar Daddy," which is some kind of candy bar he is sponsoring. He has a scruffy hairdo of no style and wears horn-rimmed glasses. He would look like your normal, everyday gas station attendant if he were not one of the great schemers and athletes in sport. And he wears sweatpants on the tennis court. All that I was to see within an hour.

I took a cab to La Costa, checked in, and immediately went to the tennis shop, where I hoped to get a line on Riggs. A line on Riggs! He was due in three minutes, they told me, to play a match on Segura's court, which is elevated and so named because that is where the great Pancho gives his lessons, often no doubt to celebrities from Hollywood. So I waited and met one of Riggs' opponents, who said he would pass the word that I was waiting. Riggs, himself, came into the clubhouse and was out on the court before I could say, "Don Budge."

I watched him play in his crazy hat and in those gray sweatpants, and I thought I was going to be in trouble. An eccentric like Riggs just might not want to hang around with another eccentric like me. Sometimes a mixture like that gets too rich. But how would he know that, I thought, and then turned my attention to a woman of such outlandish charm that I lost track of Rigg's match. For an hour, I listened to the tales of a woman surely in her late sixties named Roxie Turpin.

In one way she appeared to be the Tallulah Bankhead of the tennis world—a woman who punctuated every sentence with the word "dahlin'." She would say, "Now, I have known Bobby dahlin' for years, dahlin', and he just looks awful, dahlin', the way he dresses, dahlin'," and then she would call over to a passerby and say, "Hello, dahlin'. I am talking to a man about a book he's writing, dahlin', and I'll be with you in a minute, dahlin'." Apparently she had played a good deal of tennis in her day and had played with the best of them. She is a close friend of Alice Marble, close enough to be asked to accompany the great champion to Wimbledon for the anniversary celebration of women's tennis. But she sounded very reticent. She said in effect that she was worried about Alice's temper, which I have already described. She said she was eating spaghetti with her once, and Alice Marble took her whole plate of spaghetti and threw it at her because of something she said. "Dahlin', and there I was with spaghetti in my hair and spaghetti sauce running down my face, dahlin', and can you believe that?"

She was laughing when she told me that story, and I was laughing with her. I bought her a sandwich while we sat and watched for Bobby Riggs to end his game. She said that she was director of tennis at La Costa, and when I said that I had been spurned by Pancho Segura, she looked at me in a confidential way and said that Pancho was vain. Moments later Segura walked into the room, and I avoided an introduction because I knew he would not be happy to

408

see me. He would think that I had come all the way to La Costa against his wishes, so I backed off. I was told that he was very tired and would not do anything that day. He had just flown in from Ecuador. (He had told me on the phone that he was going to Europe. Another person told me he was in Lima, Peru, but what I heard from Roxie was that he had been in Ecuador and had returned home very tired.) He was just checking in to look over his schedule. Burt Bacharach was coming over, and there was talk of a game, but not with Segura. They would play on Segura's court, however, and he nodded his approval. Riggs, now at the end of his match, drew no attention from Segura, tanned and handsome, who just strode from the small lounge and then disappeared. He had an hauteur that was obvious. Probably considered one of the best teaching pros in the world and a man who had risen to great heights on the professional circuit, a three-time intercollegiate champion during the war, he stood within the confines of his club like a god. I stayed clear and listened to Roxie talk about getting spaghetti, dahlin', all over her face. If Segura were vain, it didn't seem to matter.

And then there was Riggs, who Roxie said "looked silly ever since he dyed his hair blond." She went on to say that both Riggs and she had taken lessons from the famous coach Eleanor "Teach" Tennant and seemed proud of the fact. However, later I was to learn that all was not rosy with Teach Tennant and her pupils. Margaret Osborne duPont subsequently told me that when Teach came down to southern California to coach Maureen Connolly (a San Diego native) there was much consternation. Indeed, Gianni Clerici in *The Ultimate Tennis Book* wrote of how they had to get the venerable Perry Jones to fly over to Wimbledon to smooth things over between Mrs. Connolly, Maureen, and Teach—the latter two at odds. The impression I drew was that the tennis community in southern California was fearful that the authoritarian Teach would do more harm than good to the great and very young Maureen Connolly. Teach Tennant may have not been a popular woman, but she coached Maureen Connolly, who won the grand slam of tennis, and the incomparable Alice Marble. A figure in the background of tennis, she remains to this writer an elusive woman, someone who knew what she was doing and perhaps made people angry because of her insistence upon doing it well.

At the end of our conversation Roxie told me another story about Ted Schroeder that I will have to reiterate from memory. Apparently Ted had been lured from retirement to play in the Alan King Pro-Celebrity Tournament in Las Vegas (or maybe Palm Springs), and as is his custom he rose to the occasion and won it. When he was presented with his winner's check— standing before the crowd of spectators he said, "I thank you very much for this check. I think I will donate it all to charity." Repeating Schroeder's remarks brought great guffaws from Roxie Turpin. "Now, if you know Ted you

409

know that charity . . . my eye! But Ted can say the damndest things and with a straight face. He is one of a kind," she said with affection. "And then later he comes down here to La Costa."

I wanted to let her go on but suddenly Riggs, who had sat down for a soda, looked like he might be getting up to leave and I had to move quickly to see him at once. He was scruffy-looking and in a state of disarray as he checked the time, finishing his soft drink. He was hurrying on to his next endeavor. I approached him and said that I had talked with his wife, and that was good enough for him. "Come on," he said. "I am going to play golf up at the El Niguel Country Club." There was no time for him to lunch, and I doubt that he *ever* has time to lunch. A whizzbang of energy, we walked hurriedly to his Lincoln and I met his wife, who had driven over to say good-bye. She warned me about Bobby's driving and indicated that I was taking a chance. I found out later what she meant. Because he is a nonstop talker, there was little evidence that he concentrated on the road, and in fact, we did get lost trying to find the country club. Miriam Riggs is much younger than Bobby and is short and energetic herself and nice-looking. She has a smiling face and a bright personality, and I felt that with her as my ally, the great Riggs would become my friend. Indeed, he did. We drove away, and I waved at my new pal, Miriam Riggs.

We drove for miles and miles into Nixon territory (San Clemente) and off into the wilds somewhere south of Los Angeles. All the while, my tape recorder was picking up Riggs' comments, but because he is slightly deaf, I had to yell at him. He didn't seem to mind my yelling, and about halfway to El Niguel, he told me I was a damn fool to spend $130 a night at La Costa when I could stay at his house for nothing. Of course, that had never occurred to me. I had never once thought of asking one of my Wimbledon winners to put me up. Looking back on it, I suppose there were a few whom I could have imposed on. I think Margaret duPont might have given me a guest room, and so might Gardnar Mulloy—not because we were great buddies, but because he loves to talk of the old days and get his version on record. I think Kramer would have given me a room as well—he, the dean of American tennis. And maybe Gussie Moran. But I was flattered to hear Riggs, who had barely met me, offer me a room in his home. Of course, I had already checked in and declined his offer.

And so it was to be a golf game, and I would have the great opportunity of observing a Riggs' hustle. What he had done in the morning on Segura's court I'm still unsure of. But by his grinning and full-of-beans personality, there is no question that he had won a small bundle. That is my impression, and I could be wrong, but I know they were not out there in the hot sun playing for fun, and Riggs was happy. But getting back to golf. He wanted me to go around the course with him, sharing his cart, and let the tape recorder go on and on. I said the hell with that. I was wearing tennis clothes and had brought my racquet. Golf and I do not get along, and a man named Sam Murad, who is president of a company called A.V.C. Specialists, was one of the fivesome that was to play. Riggs introduced me to him as his friend, and Murad then gave me guest privileges—not only to the golf club but its neighbor, the Laguna Niguel Racquet Club. I could loll about all afternoon, eat and drink and relax and perhaps play tennis while Bobby was on the course, whizzing about in his golf cart. Sam Murad had come to me as an angel. I had two private clubs to use at will—he had said just to sign his name.

And that is how the afternoon went. I had a sandwich and a beer and then walked over to the Laguna Niguel Racquet Club and introduced myself. Because it was hot and midafternoon, there was no one to play with. However, the professional, a handsome young man named Bob Bernstein, was on hand, and I hired him for an hour. We rallied for a bit and then played three sets, which (naturally) he won. But the stroking was good, and I felt pretty proud because Riggs had promised me a game later that night and I had tuned up pretty well. I knew that with Riggs there would be money on the line, and I wanted to win, yet somehow deep inside, I wanted to lose. I wanted to fall victim to his hustle. I could not pay Bob Bernstein in cash—club rules—so I signed Sam Murad's name.

57. Bobby Riggs

Meanwhile, Riggs was out there on the course, and it was getting on toward 5:30, and I was now without friend or foe. I was alone wandering about El Niguel, and so I said to myself, "I will just wander down the fairway and find Riggs and ride along with him."

Indeed. I had been watched for hours by various security people, who did not know if I were for real. It could be I was just using Sam Murad's name and having a field day. So as I strode down the fairway, a man in a golf cart wearing a uniform rode up to me and said, "We've been watching you. What are you doing here? You are not a member."

I said that I was a friend of Bobby Riggs. That was a terrible mistake because I should have said I was a friend of Sam Murad. Riggs was not a member, and the guard in the golf cart had never heard of him. "Riggs?" he said, and then I had to explain who Bobby Riggs was. He directed me into the golf cart and told me that should we find Murad and if it were true that I was his guest, then everything would be okay. Otherwise, I would have some explaining to do. And off we went, like Germans in a motorcycle with a side car, riding through the fields of France. We just steamed along, crisscrossing fairways, and then I said, "There he is. It's Bobby Riggs!" The trouble was that Bobby was relieving himself behind a tree, and the guard looked sternly and forcefully at the great Riggs taking a pee. As we tooled up to him, Sam Murad came around from his side of the fairway and clarified matters. They were now on the 16th hole. I told Sam that I had racked up a number of charges to his name, and he said, "Forget it . . . you're my guest." The guard appeared astounded by this remark and drove off, wondering what it would be like to be rich. I could feel his mind turn.

"So you're a tennis fanatic?" says Riggs as I hopped into his cart.

"Yes, I guess I am," I answered, but he cut me off.

"For these last three holes, you are going to be a golfer. I am down a lot."

So I became his caddy, and prior to making his approach shot to the 16th green, he asked me what club he should use. He was on the side of the fairway in the rough, and I said, "Take the three iron," and he used a four iron and was short. He looked at me oddly, as though he was beginning to suspect that I might know something, and because the other players were spread over the course, he salvaged the hole with a good chip shot and then sank his putt. It was possible, he told me, that if everything clicked on the last two holes, he could come back from a certain deficit to a gain. He asked me what to do. I said, "Bobby, it's just like playing doubles. You drive it down the middle and split them up. Keep your head down and concentrate." So Riggs pounced on the tee and drove one about 220 yards right down the middle. "Nice drive, Bobby," they all said, and sure enough, the other players were in trouble, their long drives hooking and slicing. Riggs parred out and then parred the 18th, and suddenly he was a rich man. Within three holes, he made about

412

$800, but I have no knowledge of how the betting went. All I know is that he was about $500 down when I joined him, and he ended with a $300 profit. It was far too complicated for me, yet Riggs was ecstatic and led us all into the locker room for a round of beers. "Best game I ever had," he said. "Best time I ever had. Great golf, great golf," he said, talking like a baseball manager whose team had just won the World Series.

By the time we left El Niguel, it was after 7:00, and the sky was beginning to turn gray. I was wondering about tennis and I knew that Bobby Riggs had yet to eat. But that would be no problem since he uses a court that has lights, and when he is enthusiastic, food is the last thing on his mind. We would play at night and on the way back in his Lincoln he worked out the handicap. Riggs had won the "sixty-fives" title on grass, clay, indoor and hard court and thus was the best player in the world for his age on all surfaces. I had made the mistake of telling him that before I hurt my knee I had taken two games from Gardnar Mulloy. My second mistake was to tell him that I had played Louise Brough even and that Bob Falkenburg and I had had a good time of it, although he had easily beat me. But I paraphrased Falkenburg when I said that last year I would have taken him. I could sense that Riggs was becoming a bit concerned. He knew that I had given a check for $40 to Sam Murad against Murad's wishes ("You are my guest. I can't take that . . ."), and that half of the money was for a tennis lesson with Bob Bernstein. So Riggs was thinking about the handicap he was going to give me, and as we drove, it got lower and lower, until at the end, it was meaningless, as I will soon explain. In the meantime, he talked and I picked up some interesting information from the man I had been waiting months to meet.

"So Falkenburg is trying to get back into the game, for the pure joy of it, for the sheer fun of it? He wants to be a competitor again?"

"I would think so," I answered.

"You think he wants to play in the senior tournaments?"

"If someone asked him, he might say 'yes.' "

"For the sheer joy of the game," said Bobby Riggs, and then he told me that Jack Kramer had a ninety-nine-year lease on a golf course in Chino, California. "It's out that way where they have dairy farms and a jail," said Bobby. "I only played it once, and it is a damn good course. Jack and I are great friends and grew up together. He was a boy champion when I was a junior champion."

I could see that names were going to fall from his mouth and that there would not be an orderly progression of thought. I had the idea that I had better step in and give some form to our conversation.

"In 1939 you won Wimbledon in singles and the men's doubles with Elwood Cooke. You also won the mixed doubles with Alice Marble. Has any other man won all three titles in the same year?"

"Not on their first try. I think Budge has done it and maybe some others, but I am the only one to do it on my first attempt at Wimbledon. [Indeed, Don Budge won the triple crown in both 1937 and 1938.] I think Sedgman did it too," he added. Then he became irritated. "Hell, you talked with Budge, didn't you?"

"Sure," I replied.

"Then you know that he won all three titles. But I bet he didn't tell you about the $100,000 match he lost to me."

"No, he didn't," I said in awe.

"It was in 1947 in the finals for the United States Professional Championship. I refer to that as the $100,000 match against Don Budge. You see," he was saying as the Lincoln was zooming down the highway, "you see, Wilson had Budge under contract, and they had me, and it was a foregone conclusion that Kramer was going to turn pro. So they were promoting the tournaments: they promoted the Perry-Vines tour, the Budge-Perry tour, and we were all with Wilson. So we knew—Budge knew and I knew—that who won this match would get the Wilson tour against Kramer, and Budge was a fantastic player. He had the working press behind him, and nobody could figure out my game. I was a tactician and a little bit of a mystery. Budge had the strokes. So we both knew that this match was to see who was going to play Kramer, who was just about to sign with Wilson. Now I had clearly outdistanced Budge by this time. I beat him in 1946 and already had beaten him in 1947, but he was so well known and had such a fantastic record and such a following that Wilson would prefer him over me. Wilson wanted *him* to play Kramer. But I won. I would play Kramer, and I will never forget it. I won in the fifth set, 6–4, one of the most memorable of all my matches. It was a hot, muggy day on the grass at Forest Hills. Now Budge could hit shots all over the place, and he is risking everything playing me. The winner gets $100,000 and the loser goes home and sits on his ass and gets nothing. And that is what happened. I played Budge in this one great match with all the stakes on it. It was one of the proudest moments in my life. I was able to stay in there and beat him in this clutch match. I had beaten Budge all over, but none of that meant anything. What counted was that the guy who wins this match gets to play Kramer, and that is the $100,000 payroll. You see?"

"Yes," I said, overcome by his words that came at me like tracer bullets. He has a gravelly voice and an ack-ack approach to talking. Shots seem to come from his soul, which seems like a munitions factory. To put it mildly, Bobby Riggs can get excited.

"Another highlight in my life was when Kramer *did* turn pro in December 1947, and we met at the old Madison Square Garden. There were twenty-six inches of snow on the ground, but 16,000 people still came to the match. They all wanted to see Jack Kramer, Wimbledon winner, Davis Cup hero, and U.S. champion, play Riggs. They saw me as a crafty player, but with Kramer and his 'big game,' he would blast me off the court. Now, there were a few people who knew me inside, but not many, so I was able to make a few side bets, and I defeated Jack in four sets *in his debut.* You didn't ask Jack about that?"

"I can't recall. I don't think so."

"He wouldn't want to talk about his debut against me."

Then I asked him a silly question I had been dying to ask. "Did you really go to the University of Miami?"

"I had an interview with Mulloy, and briefly I did go there. I went down after the nationals in late September. They had promised me a good job and all kinds of spending money, and I would play for their team. So I went down there and damn! It was so hot and muggy that you didn't even feel like going on a court. I was used to California weather, and I didn't even like to practice, so I would run over to the beach and go swimming all the time, and I didn't like school or homework. I was no student. And they didn't give me any money or anything, and I played Mulloy in a tournament and beat him, and he didn't like being a number two guy."

"But was he still in college then?"

"He was just getting out of college. He was out of college, but was recruiting and was the coach. So I found this young freshman, who turned out to be a damn good player named Harris Everett, and we took off and played an exhibition in Houston for $50 and blew out all the tires in his car, and I asked him back to California to stay with me. He then goes on to the University of North Carolina, where he beat Seixas all the time. He's a damn good senior player now. And anyway I was beating Mulloy's ass, and he didn't like it much."

I asked Bobby if it were true that his first hustle was when he went to the president of Miami University and told him that he would go around the world for four years playing tennis and winning tournaments in exchange for a diploma.

"This is just one of the Bobby Riggs' stories you're going to hear. It is pure mythology. I never even met the president. I didn't even know his name. I made $500 from different tournaments around the country—hell, Jack Kramer blew the whistle on me and wrote that I was a paid amateur. I was surprised at that because he was Perry T. Jones' fair-haired boy, and he shouldn't have exposed us. In spite of all that, he stayed in good graces with most of the amateurs, although I think some of the international fellows gave him a battle.

"Budge and Mako and Falkenburg and Kramer and I and Ted Schroeder all came out of the same kind of mold. We had thirteen-and-under tournaments, fifteen-and-under tournaments, good weather in southern California;

58. Riggs at his prime playing at the Westchester Country Club

we could see the good players play, the competition was good. At our age levels, we were the best in the country."

"Where were you born?"

"Los Angeles."

I was still yelling at him as he powered along, his car trying to strain its way back before the lights went out, so to speak, all over town. It was late. I was panicked that he would say, "The hell with tennis," and would want to eat dinner with his wife and probably me, but no tennis. By now we would need lights. Where were the courts—at La Costa? No, right behind his house, he said, but I still fretted.

"Who were your heroes?" I screamed at him.

"Heroes?"

"As a kid, did you have heroes?"

"Heroes?" (As if to say, "Are *you* crazy?")

"I mean, did you have any idols?"

"I was born with good health," he said. "I never had a hero. I had a good body that was agile and wiry and was born into a family with older brothers and sisters, into a climate that was wonderful, where all my brothers were interested in sports—football, basketball, baseball—all kinds. In my earliest memory at about four years old, I was in competition. I was playing marbles with the kids next door."

As he said that, I thought of the bridge-playing Don McNeill at Vero Beach, recalling how he and Bobby would lag for coins against the curb of a sidewalk.

"I was playing touch and tackle football with little kids my own age. I was playing baseball and basketball and going to the athletic events at the Colosseum with my brothers. They entered me into everything and always made me competitive. 'Bobby has always got to race this kid. Run around the block—give him twenty yards, ten yards. Put the gloves on and box this guy,' and that was how I was raised. I was always playing against someone in some sport."

"Where did you go to high school?"

"High school? I am talking about five, six, seven, eight years old. Okay. High school. I went to Franklin High School in Highland Park, to be exact. I was state tennis champion for three years in a row. I don't think that has been done too often. Not in California. Kramer won it as a sophomore, lost it as a junior, and won it back as a senior. So he had a chance to do it, but he got upset in his junior year."

I was trying to remember who had upset Kramer. It was either Ted Olewine or the sensational badminton champion named David Freeman. But I knew I would never go back to Kramer's long conversation and get it straight. It was one or the other, I thought, as Riggs went on, rat-a-tat, rat-a-tat.

"What about your parents?"

"My father was a preacher. I went to church every Sunday until I was playing tennis in the thirteen-and-under, and I had to play the finals at 9:00 in the morning on a Sunday."

"What was your father's denomination?"

"The Church of Christ. Their main headquarters was in Nashville, Tennessee. Pepperdine College is a Church of Christ. Abilene Christian College is a Church of Christ."

"What is the Church of Christ?"

"It's a small church. They believe, literally, everything that the Bible says. No loose translations."

"What about bad habits?"

"I never smoked except an occasional cigar. When I was a big businessman and was bored, you know, I used to light up a big Monte Cristo cigar—same as Kramer. It's what you would call being an occasional smoker. You play poker now and then or go to a big banquet, and we might take a cigar, see?"

"What about after beating Margaret Smith and then going on all those talk shows as you waited for Billie Jean King. Did you keep in training? I was told that you didn't."

"Well . . . ah. I wouldn't say that I didn't train, but I *did* take her lightly, and I didn't think she had a chance to win. I gave Billie Jean two chances—slim and none. But I knew that the indoor carpet that she liked would favor the net player. The quicker player would get to the ball quicker. I knew that, but I was so confident that I didn't think it would make any difference to me. She might win a couple of more games than Margaret, but you know . . ."

"Well, you . . ."

"I will say this. I was way overconfident. I overestimated my powers at the time, and I underestimated hers. Now, when you do that in any competitive event, it is a big mistake. So I played on her best surface and on my worst surface, and those factors all combined, and they made the difference."

"But did you train?" I was yelling again, louder than usual, because Alice Marble (who has a great affection for Riggs) had made a point of that omission on his part—that he didn't train!

"No, I won't blame it on that. I was overconfident. My training habits were in good shape. She caught me completely by surprise, and in a lifetime playing for big money in important tournaments, I have a supremely good record. Now, one of my biggest disappointments was in the 1939 Davis Cup. I beat Bromwich [6–2, 6–3, 6–3], and I have to play Quist. Quist is supposed to be worse than Bromwich and Parker, whom I can beat, had beaten Quist. I am better than Parker, and I had beaten Quist the year before in the 1938 Davis Cup, and I have to say that this was one of the few times in a big match that I came out flat. It's like Nolan Ryan without his fastball. I was like a baseball pitcher who didn't have his stuff. So I played Quist, and I played scared. I wasn't loose. I was tensed up. I was afraid to play. All I could do was hit the ball back. Quist would come to the net, and I was afraid to pass him. So I lobbed, and Quist is a good doubles player, and he ran me from pillar to post, from pillar to post. I didn't have my fastball. I didn't have my curve. All I could do was hit the ball right on his racquet and hope for an error, and he is too good for that, but *even with all of that,* he only beat me 6–4 in the fifth set.''

Somewhere out there was LaCosta and Riggs' home in Leucadia, and I could get out of all of this. I was suddenly fed up with talk and wanted to play Riggs, and by now I had heard the stories. I remember that I had heard stories about Tilden back at the Rockaway Hunting Club in October. I was going batty with stories about tennis matches. I was a player, not an oral historian. But there was no stopping Riggs.

"And I played another match similar to that, in 1936, against Johnny Van Ryn, a good doubles player. I got locked in again. I lobbed him every ball, and I lost.

"Looking back to 1939, what should have happened is that after I slaughtered Bromwich, Parker and I should have played the doubles, not Kramer and Joe Hunt. We would have lost, but I would have been hot to take on Quist, and that would have won it for us. Instead, Kramer and Hunt play and lose, and I got a day of rest, which was the big mistake. By losing in the doubles, Frank and I would have said that we were not so hot after all. I would not have been complacent. Because we did not play the doubles, my day off killed me.''

"How about the top players of all time?"

"I would say Vines and Budge, Kramer, Pancho Gonzales, and maybe Laver.''

"What about you?"

"If I had to rank only five . . . well . . .''

"What about Tilden?"

"I would rank Tilden alone. He is B.C. The others are A.D. You don't rank him. Damn, it's B.C. and A.D. In the Tilden era, who was there? Only Tilden. Only Tilden.''

But I persisted in my thoughts that Riggs, himself, was one of the great players. He had beaten everyone but Tilden, who came before his time, and if they did play an exhibition (which I am sure they did), it would hardly count. The intriguing fact was that Riggs had Budge's number after the war. Riggs had Budge's number, and they are not too much apart in age—three years? So I asked him again where he would place himself.

"Oh, maybe sixth," he admitted.

"Not ahead of Gonzales?"

"No. Gonzales and Kramer had the big serve and volley. You have to have that. Vines had it too but seldom used it. Budge did not. He tried to learn the serve and volley but couldn't do it. He didn't have the tactics. His shot had too big a flow, and he was ready to come in after the first early ball or short return, but not on the ball in the air. So did Perry."

"But what about Hoad?"

"Hoad had a two-year record. I can't rank a two-year record. He got injured. He had a chance at the grand slam but got beaten by Laver in the fourth set. He had a good head-to-head tour with Gonzales, but other than that, I don't see Hoad."

"How about the best doubles teams?"

"Doubles. Let's see. A lot of people will disagree with me, but I would rank Kramer and Schroeder very high. I would also rank Sedgman and McGregor very high. Now statistics-wise, you can make a case for Bromwich, which the Australians always do. But I saw it and was there, and I still can't believe it."

"What about Stoefen and Lott?"

"I know everyone picks them, but I can't buy it."

"Then who would you pick as your ideal doubles player?"

"Don Budge. We beat Kramer and Segura in a winner-take-all match, and we never thought we had a chance. We made $1,000 at Charlie Farrell's Racquet Club in Palm Springs. It must have been 1948. Kramer had turned pro, and I set him up with Gonzales and taught Kramer all about the touring business . . . oh damn, I missed a turn," he said. "I want a beach route," he complained, and he looked puzzled and gazed strangely at the dials of his car, as though the dials were some kind of map. He began to mumble to himself and then said, "I thought that this was the way to the beach and then the sign says 'No Left Turn' and . . ." Confused in the darkening skies, he looked at me. I shrugged.

"Look, we have driven a long way," I said. "Do you always drive miles like this from tennis to golf and back to tennis?"

"Oh, I might be hyper," he said. "I am really happiest playing golf, playing tennis, playing a game, being in competition, *doing something*—I really come alive. That kind of life is fulfilling for me. I get a kick out of that. I might be different from Jack Kramer. Jack was willing to resign and play a bit for fun but not be out on center court. He enjoys social tennis, playing over at Dr. Omar Fareeb's house, playing with selected friends [the same court that Bob Falkenburg and I had played on] but I like to play for money."

"You can say that again," I said under my breath, and let him ramble on. He started on his golf once more and was suddenly back with Kramer, on whom he likes to keep tabs. Kramer's hip had been a problem, according to Bobby, but Bobby was genuinely happy that Jack was back playing social tennis. I told him we almost had a game together, but it didn't work out. Then back to golf.

"Now tennis," he said, "I play for health reasons. But I like golf. Tennis keeps me from drinking too much and keeps the blood in circulation, and controls my weight, but I hate losing. What I hate most are guys who are my age who were never contenders—had never won Wimbledon—but are health guys and come along and beat me. So far they haven't done that. I swept all the sixties one year and all the sixty-fives this year."

"What would you do if you had to meet Frankie Parker in the over-sixty-fives?"

"Parker?"

"He says he has to spot you three games a set."

"I can beat Parker. He cannot beat me at all—especially since he had his blood clot in his leg. He's never recovered 100 percent from that. Tony Vincent* and he played me and Mulloy, and we beat them in the first round of the forty-five-and-over at the Flushing Meadows tournament. No, Frankie would not have a chance against me. Not a chance."

"What about Frankie against Gardnar Mulloy?"

"Up to a couple of years ago, he could beat Gardnar, but not now."

"How about Tom Brown?"

"Tom Brown is younger. I have not been able to beat Tom Brown since we got into senior tennis. Tom is another story. He is younger. I would consider Tom Brown and Mulloy in the same category. Tom might have been a better singles player, but he was a lousy doubles player."

At this point we began to argue. I was sticking up for Brown. I said that he had won a set against Kramer at Forest Hills. "I'll bet you $5," said Bobby. "Tom Brown never won a set against Kramer in a finals at either Wimbledon or Forest Hills."

I said, "Okay. You lose $5." But Riggs *won* $5. The scores at Forest Hills were close as in the first set (9–7) and then runaway. It was a one-sided three-set match at Wimbledon a year later in 1947. So I lost, but I didn't, because Riggs had sweetened the bet to claim that none of Kramer's wins over Brown had gone to deuce. Seven–nine implies deuce. I said, "And Tom and Jack won the Wimbledon doubles title in 1946."

Riggs said, "That just shows how good Kramer was."

I insisted on Bobby taking his $5 because his comment about deuce was really an afterthought. He then said (as he took my money), "I once won

---

* Vincent was one of the great amateurs but was never a major champion.

$2,500 against Kramer on a bet just like this. And he paid me. He bet me that Budge didn't break his serve twice in the fourth set at Forest Hills in the semifinal round of the 1948 professional championships." (Ha, ha, he laughed.)

"Okay," I said, "I want my $5 back. What school did Jack Kramer represent when he won the interscholastic championships in 1938?"

"I couldn't bet on that," said Riggs. "I know he went to Montebello High. I suppose that's whom he played for. Hell, I never went into those things because I was the best high school player in the country." (And one presumes he didn't have to prove it.)

So no bet.

I was looking through my USTA Yearbook. "It says right here— Scarborough School. Not Montebello High, and even Kramer doesn't mention Scarborough School."

"I know he went to Montebello High because I used to give him rides home from the Los Angeles Tennis Club. He arranged it so he never had to go to school in the afternoon."

"I know," I told him. "Look," I said, yelling louder than ever, "It says Scarborough School!"

"Some miserable private school. I never heard of it. Jack should have lost a year of eligibility for transferring."

"The guy right before him is a man named Edward Gillespie. Same school, Scarborough School."

"I knew him. He came from Atlanta and went to the University of Miami. Scarborough School must be some phony school that gives out diplomas. Jack never went there."

"What about the sixties seniors? I bet I know who would win that."

"Who?"

"Seixas."

"He was beaten badly by Bob Sherman. But I agree with you; he should be able to beat Sherman." (Bob Sherman is a Dodo Cheney across-the-board senior champion whom people like Riggs fear—probably because they stay in great shape and, having not won in the great amateur days, are out to prove something in their later years. Sherman's record is extraordinary on all surfaces, but nowhere as impressive as the indomitable Riggs, who has slipped into the sixty-fives and left Bob Sherman a year or so behind him. But the fear lingers. Riggs is loyal to Seixas, who played the great game on a championship level as a youngster. Then I told him that Vic was training and playing in tournaments—the forty-fives.)

Riggs switched subjects again. He said, "Look, in northern California, there was Budge, who played the way we did in southern California, where we had Mako and Stoefen and Vines and Riggs and Kramer and Gonzales and Schroeder and Falkenburg, and now the rest of the country is catching up.

We seem to have lost the dominance. There are indoor courts, and our advantages of the outdoor weather is lost. Now, you get countries like Rumania and Czechoslovakia—look, you get a dozen kids together and give them training, the way we got in southern California, and they are competitive. As for me, I went through the pipeline."

"The pipeline?"

"Yeah. I played in the twelves and the thirteens and the juniors and the Davis Cup and then into the forty-fives and the fifties. Budge wasn't hardly able to play the seniors at all."

And then we went back to the handicapping. "How old are you?" he asked.

I could see it coming. "I am fifty-four."

"Well, that's a handicap right there."

"Yes, but how about those chairs you use? You put them on the court, and if I hit one, you can't return the ball."

"But you are only fifty-four," he insisted.

I wondered how I could get him down to where I would have a chance. Imagine outhustling Riggs. But as I said, there was a crazy need to *lose* to his hustle, so we went on bargaining.

"Forget the chairs. You could hit the chairs. You got two games from Mulloy."

"Okay, forget the chairs. Then what do I get?"

"The alleys. You get both alleys."

Both alleys? Why, no sixty-six-year-old man can cover a whole doubles court against me. I knew that. I was *sure* of that.

"On second thought," said Riggs, reading my mind, "maybe you get one alley, my forehand alley."

The man had played tennis all morning for money. He had played golf all afternoon for money. He had driven at least three hours in his car. He had not eaten anything that I knew of. It was nearing 9:30 at night. I said, "One alley will do." I had been hustled, and my subconscious could now rest. He steered his Lincoln like a helmsman on a schooner, and the rasp had left his voice. Another victory for Riggs was assured. The immense automobile hummed along the superhighway like the *Bluenose*, the world's greatest racing schooner, sliding along the swells of the Atlantic, and it hummed its course with Riggs deftly fingering the wheel.

But Riggs wasn't finished. He wanted to know how I played Seixas. "Our handicap was that every ball that Vic hit that I could not possibly reach without running would be my point."

"What?" said Riggs.

I repeated myself. "My knee!" I yelled. "I have no right knee that works!"

"The only time I did that with a fellow, he beat me."

"Look, Bobby," I said, "I really want to lose."

"You want to lose?" Disbelief was in his voice.

"Look," I said, "the only man I beat was George Lott, and he is seventy-seven."

"You beat George Lott? Why, he is one of the greatest doubles players of all time."

And so it went. We had decided on the one-alley advantage, but Riggs was worried. What would be the stakes? I wondered to myself. He had bet Kramer $2,500 over a statistic. What would he expect from me?

"We'll play for $100," I said.

"Good," he answered, still unsure of my game and riddled with suspicion. Was I really telling the truth? And who in hell was I, to begin with? Would this be a setup? Riggs could sniff out a setup a mile away. He was sniffing.

By the time we got to his house, there was one thing I had learned—Riggs was still competing with Don Budge. "Budge was the greatest doubles player I ever saw," he said. And then he went into it. He told the story of how he came out of the service better than Budge.

But he digressed before he got to it. He said, "Did you see Gene Mako, Budge's partner?" I said that I had and told him that Mako may be a genius. Bobby said that he *is* a genius. I then mentioned Sidney Wood, who is supposed to be a genius. (I was talking of intellect and so was Riggs.)

"Mako is a walking encyclopedia, but I do not agree with all of Sidney Wood's viewpoints. But he is bright, and he is a genius, I will say that."

"He is an expert on Frank Shields."

"No. Mako didn't hang around with Shields. Shields was a woman guy, a party guy, a drinking guy."

"I am talking about Sidney Wood! I am yelling at you! Why don't you wear a hearing aid?"

"All they do is make things louder but not clearer."

"I am getting a little deaf myself," I said, and then I said, "I don't know the facts about hearing aids."

"I hear everything," said Riggs, "but I hear them confused. They are backways and all around and different. I have to be one-on-one, looking at you. If you are in the back seat, and I am in the front seat, forget it."

"Look, I met your wife, and she seemed wonderful. How many times have you been married?"

"Twice before this particular marriage," he said. Then he added, "I have been married two times for sure."

"What does that mean?"

"I take the fifth amendment," he replied. "I had five boys and one daughter. One boy died, just like the Kennedy boy who went under a couple of weeks ago.* I am heartsick over this. He was my favorite kid, by the way. I know you are not supposed to have favorites, but he was my favorite."

"What did he die of?"

"It looks like overdose. He was a beautiful kid, who lived on Long Island, and he wanted to be more daring than anyone else. He played golf and tennis and developed some very bad habits . . . let's face it. You see, if you are bent on self-destruction, you can pretty well accomplish it. He had the best care in the world [medical help], but it didn't work."

"If you had your life to live over again, would you make any changes?" (I was again yelling at him as the Lincoln moved ever closer to his home and our match, and I could sense that he did not want to continue talking about his son's death.)

"Yes, I would have taken Don McNeill," and then he went on to a series of matches that he should have won.

"I mean . . . would you like to have been taller or richer or wiser?"

"Look, Stoefen was tall and died at fifty-four or fifty-five," he interrupted. "I have had a beautiful life. It's been healthy and full, and I have always been able to stay in games—golf, tennis, gin rummy, backgammon— games that have turned me on."

"But don't you get worn out from all of this? Games all day long—we still have to play again tonight!"

"It's like bread and water to me."

But as this conversation was going on, I wanted to get back to Budge and Riggs, and I had set the scenario. It goes like this. Everyone agrees that Tilden was the best of his era (the 1920s) and that on his "given day" Vines was supreme. And, of course, Kramer is always lurking behind Tilden and Budge . . . but what of Riggs? Has the whole tennis world forgotten what Riggs had done? He won Wimbledon once in 1939, as well as the doubles and mixed doubles. He won Forest Hills in 1939, and then after the war, he beat everyone in sight. Now at sixty-six, there is not a soul who can top him. Why is he forgotten in the list of great champions?

The answer is simple, and he said it himself. "You need the serve and the volley. I was a tactician." So be it. Compare other players to Bobby Riggs, a Wimbledon singles winner and a Forest Hills U.S. champion in singles, a man who had come back after the war to take on Budge and win . . . I'll take Riggs. I thought, now comes the story of how he came back from the war and beat Donald Budge.

---

* A Kennedy boy had died of a drug overdose in Palm Beach, and it was still a big story in the news.

But Riggs wasn't buying—not yet. He said, "I love the pressure, be it for $50 or more. Another guy was Falkenburg. I think we were the two most competitive guys that ever played the game. I would say that. You just love the pressure. Falkenburg was very, *very* competitive."

"What about Schroeder? He would rise to the challenge."

"I am talking about Falkenburg, who can play golf and tennis and gin rummy and poker and backgammon. Schroeder was only what you would call a scrambler and a fighter and had a lot of heart, a lot of courage—a come-from-behind courage on a tennis court. But all of that was within tennis. Falkenburg and I—we take it into everything we do. Schroeder is more normal than either Falkenburg or I."

"You know that Falkenburg has a poker table right in his living room?" I said.

"Yes, Falkenburg would have that. Schroeder had all those qualities I mentioned, but I am not as high on him as a tennis player as Jack Kramer is."

We talked again about Falkenburg, and Bobby said that he had gotten $6 million from selling his old house. I said something to the effect that I had seen his new house, which was wonderful to behold. But Bobby said that at Falkenburg's old house, he had a court for a game called palota, which had cost him $200,000 to build. "He loved that game," said Bobby, "and when he sold his house, he retained a lifetime privilege to go play on his old court. Did he tell you that?"

"No," I said, astounded by even more stories and more—was it gossip?— about some of the people I had met. I was thinking of $6 million and a court for palota, which I did not know, a game they played in Brazil.

"With Falkenburg you open the door, and he carries the ball and makes a touchdown with it. With other guys, nothing comes of it. He is one of those guys," said Bobby Riggs.

Ice cream in Brazil. And now Bobby Riggs, heading home to Leucadia, in the south of California. I loved it all. You could have thrown a tennis ball into Mexico and said, "Hi!"

"We all came down the same channel at the Los Angeles Tennis Club— Jack Kramer, Falkenburg, Ted Schroeder, and me—the same opportunities. Jack and I had Ted Schroeder under contract for the professional tour, but Ted backed out of it. Jack said let him go; he'll break out in shingles if we force him to play. I hated to see him go because I had done a lot of work arranging things. Ted offered to reimburse me all the money I was out-of-pocket, but I was so mad at him I wouldn't let him give me a dime. Now I wish I had. I hardly ever see Jack now. Maybe twice a year," he said in a typical Riggsian shift of conversation from Schroeder to Kramer—which is not unusual because one is apt to keep them as a team in his mind.

426

"Looking back, whom do you respect the most—across the board, including everybody?"

"The man I respect the most is Jack Dreyfus of the Dreyfus Fund. He is a terrific competitor. Before he made his fortune on the stock market, he made his money playing bridge and gin rummy. He is worth maybe $400–500 million. He picks a partner, and we play doubles for $100 a set. We have a lot of fun doing that. So even though $100 is like a penny to him, we have a lot of fun because he is such a competitor. He is one of the best. One time he said, 'Bob, I have forgotten more about hustling than you will ever know.' "

"Is there anyone else, outside of competitors, whom you have respect for? Losers, weak people, or strong people who don't play tennis, like MacArthur or Churchill or *someone*? I am trying to get at what makes you tick!"

"I have already told you what makes me tick. I have to be in a contest."

"What about war? That's a contest."

"I was in the war. I was in Guam when the bomb went off. I was in Pearl Harbor. I was in Saipan and Tinian."

"What were you doing?"

"I was in special services. I was in the Navy. I was a physical instructor—I ran their athletic programs [which was what Gene Mako had done], and I was very fortunate. I ran a lot of tennis programs and got a lot of practice."

And that was the reason—at last—that he had come out on top of Don Budge and became the best tennis player in the world. Briefly.

"I said to myself that the difference between Don Budge and me is who is going to come out of the service *fit*. So I said that I am going to work on my game and become a better player than I was before. And knowing Budge's personality and how proud Budge was, I knew that he would consider that he was *so* good that he would not have to practice. So I studied Budge's personality, and I knew that if he did not practice, he would go backward. I turned out to be absolutely right. Budge never again achieved his prewar form.

"So I had Budge's number after the war. I beat him in 1945, 1946, and 1947.

"Now," he said, talking rapid-fire, "you asked me a question earlier about ranking players. Well, here it goes. It goes like this. From 1880 to 1930, it was Tilden. Forget about the Four Musketeers [the superb French champions—LaCoste, Brugnon, Cochet, and Borotra, who gave Tilden fits] or anyone else. After Tilden, there was Vines. He may have been the best player who ever lived. On one day, in one year, he may have been the best player who ever lived. Then there was Perry. Three times at Wimbledon and three times a winner at Forest Hills—you've got to remember Perry. After Perry we talk about Don Budge. In my opinion, we had Vines, who for one year was the best player ever, and we have Budge, who for the best three years of his life, nobody could hold a candle to—period. For the best five-year period, I give it to Jack Kramer. The best ten-year period, I give it to Laver. The best twenty-year period, I give it to Gonzales. The best twenty-five to thirty-year period, I give it to Rosewall. Now, that is the way I rank them over the period that tennis has been played."

"You mean that about Gonzales?"

"Yes. He kept up a higher level of play for that twenty-year period. He beat Laver when he was forty years old! He beat Newcombe when he was forty-one or forty-two. He held a very high level of play over a great number of years."

"Have you seen Gonzales lately?"

"Yes. He's dogging it. Once that he found out he couldn't win against Sedgman and Fraser and others, he couldn't take the pill. Too hard to swallow. Slams the ball down. Hits it into the net. I hate to say that. He dogged it and quit and threw in the towel. But he didn't do that for a long time. But when he couldn't win, he quit. I don't admire him for that. Be a good sport and go down fighting.

"But now I get confused. I want to go back to my players to remember. I go to Rosewall for thirty years, but I want to put Sedgman in there. I want him in there just before Laver. I don't want to remember Hoad," he said, as an aside.

"So suppose you had them all on their best day, playing each other. Then what?"

"Probably Vines, but here is what I want to say. Suppose you tell the losers that if they lose, they don't get any money. Suppose you say that the winner gets the money and the losers have to jump off the Golden Gate Bridge. On those terms, I would take Gonzales. He might be the meanest and might rise to the highest, and if his life depended on it, he might be the survivor."

"Well, wait a minute," I shouted. "What about women?" Riggs and Billie Jean King had broken all gross receipts in the history of tennis. His relationship with women was vital.

"We never had any interest in women. Pauline Betz was a great favorite of mine. Great backhand, great competitor . . . and then Margaret Smith Court had the greatest record in tennis and Billie Jean King had a great record and Helen Wills Moody (Roark) had a great record, but Mo Connelly may have been the best of them all. Chrissie Evert has a great record, but she is really not a good athlete, only a baseline player and a limited player. Talent-wise, she is a great ground stroker, but she herself says she is not an athlete. Now, you get a great player like Martina Navratilova, and she is beating Evert ten times in a row, and it's not because Chrissie has passed her peak. She is just limited, in my opinion. If Martina can continue, she may be the best woman player that ever lived. On her record over this last year, I don't think any woman ever played so well."

"Okay," I said. "Do you believe in God?"

"My father was a preacher. I told you that. When I was fourteen I was baptized, fully submerged. Now . . . today? I would say that I am confused."

"Do you ever go to church?"

"Yes, I do, but that doesn't mean you believe in God. It means custom. It's being in with your contemporaries. I go to the Church of Christ—the way I was brought up—but for many years I went to the Congregational Church in Manhattan. I was a Sunday School teacher."

"You were a Sunday School teacher? That's great news."

"Yeah. I believe strongly in Christianity. The doctrine is beautifully sound. I believe in the Ten Commandments. I believe in the Golden Rule. Anybody who believes in the concept of Christianity cannot help but be a better person and successful person. I really believe that if you cast your bread on the water, it comes back tenfold. I always lend a helping hand. I try to be a nice person. I always help younger people coming up without a dime. I don't cater to rich people. I was never a good politician. Kramer was a good politician in tennis circles. I never did that. I am not social at all. I don't care to go to parties. I live a cloistered life within a tight, close ring. I'm not saying that is smart. I only say that that is what I opt for. That is what I do. I am very contented in my teeny little life-style. I had a beautiful day today playing golf. I will defend all my eight championships this year. I am a very contented person, doing just what I am doing."

"Now, about those eight championships?"

"I will play in them," he said, and then he went on listing a litany of tournaments, ending up saying that this year he expects to win all the doubles with Robin Hippenstiel [to go along with his singles victories]. "Robin Hippenstiel is the guy who got Kramer going in San Bernadino years ago. Without Hippenstiel, Jack might have been a railroad man."

"Well, I'll be damned . . . hey, we are running out of gas," he said, staring at his gauge. "But we can damn near coast down to La Costa."

And so endeth the lesson. We found a station, and I insisted on paying for his fuel. We then traveled to his home. By the time we got fuel for his immense automobile, I felt I could have written a book about Riggs alone. Forget Budge and Seixas and Kramer and Brough. The man was endlessly and consistently interesting.

So we had our game. We went to his house, which sits *right* on the edge of the Pacific. The sea crashes into his front yard. He has a modest home with a living room with a vaulted ceiling. Everywhere there are photographs and mementos. The place is new and part of a complex of condominiums, one aspect of which are those outdoor tennis courts with lights. We talked to his wife, Miriam, for a few moments and then proceeded to the court.

The handicap was this. I would get two games and the forehand alley, and we would play for $100. He won 6–4. Bobby Riggs did not try for my angle shots but took my normal ground strokes and outstroked me. As far as the alley goes—that was his hustle. When you play singles at 10:00 at night, you don't think about hitting what are normally "out" balls down the alley. So I never used it. It was meaningless.

But we went head-to-head, we played well, and he won, which is what I had expected. I had seen him hours earlier. He rarely errs. My knee locked me into a situation where I could not run, and he understood that and did not drop-shot me, nor did he force me much. He played just well enough to pull it out. He just stood back there and stroked the ball until I lost the point.

Miriam was there watching. And she said to me that the two of us could take him. She liked my game and thought that in doubles, where I would not have to run too much, we could beat him. I told her that I was fearful of another hustle—after all, she is his wife! But she said, "I love to beat Bobby. Don't even *think* about that."

So here we were, at the end of a very long day, playing again. This time Miriam and I would play him even, and this time we would get *both* alleys, but no games—no handicap other than the alleys. The wondrous Riggs would play doubles against a doubles team, only he was all alone.

Miriam Riggs is a good, strong tennis player. We had Bobby's number without any doubt. We had doubled the bet—$200 was on the line for me— but I knew we could take him. He didn't even try for the alley shots, and his serve had no sting. What he had were his tactics, and we went all the way to 6–6 for a tie-breaker. I couldn't believe what I was doing. I was in a game that we should have won 6–2, and yet we had reached a tie-breaker. Tie-breakers mean pressure, and all day Riggs had said how much he loves pressure. So I blew a few overheads, and Miriam cried out loud and almost wept on the court in her frustration. I blew a final lob that anyone could have put away, and Riggs went ahead. However, there is a final comment. He took the tie-breaker on a bum call. You have to win by two points, and he was ahead by one when Miriam hit a ball flat on the outside line of the alley. I saw it and she saw it, but Riggs said, "Out!" and that was it. Miriam was furious, and so was I. We protested. But there was no compromise from Bobby. It was late. He wears glasses and is partly deaf and saw it as he saw it. And he had called an "in" ball "out"!

As Margaret Osborne duPont had told me, "Things even up in the end." Swell.

Late that night, Riggs and Miriam drove me back to La Costa. We were

430

all laughing and fooling around in the car. Just as we rolled in, I pulled out my checkbook. I said, "Bobby, I owe you $200."

He said, "Jeez, I forgot all about that. It was so much fun!"

Then he said something I will always cherish. He said, "You know, Stan, I have had such a good day with you that this is one check I won't cash. I am going to frame it."

I gave it to him, and he said, "I will just have to frame this one," and then he let me out of the Lincoln.

The next day, he showed up with two books he had written. They were inscribed as follows: "To Stan. It was fun playing tennis with you. I'll give you a rematch anytime. That's more than Billie Jean would do for me." The other book was inscribed in simpler terms: "To Stan, one of the great guys, Bobby Riggs."

And, indeed, should he frame my check, it will be on a wall in his house beside pictures of himself and Don Budge and Jack Kramer.

Imagine that?

Epilogue:

A Guilty Conscience
and John Van Ryn

John Van Ryn is the grand old man of tennis. He is the oldest living world champion among the men. And Van Ryn, now a sprightly seventy-nine years old and fairly natty in appearance, is as accessible as his club, the Everglades, is not. He lives in Palm Beach in a modest yellow apartment house no bigger than a standard suburban home, but its facade is very neat, just like its tenant, John Van Ryn. Seeing him standing there at the arc of the circular driveway waiting for me to arrive—a man who is right on the button—I looked at the slim and precise athlete of whom the writer, Richard Schickel, wrote: "John Van Ryn, everybody's favorite doubles partner." He couldn't make an error. I thought as I drove up and opened the car door for him to enter. Looking as neat as a pin, he would angle his shots onto the court with upsetting accuracy. We were to meet at noon. It was exactly noon when he took his place beside me.

In 1929, playing with his long-time partner, Wilmer Allison, he won Wimbledon in an era that boasted George Lott, John Doeg, Fred Perry, and the famous Four Musketeers of France, and William Tatem Tilden. Not only did Allison and Van Ryn win in 1929, but they also won the next two years as well, beating in the finals two teams of immense reputation: George Lott and John Doeg; Jacques Brugnon and Henri Cochet. In 1927, two years before his great win at Wimbledon, he and a fellow Princetonian won the U.S. Intercollegiate doubles, and he followed that by taking the Middle States Tennis As-

432

59. John Van Ryn at the Everglades Club

sociation *singles* title—his name enshrined in a list of great singles players including Tilden and Seixas and Pancho Gonzales.

That was a year before I was born, and I think the decade of the 1920s with its great allure must have been the spur to my conscience to try my hand at an epilogue and not lose John Van Ryn to my book. I had seen everybody else I could see. When he said, "Come on down," I went once more to the bank, took out a loan, and made my plans: All the way to Florida for a man I did not know and had forgotten about—he was a man who, in the beginning, I had thought had died. It was Gene Mako who told me that John Van Ryn was alive and living in Palm Beach. I believe George Lott had said that John was last thought to be working in Philadelphia. In any case, he was lost in the maze of people I was seeing. I wanted Bobby Riggs to conclude my book, and so he did. I mailed it in, accepted the editing, made my own corrections, and was awaiting galleys when my conscience kept probing: "If John Van Ryn is in Palm Beach, at least call information and see if you can get his number." That I did, and then I knew I was hooked.

The Everglades is a club that strikes me somewhat like the River Club in New York. I had the feeling that to join either you had to pay a fortune. (John told me that memberships in the Palm Beaches went from between twenty to forty thousand *just to get in*.) I recalled playing golf at the Everglades back in the mid-1950s. I don't know whom I played with nor why, but I had taken the place for granted. Lunching with John Van Ryn, I could see that you couldn't take it for granted anymore. If you were going to winter in Palm Beach, you had to belong to something, and the Everglades was old, with a finely honed Anglo reputation, and it fronted right on Worth Avenue, a street lined with chic stores and boutiques and where pure gold seemed to glitter in the hot, clear Florida air. It was a place where the rich got richer, yet inside the club there was a strong feeling from the old days when manners ruled over wise-cracks and nobody mentioned money.

We began talking about George Lott, who played with John for a short period in 1931 when they won the French title, Wimbledon, and then went on a tour, crisscrossing the continent. As far as John can recall, they never lost a set, and I reminded him that George Lott thinks of him as his greatest partner. "George should have been national champion [in singles], but he seemed to need a partner," said Van Ryn. "He had everything, but played better when he wasn't alone. I don't know why. He won the Juniors, and was runner-up to Ellie Vines in 1931 . . ."

"What about Wilmer Allison, your regular partner?"

"Wilmer was off his game. He didn't want to go, so George went and we beat everyone. But then we came back to the states for the men's championship [at Longwood] and Wilmer was all right again. His game was back, so Wilmer and I played and we won. That meant that I won the French, the English, and the U.S. all in one year: 1931."

"And here it's written," I said, pointing at the USTA record book, "that in 1935 you and Allison won the U.S. doubles, beating Budge and Mako. That would be your second U.S. title, and you have already won Wimbledon three times," And look here, I thought. In 1935, they almost won Wimbledon, losing to the superb doubles team in the finals—the Australians, John Bromwich and Adrian Quist. If they had beaten Bromwich and Quist—and Budge and Mako—back to back, it would have been a mighty feat, indeed. John Van Ryn smiled as I leafed through the record book.

"You know who was a fine doubles player but never got the credit he deserved? Ted Schroeder."

"Many people think that Kramer and Schroeder were the top doubles team or near it."

"But you remember Ted as a singles player first. You can forget how good he was in doubles."

He then went on to Fred Perry, whose address he did not have even though Perry lived close by in Pompano Beach. Fortunately I had it on the front of a notebook I was carrying and gave it to him.

434

Recalling Fred, he told a funny story. To mark the occasion of Fred Perry's first win at Wimbledon in 1934 and his unequaled run of three straight championships at Forest Hills ending in 1934, a statue was sculpted of the great Briton, and Van Ryn, who was there, noticed that it really bore a likeness to a fifteen-year-old boy and was not life-size and only vaguely resembled Perry. So later Fred asked John how he liked the statue, and Van Ryn with some adroitness said that he liked it all right but it was too small. Fred then said, "I was standing in front of it when an older women came up. She looked at the statue and then at me and repeated, alternating her gaze for some time. Finally she asked, 'Are you Fred Perry?' I said, 'Yes, I am.' Well, the lady stared at me and said, 'You certainly were better looking then.' " Fred, without missing a turn, replied, "Well, madam, so were you," and at that she steamed off highly insulted. Fred told that story to Don Budge as well as to Van Ryn, and they both laughed over it. I noted the age—fifteen—and remembered that at fifteen Fred was on his way to becoming a world-class table tennis player. As embodied in sculpture, somebody had erred. The very youthful Fred Perry had yet to dominate the great tennis courts of the world.

I talked for a while about how nice everybody had seemed. We got onto the subject of Vic Seixas, who once had worked as a stockbroker, as had John Van Ryn (and George Lott) in Philadelphia.

"There was some talk of Vic coming down here [to Palm Beach] but nothing came of it," said John. "But surely you couldn't find a nicer man. And the same goes for Don Budge. He's just great."

I mentioned how friendly Jack Kramer had been and how I had quite a lot of his thoughts on tape. "You couldn't have a better man than Jack on tape. He certainly was one of the great players."

"Did you play Riggs?" he continued.

"Oh, yes, I was with him all day. Had a swell time."

"Well, I wouldn't call him one of the greatest people, but I would say he is unique. But he was a bad boy. I graduated from Princeton in 1928 and went to California to learn how to play tennis. Well, there was this young kid there—at the L.A. Tennis Club—and he had some pretty good shots. So there was a teacher there at the University of Southern California named Esther Bartosh, and she took this little ragamuffin, whose mother was anxious to get rid of him, and went to his mother and asked if Bobby could move in with her. Esther Bartosh had a little boy about his age, and it seemed like a good idea.

"Esther Bartosh brought him up, and it used to make me mad because he never paid tribute to her until just a couple of years ago. I read something he had written, and he finally admitted his debt to Esther Bartosh. She taught him all his shots!"

He continued with another story about Riggs: "He came down here about ten years ago and went to Miami Beach early, before the season, and played a lot of golf. He shot a 90, a 93, a 98, and finally got an official Florida handicap of about 15. Well, he then cleaned up. He could shoot a 77 if he had to, and the rich suckers were coming on for fifty dollars Nassau and a hundred dollars Nassau, and he did all right for himself. He had that official handicap, right there on paper.''

And then he went on. "You know the Billie Jean-Riggs match. I heard that he bet against himself. Ask Gardnar Mulloy. Bobby has that brother that takes his bets.''

"I doubt that,'' I said, defending Riggs.

"Well, I *don't*,'' said Van Ryn.

"Riggs just took Billie Jean too lightly . . . that's what he told me.''

"You ask some of the tennis players,'' countered Van Ryn.

And so we left it at that. Apparently there was suspicion about that famous duel that I had not heard before. It made no sense to argue about it because I was a firm Bobby Riggs ally, and John Van Ryn was going on hearsay and years of tennis knowledge, but I was convinced that he was wrong about Riggs. Riggs had let down his guard not by design, but by accident.

At that point, my courtly host offered me dessert, but I declined. I didn't want to be chomping on cake or ice cream or fruit as he spoke. In fine understated fashion, we had eaten omelets. I looked at Van Ryn's wiry body and thought that thin men didn't eat sandwiches. Van Ryn would be eighty when this book was published. Had I come a few weeks later or seen him after Fred Perry back in the fall of 1983, I would have played him a set or two of tennis. Today he was waiting for his knee to heal, having had arthroscopic surgery. Forever amazed at the durability of some men and women, I had a suspicion that it came from diet and an orderly life. Without emotion or a touch of sneer in his voice, John could suppose that Bobby Riggs had thrown a match. A rascal, a onetime bad boy, Bobby was one kind of emotional person who thrived on his enthusiasms. Van Ryn was of another stripe, and so be it. He sat back in his chair, and the memories drifted forth. Doubtless he would outlive them all, maybe even Gardnar Mulloy. At that time in the posh Everglades, longevity seemed important.

"In 1932 both George Lott and I were working for Fitz-Eugene Dixon and Dixon and Company, a brokerage house, and Tilden came along and offered each of us fifty thousand dollars to turn professional and go on tour with him. Well, I asked Mr. Dixon what I should do, and he said that fifty thousand dollars was a lot of money (especially in those days), and if I was sure I'd get paid, to consider the offer. So Mr. Dixon, who had been Davis Cup captain and had gotten us our jobs, said, 'I don't think the tour will last.'

"He was right. The tour went to a little over a month and nobody got anything. In those days, they would go from place to place and put up some

436

kind of canvas surface and play before two or three hundred people. Hell, they had to give tickets away to fill up the house. It was a farce."

John Van Ryn, listening to the caution in his boss's voice, stayed behind in Philadelphia. George Lott went on the professional tour, and as George told me, it was the one thing he regretted more than anything else. From then on, George was hooked on tennis. Van Ryn went on to a prosperous career as a stockbroker.*

Lunch was over, and I could sense uneasiness in John Van Ryn. As though reading my mind, he explained that at the Everglades they didn't allow business interviews in the dining room, and we were stretching it a bit with my tape recorder in plain view as we ate. He told me to grab the recorder and said with a laugh, "Follow me into the locker room—used by golfers." Once more the locker room reminded me of the River Club in that you could find no metal lockers, no dirt, or even a towel dropped carelessly on the floor. The lockers were pine and had small brass numbers on them, and the walls of the room were pine. It was not a dark room with dark wood but light and airy, and we sat at a table to resume our talk. Because of the hiatus due to transferring from one room to another, whatever train of thought was going through John's mind was temporarily lost. So I asked him some questions— the same ones I had asked Budge and Kramer—and when I mentioned their names, his face lit up.

"You have gone to two of the best, obviously, that I know. What do you want," he said eyeing my sheet of questions. "My height and weight?"

"No," I told him, "just an insight into your personality. Your achievements are in the record books. What I want is an inkling of who you are, what you are like."

He grinned and sat back at the wooden table where golfers took their drinks after a game.

He was born in Newport News, Virginia, in 1905. His father was an agent for the Holland-American Line; I told him that I had passed by those huge Newport News shipyards, heading down the inland waterway.

He acknowledged that and went on. "I lived in Newport News for about five or six years, and then we moved to Chicago for another three years or so. Finally we settled in East Orange, New Jersey [Althea Gibson's adopted hometown], and I went through high school there and then on to Princeton."

---

* The year must have been 1935. George Lott continued to play as an amateur with Lester Stoefen as his partner, and in 1933 Van Ryn and Lott teamed up to beat Perry and Hughes in a losing cause against Great Britain in an Interzone Final. And in 1934, Lott and Stoefen beat their British opponents in the Davis Cup Challenge Round. Van Ryn, always an amateur, won the U.S. Doubles in 1935 with Wilmer Allison.

He was sent there by his father because it was closer to home. By now his father was working in New York as the U.S. head of the Holland-American Line. Born in Holland, the elder Van Ryn had worked his way up within the company and was able to send young John off to a top-rated school—certainly top-rated in a social sense.

"He was quite a man, my father. He was knighted by Queen Wilhemina because during the World War the line was bombed out by the Germans in Rotterdam, and my father and two other men set themselves to restoring the Holland-American Line, which they did. After the war, he was ordered back to Holland, where the queen presented him with the title Knight of the Orange Nassau. He became Sir John Van Ryn."

"How did you get mixed up with tennis?"

"My father was a pretty good athlete, and he got me to play with him. As an example, after Sunday school I would go over to the court that was between the church and our house, and he would tell one of the men, 'Okay, my son is going to play now.' I was a kid of about twelve or thirteen then, and the other men didn't want to play with a kid, so my father would say, 'Either he plays or I go home with him.' So I got to play with the men. But," he added, "I never took a lesson in my life. Had I got top instruction, I would have been a better player."

We talked about his prowess at doubles, but he stood by his singles record even though he was never ranked higher than fourth. "I was ranked number four in the country in 1931 [with Vines, Lott, and Shields before him, in descending order]. I won enough tournaments," he said, and I noted that he was ranked in the top ten for eight years from 1927 through 1937. In Davis Cup play, his record was a remarkable 29–3 in overall competition.

We went back to doubles. "Only McEnroe and Fleming play doubles now. Who else is there? And they tied my record at Wimbledon by winning it three times, and I don't like it. I was the only American to win it three times. In the old days, everybody played doubles: Kramer and Schroeder, and Vines and Gledhill, and Lott and Stoefen, and Budge and Mako, so there was great competition. Now the good singles players won't play. They save themselves for the money. It is sad," he lamented, and underlying his sorrow (or at least his concern) was a resentment that what he had done against the best that played the game, another team had equaled against inferior odds. He had to share his cherished record. We did not mention Longwood, where Mulloy and Talbert had won the doubles four times, and Van Ryn and Allison only twice. The glory seemed to rest elsewhere, in England, and now he was sharing it with some regret.

He paused for a minute, and I plunged ahead into singles. I asked him how he would compare Tilden to McEnroe. "Well, I came along a few years

438

60. Van Ryn, solo

after Tilden's prime. But to answer your question—you can't. The foot fault judge has changed everything. How Budge would serve under the new rules I can't say. But jumping two feet into the court . . . McEnroe would have double-faulted each time. You can't compare them because of the rule change. Could McEnroe have served as well under the old rules? I doubt it. And mention John Doeg [who Frank Parker said had such a fast serve that the ball appeared egg-shaped]? What would the rule change do to his serve? Think about that.''

"How would you rank the best players of all time?''

"It's hard to take number one and go down a list. But I would say Budge, Kramer, Tilden, and Gonzales.''

"What about Vines on his 'given day'?''

"He's a great friend of mine, but I wouldn't say that—[that he was the best on his given day]. Vines was tremendous when he was on, but he could be put off. Yet I would say that at his very finest, no one could beat him. But over the long haul . . . I have seen him lose to dogs. He had no margin for error. And, of course, I would have to put McEnroe up there.''

"How about Laver?''

"Yes, you have to place him with the best.''

"Hoad?''

"For a short time. But then he hurt his back.''

"Couldn't bad backs and knee problems come from hard courts? It seems that that is about all the Californians play on.''

"Yes. But nowadays people play too much. Too much strain. I play on Har-tru at the Bath and Tennis Club here in Palm Beach. Except for this knee problem, I have never been hurt in my life.''

"How about Schroeder?''

"A great volleyer and a very good doubles player, but not in the list I gave you.''

"Your own fame would rest in doubles?''

"Oh, I suppose so. But to be ranked, you have to beat somebody. I beat Perry and Riggs, and I won Seabright and almost beat Vines, who took me in five sets.''

"John Doeg. His name comes up a great deal.''

"Doeg had the greatest left-handed serve until McEnroe. With the new rules on foot faults, he'd probably be better than McEnroe. The rest of his shots were awful. Everybody said what a good volleyer he was, but he would come to the net after that serve of his, and you were lucky just to get it back. He died about ten years ago. I don't know from what. He just died. A big guy and very strong, related to the Bundys out in California.''

"What about Allison?''

"He died about five years ago. He may have drunk a little too much. As I

61. Allison and Van Ryn: the legendary team

understand it, they were naming the tennis courts after him at the University of Texas, and he made a speech and got pretty emotional and went home and died. He was the best volleyer outside of Borotra. His ground strokes weren't that good."

"Who was the best doubles player you ever played with?"

"Anyone who ever played with George Lott would say George Lott without any question. He was just great. He *had* to be great. He won the national title six times with three different partners: Hennessey, Doeg, and Stoefen. He won the French and English with me."

"Going back to Tilden. Did it bother you traveling with Tilden, knowing what he was like?"

"I wouldn't say it bothered me. All the tennis players knew it. I'll never forget the night when we were playing Davis Cup in Berlin. I think Tilden and Hunter were playing the singles, and Allison and I were the doubles team. So Tilden, and von Cramm, who was playing with Henkel, took us to this club of theirs for dinner, and there were all these tables, each with a telephone so you could call someone at the next table. Allison and I had never seen anything like it. All these woos and such. You would see these fellows with lipstick on, dialing each other and going woo-woo: we were shocked."

It was a time of fashionable decadence immortalized by Christopher Isherwood in *Berlin Stories*, and who can forget the character played by Joel Grey in *Cabaret*? But I had been under the impression that the aristocratic sportsman, Gottfried von Cramm, had been sent to jail on a rigged charge directed by Hitler because von Cramm was far from enthusiastic about the Nazis. Entrapment, a word currently in vogue, came to mind. But John Van Ryn demurred.

I said, "Wasn't von Cramm set up by the Nazis? That seems to be the common view."

"I don't believe that," said John. "He would pass you at the net, and he would say 'You're playing well today, *dear*.' But I was fond of him, and we would sit together at dinners—you know, by alphabet: Van Ryn, von Cramm. It was 1937 when he and Henner Henkel were making a world tour for the German Tennis Association, and when they got back, the Nazis put him in jail because they knew all along about von Cramm. They threw him in jail on a morals charge, and they had known about him for years. But the reason they threw him in jail was because throughout the whole tour he was telling everyone about this group, the Nazis, and how terrible they were, and he was just speaking out of school."

"In the free world, he is kind of a hero because of his speaking out, but underneath there was truth to the charge that he was a homosexual?"

"Yes, he was. But I can't say a hundred percent. AC-DC. And he *was* a hero in that he voiced his feelings. I remember playing with Allison in 1935 against Henkel and von Cramm at Wimbledon. We were in the semifinals, and they had us match point when they walked over to the net and said, 'We default.' Allison and I said, 'Please say that a little louder, please. We didn't quite hear what you said.' Well, they defaulted at match point, and that got us into the finals, and the reason they defaulted was because they and all other German nationals were ordered to report immediately to a channel ship for their crossing back to Germany. Had we gone on to beat Quist and Crawford (and we had them at match point twice), it would have been my fourth Wimbledon. But when von Cramm said, 'We default,' we were astonished. That was the year Hitler went into Czechoslovakia.''

I wanted to leave von Cramm alone. Von Cramm's "AC-DC" nature was more a footnote to history or to the culture of the time. Like the always impressive Tilden, they remain legends in the game and were beloved by many and certainly admired by most athletes who played with or against them. I suppose Hitler had to do something about the anti-Nazi von Cramm, and he found one spot in his nature where von Cramm was at least partially vulnerable. I thought of the man admired so much by Don Budge, who had referred to him quite simply as "Cramm," sitting in a Nazi jail, and it made me wince.

"In your time, how would you rank the great doubles teams?"

"George Lott and anybody: Doeg, Stoefen, Hennessey, and . . ."

"Van Ryn?"

"If you like. Allison and Van Ryn—I think you have to put us up there somewhere. And Vines and Gledhill, and Kramer and Schroeder."

"How about Talbert and Mulloy?"

"They won a lot of tournaments, and Mulloy will kill me for saying this, but I don't think they were that good."

"How about Tilden and Hunter, or Tilden and Johnston?"

"They were great. No doubt. But Tilden was not a great doubles player. He had no real net game. Like Doeg, his serve was so good, he didn't have to really develop a volley. He was a great net *rusher*. Not a great volleyer. He won the U.S. doubles three times with Vincent Richards and once with Brian Norton. Don't forget that."

"Lott writes that R. Norris Williams and Richards were the greatest doubles team of all."

"Could be. But I never saw them play."

"Did you have any heroes as a kid?"

"Oh, I guess you could say Babe Ruth and Bill Tilden and Jack Dempsey. But you wouldn't call it hero worship. My father took me to athletic contests in New York all the time, and I liked all sports."

"How about Princeton?"

"I went on an athletic scholarship. I played both tennis and baseball, and they gave me my choice. So I picked tennis and was number one for four years."

"Going back over your life—over seventy-nine years—whom do you admire the most, looking back through history?"

"I can't answer that," he said. "It's a big question. Surely not politicians. I was not a hero worshiper, as I said. I could try to come up with a doctor or someone, but, no, I can't answer that."

"You're a Republican?"

"Certainly. Most people around here are, too. Nice people with money vote that way."

"Would you say that it is your own life that matters and other people don't count that much?"

"I guess I am selfish that way. I care about my wife and her family and my family, when they were around, and what we did . . . I am not so crazy about someone else or what he did. I don't go out with a sign that says, 'Impeach this fellow' or 'I am for abortion'—or against abortion—that is not my life."

"Your philosophy is that in this country it is up to each person to do the best that he can on his own terms?"

"I'll agree with that. Everybody has an equal chance, and you have to make the best out of your opportunities."

"Do you feel compassion for poor persons?"

"Yes, I do. Certainly. And I think a lot of them will make it if they try and aren't given things instead of working for them. I had a scholarship to college, and I don't know if I could have gone without one. We were not rich people. I played in East Orange for a high school."

East Orange made me think again of Althea Gibson. I asked John, "Can you imagine Wilt Chamberlain playing tennis? How could you pass him or lob him?"

"You aim for his stomach," he said. "That was what we did with Lester Stoefen, who was very tall."

"Is there anything in your life that you would change?"

"I would be born thirty to forty years later so I could have made money playing tennis. But, no, I had a happy life. I don't ever remember being spanked. I had a very fine home life, but sure there are things I could have done better. I have had a very happy married life."

"Still married to the same woman?"

"Yes."*

---

* The former Marjorie Buck. Mrs. Van Ryn won the U.S. Indoor doubles in 1932 playing with Marjorie Merrill. She also won the same event in 1949 with Gussie Moran; 1950 and 1951 with Nancy Chaffee and, unbelievably, in 1960 as Ruth Jeffrey's partner.

"Children?"

"No. Sometimes we think we should have had children, and sometimes we think we are very lucky."

"What about business? After George Lott left Dixon and Company to go back into tennis, did you stay on?"

"No. I left in 1935 to join Wilmer Allison in Austin, Texas, to work for his father-in-law, who had his own brokerage business. We worked for a small local brokerage that did business through Fenner and Beane, and then Fenner and Beane was taken over; and we went along, and Mr. Merrill began taking over other houses, and I got in sort of through the back door."

"Would you say you are self-made?"

"Yes. And then the war came, and Allison went into the army, and I went into the navy; and after the war Mr. Merrill, who knew me from my tennis, asked me if I wanted to open an office in Palm Beach. He said, 'I think Palm Beach is going to become a year-round resort.' He said, 'I think that air-conditioning is going to make all the difference in the world,' and he was absolutely right. We opened this office in December of 1945 with five employees. I was manager for twenty-two years and stayed on until seven years ago—a late retirement."

"Then tennis was a springboard into a good life."

"Yes, it was. Had I not been known as a tennis player, Mr. Merrill would never have given me my opportunity."

"What would have happened to you had you not been a good tennis player?"

"Oh, I would still have gone into the brokerage business. I started out at Princeton as an engineering student but shifted to economics."

"Pauline Betz majored in economics, was taking her masters in it," I offered.

"Pauline is smarter than I am," he answered. "She is a smart girl. And so is Schroeder," he added.

"Schroeder is supposed to be eccentric."

"Aren't all geniuses eccentric?" he answered.

"What about God?" I asked. "Are you religious?"

"Yes. I am an Episcopalian, and my wife and I go to church every Sunday."

"What do you think will happen to you after you die?"

"We'll have to die to find out. But I *say* in church every Sunday that I believe in the resurrection and life everlasting."

I thought his answer was a dodge, but I let it go. "How do you live your life today?"

"I belong to this club and the Bath and Tennis Club, and we travel all over Europe and to Australia, and we have a lot of friends, and I don't think there is anyone out there who wants to shoot me. I was very, very lucky. I made some good investments along the way. When we are both gone, what we leave will be divided among the hospitals here and tennis associations and the Crippled Children's Society and things like that. Until then, we live the way we want to live. I don't want the government to get it. We have set up a trust so our money will go to places where we want it to go."

"What about the influence of your parents?"

"My father was a good gymnast. He had rings up in the attic, and when he came home from New York, he would exercise. My father was very smart. He came up from eighteen years old with no college education with the Holland-American Line to become a director. And he helped me with my homework in school, as did my mother. They helped me get good grades. When I came home from school, my mother would give me a hot lunch. When I came home in the afternoon, she was there to greet me. They wanted me to do well. A solid home life is important. No doubt."

"How about smoking and drinking?"

"I never smoked. I did start to drink around twenty-five or thirty, but not till then because I thought it was bad for me as an athlete."

"One last question: What was your greatest match?"

"There were two. The first one was when Wilmer Allison and I went to Wimbledon as part of the Davis Cup team. We beat Tilden and Hunter in the semis, and Gregory and Collins in the final. And we were just tagging along for the ride. Up to that time, we were the first unseeded team to ever win the tournament, and that is something, I'll tell you. That was 1929. My finest singles victory was beating Tilden in the finals at the Heights Casino in Brooklyn. I beat Hunter in the semis, and that tournament was the biggest indoor tournament in the country at that time. I think the year was 1932."

And then Frank Shields. Everyone from the pre-war days has a Shields story, and John Van Ryn had one he was dying to tell. They were at a tournament at the Piping Rock Club on Long Island, and Shields had just won the junior championships. Everyone was there, and at the dance Shields became very inebriated—"Drunk," said Van Ryn—and as the president of the club would pass him, Frank Shields would give him "the bird," which is a noise close to what an offspring of a crow and a pig might make, or what someone from Ebbets Field would emit when Van Lingle Mungo walked in the winning run. At any rate, he was barred from the dance and went into the parking lot where, having secured a golf club from the locker room, he smashed up several cars and then fled. Police chased him throughout the night, to no avail, until at about 5:30 a maid who lived in the servants' quarters screamed. She had seen a hand come out from beneath her bed. It belonged to Shields. He had passed out, awakened to screams of terror, and was banned from the circuit for a year. What the maid thought about all of this is unknown.

"He was a very naughty boy," said the finely tuned Van Ryn, and at that we rose to leave.

It was midafternoon. A good deal of tennis talk had passed between us. Previously I had taken two days to explore Boca Grove in Boca Raton, where Gardnar Mulloy is director of tennis. Mulloy had beaten me 6–1, 6–1, as I fell apart against his smooth, effortless accuracy. But I'd met others—members of the club, the Boca Grove Golf and Tennis Club—and had a fine series of matches, leaving undefeated. Van Ryn had an appointment, and I was ready to fly home. I'd seen him, and we had lunched. As with Gardnar at Boca Grove, he insisted on picking up the tab. It was a royal time, but time to call it quits. Tennis stars enthralled me, as did the old times—the grand, splendid times of their youth. I said good-bye to John Van Ryn and was again reminded of my father. Van Ryn stood in front of his apartment and waved farewell the same way my father used to: no emotion to speak of, but with a swell smile on his face.

John Van Ryn was my twenty-fifth champion. Though each was in a class by himself—or herself—they shared similarities that emerged as they grew to the top. Politically, they were pretty much the same. All were tough, resilient Americans, the kind you cheer for in movies. But I was not like them. I could never have made the grade. I had been a member of the junior varsity, who had stumbled into the wrong locker room and had seen a team of winners. I had stumbled upon the first team.

Afterword

Of course, I want to thank all of the champions who opened their minds and their hearts to me. I realize that in some cases, they may feel slightly offended. But my affection for them should overrule any such feelings of discontent. As they all knew, I had to tell the truth as they told it to me, and as I felt it while I was in their presence.

I want to say that when I started out, I was thinking of perhaps twelve players. I knew little about the game of tennis other than that I played it and had won a few local tournaments. I was usually in bad physical shape whenever I played any of the champions in this book and that fact, combined with my abysmal lack of knowledge of the minutiae of the game, must have upset several of my interviewees. For that I apologize.

Indeed, I missed a few great individuals. Helen Wills and Helen Jacobs and Doris Hart come to mind, but they did not want to be involved with my book—although Helen Jacobs did say that she would correspond with me by letter. I didn't want letters—I wanted contact—and so I shelved her kind offer.

Segura and Gonzales . . . well, what can I say? Perhaps I could have gotten to Segura by pulling strings. Jack Kramer might have intervened. Gonzales I saw anyway. I would not choose him as my doubles partner, but I have a sparkling picture of him talking to a young woman. And seeing him perform was better than watching any movie star.

And that's all there is. I went as far as I could go and made a few blunders. I thank Ted Schroeder for his insistence upon my getting a taxi to the hospital. A great player, he worked, and he sporadically left his job and played—and he won. When he stopped winning, he quit and went back to work. Tennis is a game and some people place their jobs first. Ted Schroeder did that. He chose his path and when I write that he looks like a milkman or a dairy farmer, I hope that it will make him smile.

As for Kramer and Budge and Riggs—Good grief! What can you say? Everyone I saw was a giant in his or her time. I cannot add anything else to that statement except that Gardnar Mulloy stands out in my mind as a pal whom I can like without reverence. A great player, and surely the greatest at his age who ever played the game, his humanity defies exaltation. He is the kind of man you can be with and actually forget his grand accomplishments.

Next stop—Australia and then on to Switzerland to play the amazing Budge Patty. But all that depends . . . will anyone read this book? The writer's worry is not too far from the anxiety that must run through the mind of a man like Kramer who will be meeting Don McNeill in the morning. Will he sleep well that night? I suspect it is the same sort of thing. And Tom Brown—we should have won. And Shirley Fry: I'll get you in time, in time. As I said, I have nothing to add . . . but, but, but. I'd like to start all over again. I'd do it better. I'd be better just the way it is in tennis when you rehash a match you have lost.